At the Dark End of the Street

At the Dark End of the Street

Black Women, Rape, and Resistance—A New History
of the Civil Rights Movement
from Rosa Parks to the Rise of Black Power

Danielle L. McGuire

ALFRED A. KNOPF
NEW YORK
2011

Copyright © 2010 by Danielle L. McGuire
All rights reserved. Published in the United States by Alfred A. Knopf,
a division of Random House, Inc., New York, and in Canada by Random House
of Canada Limited, Toronto.

www.aaknopf.com
Knopf, Borzoi Books, and the colophon are registered trademarks
of Random House, Inc.

Library of Congress Cataloging-in-Publication Data
McGuire, Danielle L.
At the dark end of the street / by Danielle L. McGuire. — 1st ed.
p. cm.
"Borzoi Book."
Includes bibliographical references and index.
ISBN 978-0-307-26906-5 (alk. paper)
1. African-American women—Civil rights—Alabama—History—20th century.
2. African-American women—Violence against—Alabama—History—20th
century.   3. Rape—Political aspects—Southern States—History—20th century.
4. Civil rights movements—Southern States—History—20th century.
5. Southern States—Race relations—History—20th century.   I. Title.
E185.61.M4777 2010
323.1196'0730761—dc22   2010012072

Manufactured in the United States of America
Published September 9, 2010
Reprinted One Time
Third Printing, February 2011

For Recy and Ruby

Sex is the principle around which the whole
structure of segregation . . . is organized.

—GUNNAR MYRDAL, 1944

Contents

Illustrations

Prologue

ON SEPTEMBER 3, 1944, the Rock Hill Holiness Church, in Abbeville, Alabama, rocked late into the night. It was nearly midnight when the doors of the wooden, one-story church swung open releasing streams of worshippers, all African American, into the moonlight. After a night of singing and praying, Recy Taylor, Fannie Daniel, and Daniel's eighteen-year-old son, West, stepped out of the country chapel and strolled toward home alongside the peanut plantations that bounded the Abbeville-Headland highway. Taylor, a slender, copper-colored, and beautiful twenty-four-year-old mother and sharecropper, noticed a rattletrap green Chevrolet pass them at least three times, young white men gawking from its windows.

"You reckon what they are up to?" Taylor asked.

Taylor and Daniel, a stout sixty-one-year-old woman, watched the car creep by one last time and roll to a stop a few feet ahead of them. Seven men, armed with knives and guns, got out of the car and walked toward the women.

Herbert Lovett, the oldest of the crew at twenty-four and a private in the U.S. Army, shouted, "Halt!"

When they ignored the order, Lovett leveled his shotgun. West tugged at his mother's sleeve, begging her to stop. "They might shoot you," he whispered.

As the circle of men closed in, Lovett waved his gun at Taylor.

"We're looking for this girl, right there. She's the one that cut that white boy in Clopton this evening," Lovett said, adding that the local sheriff, George H. Gamble, had dispatched the group to find the alleged assailant.

"You're wrong," Fannie insisted. "She's been to my house all day."

The men crowded closer, nodding their heads in agreement. "Ain't this her?" Lovett asked.

"Yep, this the one," Joe Culpepper said. "I know her by the clothes she got on."

"That's her," Luther Lee agreed. "Get her!"

Lovett lurched toward Taylor and grabbed her arm. Then he turned to West and asked if Taylor was his wife.

"No," West replied, "she's Willie Guy Taylor's wife." Undeterred, Lovett extended his hand to the teenager, ordered him to shake it, and promised not to hurt Taylor.

"We're going to take her up here and see if Mr. Gamble knows her," Lovett claimed. "If she's not the one, we'll bring her right back."

As Lovett spoke, Taylor managed to wrest her arm from his grasp and bolted toward a stand of trees behind a cabin.[1]

"Come back! Come back!" Fannie yelled. "They going to shoot you. Come back!"[2]

"Stop!" Lovett shouted. He cocked the gun at the back of her head. "I'll kill you if you run."

Lovett walked Taylor to the car and shoved her into the backseat. Three men piled in behind her, while four others squeezed into the front. The headlights switched off and the car crept away. After a few miles, the green sedan turned off the main highway, rattled down a red-clay tractor path into the woods, and stopped in a grove of pecan trees. "Y'all aren't carrying me to Mr. Gamble," Taylor shouted. The men in the backseat clasped her wrists and ordered her to be quiet. Lovett grabbed his gun and waved Taylor and his companions out of the car.

"Get them rags off," he barked, pointing the shotgun at her, "or I'll kill you and leave you down here in the woods."

Sobbing, Taylor pulled off her clothes.

"Please," she cried, "let me go home to my husband and my baby."

Lovett spread an old hunting coat on the ground, told his friends to strip down to their socks and undershirts, and ordered Taylor to lie down. Lovett passed his rifle to a friend and took off his pants. Hovering over the young mother, he snarled, "Act just like you do with your husband or I'll cut your damn throat."

.   .   .

Lovett was the first of six men to rape Taylor that night. When they finished, someone helped her get dressed, tied a handkerchief over her eyes, and shoved her back into the car. Back on the highway, the men stopped and ordered Taylor out of the car. "Don't move until we get away from here," one of them yelled. Taylor heard the car disappear into the night. She pulled off the blindfold, got her bearings, and began the long walk home.[3]

A few days later, a telephone rang at the NAACP branch office in Montgomery, Alabama. E. D. Nixon, the local president, promised to send his best investigator to Abbeville. That investigator would launch a movement that would ultimately change the world.

Her name was Rosa Parks.[4]

In later years, historians would paint Parks as a sweet and reticent old woman, whose tired feet caused her to defy Jim Crow on Montgomery's city buses. Her solitary and spontaneous act, the story goes, sparked the 1955 bus boycott and gave birth to the civil rights movement. But Rosa Parks was a militant race woman, a sharp detective, and an antirape activist long before she became the patron saint of the bus boycott. After meeting with Recy Taylor, Rosa Parks helped form the Committee for Equal Justice. With support from local people, she helped organize what the *Chicago Defender* called the "strongest campaign for equal justice to be seen in a decade." Eleven years later this group of homegrown leaders would become better known as the Montgomery Improvement Association. The 1955 Montgomery bus boycott, often heralded as the opening scene of the civil rights movement, was in many ways the last act of a decades-long struggle to protect black women, like Taylor, from sexualized violence and rape.

The kidnapping and rape of Recy Taylor was not unusual in the segregated South. The sexual exploitation of black women by white men had its roots in slavery and continued throughout the better part of the twentieth century.

When African Americans tested their freedom during Reconstruction, former slaveholders and their sympathizers used rape as a "weapon of terror" to dominate the bodies and minds of African-American men and women.[5] Interracial rape was not only used to uphold white patriarchal power but was also deployed as a justification for lynching black men who challenged the Southern status quo. In addition to the immediate physical danger African Americans faced, sexual and racial violence functioned as a tool of coercion, control, and harassment.[6] Ida B. Wells, the gun-toting editor of the *Memphis Free Press* who led a crusade against lynching in the 1890s, argued that white men accused black men of rape as part of a larger "system of intimidation" designed to keep blacks "subservient and submissive." Worse, Wells argued at the turn of the century, white men used the protection of white womanhood to "justify their own barbarism."[7]

The rape of black women by white men continued, often unpunished, throughout the Jim Crow era. As Reconstruction collapsed and Jim Crow arose, white men abducted and assaulted black women with alarming regularity. White men lured black women and girls away from home with promises of steady work and better wages; attacked them on the job; abducted them at gunpoint while traveling to or from home, work, or church; raped them as a form of retribution or to enforce rules of racial and economic hierarchy; sexually humiliated and assaulted them on streetcars and buses, in taxicabs and trains, and in other public spaces. As the acclaimed freedom fighter Fannie Lou Hamer put it, "A black woman's body was never hers alone."[8]

Black women did not keep their stories secret. African-American women reclaimed their bodies and their humanity by testifying about their assaults. They launched the first public attacks on sexual violence as a "systemic abuse of women" in response to slavery and the wave of lynchings in the post-Emancipation South.[9] Slave narratives offer stark testimony about the brutal sexual exploitation bondswomen faced. For example, Harriet Jacobs detailed her master's lechery in her autobiography to "arouse the women of the North" and "convince the people of the Free States what Slavery really is."[10] When African-American clubwomen began to organize antilynching campaigns during the late nineteenth century, they testified about decades of sexual abuse.[11] On October 5, 1892, hundreds of black women converged on Lyric Hall in New York City to hear Ida B. Wells's thunderous voice. While black men were being accused of ravishing white women, she argued, "The rape of helpless Negro girls, which began in slavery days, still continues without reproof from church, state or press."[12] At the 1893 World's Fair in Chicago, Fannie Barrier

Williams told an audience of black and white clubwomen about the "shameful fact that I am constantly in receipt of letters from the still unprotected women of the South. . . ." Anna Julia Cooper, a Washington, D.C., educator, author, and respected clubwoman, echoed Williams's testimony. Black women, she told the crowd, were engaged in a "painful, patient, and silent toil . . . to gain title to the bodies of their daughters."[13]

Throughout the twentieth century, black women persisted in telling their stories, frequently cited in local and national NAACP reports. Their testimonies spilled out in letters to the Justice Department and appeared on the front pages of the nation's leading black newspapers. Black women regularly denounced their sexual misuse. By deploying their voices as weapons in the wars against white supremacy, whether in the church, the courtroom, or in congressional hearings, African-American women loudly resisted what Martin Luther King, Jr., called the "thingification" of their humanity. Decades before radical feminists in the women's movement urged rape survivors to "speak out," African-American women's public protests galvanized local, national, and even international outrage and sparked larger campaigns for racial justice and human dignity. When Recy Taylor spoke out against her assailants and Rosa Parks and her allies in Montgomery mobilized in defense of her womanhood in 1944, they joined this tradition of testimony and protest.

Montgomery, Alabama, was not the only place in which attacks on black women fueled protests against white supremacy. Between 1940 and 1975, sexual violence and interracial rape became one crucial battleground upon which African Americans sought to destroy white supremacy and gain personal and political autonomy. Civil rights campaigns in Little Rock, Arkansas; Macon, Georgia; Tallahassee, Florida; Washington, North Carolina; Birmingham and Selma, Alabama; Hattiesburg, Mississippi; and many other places had roots in organized resistance to sexual violence and appeals for protection of black womanhood.

And yet analyses of rape and sexualized violence play little or no role in most histories of the civil rights movement, which present it as a struggle between black and white men—the heroic leadership of Martin Luther King confronting intransigent white supremacists like "Bull" Connor. The real story—that the civil rights movement is also rooted in African-American women's long struggle against sexual violence—has never before been written. The stories of black women who fought for bodily integrity and personal dignity hold profound truths about the sexualized violence that marked racial politics and African American lives during the mod-

ern civil rights movement. If we understand the role rape and sexual violence played in African Americans' daily lives and within the larger freedom struggle, we have to reinterpret, if not rewrite, the history of the civil
rights movement. *At the Dark End of the Street* does both.

It is no surprise that buses became the target of African-American resistance in Montgomery during the 1955–56 boycott. It was much easier,
not to mention safer, for black women to stop riding the buses than it
was to bring their assailants—usually white policemen or bus drivers—
to justice. By walking hundreds of miles to protest humiliation and testifying publicly about physical and sexual abuse, black women reclaimed
their bodies and demanded to be treated with dignity and respect. Cou-
pling new historical evidence with a fresh perspective, Chapters 2 and 3
reveal the history of the Montgomery campaign as a women's movement
for dignity.

Issues of sexual violence were crucial both to the civil rights movement
and to the white supremacist resistance. Segregationists responded to the
nascent African-American freedom movement with a sexually charged
campaign of terror to derail the freedom movement. Between 1956 and
1960, black Southerners braved the Ku Klux Klan, the White Citizens'
Council, and other extremist groups, sparking some of the fiercest struggles for black humanity of the modern civil rights movement. These battles, highlighted in Chapter 4, exposed the power of sex in maintaining
the South's racial hierarchy and underscored the extent to which whites
would fight to preserve it.

Often ignored by civil rights historians, a number of campaigns led to
trials and even convictions throughout the South. These cases, many virtually unknown, broke with Southern tradition and fractured the philo-
sophical and political foundations of white supremacy by challenging the
relationship between sexual domination and racial equality.

Nowhere was this more apparent and more important than in Tallahassee, Florida, where Betty Jean Owens, an African-American college student, stood in front of an all-white jury in 1959 and testified about being
kidnapped and gang-raped by four white men. The extraordinary trial, the
subject of Chapter 5, focused national attention on the sexual exploitation
of African-American women. For perhaps the first time since Reconstruction, black Southerners could imagine government as a defender of
their manhood and womanhood. The Tallahassee case led to rape convic-

tions elsewhere that year in Montgomery, Alabama; Raleigh, North Carolina; and Burton, South Carolina. The 1959 Tallahassee rape was a watershed case that remains as revealing now as it was important then.

Black women's testimonies revealed their vulnerability across the South, especially in Mississippi. Most accounts of the Mississippi movement focus on racist brutality directed at men—from Emmett Till and Medgar Evers to Andrew Goodman, Michael Schwerner, and James Chaney. Chapter 6 challenges the dominant historical narrative of the Mississippi freedom struggle by documenting black women's resistance to racial *and* sexual abuse.

The 1965 Selma, Alabama, campaign, like the Montgomery movement, has an important history rooted in sexualized violence that historians have not yet explored. Federal intervention and congressional action on behalf of African Americans in 1964 and 1965—especially the Civil Rights Act and the Voting Rights Act—constituted the most dangerous threat to white dominion and left segregationists reeling. But the segregationists fired back with traditional ammunition of sexual slander and the "black beast rapist." Chapter 7 documents how white supremacists in Selma and across the South used the rhetoric of rape and "miscegenation" to resuscitate and revive massive resistance, underscoring the importance of sex and sexual violence to the maintenance of white supremacy. Civil rights activists were not only "outside agitators" or Communists intent on destroying the Southern way of life; now they were sexual fiends. It was within this storm—and because of it—that the Ku Klux Klan murdered Viola Liuzzo, a white housewife from Detroit who embraced the black freedom struggle. Her detractors, of course, accused her of embracing black men.

An analysis of sex and sexualized violence in well-known civil rights narratives changes the historical markers and meanings of the movement. Like the Tallahassee case, the 1965 trial of Norman Cannon, a white man who abducted and raped a black teenager in Hattiesburg, Mississippi, had broad implications for both the Mississippi movement and the African-American freedom struggle as a whole. The verdict was recognized nationally as a major victory. It ought to be considered one of the bookends of the modern civil rights movement. And yet the story has never been told. While the Voting Rights Act is often referenced as the culminating achievement of the modern civil rights movement, a pillar of white supremacy fell in 1967 when the Supreme Court banned laws prohibiting interracial marriage in the landmark *Loving v. Virginia* decision. Only when we place the *Loving* decision within the long struggle for black women's bodily integrity and freedom from racial *and* sexual terror can it be properly recognized as a major marker in the African-American freedom movement.

The struggle did not stop with that landmark victory. The right of African-American women to defend themselves from white men's sexual advances was tested in the 1975 trial of Joan Little, a twenty-year-old black female inmate from Washington, North Carolina, who killed her white jailer after he allegedly sexually assaulted her. The broad coalition of supporters who rallied to Little's defense—from the National Organization for Women to the Black Panther Party—reflected the enormous social, political, and economic changes wrought by the civil rights movement, the women's movement, and the emergence of the New Left and Black Power. But it also showed continuity with the past—the Free Joan Little movement mirrored the eclectic coalition that formed to demand justice for Recy Taylor in 1944. They were both led primarily by African-American women and helped serve as catalysts for larger struggles. The stunning verdict, announced by a jury made up of whites and blacks, signaled the death knell of the rape of black women that had been a feature of Southern race politics since slavery.

Like the kidnapping and rape of Recy Taylor in Abbeville, Alabama, in 1944; Betty Jean Owens in 1959; Rosa Lee Coates in 1965; and hundreds of other African-American women throughout the segregated South, these brutal attacks almost always began at the dark end of the street. But African Americans would never let them stay there.

At the Dark End of the Street

CHAPTER 1

"They'd Kill Me If I Told"

THE ROAD TO ABBEVILLE, a rural county seat ninety miles southeast of Montgomery, was familiar territory for Rosa Parks. Her father, James McCauley, a handsome, barrel-chested builder and expert stonemason, was one of eleven children reared by Anderson and Louisa McCauley in the hardscrabble town. The sprawling McCauley clan squeezed into a tiny, wood-frame home with dirt floors. Similar cabins provided shelter for the bulk of Abbeville's two thousand souls—mostly sharecroppers and tenant farmers who scraped a living out of the peanut and cotton fields that quilted the countryside.[1]

While Rosa's grandmother, Louisa McCauley, maintained the homestead and tended to her growing family, her husband and oldest sons built big, beautiful homes throughout Alabama's Black Belt, a band of inky, fertile soil stretching across the middle of the state.[2] The region was known for its bumper cotton crops and punishing plantations. As skilled laborers and contract workers, the McCauley men maintained a sense of independence that few African Americans could claim. Despite the promises of a progressive New South, the legacy of slavery in the Black Belt was palpable. Tenant farming and debt peonage dominated the economy, and the ghosts of the "peculiar institution" haunted the rolling landscape, where the children and grandchildren of slaves and slave owners eyed each other with fear and familiarity.[3]

That familiarity was visible in James McCauley's pale almond skin and dark, wavy hair. The grandson of a fair-skinned slave woman and a "Yankee soldier," he had a light coloration that mocked the new segregation laws that white legislators passed at the turn of the century.[4] City workers nailed wooden signs proclaiming "Colored" or "Whites Only" between seats in streetcars and above doorways in theaters, restaurants, and boardinghouses. Toilets, water fountains, telephone booths, waiting rooms, and ticket windows were all similarly marked. In Birmingham, Alabama, Jim Crow laws barred whites and blacks from being together in "any room, hall, theatre, picture house, auditorium, yard, court, park or other indoor or outdoor place." Black nurses could not care for white patients, and black students dared not use "white" textbooks. In Texas, circuses were segregated, and "Caucasians" and "Africans" could not watch a boxing or wrestling match together. Some states prohibited black and white workers from laboring together in the same room, while others barred blacks from certain trades altogether.[5] For the most part, the McCauleys pursued their daily affairs without giving much thought to these laws.

One Sunday, in the spring of 1912, James McCauley decided to go hear his brother-in-law preach at the white-framed Mount Zion African Methodist Episcopal Church in Pine Level, Alabama. Across the pews, he saw a striking woman with diaphanous skin, high cheekbones, plum lips, and flowing waves of dark, shiny hair. She was twenty-four years old, had attended Payne University in Selma, Alabama, and taught school nearby. Her name was Leona Edwards.

Like many black Southerners, McCauley and Edwards shared a family history that involved interracial couplings ranging from tragic love to brutal rape. Leona was the daughter of Rose Percival, born a slave; and Sylvester Edwards, whose milky-white complexion and straight brown hair were the product of an illicit relationship between a white plantation owner and his slave mistress. After his mother and father died, Sylvester became an object of mistreatment in the plantation household. The white overseer beat him mercilessly, starved him, and refused to let the boy wear shoes. Years of cruelty hardened Sylvester until he felt what his granddaughter Rosa would describe as an "intense, passionate hatred for white people."[6]

After slavery ended, despite his disdain, Sylvester often passed for white. After shaking Sylvester's hand and speaking to him as an equal, whites occasionally discovered he was "black" and became angry or embarrassed. In a kind of tragicomic retribution for years of mistreatment, Edwards enjoyed watching whites squirm over the unspoken absurdities of the color line. Though he used his apparent whiteness to his advantage when necessary, he remained pugnacious toward whites and taught his three daughters to be especially wary of white men. Leona inherited both her father's pigmentation and his pride—she became a teacher so she would never have to cook or clean for whites.[7]

It didn't take long for Leona and James McCauley to fall in love. They were married "right there in Pine Level" on April 12, 1912, and moved to Tuskegee, Alabama, home of Booker T. Washington's famed Tuskegee Institute. Their daughter, Rosa, was born roughly nine months after the wedding. Leona hoped her itinerant husband would land a job at Tuskegee and settle down, but the "citadel of black intellectual life" was not as appealing to James as it was to his wife.[8] He saw himself as a rambling man, more interested in making good money than putting down roots. His long trips away from home left Leona depressed and tearful, alone with her new baby. When James decided he wanted to move back to Abbeville to be closer to his family, Leona had no choice but to leave Tuskegee and abandon her dream of racial uplift.

Rosa was two years old when they moved in with her father's extended family in Abbeville. Surrounded by playmates, she quickly became the center of attention. Over time, however, the dirt floors and crowded beds were too much for Leona, who was not particularly fond of her in-laws. James announced in 1915 or 1916 that he planned to move north, joining the millions of African Americans fleeing the South in search of better jobs and the promise of freedom. Leona decided to stay behind. She and little Rosa left Abbeville and returned to her parents' farm in Pine Level, where Sylvester Edwards taught his granddaughter, who the world would come to know as Rosa Parks, "not to put up with bad treatment from anybody."[9]

When Rosa Parks returned to Abbeville almost thirty years later to investigate the rape of Recy Taylor, she was, in a sense, coming home. Though she had not seen her father in years, she remained kin to a sizable portion of the black community there. She could count on the McCauleys for a hot meal, a warm bed, and all the local gossip. News of the gang rape of Mrs. Taylor had reverberated through the sharecroppers' cabins and the tattered gray shacks in the colored section of town. Taylor, her husband, and their three-year-old daughter, Joyce Lee, rented one of these cabins at the bot-

tom of a rust-colored hill just outside of town. Here Parks scribbled notes
as she listened to Taylor testify about the vicious attack.[10] Her time was
limited. Deputy Sheriff Lewey Corbitt, known among blacks in Abbeville
as a mean man with a propensity for violence, drove repeatedly past the
house. Finally, he burst into the cabin and ordered Parks out of town. "I
don't want any troublemakers here in Abbeville," he said. "If you don't
go," he said, "I'll lock you up."[11]

Parks gathered up her notes and carried Taylor's story back to Montgomery, where she and the city's most militant black activists organized
a campaign to defend Recy Taylor.[12] Eleven years later, this group of homegrown leaders would take history in their hands and become heralded as
the Montgomery Improvement Association, eventually vaulting its first
president, Dr. Martin Luther King, Jr., to international prominence during the Montgomery bus boycott. But when the coalition first took root,
King was still in high school in Atlanta.

Alone on the dark highway after her assailants dumped her out of the car,
Recy Taylor pulled off the blindfold and got her bearings. In the moonlight, she recognized the silhouette of Judge Charlie Nordan's barn and
knew which way to turn. Staggering along the edge of the road, she saw
the deputy sheriff's car whiz past. As she approached Three Points—the
intersection of three main roads near the center of Abbeville—she saw
another familiar vehicle. Will Cook, the former chief of police and a local
shopkeeper, pulled his automobile to the side of the road. Taylor's father,
Benny Corbitt (no relation to the deputy sheriff), called to his daughter,
the oldest of seven children, and she crawled into the car. As the dark, open
space of the highway receded behind small storefronts, Taylor saw her husband, Willie Guy Taylor, and her friends Fannie and West Daniel, hud-
dling with two police officers in front of Cook's store.[13] It was nearly three
in the morning.

Recy Taylor had no way of knowing that Fannie Daniel had immediately reported the abduction to Cook, who must have felt the fear and
urgency in the older woman's voice. Her son's description of the green
Chevrolet assured Cook's assistance. He "knew at once," he said, who
owned it. Cook fired off a series of orders to get the investigation under
way, sending Fannie and West to rouse George Gamble, the Henry County
sheriff; then driving to Benny Corbitt's house to notify him about the

abduction of his daughter. Benny grabbed a pistol, slid it into his waist-band, and ran outside. First he went to Price's lumber, where white men had taken black women before, and searched desperately between the stacks of wood. When he could not find her there, he began walking through town. Finally, he headed east, toward "lovers' lane," a wooded area outside town where white teenagers were known to congregate after hours. His shirt was soaked with sweat when he finally spotted the silhouette of his daughter staggering on the roadside. Her clothes were tattered and torn, and she was shaking with sobs.[14]

After such a brutal gang rape, Taylor must have been in extreme pain and shock. There was no telling what physical injuries she sustained, how many bruises would mar her skin the next morning. The psychological wounds were bound to last a lifetime. That she could walk a distance after the attack indicates only a dogged determination to return home alive.

When Taylor stumbled into the arms of her husband, he was standing outside Cook's store. Taylor's family and friends crowded around her, lis-tening quietly as she told them what happened. She told Sheriff Gamble that she could not name any of her assailants, but her description of the car pointed to one suspect. "There's only one car in the county that fits that description," he said. Telling Taylor to stay put, he quickly walked to his car.

Thirty minutes later the sheriff returned with Hugo Wilson, his father, and their big green sedan. Taylor identified the car and pointed to Wil-son as one of the rapists. Fannie and West Daniel backed Taylor up. West identified Wilson's car as the one "that the white boys were in when they stopped me, my Mama and Recy Taylor." Wilson, he said, pointing to the young white man, "made Recy Taylor get in the car and drove off with her." Sheriff Gamble took Wilson to the jailhouse, and Willie Guy Tay-lor walked his wife home.[15]

Under questioning from Gamble at the Henry County jail, Wilson admitted picking Taylor up and, as he put it, "carrying her to the spot," and gave up the names of his accomplices. Dillard York, Billy Hower-ton, Herbert Lovett, Luther Lee, Joe Culpepper, and Robert Gamble, he said, "all had intercourse with her." Wilson swore that they did not use force. "We all paid her."[16]

Wilson's defense was certainly plausible; it was not uncommon for white Southerners—even die-hard segregationists—to visit black prosti-tutes under the cover of darkness. African Americans called white men

who surreptitiously searched for coerced or consensual interracial intercourse "alleybats."[17] Still, Gamble must have known Wilson was not
telling the truth. He himself had seen Taylor distraught, disheveled, and
trembling. Three eyewitnesses identified Wilson as the driver of the car
used in the armed abduction. Sheriff Gamble could have justified arresting Wilson without difficulty. At the very least, he might have called the
other men Wilson named and brought them in for questioning. Instead,
Gamble sent Wilson home with a $250 bond and instructions to have
his parents sign and return it at their leisure. The sheriff did not call the
other men in, issue any warrants, or make any arrests.[18]

If Sheriff Gamble hoped the case would quietly disappear, he was disappointed. Rosa Parks had been a member of the Montgomery NAACP for
only a year when she met with Recy Taylor in 1944, but she was already
a seasoned activist. Her quiet demeanor hid a steely determination to battle white supremacy. Rosa's grandfather taught her to stand up for herself and others and introduced her to the boisterous exhortations of the
Jamaican-born black nationalist Marcus Garvey when she was in grade
school. Garvey's condemnation of white supremacy and his calls for a
"Back to Africa" movement were common topics of conversation in the
Edwards household. Garvey's fearless race pride rallied millions into the
ranks of his Universal Negro Improvement Association. From its auspi-
cious beginning in 1914 to its stark demise eleven years later, the UNIA
was the biggest and brassiest organization for black human rights in the
world. Garvey's call for a "new world of *Black* men, not peons, serfs, dogs,
or slaves," resonated with Edwards, who refused to be cowed by white
men, even when they wore hoods and carried guns.[19] Perhaps her grandfather took young Rosa to Tuskegee in 1923, where Garvey enjoyed
a warm reception from students and faculty and impressed African-
American ministers from Birmingham.

Sylvester Edwards became his granddaughter's political mentor at a
time when Garvey's rise coincided with a national resurgence of the Ku
Klux Klan, a terrorist organization dedicated to "100 Percent Americanism" and the supremacy of white Anglo-Saxon Christians. Though they
hid behind masks when committing acts of terrorism, businessmen, police
officers, civic leaders, and state politicians north and south proudly proclaimed their loyalty to the hooded order. By 1924 the KKK counted four
to six million members nationwide. Alabama boasted 115,000 men and

women in 148 separate klaverns. Even Governor Bibb Graves held a membership card.[20]

After World War I the Alabama Klan unleashed a wave of terror designed to return "uppity" African Americans to their proper place in the segregated social order. The war to "make the world safe for democracy" had upended the racial status quo in the South. The promise of a better life in the North encouraged thousands of domestics and sharecroppers to flee low-paying jobs and the constant threat of racial violence, launching the Great Migration. Meanwhile many black soldiers returned to the South expecting that their military service would be rewarded with better treatment. "Whites didn't like blacks having that kind of attitude," Rosa Parks recalled years later, "so they started doing all kinds of violent things to black people to remind them that they didn't have any rights . . . I heard a lot about black people being found dead and nobody knew what happened," she said. "Other people would just pick them up and bury them."[21] In 1919 the Alabama Klan lynched four African Americans in Montgomery in less than twelve hours. In Ensley Klansmen flogged a black doctor who treated white patients; the Klan murdered two black men in Shelby County who decided to quit their low-paying farm jobs; and in Houston County an angry horde of hooded vigilantes shot and killed a black man as he waited on a platform for a northbound train.[22]

Sylvester Edwards refused to be the Klan's next victim. Cradling his double-barreled shotgun as the robed rebels paraded on the street outside his home in Pine Level, he positioned himself between the front door and the yawning fireplace. Rosa remembered kneeling beside his chair as he waited, rocking slowly back and forth. "I don't know how long I would last if they came breaking in here," he said to Rosa, "but I'm getting the first one who comes through the door." Rosa sat with her grandfather each night, waiting for the danger to pass. "Whatever happened," she said later, "I wanted to see it. I wanted to see him shoot that gun. I wasn't going to be caught asleep."[23]

By the time she was ten years old, Rosa was as defiant as her grandfather. "I saw Franklin," she announced to her grandmother one summer day, referring to a notorious white bully. "He threatened to hit me," she said. "I picked up a brick and dared him to hit me." Her grandmother scolded her and insisted that black children could not "talk to white folks that way . . . You'll be lynched before you're twenty years old." The sharp reprimand hurt young Rosa's feelings, but it did not curtail her feisty behavior: "I felt that I was very much in my rights to try to defend myself if I could." When another white boy on skates whizzed past and tried to push Rosa off the sidewalk, she pushed him back. The boy's mother saw the infraction and threatened to have Rosa arrested. "He pushed me," Rosa snapped, "and I didn't want to be pushed."[24] "It had been passed down almost in our genes," she said later, "that a proud African American can simply not accept bad treatment from anybody."[25]

As a young woman, Rosa McCauley was drawn to Raymond Parks, a spirited and brazen barber who lived in Montgomery, soon after she met him in the spring of 1931. At first his light complexion turned her off, and she rebuffed his flirtations. "I thought he was too white," she admitted; "I had an aversion to white men." But when she found out that Parks was a charter member of the Montgomery NAACP who carried a pistol in his pocket so that he could stand up to whites without fear, she relented and agreed to a date. Over the next year, they spent hours sitting in the rumble seat of his little red Nash, talking about injustice in Alabama. "He was the first man of our race, aside from my grandfather," she said, "with whom I actually discussed anything about the racial conditions."[26]

Raymond and Rosa had plenty to talk about. Rape and rumors of rape preoccupied Alabamians during the Depression years, and stories of racialized sexual violence echoed out from Alabama to the rest of the world. It is likely Rosa and Raymond discussed the brutal rape of Murdus Dixon, a twelve-year-old black Birmingham girl raped at knifepoint in the early 1930s by a white man who hired her as a domestic. Police refused to arrest the man, and the case languished until it finally disappeared from public conversation.[27]

By the spring of 1931, most conversation in Alabama centered on what had happened in the small town of Scottsboro. On March 25 hundreds of white men in dusty overalls, with shotguns slung over their shoulders, crowded around the crumbling two-story jailhouse. Inside were nine African-American boys, none older than twenty, who had been kicked off a Memphis-bound freight train and arrested after roughhousing with a handful of white hoboes. But when Ruby Bates and Victoria Price, two white women working as prostitutes, were also taken off the train, they accused the black youths of rape. By late afternoon, their accusation had been transformed into a lurid tale. Rumors spread that nine "black brutes" had "chewed off one of the breasts" of Ruby Bates. By the time the young men were brought to the Scottsboro jail, an incensed mob had already decided they were guilty. "Give 'em to us," someone shouted, as the mob pushed toward the jailhouse door. "Let those niggers out!" "If you don't," another threatened, "we're coming in after them." Fearing a mass lynching, the sheriff asked Governor B. M. Miller to send in the National Guard.[28]

Denied a lynching, white Scottsboro clamored for a quick hearing and a quicker execution. The "nigger rape case," as locals called it, began the day after the arrests. Within two weeks the young men had been tried, convicted, and sentenced to die in Alabama's electric chair. The instant trial and harsh sentences aroused anger and protest around the country. The Central Committee of the Communist Party of the United States issued a statement calling the ruling a "cold blooded 'illegal' lynching." The Interdenominational Ministers Alliance, a group of black clergymen from Chattanooga, Tennessee, raised fifty dollars for their defense, and the Alabama Interracial Commission passed a resolution calling for a careful review of the facts. In the months after the trial, the International Labor Defense, the NAACP, trade unions, leftist groups, and outraged individuals flooded the governor's office with letters of protest.

In Montgomery, Raymond Parks joined other black activists in secret meetings to raise money for the Scottsboro defense. "It gnawed at him to see those innocent kids were framed," Rosa said. "He'd say, 'I'll never sleep until they're free.' "[29] After Rosa and Raymond were married in 1932, they hosted gatherings of local Scottsboro defenders in the front room of their little shotgun house in Montgomery's Centennial Hill neighborhood near Alabama State College. "Whenever they met," Parks recalled, "they had someone posted as lookout and someone always had a gun." At one meeting, the men sat around a small card table covered with guns plotting to save the youths from the electric chair. "This was the first time I'd seen so few men with so many guns," Parks remembered fondly. "I didn't even think to offer them something to drink . . . I don't know where I would have put any refreshments. No one was thinking of food anyway."

Rosa Parks spent the rest of the evening on the back porch with her legs folded into her chest, her chin resting gently on her knees. After the men left, Raymond lifted his wife from the porch and assured her everything was all right. Even though the immediate danger had passed, she was sad and angry "about the fact that black men could not hold a meeting without fear of bodily injury or death." It would take Parks and other activists, mainly the International Labor Defense and the NAACP, almost twenty years to free the Scottsboro boys. When the last of the nine men walked out of prison in 1950, Scottsboro was "synonymous with Southern racism, repression, and injustice," and Montgomery was heading for the history books.[30]

In the early 1940s, Rosa and Raymond Parks hosted Voters League meetings, where they encouraged their friends and neighbors in Montgomery to register to vote, even though it was a dangerous proposition. These clandestine meetings, like the Scottsboro gatherings, introduced Parks to Alabama's underground network of black activists who worked for racial justice during the dark days of the Depression.[31] That support network became indispensable when Rosa Parks tried and twice failed to register to vote. Unlike whites, blacks had to pass a literacy test to prove their intellectual fitness to vote. County registrars routinely failed the South's most-educated blacks and passed illiterate whites as a way to maintain lily-white voter rolls. Parks persisted, however, and finally received her registration certificate in 1945, after taking the qualifying exam three times. She was so sure she passed the third test that she copied her answers on a separate sheet of paper in case the registrar claimed she failed. She kept that copy, she said later, so she could "bring suit against the voter registration board."[32]

It was after her second attempt to register, in 1943, that Rosa Parks first collided with a burly white bus driver named James F. Blake. Blake was known around town as a "vicious bigot" who targeted black women for mistreatment, calling them "bitches" and "coons." When Parks refused to reenter Blake's bus from the rear door after paying up front, a humiliating Jim Crow practice, he threatened to throw her off the bus. She refused. "I [don't] see the need of getting off and getting back on," she protested, "when people were standing in the stepwell." Besides, she added, "how was I going to squeeze in anyway?" Parks's behavior infuriated Blake. He lunged at her, grabbed her by the coat sleeve, and pulled her toward the door. "I know one thing," she warned as he dragged her out, "you better not hit me." As she was about to disembark, she pretended to drop her purse and quickly sat down in the front seat to retrieve it. Her spurt of defiance enraged the bus driver. "Get off my bus!" Blake roared as she finally stepped into the street. As the bus pulled away from the curb, Parks vowed to never ride on Blake's bus again.[33]

Rosa Parks joined the Montgomery NAACP chapter shortly after the 1943 bus incident with Blake. At the first meeting she attended, she was elected branch secretary.[34] The humble title obscured the importance of the job, which required Parks to spend much of her time traveling down dusty Alabama roads interviewing people and documenting acts of brutality, unsolved murders, voter intimidation, and other racial incidents. Her belief in racial equality and her ingrained sense of self-worth helped Parks become known as someone who could be trusted with delicate or dangerous information. "Rosa will talk to you," folks quietly assured victims of racial violence.[35] Having been politicized and deeply affected by the injustice in the Scottsboro case, Parks was especially interested in interracial rape cases.[36]

Rosa Parks carried Recy Taylor's story from Abbeville to Montgomery, where she helped organize her defense.[37] E. D. Nixon, a union man who headed the Alabama Brotherhood of Sleeping Car Porters; Rufus A. Lewis, who directed both a local funeral home and the football team at Alabama State; and E. G. Jackson, who served as editor of the *Alabama Tribune,* all signed on to help. With support from national labor unions, African-American organizations, and women's groups, Rosa Parks and her local allies formed the Alabama Committee for Equal Justice for Mrs. Recy Taylor. By the spring of 1945, they had recruited supporters around the country and had organized what the *Chicago Defender* called the "strongest campaign for equal justice to be seen in a decade."[38]

When the Henry County Grand Jury took up Recy Taylor's case on October 3 and 4, 1944, no one expected equal justice, but Taylor's family and friends hoped for an honest hearing. Once there, Taylor discovered that none of the assailants had actually been arrested. That meant the only witnesses present, when the all-white, all-male jury came together during the fall session, were Taylor's loved ones, none of whom could provide the names of the white men who assaulted her. Aside from identifying Hugo Wilson and his car the night of the attack, Sheriff Gamble never arranged a police lineup, so Taylor could not point to her attackers in court. He claimed he placed Hugo Wilson and his accomplices under a $250 appearance bond, but court records indicate that the bonds were issued late in the afternoon, a day *after* Taylor's hearing.[39] Circuit solicitor Keener Baxley, whose son Bill would eventually become attorney general of Alabama in 1971 and pardon the last Scottsboro defendant, appeared to go through the motions of a legitimate trial. It was clear that the proceeding was a farce designed by Baxley and others to protect themselves from outside criticism and to remind black women that they could not rely upon even the most basic protections under the law.[40]

By creating a faint shadow of judicial procedure, white leaders could dismiss complaints of racial discrimination by arguing that Recy Taylor received every consideration the law allowed. White Alabamians were so sensitive to the national and international outrage over the near lynching and subsequent trials of the Scottsboro nine that state and county leaders had to at least give an appearance of equal justice. Baxley and Gamble knew exactly what they were doing. Without an indictment from the grand jury, Taylor's case would never make it out of Henry County. There would be no further hearings, and they expected that the matter would eventually die.

For nearly a month after the grand jury met, Baxley and Gamble's strategy appeared to be working. Taylor and her husband quietly returned to their jobs and daily burdens, resigned to the bitter truth that her assailants roamed freely through town. They did not have much of a choice. After reporting the rape, Taylor received multiple death threats. The night after the attack, for example, white vigilantes firebombed Taylor's home while the family slept, setting the front porch on fire. Taylor's husband rushed outside and quickly put out the flames, saving his wife and toddler. They moved in with her father and six siblings the next morning, and Taylor stayed close to home. "I haven't gone up into the town since it happened," she told a reporter later. "I'm afraid they'll kill me. They said they'd kill me if I told on them."[41] The entire family took precautions as well. "Nobody would walk at night," Taylor's brother, Robert, recalled. "Everybody tried to make sure that they done what they had to do in the daytime." And each night, after everyone was tucked safely into bed, Benny Corbitt climbed a tree in his backyard. Cradling a double-barreled shotgun and a sack of shells, he guarded the cabin until the sun broke on the horizon, and then went inside to sleep.[42]

As the crisp fall days passed, however, the story of the brutal rape and the phony hearing spread across the state and then the nation, passed on in union halls, churches, NAACP chapters, barbershops, pool halls, and juke joints, through the underground networks of African-American activists, and along the infrastructure built by the defenders of the Scottsboro youth. Bolstered by a rising black militancy fueled by the global war against fascism, black activists in Alabama and their allies in national labor unions and leftist and liberal organizations joined in coalition to defend

Taylor and demand punishment for the white men who kidnapped and raped her.[43]

Many of these activists came together at the Negro Masonic Temple in Birmingham, the nerve center of Alabama's black political community. Here, militant members of the Birmingham and Montgomery NAACP chapters swapped organizing strategies with sharecroppers and steel-fisted union men whose battles for better wages and human dignity in the 1930s had laid a solid foundation. Editors and reporters from Alabama's black newspapers, mainly the *Alabama Tribune* and the *Birmingham World,* could interview members of the middle-class, progressive, and Communist-infused Southern Negro Youth Congress (SNYC), or catch up on regional news with the leading lights of the Alabama branch of the Southern Conference for Human Welfare (SCHW), the South's most prominent inter-racial liberal organization. Labor organizers passing through Birmingham could stop in to make a connection, gather information, or have a friendly chat. Together these eclectic groups and individuals turned the Masonic temple into a hive of activity. They coordinated campaigns, investigated police brutality, condemned the poll tax, pushed for the ballot, and fought for human rights.[44]

The SNYC, an outgrowth of the left-wing, New York–based National Negro Congress, was just nine years old in 1944, but it was perhaps the most promising civil rights organization in Alabama at the time.[45] At first, the SNYC attracted mostly young, college-educated black Southerners, but it quickly gained attention and support from prominent African-American leaders with national political reach. The list of SNYC board members included conservatives like Charles Gomillion and F. D. Patterson, the dean and president of the Tuskegee Institute; Percy Sutton, a Tuskegee Airman and well-known lawyer; Atlantans Reverend Martin Luther King, Sr., and Benjamin Mays, president of Morehouse College; Ralph Abernathy, a powerful young preacher in Montgomery; Modjeska Simkins, an outspoken and fearless NAACP leader in South Carolina; and Nannie Burroughs, a nationally known educator and women's club leader from Virginia. This broad-based coalition helped publicize the SNYC's activities.[46]

In Alabama the SNYC leadership included black women, many of whom practiced a tradition of collective organizing rooted in sharecroppers' struggles to win the most rudimentary rights from white landlords in the early 1930s.[47] Other members were middle-class, college-educated

African-American women played a prominent role in the Southern
Negro Youth Conference, a leftist organization committed to fighting
racial injustice. Members of the SNYC's Third Conference
Preparation Group gather at Miles College in Alabama, 1940.

black women who saw the SNYC as providing more opportunities for
women than traditional black organizations. Esther V. Cooper, a feisty
organizer and women's rights advocate, was only twenty-three years old
in 1940 when she helped lead the Birmingham chapter of the SNYC. Just
before she moved there, Cooper wrote a master's thesis at Fisk University
devoted to the "special issues that confronted working-class black
women," especially domestics and sharecroppers.[48] Dedicated to culti-
vating black female leadership throughout Alabama and building bridges
with existing women's networks, she was the SNYC's executive secretary
by 1942.

Rosa Parks and the SNYC women were natural allies. By leveraging
their relationships with CIO-affiliated unions, Communist networks, and
local and national civil rights organizations, Parks, Cooper, and their
cohorts helped spread Recy Taylor's story from the back roads of Alabama
to the street corners of Harlem. Reaching out to friends and affiliates
around the country, they sought publicity, funding, and legal assistance.[49]
By the end of October, Taylor's story had traveled all the way to Pennsylvania, where the widely read and respected black newspaper the *Pittsburgh
Courier* ran it on October 28, 1944. Strategically placed beneath a banner headline that declared "Treatment of Negro Called Greatest Evil in
America," the succinct front-page article, "Alabama Whites Attack
Woman; Not Punished," highlighted sexual violence as one of those

As executive secretary of the SNYC, Esther Cooper, seated right, organized committees, lobbied government officials, published newsletters, and investigated racial crimes. She visited Recy Taylor in Abbeville, Alabama, in July 1945.

evils.[50] The prominent article and provocative headline reflected the *Courier*'s "Double V" strategy. During the war years, the black press, led by the *Pittsburgh Courier,* urged African Americans to adopt "double victory" as a wartime battle cry. "The first V [is] for victory over our enemies from without," a *Courier* reader argued in a letter to the editor. "The second V [is] for victory over our enemies from within. For surely those who perpetuate these ugly prejudices here are seeking to destroy our democratic form of government just as surely as the Axis forces."[51] Readers responded to the black press's drumbeat to "Defeat Mussolini and Hitler by Enforcing the Constitution and Abolishing Jim Crow," devouring 200,000 copies of the *Courier* each week. The *Courier* was not alone in its success; wartime readership of black newspapers increased nearly 40 percent.[52]

The *Courier* article made the rape of Recy Taylor a national example of Southern injustice. It immediately sparked nationwide interest. Eugene Gordon, a prominent black Communist and writer for the *New York Daily Worker,* followed up on the *Courier*'s lead by traveling to Alabama to interview Taylor.[53] Gordon's November 19 article, "Alabama Authorities Ignore White Gang's Rape of Negro Mother," reported that since the attack, "Alabama justice has been blind, deaf, and mute." Gordon blasted segregationists' long-standing defense of white womanhood and their manipulation of interracial rape to justify violence against black men.

$600 To Rape Wife? Ala. Whites
Make Offer To Recy Taylor Mate!

By FRED ATWATER
(Defender Staff Correspondent)

MONTGOMERY, Ala. —
"Nigger—ain't $600 enough
for raping your wife?"

Stocky Willie Lee Taylor
considered it.

He talked to white Marvin
White, who wanted him to forget
prosecuting the six white men who
raped and ruptured Recy, his 24-
year-old wife.

White spoke for his clients, all
youths from prominent Abbeville
families who had been identified by
Recy. They were Hugo Wilson,
Penute Hastings, Sam Skippy,
Billie Hilder, Dillard York and
Luther Lee.

They were willing to pay $100
each if Recy Taylor would forget
it, White said.

By then the rape of Recy, mother
of a two-year-old daughter, had
become known in every town in
Alabama and every Negro community in the nation. The Grand
Jury was to meet within a week
to act upon one of the few cases
ever to be brought to court of white
youths raping a Negro woman.

White repeated his offer of $100
for each man as a "settlement."

Willie blurted out "No." But that
didn't end it. White came back
and again after more pressure and
threats had been leveled at the
Taylors and Willie said, "Come
back later and I'll tell you." He
came back later and Willie answered "Yes."

Defendants Dismissed

Willie may as well have stuck to
his first no. For the Grand Jury
called on October 9, 1944, dismissed

VICTIM OF WHITE ALABAMA RAPISTS

First published photo of Mrs. Recy Taylor,
victim of six white rapists in Alabama, and
her little family is this picture received from
their refuge in an Alabama city some distance
from their hometown of Abbeville, where the
crime occurred. With the young mother is her
daughter, little Jayce Lee Taylor and her husband, Willie Guy Taylor.

Recy Taylor, Willie Guy Taylor, and their child, Joyce Lee Taylor.

Pointing to the most recent example, Gordon argued that "every southern newspaper played up the rape of the unnamed wife of a white soldier
in Florida" but failed to report the crime against Recy Taylor. Worse, he
fumed, Southern editors stood silent as the alleged black rapists of a white
woman "were burned to death in Florida's electric chair," while Taylor's
assailants weren't even questioned. "The whole country must be aroused
to action," Gordon thundered, "against this and other similar outrages
against Negro womanhood."[54]

In New York City black activists, embroiled in their own grassroots struggles against segregation, police brutality, and housing discrimination, read
Gordon's article and were outraged.[55] They heeded his call to arms by
flocking to Harlem's Hotel Theresa on November 25 for a mass meeting.
Called by the New York branch of the SCHW, and the SNYC's parent
organization, the National Negro Congress, the meeting hoped to draw
attention to the double standard of justice in the South and "find ways and
means of centering nationwide attention on Mrs. Taylor's case and forcing

legal action" in order to "lay a basis for ending this southern practice of degrading Negro womanhood."[56] Their allies in Alabama provided crucial assistance.

More than one hundred people, representing middle-class mainstays like the YWCA, the NAACP, and the National Council of Negro Women, as well as leftist labor unions like the CIO and the Negro Labor Victory Committee, came to the emergency meeting.[57] Audley Moore, a spirited black nationalist who had a long history of defending black women from sexual violence, came as the Harlem representative of the International Workers Order.[58] Prominent black Communists like Benjamin J. Davis and James W. Ford, as well as leftist and Communist-affiliated organizations like the International Labor Defense, filed into the hotel and found seats. Reporters from the leftist *Daily Worker;* the New York tabloid *PM;* the progressive West Coast paper the *California Eagle;* and Adam Clayton Powell, Jr.'s, weekly, *The People's Voice,* clustered around the dais, pencils and notepads at the ready. Alabama SNYC delegates provided local information about the Recy Taylor case.

The assembly of such an eclectic group of activists yielded incredible results. After being briefed on the "Abbeville Affair," participants agreed to partner with the Alabama branches of the SNYC and the SCHW to form the Committee for Equal Justice for Mrs. Recy Taylor. They chose delegates who would immediately travel to Abbeville to investigate the crime and report their findings at the Sixth All-Southern Negro Youth Congress conference, to be held in Atlanta the following week. There they planned to create a "Negro-rights, Negro-white unity campaign throughout the South."[59] When the call for donations came, activists dug into their pockets and contributed close to one hundred dollars. They agreed to use the money to flood the South with flyers decrying white attacks on black women and promised a publicity campaign aimed directly at the governor of Alabama, Chauncey Sparks.[60] As one newspaper article put it, "The phrase 'protection of Southern womanhood' had life and meaning injected into it."[61]

Almost immediately letters and postcards trickled in to Governor Sparks's office. Known as the "Bourbon from Barbour," Chauncey Sparks won the governorship in 1942 by promising to "padlock the state treasury" and keep the federal government's nose out of Alabama's business.[62] Though he eventually started spending money on schools, agricultural programs, and hospitals, he was no Franklin Roosevelt liberal. A tight-lipped and pragmatic conservative, he was also an ardent white suprema-

Alabama Committee for Equal Justice
P. O. BOX 1589, BIRMINGHAM, ALABAMA

Hon. Chauncey Sparks,
Governor of Alabama
State Capitol
Montgomery, Alabama
Dear Governor Sparks:

 I wish to commend you for the action you have so far taken on the Recy Taylor case of Abbeville, Alabama. As a citizen of Alabama, I urge you to use your high office to reconvene the Henry County Grand Jury at the earliest possible moment. Alabamians are depending upon you to see that all obstacles, which are preventing justice in this case, be removed. I know that you will not fail to let the people of Alabama know that there is equal justice for all of our citizens.

Respectfully yours,
Rosa L. Parks
22 Mill St. Montgomery, Ala.

17

Rosa Parks wrote letters, signed petitions, and sent postcards in an effort to secure justice for Recy Taylor.

cist like other anti-tax, anti-labor elite Democrats, known as the Big Mules, in Alabama.

In 1946 Sparks helped lead a campaign to ratify the Boswell Amendment, which made it all but impossible for most African Americans and poor whites to register to vote. He was George Wallace's first mentor and benefactor. In the fall of 1945, Sparks offered the skinny twenty-six-year-old a job as an assistant in the attorney general's office, giving rise to Wallace's storied career.[63]

By mid-December 1944 hundreds of letters protesting the rape of Recy Taylor poured in from all over the country and stacked up on Sparks's desk.[64] "I've heard a great deal of how the South prides itself on protecting its womanhood," Mrs. Gretchen Coon told Governor Sparks. "How do you square this vaunted theory with the practice and the kind of justice evidenced in Abbeville on September 3rd and subsequently?"[65] A "friend of the South" tried to appeal to Sparks's sense of racial duty, pointing out the irrational defense of white supremacy while doing nothing to prevent whites from having sex—coerced or otherwise—with black women.

You are justly and earnestly striving for the purity of your race, yet you openly permit a great many of your men to freely cohabit with women of the Negro race. This is encouraged by your laws. Ironically enough, the Negro man does not seem as desirous of cohabiting with the white woman as the white man is pleased with cohabitation with Negro women . . . The failure to indict the white men [who assaulted Recy Taylor] says to the white youth of the South that it is alright to have sexual intercourse with the Negro . . . [The rapists] in Abbeville Alabama . . . have made your lofty and noble principles of race and good clean society a *joke*.[66]

Charles Collins, executive secretary of the Negro Labor Victory Committee, a leftist labor union, agreed. "The rapists are known, identified, and yet allowed to go unpunished in your state," Collins argued. "This brazen denial of the simple rights of humanity, exposes, more than ever, the emptiness of the white supremacy advocates who employ the charge of 'rape' in order to attack the Negro people."[67]

Unsubstantiated charges of the rape of white women by black men had been part of the Southern political culture for decades. Rumors of rape were rooted in Reconstruction-era stereotypes, in which white Southerners portrayed black men as the mythological incubus, a beast that attacks women while they sleep, to disfranchise African Americans and justify racial violence. Between 1880 and 1920, Southern Democrats fueled rumors of "black beast rapists" defiling pure, white womanhood, in an effort to "redeem" Dixie from the grip of Republican rule. Most often these campaigns amounted to one-sided racial pogroms, as white supremacists used white fears of black male sexuality to seize political control of the state and subjugate African Americans.[68] Even after the white supremacy campaigns secured state legislatures and sanctioned Jim Crow, rumors of black-on-white rape conveniently surfaced whenever African Americans asserted their humanity or challenged white supremacy. "Any assertion of any kind on the part of the Negro," as Southern historian W. J. Cash put it, "constituted in a perfectly real manner, an attack on the southern white woman."[69]

During the 1940s, virtually any self-assertion among African Americans conjured images of "amalgamation" and fears of "social equality," a euphemism for interracial sex.[70] In a rant against wartime black activism, Mississippi senator Theodore Bilbo, perhaps the most acrimonious segregationist in Congress, argued that "every Negro in America who is behind [civil rights] movements . . . dream[s] of social equality and intermarriage between whites and blacks."[71]

Howard Odum, a prominent sociologist from the University of North Carolina, argued that white fears of interracial sex sat at the center of wartime racial tension. In his 1943 study, *Race and Rumors of Race,* Odum documented the "weird, wild stories" whites told one another about blacks.[72] Whites, he said, worried that demands for black equality heralded a bloody insurrection, similar to Nat Turner's murderous slave rebellion in Virginia in 1831.[73] "Negroes are buying up all the ice picks," whites told one another, "waiting for the first blackout" to attack. Many whites believed that blacks were also hoarding guns, stashing them in coffins and church basements, waiting for the right moment to "turn the tables" and "overrule the South."[74]

The most incendiary race rumors were about black men's insatiable lust for white women. According to Odum, these near-hysterical stories reflected white beliefs that rising black activism indicated African Americans' "bold intention" to achieve the hated "social equality."[75]

Everyone had their own version of this story.

"Negro Men were all planning to have white wives," whites whispered to one another in wartime North Carolina. "And when all the white men have gone to war," they said, "the white women will be left for the Negro men."[76] Another tall tale traded among friends in Georgia told of a black man who warned a white couple that they "better be necking now because after the war we'll be doing the necking."[77] In Louisiana whites warned schoolgirls to never walk alone since there was apparently an "outbreak of Negroes attacking white women."[78]

Unsubstantiated rumors of black men attacking innocent white women sparked almost 50 percent of all race riots in the United States between Reconstruction and World War II. In 1943 alone there were 242 violent interracial clashes in forty-seven cities.[79] Beaumont, Texas, was typical of small manufacturing towns reeling from changes wrought by the war. As blacks and whites from surrounding areas poured into the Gulf Coast town for defense jobs, racial tension increased. Lack of housing and health care, overstretched social service providers, and overcrowding on buses and public transportation all threatened the segregated social order. But it was the rumors that a black man brutally raped, beat, and stabbed an eighteen-year-old white telephone operator in Beaumont on June 5, 1943, coupled with reports of a plan among black soldiers to "invade the city in search of unprotected white women," that triggered a riot in the tinderbox town.[80]

When a twenty-four-year-old white woman claimed she was attacked by a black man in her "victory garden" a few days later, a mob of more than two thousand white men, mostly bulky stevedores, rampaged through the black neighborhood, beating pedestrians and burning businesses. In their wake, they left hundreds injured and three dead and destroyed more than two hundred buildings.[81] The Beaumont riot was hardly unusual; racial disturbances in Wilmington, North Carolina, in 1898, Atlanta in 1906, Springfield, Illinois, in 1908, Omaha, Nebraska, and Washington D.C., in 1919, Tulsa, Oklahoma, in 1921, and Mobile, Alabama, in 1943 were all sparked by rumored incidents of rape or manufactured "rape epidemics" involving black men and white women.[82]

Rumors about the mistreatment and rape of *black* women by *white* men started plenty of brawls throughout the South, too, but none caused as much violence and bloodshed as the rumor that made Detroit explode in the summer of 1943. Three days of rioting left thirty-four people dead, nearly seven hundred injured, and an estimated $2 million in property damage.[83] During World War II, Detroit, like Beaumont, teetered on the edge of racial cataclysm. Five hundred thousand black and white migrant workers poured into the Motor City, clashing over defense jobs, housing, and access to transportation, public parks, and education. On June 20, 1943, the temperature soared past ninety degrees, and thousands of Detroit's working-class residents sought relief on the beaches of Belle Isle. Throughout the day, isolated scuffles broke out between black and white picnickers who competed for grills and tables. These minor skirmishes erupted into a full-scale riot after rumors that a white Southerner had thrown a black mother and her baby off the Belle Isle Bridge sent hundreds of black men streaming into the streets to defend and protect black womanhood.[84]

The rumor that sparked the Detroit riot was one of many sexual stories detailing the widespread mistreatment of black women during the 1940s. The most oft-repeated tale insisted that "white soldiers in the South were mistreating Negro women." One rumor told of a white MP who "had beaten the wife of a Negro soldier in a Georgia camp." Another story, from Mississippi, described the beating of black soliders while police attacked their wives and girlfriends. There were also plenty of stories circulating about black women who had been arrested and beaten by policemen after protesting mistreatment on buses.[85]

As a kind of cultural narrative, rumors of rape and sexualized violence had enormous symbolic power and political potency. Whites used outrageous racial rumors and rape scares to justify strengthening segregation and white supremacy. Meanwhile the stories of sexual subjugation and racial terror that circulated among African Americans exposed white hypocrisy about interracial sex and spurred demands for equal justice and bodily integrity. Given the tenuous social and political environment into which the Recy Taylor story quickly spread, it was bound to spark similar fears and anxieties, if not violent clashes.

Perhaps few understood this better than members of the U.S. military. Thirty-three soldiers from "somewhere in Belgium" put down their guns and picked up pens to sign a petition addressed to Governor Sparks. They demanded he use his gubernatorial powers to intervene in the case. "Failure to act in any such case," the soldiers argued, "is a matter of grave concern to everyone believing in the principles of American democracy—the principle of the equality of all before the law, regardless of race, color or religion; particularly to those of us who face a ruthless enemy to preserve that democracy." The failure to hold white men accountable was irresponsible: "we are engaged in a war for freedom," they insisted, "which requires the united support of all Americans, Negro and White."[86]

In a letter to Governor Sparks, Eugene Henderson, an African-American merchant seaman, noted the irony of America's role as defender of democracy abroad while it denied justice at home. "I have risked my life many times to deliver supplies to our armed forces and our allies," he said. "My morale drops when I learn that a woman of my race has been brutally raped by six white men and nothing done about it." Why, Henderson asked, "isn't Negro womanhood as sacred as white womanhood?"[87] Ernest Scott, president of the Transport Workers of America, echoed Henderson's sentiments and feared that the "effect of such lawlessness on the morale of our men in the armed services . . . cannot but be bad . . . [T]he least we can do for our servicemen and women is to assure them that while they are fighting our country's battles . . . their families back home are safe."[88]

Enough black troops were upset by the gang rape of Recy Taylor that Charles S. Seely, the editorial director of the *Army News,* felt compelled to urge Governor Sparks to act. "If this pamphlet reaches any considerable number of Negroes in our armed services, and I have no doubt it will," he warned Sparks, "it will greatly affect their efficiency . . . This of course will be very bad for the war effort," he argued, "for it is senseless to fight

fascism abroad if fascistic influences are to be protected here at home."
Seely asked Sparks for a statement "that assures Negro soldiers that you
will see to it that the 'degenerate and ruthless persons who attacked Mrs.
Taylor are brought to justice and severely punished.' " If Sparks would
commit to a similar statement, Seely argued, he could "publish it in all
three of our papers . . . This way," he insisted, "it will reach a great many
of the million or so American Negroes who are fighting for democracy"
and "help keep up the morale of the Negroes in our services."[89]

As the "Abbeville Affair" threatened America's war effort, Governor
Sparks worried about the negative publicity the assault would have on his
state. Mr. and Mrs. Scott McCall told Sparks that the rape of Recy Taylor
"was as bad as what we would expect from the Nazis."[90] Julius Crane, the
vice president of the United Shoe Workers of America, demanded Governor Sparks take "immediate steps" to try Taylor's assailants "before
Alabama is placed on Hitler's list as a possible postwar refuge."[91] Perhaps Crane knew that Fort Rucker, a military base just outside Abbeville,
was already home to German prisoners of war, who were often treated better than African-American citizens.[92]

Letters and petitions continued to pour in from concerned Alabamians,
and Sparks worried that he faced "another Scottsboro," as one correspondent after another called it. The governor knew that in places like Birmingham, Mobile, and Montgomery, where fierce labor competition,
union battles, and rabid racism created a volatile climate, the failure to
prosecute Recy Taylor's assailants could easily cause an explosion.[93] Of
course, prosecuting them also carried risks, but Taylor's defenders seemed
considerably better organized than her antagonists. Just before Christmas,
Eugene Gordon from the *Daily Worker* teamed up with E. G. Jackson,
Montgomery activist and editor of the popular black newspaper the
Alabama Tribune, to confront Sparks. Inside the imposing white marble
capitol, where Jefferson Davis pledged his loyalty to the Confederacy in
1861, Governor Sparks reluctantly agreed to launch an investigation.
Sparks hedged, making no commitments to a just outcome. Still, Gordon
and Jackson sensed the governor's responsiveness to outside pressures. In
an article about their meeting, Gordon reported that "the Governor . . . agreed with his Attorney General that they wanted no publicity.
They wished to make their investigations and decide on what action to
take, all without the *Daily Worker* or the Negro press saying anything
about the fact that the state's highest officers were interested."[94]

If Governor Sparks hoped to keep his decision a secret, members of the Committee for Equal Justice proclaimed the news far and wide. Talk of Sparks's interest propelled local leaders into action, many of whom formed local branches of the Committee for Equal Justice for Mrs. Recy Taylor. "I found people in Birmingham, Montgomery and other Alabama cities and towns," Gordon noted, "talking about the case as a result" of the official investigation. "Young people," he boasted, "were asking their churches to get in on the case."[95]

In Montgomery, Rosa and Raymond Parks joined E. D. Nixon; Rufus A. Lewis; Johnnie Carr and her husband Arlam Carr, Sr., both longtime NAACP members; E. G. Jackson; and Mrs. Irene West, the wife of Montgomery's only black dentist, to raise money for Taylor's defense. They organized mass meetings, canvassed neighborhoods, signed petitions, and sent postcards to the governor and attorney general.[96] These networks—these very people—would lift Martin Luther King, Jr., to international prominence a decade later, after their leading organizer was arrested on a Montgomery bus. The protection of the dignity of black women's bodies, begun in a long twilight struggle in causes like the Abbeville crusade, would alter the arc of human history, making the word *Montgomery* an enduring metaphor for the power of nonviolent direct action.

Montgomery was not the only city with a local chapter of the Committee for Equal Justice. By January, the *Worker* reported that the "Taylor Case Is Now Nationwide," with branches in sixteen states and Washington, D.C.[97] Distinguished activists, artists, and political leaders added their names to the growing board of advisers. Such luminaries included W.E.B. Du Bois; Mary Church Terrell, a suffragist and founder of the National Association of Colored Women; Charlotte Hawkins Brown, a popular clubwoman and respected educator; Ira De A. Reid, a sociologist and assistant director of the newly formed Southern Regional Council; John Sengstacke, the publisher of the *Chicago Defender*; Countee Cullen and Langston Hughes of Harlem Renaissance fame; Lillian Smith, author of the controversial interracial love story *Strange Fruit*; and Broadway impresario Oscar Hammerstein II. Such an illustrious roster raised eyebrows—especially among anti-Communists, who suspected the Committee for Equal Justice was nothing but a front for the Communist Party.

J. B. Matthews, one of the most well-known professional anti-

Communists who worked for the House Un-American Activities Committee and named names for the Hearst Corporation, warned the FBI that the Committee for Equal Justice for Mrs. Recy Taylor (CEJRT) contained more than "400 names" and was the "chief large-scale agitation of the communists in the South at the present time." The Communist Party, he said, was engaged "in one of their typical agitational campaigns to exploit the incident of Mrs. Taylor's rape, just as they agitated for many years on the subject of the Scottsboro case."[98] While Matthews was correct that some members of the CEJRT were Communists or "fellow travelers," it was not a front for Communism. But its glaring spotlight on white men who raped black women did smack of subversion. Exposure of this historic relationship threatened to unravel the racial and sexual status quo that held the segregated social order together. For Montgomery's black activists, the prospect of striking at the heart of the matter was invigorating.

"With the people, black and white, North and South mobilized for a fight for justice around Mrs. Taylor," E. D. Nixon told Earl Conrad, a reporter for the *Chicago Defender,* "we now have the strength and power to do something with it." Nixon lamented that cases "like this or cases almost as serious as this are so frequent down here that we almost take them as a matter of course. It's a question of choice sometimes—which we can concentrate on for a fight."[99]

Nixon was Montgomery's most outspoken black activist. According to Roy Wilkins, he was "straight as a ramrod, tough as a mule and braver than a squad of marines." In addition to leading the Montgomery NAACP, Nixon served as head of the Alabama Voters League. In 1944 he led nearly eight hundred African Americans on a march to the registrar's office, demanding the right to vote. His fearlessness and constant agitation caught the attention of the city's white newspaper, the *Montgomery Advertiser,* which referred to him later as the "NAACP Mau Mau Chief."[100] As president of the Alabama branch of the nation's largest all-black labor union, the Brotherhood of Sleeping Car Porters, Nixon was connected to militant unionists who knew how to organize. Led by the powerful and imposing A. Philip Randolph, the Brotherhood of Sleeping Car Porters was one of the most successful labor unions during the 1940s. In 1941 Randolph threatened to bring his army of sleeping car porters to Washington unless President Franklin Delano Roosevelt ended segregation in defense industries. Fearing global embarrassment on the eve of America's entry into World War II, Roosevelt capitulated and signed Executive

Order 8802, creating the Fair Employment Practice Committee. Randolph recognized Nixon's indomitable energy and political talent early on and served as his mentor for many years.

E. D. Nixon told the *Defender* reporter that he had "a dossier of fifty cases of rotten violence against Negroes in Alabama in the past couple years—we hardly know where to begin in approaching this question." Since Rosa Parks lived next door to Nixon, served as his personal secretary, managed his union office, and did field work for the Montgomery NAACP, she almost certainly prepared the file Nixon referenced. E. G. Jackson, editor of the *Alabama Tribune,* sat next to Nixon as the reporter from the *Defender* took notes. Nixon provided grisly details of what he called "one horror tale after another of white male degradation of the Negro women of Montgomery and lower Alabama." "We have numerous reports from our women," Jackson said, "of assaults by white taxicab drivers . . . The cabbies take them into their cars at the railroad depot, but before taking them home, drive them outside the town, and subject them to attacks." Jackson and Nixon told the *Defender* that what happened to Recy Taylor was hardly unusual—it was part of a ritual of rape in which white men in the segregated South abducted and assaulted black women with alarming regularity and stunning uniformity. "We Negro men feel powerless," Jackson confessed. "The weight of hundreds of years hangs over us like so much iron . . . [W]e would be superhuman if we alone could lift it off of our shoulders."[101]

During the 1940s, reports of sexual violence directed at black women flooded into local and national NAACP chapters. Women's stories spilled out in letters to the Justice Department and appeared on the front pages of the nation's leading black newspapers. The stories told how white men lured black women and girls away from home with promises of steady work and better wages; attacked them on the job; abducted them at gunpoint while they were traveling to or from home, work, or church; and sexually humiliated and harassed them at bus stops, grocery stores, and in other public places. John McCray, a spirited advocate for black voting rights in South Carolina and editor and publisher of the *Lighthouse and Informer,* the Palmetto State's most important black newspaper, argued that it was a "commonplace experience for many of our women in southern towns . . . to be propositioned openly by white men. You can pick up accounts of these at a dime a dozen in almost any community."[102]

The stories followed similar patterns. In January 1940 John H. Davis, a white man from Fayetteville, North Carolina, lured sixteen-year-old Mary Poole from her home by promising her a job "as a nurse girl for his wife." Instead, as she put it, he "drove her to some woods" and "forced her to submit." As he drove away, abandoning her in the woods, he tossed her clothes out of the car window.[103] In May 1942 Sadie Mae Gibson, a twenty-three-year-old black schoolteacher in Decatur, Alabama, was walking home one sunny afternoon when Dan Olinger, a white teenager, forced her into a clump of bushes and at rifle point raped her.[104] Two months later, as Rosa Lee Cherry, a black high school student, walked home from church in Little Rock, Arkansas, three uniformed police officers threatened to throw her in jail unless she got in their patrol car. They drove her behind a railroad embankment and sexually molested her. She escaped after promising to "get them another girl."[105]

Lila Belle Carter, a sixteen-year-old girl from Pine Island, South Carolina, never escaped. She was abducted in October 1945, on her way to the store for some rice. After a white insurance collector raped her, he murdered her and left her lying face down in a puddle of mud.[106] While most victims did not share Lila Belle Carter's fate, the method her assailant used—abduction—was quite common. Nannie Strayhorn, a thirty-two-year-old mother of two from Richmond, Virginia, accepted a ride home from two white police officers in October 1946. Instead of taking her home, officers Carl R. Burleson and Leonard E. Davis drove to an isolated area outside town and took turns raping her at gunpoint.[107] In Clio, Alabama, in 1948, a white man offered Janie Mae Patterson, an eleven-year-old girl, some money in exchange for help finding a well to slake his thirst. She eagerly climbed into his car and promised to show him the way. Instead of following the girl's directions, he drove to a mill about five miles away, "took a blanket out of his car," and then "ravished the girl."[108]

The sexual violence enacted and enforced rules of racial and economic hierarchy. When Herschel Gasque and Charles Berryhill, two white farmers brandishing guns, knocked on Mrs. Mamie Patterson's door in Tuscumbia, Alabama, in February 1948 to "collect a debt from [her] husband," she refused to divulge his whereabouts. When she demanded that they leave, they pushed Patterson aside and barreled into her house, where they found her husband hiding. Gasque and Berryhill, a "200-pound former professional wrestler," brutally beat Patterson's husband, then turned their pistols on her and slowly backed her outside into their car.[109] In retaliation for Patterson's defiance, the white men drove the mother of six into the woods, where "they both raped [her]" and told her to "perform abnormal acts."[110]

In order to reclaim their bodies and their humanity, African-American women called on a tradition of testimony and truth-telling that stretched back to slavery. "We colored women are tired of such things," Mrs. Joy B. Jones proclaimed in a 1947 letter to NAACP founder Arthur Springarn. She attached a news clipping that described the sexual molestation of a black girl by a white businessman in Macon, Georgia. "Seems like all the money we pay in organizations," Jones argued, "doesn't remedy the matter. This man should be given the same conviction that a colored man would have got."[111]

Failure in the courts did not stop black women from speaking out, decades before the women's movement. These testimonies helped bring attention to the issue of sexual violence and often ignited local campaigns for equal justice and civil rights. When James Lee Perry, a "well-to-do white oil dealer" from Meridian, Mississippi, raped Ruby Atee Pigford, a black teenager, he never expected her to report the crime. Even if she did, he could be fairly confident that white authorities would not take her complaint seriously. Perry lured the girl away from home by promising her a babysitting job that paid seventy cents an hour—good money at the time. After picking her up on August 7, 1947, Perry drove Pigford to a nearby roadhouse, instead of taking her to his home. Angered by her refusal to accompany him into the bar, he beat her until she was unconscious. He then raped her, tied her to the bumper of his car, and dragged her bound body through town. He dumped her, bruised and battered, outside her home later that evening.[112]

She told her parents what happened, and they told their friends. By the next day, African Americans throughout town demanded punishment for the crime. Edward Knott, Jr., the secretary of the Meridian, Mississippi, NAACP, wired the story to the *Pittsburgh Courier* and airmailed a letter to the national NAACP office. Assistant special counsel Marian Wynn Perry responded immediately. "We have discussed the case here in this office in light of the conditions in Mississippi and action which is possible there," she said. "It is our suggestion that as much publicity as possible be given to the case." Perry knew that accusing a white man of raping a black woman in Mississippi, the most violent state in the South, was dangerous, if not deadly.

In Mississippi, African Americans understood that their lives "could be snuffed out on whim."[113] Aside from the daily indignities of segregation, between 1943 and 1949, white men in Mississippi castrated, mutilated, and lynched two fourteen-year-old black boys for playing tag with a white girl near the town of Quitman; murdered a dairy farmer, who had used self-defense when his white employer attacked him; killed Reverend Isaac Simmons and cut off his tongue for refusing to sell his land; whipped Leon McTate to death for allegedly stealing a saddle; and beat Malcolm Wright to a bloody pulp because they didn't like the way he drove a wagon.[114]

"The only chance you have to secure redress for this terrible attack," the NAACP assistant counsel asserted in the rape and dragging of Ruby Pigford, "is by publicity and pressure within the State of Mississippi, and you, of course, who are in Mississippi, will know how much can be done." Perry encouraged Knott and other concerned citizens to get the local black newspaper, the *Jackson Advocate,* and its editor, Percy Greene, on board. She also promised assistance from the national office, which eagerly protested lynching but rarely got involved in rape cases. After signing off, Perry sent a picture of a bloodied and battered Ruby Pigford in her hospital bed to the *Pittsburgh Courier* for an exclusive report.[115] Perry seemed to understand that justice in the Pigford case, like so many others, was unlikely. The only feasible way to hold white men accountable for raping black women—since Southern courts would not—was to draw outside attention to the crime.[116]

"If the state of Alabama does not handle [the Recy Taylor] case in the way it ought to," E. G. Jackson thundered from the pulpit of the Dexter Avenue Baptist Church in December 1944, "if the right-minded citizen[s] of the state do not demand indictment in this situation, then . . . the Negro people will welcome and invite all of the assistance that they can get from the North."[117] It was no idle threat. The *Chicago Defender* called the attack on Recy Taylor "Dixie's most blatant rape case." When the *Defender* argued that the CEJRT had launched the "strongest campaign for equal justice to be seen in a decade," they meant that Rosa Parks's trip to Abbeville had grown into the most successful national campaign for racial justice since the Scottsboro trials, where Parks had first learned how to organize.

Prominent white Alabamians took the growing movement seriously. Like Parks, they too remembered Scottsboro. Mrs. Margaret H. Moss, pres-

ident of Alabama's Federation of Women's Clubs, wrote to Governor
Sparks for advice. Fretting about the effect the "northern press" and "out-
siders" could have on her beloved state's reputation, she offered the governor some advice. "Some years ago, when visiting my brothers in
Washington," she wrote, "I found that many people knew little of the conditions in our state beyond 'Stars Fell on Alabama,' the football team and
the Scottsboro case." Fearful of "another misrepresentation of Alabama"
caused by the "delay and inaction of government in the Abbeville affair,"
she asked Sparks for a statement promising equal justice. That way, she
said, "I can be armed with something to say when rumors and mistaken
information come to me." For example, she said, "I am told, that the assistant attorney general is quoted as saying that 'he hates niggers and would
as soon run over one in his car as to speak to one.' I am also told," Moss
continued, "that the case is being discussed in the Negro National Press
and committees are being formed in a number of other states to see the
matter through. This all sounds so unnecessary." At least, she added, they
agreed that "the less publicity the better."[118]

Governor Sparks hoped that promising a separate investigation would
hold back protests, but it did not stem the tide of petitions and letters
pouring into the governor's office, especially after the *Pittsburgh Courier*
ran the erroneous headline "Sparks to Press Charges Against Rapists Following Protests" in a front-page article two days before Christmas.[119] As
time wore on without any major arrests or trials, Sparks became the protesters' number-one target.

Instead of targeting Sparks, who followed through on his promise to
launch an investigation, the Committee for Equal Justice should perhaps
have directed national attention to G. D. Halstead and Keener Baxley, the
less visible but, in this case, more powerful county and circuit solicitors,
whose intransigence kept the case bottled up. In order to get a sense of
what was going on in Henry County, Sparks sent his private investigators,
J. V. Kitchens and N. W. Kimbrough, to Dothan, Alabama, on December 9, 1944, to interview Halstead, Baxley, and Sheriff George H. Gamble. While Baxley readily admitted that "in his opinion the crime was
committed as alleged by the victim," he feigned ignorance about how to
move forward. "No further facts could be ascertained," he claimed,
"because the victim stated . . . that she did not know any of the boys that
she claimed to have ravished her." Halstead seconded Baxley's defense. He
"had come to a block," he said, and did not know "how any additional
information could be obtained . . . It would be free-lancing," Halstead

insisted, "as no one else knew any of the facts in this case" and "neither of the witnesses had identified the boys who were alleged to have ravished Recy Taylor." When the investigators reminded them that Recy Taylor had identified Hugo Wilson as one of her assailants and owner of the car used in the attack, Baxley grew visibly upset. He "would not consent for any of them to be interviewed," Baxley stammered.[120] Baxley's bluster did not scare Kimbrough and Kitchens, who had not come to ask permission.

In Abbeville the next day, Sheriff George Gamble, who claimed to have started an investigation immediately after the crime was alleged, told the investigators that he placed Hugo Wilson under a five-hundred-dollar bond. He also assured them that he arrested "all of the boys except Wilson" two days after the assault. Taking the investigators aside, Gamble warned them that the "victim was nothing but a whore around Abbeville" and had "been treated for some time by the Health Officer of Henry County for venereal disease." Gamble claimed he even had to put Taylor in jail "once or twice . . . upon written request from the County Health Officer." To further discredit Taylor and discourage the investigators from pursuing the case, Gamble added that Taylor's husband "would not work and lay around Abbeville practically all the time." He even threatened to throw him "in jail and charge him with vagrancy."[121]

Will Cook, the former police chief and white store owner who said he launched a search for Taylor after she was abducted, told the investigators the same story Gamble had just peddled. After detailing his role in the search that night, Cook smeared Taylor as a prostitute. She "was nothing but a whore around Abbeville," he insisted. She worked at Fort Rucker, a nearby army training base, he said, "but they ran her away from there [after she] had given a number of soldiers . . . the clapp."[122]

Other whites with whom Kimbrough and Kitchens spoke contradicted Gamble's and Cook's stereotypical descriptions of the Taylors. Mr. W. H. Carr, Recy Taylor's neighbor and occasional boss, told investigators that Recy and her husband "were good workers." In more than three years, he said, he had "never seen any strange Negroes hanging around their home." They "always stayed in their place," Carr said, and had "never been involved in any disturbances of any kind."[123] Other white men in Abbeville corroborated Carr's characterization of Recy Taylor as an upstanding, respectable woman who abided by the town's racial and sexual mores. Marvin White, L. D. Smith, Robert Sowell, and M. B. Clark, all honorable white men in the community, stated that they knew Taylor and "knew nothing detrimental as to her character." Most folks, they said, "consider her above the average Negro as to her conduct as a Negro woman in the community."[124] Major L. A. Hamilton at Fort Rucker told the investigators that there was nothing in Taylor's file "regarding any misconduct of any nature."[125]

Kimbrough and Kitchens soon found proof that Sheriff Gamble was lying. Searching through the bonds filed at the Henry County Circuit Court, they discovered that Gamble never placed any of the assailants under arrest, not even Wilson, who admitted having sex with Taylor.[126] After confronting Gamble with the conflicting information, the sheriff stonewalled. "It's a bad case," he said.[127]

Despite Gamble's intransigence, Kimbrough and Kitchens returned to Abbeville with the assistant attorney general, John O. Harris, on December 18, 1944. When they arrived, they contacted Sheriff Gamble, whose story quickly changed in front of the governor's deputy. Gamble told the assistant attorney general that he "never arrested [Taylor] or committed her to jail for any offense." Nor did he ever have "any trouble with her or her husband." Taylor's reputation, Gamble now claimed, "is as good as any Negro's in that community." While Gamble still insisted he had arrested the assailants, Kimbrough and Kitchens decided to go directly to the source and ask the suspects what happened the night they picked up Recy Taylor.

Almost all of them told the same story. Four of the seven men admitted having intercourse with Taylor, but argued that she was essentially a prostitute and a willing participant. They took up a collection to pay her, they said. All but two of them said Taylor got into the car of her own volition and that there was no force or coercion used. Hugo Wilson, whom Taylor and other witnesses identified on the night of the crime, said he had had nothing to do with her, denied being present, and claimed to know "nothing in the world about it." Recy Taylor, he added, was a "damned liar," and so were the sheriff and anyone else who claimed they saw him that night. Herbert Lovett, who cradled a shotgun during the attack on Taylor, claimed he "was never arrested" and "knew nothing of the affair." Furthermore, he said, he was not with any of the other suspects that night and did not know why his friends "would want to bring him into something of which he knew nothing and was innocent."[128]

Joe Culpepper's version of events corroborated Recy Taylor's testimony in considerable detail. Culpepper said that he and the other men "were talking about getting a woman" on that September night and "rode out on the highway toward Dothan . . . We saw two women and a man walking along the highway," he said, and decided to pull over. "All of them except one got out of the automobile." Herbert Lovett, he added, took his shotgun "down the road and was talking to Recy Taylor." A few moments later, Culpepper said, "Recy Taylor came to the automobile with Lovett behind her with the shotgun in his hand." After turning off the highway, Culpepper recalled that Taylor yelled, "Yo'all are not carrying me to Mr. Gamble." When they stopped beneath a patch of trees, Lovett forced her out of the car at gunpoint and made her undress. "She was crying and asking them to let her go home to her husband and her baby," Culpepper said. When it was over, he said, "someone . . . put a blindfold on Recy's face, got her in the car and put her out near a street light." Culpepper added nothing about paying her, but when asked directly by the detectives, he quickly corrected himself. "Yes," he said, "they paid her money." He could not remember who took up the collection, however, or how much she received.[129]

With the suspects' statements, Culpepper's admission of coercion, signed affidavits from at least three eyewitnesses, and Sheriff Gamble's recantations and lies, Governor Sparks had enough ammunition to order a second grand jury hearing. He appointed Assistant Attorney General William O. Harris to lead the charge. After meeting with Harris to go over the case, members of the Committee for Equal Justice gathered to debate hiring a new attorney. According to Pauline Dobbs, a SNYC worker present at the meeting, Harris seemed "more concerned about the representative . . . sent by the *Daily Worker* to investigate the case" and the "deluge of letters and telegrams received from northern pressure groups" than he was about the "guilt of the criminals or the crime itself." The whole "purpose of presenting the case to the grand jury in Abbeville," Dobbs noted, "was to give the defendants light sentences in order to close the case."[130]

Dobbs was right to worry. The attorney general failed to convince the jurors of Henry County that there was enough evidence to indict the seven suspects when he presented Taylor's case on February 14, 1945. With at least one confession and corroborating testimonies among the suspects, not to mention the sheriff's blatant attempt to stuff the entire affair under the carpet, it seemed like a relatively easy case to close. But the all-white, all-male jurors sat stony-faced and silent. For a second time, they refused to issue any indictments.

News coverage of the second hearing was more hostile to Taylor. The *Dothan Eagle* repeatedly referred to Recy Taylor as "the Taylor woman" and dismissed her testimony—arguing that she was essentially a prostitute. The *Birmingham News* expressed concern, but not for justice or for Recy Taylor. Instead, editors worried that the outcome would only aid "those disposed to think ill of Alabama because of the Scottsboro case." The Recy Taylor case, the *News* noted, "was certain to become a *cause célèbre*" and "*that* is why all Alabamians should be interested." Already, the editors proclaimed, "this ugly business has drawn national attention." The ghosts of Scottsboro haunted every discussion. Residents of Henry County "ought to know by this time what agitation for justice by disadvantaged persons can do to bedevil the life of the state."[131] The assistant attorney general told the *Dothan Eagle* there was nothing more that could be done. "This case has been presented to two grand juries in Henry County," he said, and "both grand juries have not seen fit to find an indictment." Harris argued that he made a "full disclosure . . . and no facts or circumstances connected with this case have been suppressed."[132]

Members of the Alabama Committee for Equal Justice were disheartened by Harris's statement, which implied that the state no longer planned to intervene on behalf of Recy Taylor. It all seemed a little too tidy. E. G. Jackson, E. D. Nixon, and Rosa Parks worried that the state's public resignation put Taylor and her family in imminent danger. Esther Cooper of the SNYC checked in on Recy Taylor after the trial. Taylor "shows in her face the terror of her experience," Cooper said. Taylor told Cooper that their mail often arrived already opened and that she was afraid to go into town.[133] Fearful of white retaliation, Parks, Nixon, and other members of the Alabama Committee for Equal Justice moved Taylor and her family to Montgomery, where they provided an apartment and secured a job for her husband.[134] Clara Hard Rutledge, who was one of a handful of liberal white women in Montgomery who supported the Taylor case and the bus boycott ten years later, helped to organize other sympathetic whites. She told Earl Conrad, the reporter for the *Chicago Defender,* that the "only possible approach at the present time is letters to the Governor."[135] Local members of the Alabama Committee for Equal Justice followed Rutledge's advice and redoubled their efforts to persuade Governor Sparks to intervene. Henrietta Buckmaster, a historian and the new chairwoman of the national Committee for Equal Justice, also urged supporters across the nation to contact Sparks and send money to the committee. "We can bring these criminals to justice," she proclaimed, "because the Recy Taylor case is the people's case."[136]

Alexander Nunn, the white editor of the *Progressive Farmer,* a conservative magazine, watched the case "with apprehension" and worried that the failure to indict would hurt Alabama in the long run. In a letter to Governor Sparks, Nunn encouraged him to send the attackers to jail. "We had a similar case," Nunn wrote, "though not so disgusting, in my home county of Lee several years ago and the white man, a taxicab driver, was set free at that time. I said then and I say to you now, that for the good of both races, I think I would punish even more quickly and severely, white men for criminally attacking Negro women than I would Negro men." Lest Sparks mistake him for a wishy-washy liberal, Nunn reminded him that "no one in this state would be more severe on a Negro in such cases than I would." Sparks replied that his hands were tied: "Nothing further can be done without a grand jury indictment. As you know, the grand jury of any county is all-powerful in the matter of criminal investigation and prosecution. No trial can be had until a grand jury returns an indictment."[137] While letters still urged Sparks to intervene, by springtime it was apparent that the "people's case" was going nowhere.

As time passed without an indictment, Henrietta Buckmaster and members of the executive board of the Committee for Equal Justice quietly agreed to shift their attention away from the Taylor case and "broaden the scope of [their] work."[138] At the end of March, the CEJRT issued a press release for a different rape case: "Another young Negro girl has been raped under circumstances of almost incredible brutality. This committee was organized to fight for equal justice for Recy Taylor, but we cannot ignore another such case." The press release referenced a recent case in which three white men in Decatur, Georgia, kidnapped and raped a seventeen-year-old black high school girl. Unlike the Taylor case, a grand jury indicted the assailants, but an all-white jury acquitted the three men at their criminal trial on March 23, 1945, after deliberating for only six minutes.[139]

In a letter to board members on April 2, 1945, Buckmaster acknowledged defeat in the Recy Taylor case. It was time, she said, to "put all [our] forces behind the demand for punishment of the rapists of a 17 year old Negro girl in Decatur."[140] Shortly thereafter they sent out flyers screaming, "The Terror Spreads!" In Memphis, Tennessee, the committee announced, "Two Negro girls were forced into a police car, taken for a ride in the country and criminally assaulted by two uniformed policemen." And in Bennettsville, South Carolina, "a respectable Negro woman was ordered off the streets by four white men and forced to pay a five dollar fine." By referring to these very different incidents as "terror," the CEJRT signaled its intent to wage war not only upon the ritual of rape but also upon the everyday assaults African-American women faced.

In a pamphlet promoting the committee's broader approach, Buckmaster argued that despite the lack of a legal conviction, the successful mobilization of activists across the nation on behalf of Recy Taylor represented a major victory. "Our hope of a free new world," she said, "our passionate conviction that the day has almost come when women everywhere may raise their children without fear and love their husbands with assurance and be the individuals to which their highest hopes and capacities entitled them. This is what we're fighting for . . . When we say 'Equal Justice for Recy Taylor,'" Buckmaster wrote, "we are also saying Equal Hope, Equal Joy, Equal Dignity for every woman, child and man the wide world over . . . Is that too much to ask?"

The announcement of the Committee for Equal Justice's new aims came on the eve of the greatest red scare in American history.[141] Coupled with the legal dead-ends it hit in Alabama, the committee's ability to mobilize local people and rally nationwide support slowed as Southern segregationists combined white supremacy and vicious red-baiting to attack African-American activism as a Communist plot to destroy "the Southern way of life." These bitter attacks forced the more radical leaders of the Alabama branch of the CEJRT, like the SNYC women, to seek shelter in other states or less tainted organizations, where they continued to press for racial justice. Mainstream black activists who were involved in the campaign for equal justice for Recy Taylor, but were otherwise not affiliated with the Communist Party, like E. D. Nixon, Rosa Parks, E. G. Jackson, Rufus Lewis, and Johnnie Carr in Montgomery, distanced themselves from their more radical allies. In later years, they would use the international Cold War as a political lever to expose the deep canyon between the United States' boasts of freedom and democracy and the brutal reality of segregation. But when the Red Scare began, they did what was necessary to survive politically and continue their assault on Jim Crow.[142]

Although the struggle to secure justice for Recy Taylor did not succeed in the short term, it was the largest and best organized of many efforts to draw attention to the ruthless heart of the racial caste system. Decades later, when radical feminists finally made rape and sexual assault political issues, they walked in the footsteps of generations of black women. If they did not always know this, it was hardly the fault of African-American women in the South, who testified both in the nation's courts and in its newspapers that their bodies were not their own. The Recy Taylor case brought the building blocks of the Montgomery bus boycott together a decade earlier and kept them in place until it became Rosa Parks's turn to testify. When that boycott took off, no one called it a women's movement, though many observers then and since have noted the centrality of women in its ranks. Even Dr. King credited "the zeitgeist" when asked to comment on the strange, spontaneous combustion of the bus protest. But the Montgomery bus boycott was not a prairie fire, or a rising tide, or a gear that tumbled in the cosmos. It was another in a series of campaigns that began when Rosa Parks rode up to Abbeville in 1944 to gather the facts in the Recy Taylor case, so that black women could tell their stories.

Indeed, many of the African Americans who cut their political teeth defending black women like Recy Taylor who were raped by white men in Alabama in the 1940s brought their experiences and organizational insight to other struggles for dignity and justice in the 1950s and 1960s. Like E. D. Nixon and Rosa Parks in Montgomery, they often became pillars of the modern civil rights movement.

The national campaign to defend Recy Taylor highlighted the power of sexual stories to mobilize communities and build coalitions. African Americans throughout the country risked their lives and livelihoods on behalf of black women's right to bodily integrity. This cut to the heart of people's lives. It was deeper than voting rights, deeper than the poisons of stigma and exploitation, though those cruelties were also fundamental to the racial caste system.

While the survivors of sexualized violence rarely received justice in Southern courts, black women like Recy Taylor who were raped by white men in the 1940s used their voices as weapons against white supremacy. Their testimonies were a form of direct action. Taylor's refusal to remain silent helped expose a ritual of rape in existence since slavery, inspired a nationwide campaign to defend black womanhood, and gave hope to thousands suffering through similar abuses. Because of the campaign for equal justice for Recy Taylor, sexual violence and interracial rape became the battleground upon which African Americans sought to destroy white supremacy and gain personal and political autonomy. That battleground is where the modern civil rights movement began, though its roots were as deep as the Atlantic slave trade.

As World War II came to a bloody close, another war was about to begin on the buses in Montgomery, Alabama.

CHAPTER 2

"Negroes Every Day Are Being Molested"

AFTER SPENDING a hot July day in 1942 studying at Alabama State Teachers College in Montgomery, Ella Ree Jones decided to catch the earliest bus home. She felt ill all morning and was in no mood for a fight. She boarded the Cleveland Avenue bus, the same one Rosa Parks would make famous thirteen years later, and quietly slipped into a seat opposite the rear door, in the section reserved for colored passengers. The bus filled to capacity as it rumbled through downtown Montgomery. Glancing into his rearview mirror, the bus driver noticed one white man standing. At the next stop, he turned and glared at Jones.

"Girl, get up and let this passenger sit down," he said.

"I am sick," Jones replied. "And I don't feel able to stand up for that man to sit down. Besides," she added, "I am over halfway to the back of the bus."

Unwilling to engage in a debate about the subtleties of segregation, the driver became agitated. "Do you want to stand up," he shouted, "or do you want me to put you off?"

"Neither," Jones said.

Suddenly the bus lurched to the curb, and the driver scurried out. He made sure he locked the back door before he called the police.[1]

The trapped black and white passengers collectively held their breath. Granted police powers, bus drivers enforced segregation with an iron fist.

Many kept blackjacks and pistols under their seats, wielding them whenever their authority was challenged. It was not unusual for black passengers to defy drivers, whose penchant for cruelty angered even the most accommodating customers, but it carried enormous risk.[2] The complaint records of the Birmingham buses are riddled with reports of drivers beating, shooting, and even killing black passengers.[3] When Jones ignored the driver's direct order, everyone on the bus knew she sat in the path of peril.

As the driver waited for the officers to arrive, a white man carrying carpenter's tools walked over to Jones and pulled out a shiny, sharp saw. Standing over her with the saw drawn back, he told the student he had a "notion to slap [her] brains out." Just then the driver returned, flanked by two Montgomery police officers. Pointing toward Jones, the driver sneered, "I'm going to teach you to do what the white man tells you to do." The officers lunged and pulled the student out of her seat and down the back steps, scattering her school supplies. They grabbed her arms, twisted them until she screamed, and pushed her toward the waiting police car. When one officer loosened his grip long enough to open the back door, she clawed his face with her fingernails. "He threatened to kill me then," she recalled later. "They cursed me all the way to City Hall."

When they arrived at City Hall, the officers dragged Jones behind the building and beat her with a pipe until she was, as she put it, "too weak to get off the ground without help." She struggled to stand, but they kicked her repeatedly. As she writhed on the ground, one of the officers grabbed Jones's head between his hands and propelled it into the brick wall. She collapsed and crumbled to the ground. Clenching her arm, an officer pulled her toward the back steps, then "twisted his hand in [her] hair and picked [her] up off the ground by [her] hair." When she was finally on her feet, the officers pushed Jones up the stairs, poking her with a walking stick until she was in a jail cell. "What am I being charged with?" Jones asked before the officer slammed the door. "Suspicion," he said.[4]

The police held Jones overnight, denied her medical attention, and took her to court the next morning, where she was fined twenty-eight dollars. Standing before a judge in a bloodied and torn dress, she demanded to know the reason for the exorbitant fine. "Case closed," the judge said, and dismissed Jones with a flick of his wrist.

The next day Jones filed a complaint with the national NAACP. Thurgood Marshall, a young attorney working for the NAACP Legal Defense Fund, was appalled by the beating and the trumped-up charges. Despite

his age, Marshall was the most celebrated black lawyer in America, having won a number of high-profile cases, including the integration of Missouri Law School in 1938.[5] His growing status as a civil rights warrior led
thousands of people to flood his New York office with complaints of racial
discrimination and police brutality. "There is no question in my mind,"
Marshall said in a letter about Jones to T. T. Allen, the president of the
Montgomery branch of the NAACP in 1942, "that we should bring suit
against the bus company, and take whatever steps we can against the
policemen."[6] Apparently the case never went to court.

Thurgood Marshall's problem was that there were too many cases and
too few resources. Marshall and his colleagues performed a cruel triage to
determine which cases to pursue. African Americans choosing to testify
in racially charged cases placed themselves and their loved ones at great
risk. Sometimes the victims scratched out shaky lives among the down-
trodden that could easily be caricatured to discredit them. Sometimes the
cases were heart-wrenching but hopeless from a legal standpoint, given
the realities of judicial practices in a hard racial caste system. Finding the
right combination of strong documentation, brave witnesses, sympathetic
victims, and legal resources tested Thurgood Marshall's legal and political acumen.

In a letter to his mentor, Judge William H. Hastie, the dean of Howard
Law School, Marshall asked for advice on how to respond to the brutal mistreatment and sexual harassment of two black women on a bus at an
Alabama military camp in 1945. The two women, Private Roberta
McKenzie and Private First Class Gladys Blackmon, boarded an empty
bus and sat down in the rear. When asked to stand so that a white man
could sit, they both refused, arguing that there were plenty of seats
remaining in the white section. The bus driver grabbed his nightstick,
walked toward the two Women's Army Corps (WAC) members, and
knocked off their hats. He then slapped both women and, they alleged,
"punched them in the breast," while uttering profanities.[7] After he pushed
them off the bus, they reported the attack to the NAACP. In the midst
of a "War for Democracy," Marshall knew that the beating of black WACs
in uniform would be explosive. "This is one of the worst cases we have had
in this office for some time," he said. It "looks like dynamite to me."[8]

Ten years later thousands of working- and middle-class women, fed up
with decades of abuse, took to the streets to protest their mistreatment
and demand the right to "sit with dignity." The Montgomery bus boycott, frequently regarded as the spark plug of the modern civil rights

movement, was actually the end of a drive chain that ran back into decades of black women's activism. That supposedly "spontaneous" event was, in fact, the culmination of a deep history of gendered political appeals—frequently led by black veterans—for the protection of African-American women from sexual and physical assault. Only by understanding the long and relatively hidden history of sexualized violence in Montgomery, Alabama, and African Americans' efforts to protect black womanhood, can we see that the Montgomery bus boycott was more than a movement for civil rights. It was also a women's movement for dignity, respect, and bodily integrity.

Rosa Parks left Alabama for the first time in 1946. Atlanta was less than two hundred miles away, but it seemed a world away from the rickety rural shacks that still dotted the Alabama countryside. The New South city promised great change and possibility for the future. Skyscrapers sparkled against the sky and served as a backdrop for the bustling business district anchored by the headquarters of Sears, Roebuck and Coca-Cola. Streams of automobiles roared through the city on viaducts high above the busy rail lines. Airplanes took off and landed just outside town. Though Atlanta was thoroughly segregated, it seemed to be the perfect setting for an NAACP meeting dedicated to training future leaders who would seize the opportunities of the postwar period to wage war against Jim Crow.

Thurgood Marshall, known as "Mr. Civil Rights" since he persuaded the Supreme Court to strike down the white-only Democratic primary as unconstitutional in 1944, was the keynote speaker. Though African Americans won some concessions during World War II, there was much work to be done, he said, listing the primary problems plaguing African Americans throughout the South. Much of what he focused on—police brutality, discrimination in public facilities, job discrimination, and segregation—resonated with Rosa Parks, who had reams of notes on such abuses in Montgomery.[9] But his final topic, the heinous treatment of returning black veterans, was on everyone's mind that year.

For the approximately one million African Americans who served in the armed forces, victory over totalitarianism abroad meant little without real change at home. Having helped topple Hitler, black soldiers were not about to bow before the Bilbos and Talmadges of the South. Instead, they returned home with a new sense of pride and purpose and often led campaigns for citizenship rights, legal equality, and bodily integrity.[10] In small towns and cities across the South, black veterans became the "shock troops" of an emerging civil rights movement.[11]

White Southerners responded to postwar black activism with a wave of violence that reasserted white supremacy.[12] In Birmingham, Alabama, police commissioner Eugene "Bull" Connor directed a force that was responsible for untold numbers of racially motivated beatings, bombings, and murders in the years immediately after World War II. Within the first six weeks of 1946 alone, uniformed officers reportedly killed five black men, all veterans, because they had taken part in voter registration drives.[13] On February 12, 1946, Linwood Shull, the chief of police in Aiken, South Carolina, jammed his billy club into Sergeant Isaac Woodard's eye sockets after the black serviceman, home from a fifteen-month stint in the South Pacific, got into an argument with a white bus driver. The beating permanently blinded Woodard. After an all-white jury in Columbia, South Carolina, acquitted Shull of any charges, white spectators in the crowded courtroom roared with approval.[14]

Fearful of black veterans' refusal to stay "in their place," whites in Georgia warned African Americans, especially vets, to stay away from the polls in 1946. Since Thurgood Marshall helped persuade the Supreme Court in *Smith v. Allwright* to outlaw the white primary two years earlier, strict adherence to the Court's ruling would have transformed the political landscape. Whites across the region turned to extralegal terror. In Greenville the Ku Klux Klan planted a fiery cross in a black neighborhood, hoping it was enough to scare away any potential voters. In Cairo masked men fired shots at the homes of prominent blacks. Throughout the state, white men nailed warnings and death threats on the doors of black homes and slipped them inside black newspapers.[15] On July 17, 1946—Election Day—veteran Maceo Snipes walked past armed thugs patrolling the ballot box to cast his first and last ballot. Later that night, four white men dragged him out of his house and murdered him.[16]

A few weeks later, a white mob led by the Georgia state police shot two black couples to death in broad daylight. Roger Malcolm, one of the victims, had stabbed his white landlord earlier that summer, allegedly because he showed sexual interest in Malcolm's pregnant wife, Dorothy. Dorothy's brother, George Dorsey, a veteran, defended his sister's womanhood and his brother-in-law's actions, insisting black men had the same right as white men to protect their women. Enraged whites gathered on July 25, 1946, beneath Moore's Ford Bridge. Along the sloping banks of a river, a mob lined up the two couples and peppered their bodies with bullets.[17] "Up until George went into the army," Loy Harrison, one of the murderers, said years later, "he was a good nigger. But when he came out, they thought they were as good as any white people."[18]

It did not take long for white Southerners to claim black efforts to gain equality were a mask for more sinister, sexual desires, an argument rooted in Reconstruction-era politics. During the 1890s, former slaveholders and their Democratic political allies used the rhetoric of black-on-white rape and fabricated rape scares, as Glenda Gilmore put it, as "a politically driven wedge powered by the sledgehammer of white supremacy" to seize power from the biracial coalitions of Republicans and Populists that swept elections in Southern states.[19] Black activists in the post–World War II period often joked that "the closer a black man got to a ballot box, the more he looked like a rapist."[20] However, African-American men did not actually have to vote or threaten political overthrow to be accused of rape. As Frederick Douglass noted nearly a century earlier, the myth of the black man as a rapist was an "invention with a well defined motive."[21] These ghosts were easily conjured in the uncertain years after the war. Whites used rape as a catchall charge to justify violence against African Americans and undermine their political, social, and economic rights.

For example, in August 1946, police in Minden, Louisiana, arrested and jailed John C. Jones, a twenty-eight-year-old black veteran, and his seventeen-year-old cousin, Albert Harris, for acting "uppity" after they protested an unfair land deal. However, police claimed the two men were "prowling" around a white woman's window, though she refused to press charges. After several days in jail, police released them into a mob of armed white men. The mob drove Harris and Jones down a country road, where they tortured and beat Harris until they believed he was dead. Then the mob mutilated Jones with a meat cleaver and a blowtorch.[22] When they were satisfied with their work, the mob left the mangled men in a ditch, ostensibly dead.[23] Jones died, but Harris managed to survive and eventually identified five of the murderers in court, though an all-white jury quickly acquitted them.

The brutal beating of Isaac Woodard and Albert Harris, the murder of Maceo Snipes and John Jones, the lynching on Moore's Ford Bridge, and dozens of other incidents across the South in 1946 were designed, as one white man put it, to "keep Mister Nigger in his place."[24] Walter

White, head of the NAACP, called the violence "a rabies of the spirit . . . a mob sickness." This disease, he said, was "a dread epidemic" that was "rampant in our land."[25] In an effort to end the violence, the national NAACP and forty other civil rights groups formed the National Emergency Committee Against Mob Violence on August 6, 1946, to focus national and international attention on racist brutality.[26] The committee met with President Harry Truman a month later and urged him to use the power of the federal government to end mob violence in the South.

They believed Truman would act, if only to boost the United States' image in the world at the dawn of the Cold War. Images of lynchings and racial violence scarred the front pages of newspapers around the world, mocking American ideals of democracy. The Soviet newspaper *Trud* pointed to the "increasing frequency of terroristic acts against Negroes," as part of an exposé on the "Position of Negroes in the USA."[27] Segregation, a reporter for a Sri Lankan newspaper noted, "is the greatest propaganda gift any country could give to the Kremlin in its persistent bid for the affections of the coloured races of the world."[28] Federal action would not only shore up America's image abroad, the committee assured Truman, but would also give black voters in the urban North, whose ballots could tilt the election in his favor, an incentive to vote for Truman in the 1948 presidential election.[29]

Truman responded with Executive Order 9808, creating the President's Committee on Civil Rights (PCCR), on December 5, 1946. He hailed their report, *To Secure These Rights,* as "an American charter of human freedom in our time" and a "guide for action."[30] The report condemned lynching, disfranchisement, and racial discrimination in public accommodations, housing, and employment and issued concrete prescriptions for change. Nearly a decade before the *Brown v. Board of Education* decision, *To Secure These Rights* asserted unequivocally that segregation was "inconsistent with the fundamental equalitarianism of the American way of life in that it marks groups with the brand of inferior status." Most important, the report argued that it was the job of the federal government to protect individuals from racial violence and discrimination, something that would not be codified until the Civil Rights Act of 1968.[31]

At the 1948 statewide NAACP convention in Mobile, Alabama, African Americans praised Truman's new commitment to civil rights. But Rosa Parks, who attended the meeting as a delegate from the Montgomery branch, was more cynical. She knew sexual violence sat at the core of white supremacy, and she feared a terrible backlash as segregationists, whose anger had already been roused by rising black activism, came unhinged. They viewed the report as a federal attack on the Southern way of life and an open invitation for interracial sex. Truman's actions, segregationists argued, would lead to intermarriage, "amalgamation," "miscegenation," and the rape of white women. Led by Strom Thurmond from South Carolina, Southern legislators raced to vilify the president. In a fiery diatribe on the U.S. Senate floor, Mississippi's James Eastland and his state colleagues accused Truman of "turning over the government to the mongrelized minorities."[32]

In popular memory, Rosa Parks leaves the speechifying to Dixie demagogues and Dr. King, but at the 1948 NAACP convention in Mobile, Parks gave an impassioned speech warning her colleagues to be wary of any federal civil rights promises. With Southern Democrats like Eastland and Thurmond threatening to bolt the Democratic Party, Parks suspected that few, if any, of Truman's initiatives on civil rights would become law. Besides, she argued, no matter how promising the report was, it would not end the wanton abuse and harassment of African Americans. "No one should feel proud," she said, "when Negroes every day are being molested and maltreated." Parks's fiery speech got her elected secretary of the Statewide Conference of the Alabama NAACP, a job she took on in addition to her work for the Montgomery branch, the Brotherhood of Sleeping Car Porters, and her employment as a seamstress.[33]

The new state NAACP position expanded the scope of Parks's work documenting racial incidents, discrimination, and violence in Alabama. "There were many, many cases to keep records on," she recalled later.[34] The failure to secure justice for Recy Taylor in 1944—one of the first cases Parks worked on as secretary of the Montgomery NAACP—weighed heavily on her memory. "There wasn't much we could do," she admitted in her memoir. "The NAACP and the Committee [for Equal Justice] managed to get Governor Sparks to commence a special grand jury to investigate the case—though that grand jury also refused to indict the men." "Of course," Parks noted, "the opposite was true if a white woman cried rape and accused a black man."[35]

Parks clearly understood, as historian Timothy B. Tyson puts it, that the "much traveled back-road between the races was clearly marked 'one-way.' "[36] When white women violated these Southern signposts, it was not uncommon for them to sacrifice their black lovers to save themselves from the stigma of violating the South's most sacred taboo. No one traveling in Parks's political circles, for example, could have failed to hear about the tragedy of Willie McGee.

McGee, a married African-American man from Laurel, Mississippi, entered into a long sexual relationship with his white employer, Mrs. Willametta Hawkins, after she threatened to cry rape if he refused her flirtatious advances. Hawkins first propositioned McGee, who often did odd jobs around her house, in 1942. "I was waxing the floors with her in the house and she showed a willingness to be familiar and let me have intercourse with her in the back room," McGee said. "After that, she frequently sent for me to do work which gave opportunities for intercourse, which she accepted, and on occasions after dark," he said, "she took me in her automobile out to a place in the graveyard where we had intercourse."[37] The illicit relationship smacked of coercion from the start, but it turned brutal when word leaked out.

McGee's wife, Rosalee, figured out what was going on when Mrs. Hawkins surprised McGee as he and his wife walked home from a movie theater. "All of a sudden," Rosalee said, "Mrs. Hawkins come out of an alley, and she says to Willie, 'I got my car over here. Come on into my car with me.' " Rosalee protested, and McGee told Hawkins to "go away."

An all-white jury in Laurel, Mississippi, sentenced Willie McGee, a thirty-one-year-old father of four, to death for allegedly raping a white housewife. The Civil Rights Congress protested the decision and launched an international movement to free McGee.

"This is my wife," he said, shocked at the woman's audacity. "I'm with my wife!!"

"Don't fool with no Negro whores," Hawkins shouted, angry at being rebuffed.[38]

McGee reluctantly went with Hawkins, fearing the tragic consequences of turning her away. "People who don't know the South don't know what would have happened to Willie if he told her no," Rosalee told a friend. "Down South you tell a woman like that no, and she'll cry rape anyway. So what else could Willie do?"

McGee finally broke off the relationship with Hawkins in November 1945, just before her husband, Troy, discovered the affair. After Troy and Willametta had a terrible fight, she called the police to report that a black, kinky-haired intruder had raped her. Within a few hours, police held McGee in custody.[39]

Nothing could have convinced white Southerners that Willametta Hawkins seduced McGee or that they had had a long-term sexual relationship. While it was perfectly reasonable, if frowned upon in some circles, for a white man to have a sexual relationship with a black woman, the segregated social order strictly forbade white women and black men from association, let alone sex. The chief justice of the Mississippi Supreme Court called the suggestion of a mutual love affair between a black man and a white woman a "revolting insinuation" that he "could not entertain" or "even consider in court." He sent McGee to the electric chair without hesitation.[40] That McGee received the death sentence for what was a relatively common, if covert, practice among white men and black women underscored the hierarchy of race and sex in the segregated South. It also helped launch an international protest movement.

The Civil Rights Congress (CRC), a leftist legal defense and protest organization, led the worldwide efforts to free McGee.[41] Despite three interventions by the U.S. Supreme Court and overwhelming evidence of racial bias in sentencing in Mississippi, officials readied the portable electric chair at the Jones County courthouse and scheduled McGee's execution for May 8, 1951.[42] Anne Braden, a white activist from Louisville, Kentucky, who protested the public execution, demanded that "no more innocent men . . . die in the name of protecting southern white womanhood. We have been made a party to this injustice too long."[43] Willie McGee understood the political purpose of his execution. "You know I am innocent," he told his wife in a letter the night before he was scheduled

On May 8, 1951, more than five hundred white men, women, and
children gathered outside the Jones County courthouse in
Ellisville, Mississippi, to cheer the execution of Willie McGee.

to die. "The real reason they are going to take my life is to keep the Negro
down in the South."[44]

Near midnight on that fateful May evening, state officials delivered two
deadly currents of electricity to Willie McGee as an ecstatic, almost all-
white audience of five hundred men, women, and children gathered outside. Troy and Willametta Hawkins stood among their neighbors and
cheered McGee's death.[45]

Willie McGee was not the first nor the last black man executed for violating the South's racial and sexual rules. On February 2, 1951, officials at
the Virginia State Penitentiary executed seven black men convicted of raping a white woman in Martinsville two years earlier.[46] On January 8, 1949,
Ruby Floyd, a thirty-two-year-old white woman, accused the seven black
men of violently raping her. The police rounded up some suspects, and
within a matter of days, seven men sat in jail. By the end of January, the
Martinsville Seven had been tried, convicted, and sentenced to death.[47]

As African Americans in Martinsville dealt with the shock of "seven
rapid-fire consecutive death sentences," they faced the stark reminder that
white men guilty of the same crime almost never received the same punishment. The *Pittsburgh Courier* highlighted this discrepancy on May 14,
1949, by juxtaposing the front-page announcement of the Martinsville

Seven death sentences with an article detailing the rape of a black woman by two white police officers in Richmond, Virginia. The policemen, Carl R. Burleson and Leonard E. Davis, who were tried and convicted of raping a black woman in 1946, kidnapped the black woman, a waitress and mother of two, then drove her to a construction site and sexually assaulted her. Judge John L. Ingram found Burleson and Davis guilty and sentenced them to seven years in prison. The guilty verdict was surprising, but the paltry sentence reminded black women that society did not consider them worthy of the same protection afforded white women.[48]

During the late 1940s and early 1950s, "protection" of white womanhood often meant shielding them from any kind of contact with African-American men, sexual or otherwise. In Yanceyville, North Carolina, the collision of race and sex was so combustible in the summer of 1951 that even a glance in the wrong direction could land a black man in jail. On June 4, Mack Ingram, a forty-two-year-old black farmer and father of nine children, walked through a tobacco field on the Boswell farm to ask the white owner if he could borrow a trailer. About seventy-five feet ahead of him walked the farmer's eighteen-year-old daughter, Willa Jean Boswell, who wore overalls and carried a hoe. Willa Jean screamed and began running when she saw Ingram walking in the same direction. She ran as fast as she could until she reached her brother. Exhausted and clearly terrified, she informed him that Ingram was "looking at her in a leering manner."[49] Her father called the police, who arrested Ingram later that afternoon. At the trial two weeks later, Willa Jean admitted Ingram never spoke to her; nor could he have since he was always at least seventy-five feet away. Still, her father argued, Ingram's "eyes were all over her."

A charge of "eye rape" was enough for Judge Ralph Vernon of the Caswell County Recorder's Court to sentence Ingram to two years of hard labor. According to the NAACP, which launched a campaign to defend Ingram, it was "as fantastic a story as has ever been enacted in an American court." It ought to be "sold to *Ripley's Believe It or Not*," they said.[50] Although the charge of "eye rape" seemed utterly absurd, it was deadly serious. "The big issue," according to the *Chicago Defender*, "is the right of a Colored man to walk across a farm road or walk the streets of Yanceyville" without the fear of being killed or sent to prison "because [a white woman] doesn't like the way he looks at her." The North Carolina Supreme Court finally dismissed the case in 1953.[51]

While the CRC, NAACP, and other organizations lost the Martinsville Seven and Willie McGee cases, they helped expose the South's legal double standards. At the same time, they revealed to the world the South's tendency toward hysteria when black men and white women crossed paths, whether in a bedroom or a wide-open tobacco field. Though McGee lost his life, his defenders worked to make audible the "whispered narrative of consensual interracial sex that had been the real story behind too many southern lynchings."[52]

Rosa Parks labored tirelessly on similar cases in Montgomery, but one in particular haunted her. In 1952 a white Montgomery woman cried rape after a nosy neighbor caught her undressing with her sixteen-year-old black lover, Jeremiah Reeves. Shortly thereafter Montgomery police arrested Reeves and beat a confession out of him. The lower courts found Reeves guilty of rape and sentenced him to die. Reeves's mother, Parks recalled, "brought the case to the NAACP." The Montgomery branch, she said, "struggled for quite a few years" to save the young man.[53] They challenged his sentence all the way to the U.S. Supreme Court, to no avail. Alabama officials executed Reeves in 1957.[54] "It was a tragedy he lost his life," Parks said. "I tried to find some way of documenting that [the white woman had] lied but I was never able to do so . . . [S]ometimes it was very difficult to keep going when all our work seemed to be in vain."[55]

Cases like Jeremiah Reeves's and Willie McGee's taught African Americans, as Martin Luther King, Jr., noted in *Stride Toward Freedom,* to "fear and mistrust the white man's justice." "In the years that [Reeves] sat in jail," King wrote, "several white men in Alabama also had been charged with rape, but their accusers were Negro girls." White men were seldom arrested, and if they were, King said, "they were soon released by the grand jury. No one was ever brought to trial."[56] This was mostly true throughout the South, but Montgomery seemed to get more than its share of what NAACP leader Roy Wilkins called "sex cases."[57]

Laboring patiently for the NAACP in Montgomery, Rosa Parks felt that 1949 in particular was a "very bad year." "There was a lot of white violence against blacks," she recalled. "Things happened," she said, "that most people never heard about."[58] Even if the stories never got their due in the mainstream press, it was the misfortune and courage of a number of unknown women who helped mobilize the African-American community in the late 1940s around issues of sexualized violence. These campaigns sparked larger protests for dignity and bodily integrity that culminated in the Montgomery bus boycott. The truly decisive moment came in 1949, when two white police officers attacked a young woman named Gertrude Perkins. "Gertrude Perkins is not even mentioned in the history books," Joe Azbell, former editor of the *Montgomery Advertiser,* said, "but she had as much to do with the bus boycott and its creation as anyone on earth."[59]

The moon illuminated the dark street as Gertrude Perkins, a twenty-five-year-old black woman, walked home, a little unsteady on her feet after a night of partying. It was after midnight on March 27, 1949, when a squad car inched toward her and stopped. Two Montgomery police officers, their badges glimmering in the moonlight, told Perkins to halt, then walked toward her. Smelling beer on her breath, they accused her of public drunkenness and ordered her to get into their car. When she refused, they grabbed her and pushed her into the backseat. They drove to the edge of a railroad embankment and dragged her behind a building, where the uniformed men raped her repeatedly at gunpoint and forced her to have "all types of sex relations." When they finished, they shoved Perkins back into the car, then dumped her out in the middle of town and sped away.

Alone on the dark roadside, terrified and shaken, Perkins nevertheless mustered the clarity and courage to report the crime. Instead of going home to her three children, she went directly to Reverend Solomon S. Seay, Sr.'s, house. Seay was the prominent and rotund minister of the Mt. Zion AME Zion Church. A newcomer to Montgomery, Seay was already regarded as one of the most outspoken black ministers in town. She knocked on the door of the Holt Street parsonage, where Seay and his family lived. Waking him, Perkins told Seay the details of her assault through sobs and tears. He could smell the alcohol and wondered if perhaps she was lying. "If you're not telling the truth," he said, "you're going to be in big trouble."

"I'm telling you the dying truth," she insisted. Seay decided that even if she had had too much to drink, she did not deserve to be attacked. "No white or black man," he said, "had a right to rape her." Seay consoled Perkins and listened as she spoke. "We didn't go to bed that morning," he recalled. "I kept her at my house, carefully wrote down what she said, and later had it notarized." He sent Perkins's horror story to syndicated columnist Drew Pearson, who let the whole country know what happened in his daily radio address before Montgomery's white leaders knew what hit them.[60]

Early the next day, Seay escorted Perkins to the police station so she could report the crime. She asked Mayor John L. Goodwyn to arrest her assailants. He quickly rebuffed her. Goodwyn, who also served as police commissioner, refused to hold a lineup so Perkins could identify her attackers. He denied her request to see a log of who was on duty the previous evening. Goodwyn claimed that providing access to that information would "violate the Constitutional rights of the members of the Police Department as individuals."[61]

As word of the attack spread, E. D. Nixon and Reverend Seay, the leaders of the local Ministerial Alliance, the Negro Improvement League, and the NAACP, organized the Citizens Committee for Gertrude Perkins. Dozens of active black citizens joined to demand equal justice and protection for black women.[62] Mary Fair Burks, an English professor at Alabama State, and her newly formed middle-class organization, the Women's Political Council, may also have been involved, since one of their early goals was to "come to the defense of women who had been victimized by rape and other physical assaults."[63]

At the first meeting of the Citizens Committee, members elected Reverend Seay chairman of the "investigating committee." His job was to find the police officers who attacked Perkins. When the meeting adjourned, members of the Citizens Committee poured out of the YMCA and ran into a wall of police cars and blinding headlights. Seay stepped forward. "Why are you flashing your lights into my face?" he asked. An officer stepped out of his car, grabbed his club with one hand and pulled at his gun with the other, and walked over to Seay. Without saying a word, he threw his arm back and hurled the club into Seay's chest.

"You're under arrest," the officer said as Seay recoiled in pain. Members of the Citizens Committee rushed around Seay.

"Y'all ought to leave this man alone," someone said, "he ain't doing anymore than you do . . . trying to defend his women." Police grabbed Seay, pushed him into their squad car, and drove him downtown. At the jailhouse, the chief of police recognized the minister. "Pull your hat off," he ordered. "We gonna teach you that *we* run this town. Niggers don't run it." The next day E. D. Nixon helped bail Seay out and promised that the NAACP would defend him in court.[64]

As the ministers and the NAACP rallied around Seay and Perkins, white

officials publicly dismissed Perkins's case. The mayor claimed Perkins's
rape charge was "completely false." He insisted that holding a lineup or
issuing any warrants would set a bad precedent since, as Goodwyn argued,
"charges of this nature, even though untrue . . . are often used to destroy
goodwill between the races."[65] Besides, he added, *his* "policemen would
not do a thing like that."[66] Since black prostitutes had routinely serviced
white police officers in the past in exchange for allowing the existence of
brothels in Montgomery, perhaps Mayor Goodwyn thought there was no
need to resort to violence or force for interracial intimacies.[67]

Blacks in Montgomery knew better. The city's police force had a reputation for physical and sexual violence. Police brutality plagued the black
community. The Perkins case was just the tip of the iceberg.[68] E. G. Jackson, editor of Montgomery's black newspaper, the *Alabama Tribune,* urged
action on the Perkins case and reminded readers of a similar assault three
years earlier.

In 1946, Viola White, an African-American woman who worked at
Maxwell Air Force Base, had refused a bus driver's order to move out of
her seat. The driver threatened to physically remove her, but she would
not budge. Finally he called the police and asked them to arrest her. When
the officer arrived, he beat White into submission and took her to jail. The
next day a judge found White guilty of "disobeying a bus driver." White
was so incensed that she hired a lawyer to appeal her case. Not long after
she filed suit, Montgomery police retaliated. One afternoon Officer A. A.
Enger seized White's sixteen-year-old daughter, drove her to a cemetery,
and raped her. As the officer thrust himself inside her, she stared at his
car and focused on memorizing the tag number. The next day she reported
the crime. After many attempts, E. D. Nixon was finally able to get a
judge to sign a warrant for Enger's arrest. Instead of detaining Enger or
firing him, however, the police chief decided to let him slip quietly out
of town.[69]

While E. G. Jackson recalled other unsolved crimes against black
women, the assault on Gertrude Perkins, he said, was "one of the worst
crimes ever committed in . . . Montgomery." "The head officials," he complained, were still "trying to keep it quiet."[70] But nothing could silence
the voices of protest coming from the Citizens Committee for Gertrude
Perkins. Their public protests, sensational newspaper headlines, and a
flood of "inflammatory" pamphlets garnered massive attention throughout the city. Even the *Montgomery Advertiser,* the "white" daily newspaper,
followed Perkins's case for nearly two months, often featuring the latest

news on the front page.[71] Because of the media attention, unrelenting protests from the Citizens Committee, and the dogged determination of Perkins's white liberal lawyers, John and Virgil McGee, the mayor finally relented and brought the case in front of the grand jury.[72]

Reverend Seay accompanied Perkins to court on May 20, 1949, nearly two months after police assaulted her. Seay waited outside the closed courtroom, where he could hear county solicitor Temple Siebels berate Perkins with his "roaring, shaking and loud voice." "Aren't you lying?" he bellowed repeatedly. "No," Perkins said plainly. "I am not lying."[73] The fact that she did not say "sir" must have unsettled Siebels, who continued to verbally assault her. His bellicose style did not seem to rattle Perkins, who walked out of the courtroom, according to Seay, "as calm as anybody you've ever seen in your life."

Perkins's dignified self-defense belied white portrayals of her as a drunk and an "ignorant, almost illiterate black woman," but that did not stop Siebels from presenting her as a prostitute.[74] "Reverend," Siebels said to Seay when he was questioned in front of the jury, "did you know that Gertrude Perkins was . . . that she's just a common street woman?" Seay argued that Perkins's character was not the issue. "Whatever she [is]," Seay said, "she had rights that no man had a right to violate." Besides, Seay argued, "since when did policemen gain the special liberty, on or off duty, to be entertained in such a fashion?"[75]

Perkins's testimony and Seay's defense did not move the all-white, all-male jury. Convinced that "there was no evidence of rape in the Perkins case," the jurors refused to indict anyone. In an interview with the *Montgomery Advertiser,* the lead juror declared Perkins's testimony full of "manufactured lies." Then, scolding the Citizens Committee and the NAACP, he argued that "the publicity of this case has not been helpful to the racial relations of the city."[76] In order to stave off any protests, the editor of the *Montgomery Advertiser* felt compelled to report that the men serving on the jury were "prominently identified" with Montgomery's different churches, including "five Methodists, seven Baptists, three Presbyterians, and three members of the Church of Christ."[77] "You could see what the point was," Reverend Seay stated in response to the newspaper's reference to ecumenical diversity. Perhaps the editor hoped this tactic would stave off any criticism of the verdict.

In an editorial designed to put any hard feelings to rest, the *Advertiser* argued that "those colored people who have felt humiliated or angered over the Perkins case can now abate those emotions." It pointed to a similar case seventeen miles north, in Wetumpka, Alabama, in which two white men, John C. Howard and Jack Oliver, received forty-five-year sentences for raping two black women, as proof that African Americans could get justice in the courts.[78] "We have no doubt," the *Advertiser* insisted, "had there been evidence, the same would have happened here." After all, the *Advertiser* continued, "the case ran the full process of our Anglo-Saxon system of justice. What more could have been done?"[79]

Certainly Seay and other members of the Citizens Committee would have preferred an indictment. White people, Reverend Seay noted, "had not accepted black people as really human." The lack of justice in the Perkins case, he said, only "increased the resentment of ordinary black people about how they were being treated."[80] Still, many were pleased with the "groundswell of unrest" that their protest yielded, including the fact that, according to Seay, it was "the first time all the ministers in the city were shaken up."[81] It would not be the last time, of course: when Rosa Parks's arrest in 1955 stirred the black community into a truly mass protest, Seay would be a pivotal leader. The public outcry in the Perkins case was "a bold expression," Seay said, "on the part of black people in this town to say to the courts and others 'We protest what is going on.' "[82]

The Perkins protest did not occur in isolation. In February 1951 a white grocery store owner raped a black teenager. Sam E. Green regularly employed Flossie Hardman, a black fifteen-year-old, as a babysitter and frequently drove her home at the end of her shift. One night, instead of taking Flossie directly home, Green pulled to the side of a quiet road and raped her.[83]

Flossie immediately informed her parents of the assault. Despite the odds of bringing Green to justice, they decided to press charges. Meanwhile Rufus A. Lewis, a World War II veteran and celebrated football coach at Alabama State University, launched a campaign to bring Green to trial. Backed by Lewis and many of his fellow veterans, the Hardmans succeeded in bringing Green to court. But when an all-white jury returned a not guilty verdict after deliberating for only five minutes, African Americans decided to take the matter into their own hands. Lewis led the charge.[84]

As one of the principal spokesmen for voter registration efforts in Montgomery, Lewis had enormous respect and support within the black community; he belonged to the mostly middle-class Dexter Avenue Baptist Church and was a member of many of the "best" clubs and associations in town.[85] Additionally, as the owner of Montgomery's largest black funeral home, he was financially independent and not easily intimidated by white economic reprisals. Lewis parlayed his social and economic wealth into a spacious brick clubhouse, named the Citizens Club. It functioned as the headquarters for many of the city's community organizations. Here Lewis taught veterans and others the ins and outs of voter registration and created a safe space where African Americans could "come and socialize" and, in the process, get politicized.[86] Lewis knew that a large swath of the black community was outraged by the attack on Flossie Hardman and the unjust ruling. Since Green's grocery store was located in a primarily black community, Lewis figured an economic boycott could destroy Green's livelihood.

Lewis organized the "Citizens Committee" to lead the boycott. The committee brought together veterans groups, the Women's Political Council, and the NAACP under the banner of protecting black womanhood. The campaign to shut down Green's store was a success. Within a matter of weeks, African Americans delivered their own guilty verdict by driving Green into the red.[87] The campaign established the boycott as a powerful weapon for justice and sent a message to whites that African Americans would not allow white men to disrespect, abuse, and violate black women's bodies with impunity.[88] Soon enough an even larger boycott would be imaginable for the African-American community.

Many whites chose to ignore this message, notably the city's bus operators, who snubbed, bullied, and brutalized black passengers daily. Drivers shortchanged African Americans, then kicked them off the bus if they asked for correct change. Half-empty buses often bypassed blacks waiting at bus stops. And bus drivers never hesitated to use violence to enforce segregation. In a sense, the ruthless beatings that Ella Ree Jones, Roberta McKenzie, and Gladys Blackmon received when they defied Jim Crow in the early 1940s represented relatively light punishment, considering the price paid by Hilliard Brooks.

On August 12, 1950, Brooks, an African-American veteran of World War II and neighbor of Rosa Parks, attempted to board a bus driven by C. L. Hood. Hood refused to let Brooks on his bus, claiming he was too intoxicated. Brooks put up a fuss and demanded to be allowed to ride.

Hood waved a police officer over, then pushed the veteran off the front steps, knocking him to the ground. As Brooks struggled to stand, the police officer, M. E. Mills, pointed his pistol at Brooks and, in the bright afternoon sun, shot him dead. Satisfied with the assailants' claim of self-defense, the mayor cleared them of any wrongdoing.[89]

There were at least thirty complaints by African Americans in Montgomery in 1953, indicating a growing sense of impatience with the grim conditions on city buses.[90] Most of these complaints came from working-class black women who made up the bulk of Montgomery City Lines' riders, over half of whom toiled as domestics.[91] With a median salary of just $523 per year, domestics could not afford automobiles and had no choice but to ride the city buses to and from the white homes in which they worked.[92] Their workplace could be just as dangerous: domestic workers faced sexual and physical abuse by their white employers. While domestics could and often did resist sexual harassment and abuse on the job by quitting, they could not easily find other transportation. They were stuck with the buses. As black lawyer Fred Gray put it, bus transportation was not "something optional, like restaurants."[93]

African-American women constantly complained about the atrocious treatment they received on the buses. Gladys Moore remembered that Montgomery's bus operators treated black women "just as rough as could be . . . like we are some kind of animal."[94] Jo Ann Robinson, an English professor at Alabama State and member of the increasingly militant Women's Political Council, argued that mistreatment on the buses was degrading, shameful, and humiliating. "Black Americans," she insisted, were "still being treated as . . . things without feelings, not human beings."[95] Bus drivers, Robinson recalled, disrespected black women by hurling nasty sexualized insults their way. Ferdie Walker, a black woman from Fort Worth, Texas, remembered bus drivers sexually harassing her as she waited on the corner. "The bus was up high," she recalled, "and the street was down low. They'd drive up under there and then they'd expose themselves while I was standing there and it just scared me to death."[96] Aside from direct sexual harassment, drivers referred to black women with contemptuous names like "black niggers," "black bitches," "heifers," and "whores."[97] Della Perkins remembered a driver who regularly referred to her as an "ugly black ape."[98]

In addition to slinging insults, bus drivers often slapped black women who crossed them. They refused to stop at every corner in black neighborhoods, allowed white children to board before black adults, demanded blacks give up their seats for whites, and forced them to pay their fare at the front of the bus and then enter via the rear.[99] The latter practice was designed to eliminate any chance that black bodies might accidentally come in contact with white bodies, thus removing the opportunity for any inadvertent move toward "miscegenation" or "social equality." This was especially important if black men boarded the bus when white women sat in the front seats, but drivers imposed the rule on black women as well. One black woman recalled that a bus driver demanded she relocate "because a white man could not sit opposite a colored lady."[100] Considering white men's long history of "integrating" with black women, this rule was particularly galling.

Georgia Gilmore, a plucky and spirited black cook, decided not to ride the buses after a driver insisted she enter the bus through the rear after paying her fare in the front. Gilmore protested, but the red-faced, redheaded driver hollered, "I told you to get off and go to the back, Nigger!" Since the bus was her sole transportation, Gilmore retreated. As she was about to enter the back door, the driver slammed it shut and pulled away.[101] Such malicious acts often resulted in injuries. "There had been several reported incidents," Ralph Abernathy, a Baptist minister, recalled, "of persons being caught in the doors . . . [and] dragged for some distance."[102]

Verbal, physical, and sexual abuse maintained racial hierarchy in an enclosed space where complete separation of whites and blacks was all but impossible. A big arrow pointing to the rear of the bus for "colored" and another pointing to the front of the bus for whites provided some guidance. But the Jim Crow line could vanish just as easily as it appeared, as the racial composition of riders changed at each stop.[103] "The bus driver could move colored people anywhere he wanted on the bus," E. D. Nixon recalled. "If a white person came into the bus and sat way back in it, no Negro was permitted to stand or sit between the motorman and that person."[104] As a rule, the first ten of the thirty-six seats on a Montgomery city bus were reserved for whites, no matter how many people were actually on the bus.[105] This frequently left black passengers, who almost always outnumbered white passengers, in the humiliating position of having to stand over empty seats.

This policy fueled resentment and anger among African Americans, especially domestics and day laborers who spent hours on their feet cooking, washing, and ironing for white people. "You spend your whole lifetime in your occupation . . . making life clever, easy and convenient for white people," Rosa Parks recalled, "but when you have to get transportation home, you are denied an equal accommodation."[106] Mistreatment on the buses, she argued, emphasized the fact that "our existence was for the white man's comfort and well being; we had to accept being deprived of just being human."[107] Like sexualized mistreatment, it was an all-too-familiar part of being a black woman in Montgomery.

With abuses piling up like cordwood and memories of previous crimes smoldering, a group of black women decided to take on the bus drivers by demanding to be treated like ladies. The Women's Political Council led the charge. This militant women's group was one of over fifty active and vibrant black benefit associations, mutual aid societies, and social clubs in Montgomery that stitched together the social fabric of the African-American community. Professional black men belonged to one or more of the traditionally black fraternities like Alpha Phi Alpha, Kappa Alpha Psi, or Omega Psi Phi, while small businessmen and laborers held membership in the fraternal orders and benefit associations like the Prince Hall Free Masons, the Knights of Labor, the Elks, or the Knights of Pythias. There were also neighborhood associations, church clubs, and political organizations like the NAACP and its youth division, E. D. Nixon's Progressive Democrats, and Rufus Lewis's Citizens Club.[108]

Black women of a certain class in Montgomery found camaraderie in sororities like Alpha Kappa Alpha, Zeta Phi Beta, Delta Sigma Theta, or Sigma Gamma Rho, or they belonged to one of eighteen clubs that made up the Montgomery City Women's Federated Clubs, including the Crusaders, Anna M. Duncan, Excelsiors, Home Makers, Phillis Wheatley, Cosmopolites, and Sojourner Truth clubs—most of which featured junior versions for young women. In addition to these civic, professional, and social clubs, many black women belonged to societies affiliated with the more than fifty black churches in Montgomery.[109]

Meetings occurred in church basements, at women's homes, at the black-owned Ben Moore Hotel, which had a large ballroom and rooftop garden, or at any one of the dozen or more lounges, bars, and clubs where blacks could drink, dance, or eat a hearty meal. The most popular gathering places were the Elks Club, the Reno Café, Pics Café, the Afro-Club, Rufus Lewis's Citizens Club, Club 400, and the Tijuana Club.[110] These clubs provided spaces where black men and women, free from white surveillance and racial domination, could work out community problems, organize politically, or just relax.

The rich network of social and political organizations kept Montgomery's class-divided black community relatively connected. In addition, they served as information hubs, where news could travel easily from one neighborhood to the next.[111] The sheer number and diversity of organizations explains the relative speed with which the 1955 boycott began; after all, blacks in Montgomery were *already* organized. It only seemed "spontaneous" from a distance.

Even though they were knit together socially, African Americans in Montgomery rarely came together to protest white supremacy en masse. With the exception of E. D. Nixon and Rufus Lewis's voter registration efforts, Rosa Parks's investigations on behalf of the NAACP, and the mass mobilization on behalf of Gertrude Perkins and Flossie Hardman, most clubwomen preferred to work on racial uplift and charitable causes within the black community instead of agitating for political and civil rights in the city at large. Direct protests proved dangerous throughout the South, and Montgomery was no exception. Few people were willing to risk their lives or their livelihoods for something that seemed as immutable as segregation.

And yet there were always a handful of fearless individuals, like E. D. Nixon and Rosa Parks, who pushed for more direct political engagement. Vernon Johns, the irascible and outspoken preacher at Dexter Avenue Baptist Church in the 1940s and early 1950s, regularly chastised his "silk stocking" congregation for their apparent resignation to Jim Crow.[112] But Johns was not an ordinary man. He seemed to be hardwired to resist segregation. The preacher loved to shock his congregants and scare white Montgomerians. In response to the ruthless beating of a black man by white police officers in the early 1950s, he posted "It's Safe to Murder Negroes in Montgomery" on the church marquee. The next week his advertised sermon title was: "When the Rapist Is White."[113] One Sunday morning he stunned his middle-class audience by beginning his sermon with a horrific tale. "When my grandfather was hanged for cutting his master in two with a scythe," he said, "they asked him on the gallows if he had anything to say." "Yes," his grandfather said, "I'm just sorry I didn't do it thirty years before."[114] The story was not true, but Johns had a point. He wanted his flock to become as fearless as was his fictional grandfather.[115]

Johns's tactics made most of Dexter's members uncomfortable, but Mary Fair Burks felt the call one morning when Johns mounted another scathing attack on the complacency of his affluent parishioners. Burks had waged her own private "guerrilla warfare" by refusing to abide by Jim Crow signs throughout the city. After a run-in with a white police officer, however, Burks decided to broaden her attack and form an army of women dedicated to destroying white supremacy. She needed foot soldiers. "I looked around and all I could see were either masks of indifference or scorn," she recalled. Being a "feminist before [she] really knew what the word meant," she said, she "dismissed the hard-faced men." They "would take it over," she said, "and women wouldn't be able to do what they could do."[116]

Instead, Burks focused on the women in her church and social circles, hoping she could convert them into activists. "I played bridge with them," she reasoned, "but more important, I knew that they must suffer from the same racial abuse and the indignity."[117] She left church that day with a plan. Over the next week, she contacted fifty women. When forty showed up for the first meeting of the Women's Political Council (WPC) in the fall of 1946, she was pleasantly surprised.[118] Burks started the meeting by testifying about her run-in with a club-wielding police officer. When she finished, nearly every woman at the meeting chimed in with similar stories of brutalization.[119]

In order to gain political leverage with the city's leaders, members of the newly formed WPC, many of them public school teachers and faculty members at Alabama State College, decided they needed to become registered voters. After a number of them cleared the various hurdles designed to keep the voting rolls lily white, they set up workshops throughout the city to help others get registered. The WPC set up "registration schools" in churches, where they taught weekly classes on how to fill out voter registration forms and, if necessary, on basic literacy. When participants were ready, WPC members accompanied them to the courthouse and helped them fill out registration applications, then returned a few days later to check on the results.[120] More than anything, they taught ordinary women how to assert themselves in front of white authorities.

By teaming up with Rufus Lewis's veterans organization and E. D. Nixon's Progressive Democrats, both of which had been active in voter registration efforts since the early 1940s, the WPC muscled its way into city elections.[121] By the early 1950s, there were enough African Americans registered to vote in Montgomery that they could easily tip the scale in close elections.[122] Over the next few years, the Women's Political Council grew as well. By 1955, it had three chapters in Montgomery and more than three hundred female members. During this remarkable growth period, the WPC earned a reputation as the "most militant and uncompromising voice" for blacks in the Cradle of the Confederacy.[123]

The militant reputation rested upon the WPC's new leadership and new focus: mistreatment on the city's buses. Mary Fair Burks handed Jo Ann Robinson, her colleague at Alabama State College and a fiery advocate of human rights, the reins of the radical women's organization in 1950, just a year after she moved to Montgomery. Despite being a newcomer, Robinson easily fell in with Montgomery's middle-class clubwomen, among whom she quickly became a "much sought after dinner guest."[124] Born and raised in Georgia, Robinson was no stranger to white supremacy. As a middle-class woman with a vehicle, though, she was unaware of the intricacies of the segregated seating policies on Montgomery's buses.

Her introduction came at the end of her first full semester teaching, as she was preparing to visit family for Christmas in December 1949. Robinson boarded a near-empty city bus and sat down in the fifth row, two rows behind the only white woman on the bus, closed her eyes, and imagined "the wonderful two weeks [of] vacation" ahead. Suddenly startled by the bus driver's roaring voice, Robinson sat straight up.

"If you can sit in the fifth row from the front of the other buses in Montgomery," he bellowed, "suppose you get off and ride in one of them."

Being a respectable, professional woman who was used to being treated like a lady in the black community, Robinson did not realize the driver was speaking to her until he pulled to a stop and stormed over to where she was seated.[125]

"Get up from there!" he yelled, drawing his arm back as if he were about to strike her. "Get up from there!"

Robinson leaped to her feet, fearful of being beaten, and ran to the front of the bus. She stumbled off the bus in a daze. "Tears blinded my vision," she recalled, and "waves of humiliation inundated me."[126]

Recalling the shame and embarrassment she experienced that December day, Robinson readily accepted the leadership of the WPC. Utilizing the political leverage the WPC had built up over the previous years, Robinson and her army of militant women—Mrs. A. W. West, Mrs. N. W. Burkes, Mrs. J. E. Pierce, Georgia Gilmore, Mrs. Edwyna Marketta, Ella Mae Stovall, Lettie M. Anderson, Mrs. Horace Burton, Mrs. Ruby Hall, and Ella Mae Henderson, to name a few—canvassed black neighborhoods. According to Robinson, they gathered "thousands of signatures on hundreds of petitions" that demanded the city do something about the "shameful and deplorable one-sidedness" of the city's segregated parks and recreation system. They repeatedly confronted the city commissioners with complaints about police brutality. In the early 1950s, Jo Ann Robinson led her band of women warriors to directly attack abuse on the city's buses.[127]

In 1952 members of the WPC packed a public hearing regarding a bus fare increase, where Zolena Pierce and Sadie Brooks testified about their mistreatment on the buses. One year later a group of WPC members stormed a meeting with the City Commission, where Jo Ann Robinson railed against the abuses heaped upon black female bus riders and argued that African Americans should not have to stand over empty seats when the black section was filled and the white section was empty. Nor should they have to pay at the front, she said, and then disembark and get on in the back. The WPC demanded that black riders be treated with dignity and respect.[128] "We were not fighting segregation," Mary Fair Burks pointed out, "as much as abuses of Negroes."[129]

Black women across the country spoke out against similar abuses. Besides the WPC, no organization did this better or more explicitly than the Sojourners for Truth and Justice (STJ), a short-lived but important national black women's organization dedicated to "the full dignity of Negro womanhood."[130] Two African-American women, Louise Thompson Patterson, a Communist and wife of William Patterson, the head of the Civil Rights Congress, and Beulah Richardson, a poet and Progressive Party activist from Mississippi, organized the STJ in the fall of 1951. Patterson and Richardson sought to unite black women across social, political, and economic lines in an effort to end white violence and terror. "We will no longer in sight of God or man," the women proclaimed, "sit by and watch our lives destroyed by an unreasonable and unreasoning hate that metes out to us every kind of death."[131]

Speaking as mothers, wives, daughters, sisters, and witnesses to sexualized violence, the members of the STJ issued a pamphlet that assailed white supremacy and called for a national meeting of black women in Washington, D.C., "We have seen our brothers beaten, shot, and stamped to death by police [and] we have seen our daughters raped and degraded, and when one dares rise in defense of her honor she is jailed for life."[132] By inviting black women to come "speak [their] mind" and issuing the call in the "spirit of Harriet Tubman and Sojourner Truth," the STJ rooted themselves in a "radical black feminist tradition of resistance" and the tradition of testimony.[133]

Members of the Sojourners for Truth and Justice—a national black women's
organization dedicated to the protection of "Negro Womanhood"—pose for a photo
with celebrated athlete, singer, and actor Paul Robeson in 1952.

On September 29, 1951, more than one hundred African-American
women from fifteen states gathered in the nation's capital to testify and
bear witness to one another's horror stories. Mary Church Terrell, the aged
and sagacious "dean of Negro women," presided over the weekend gathering and encouraged participants to "fight for our country" and make it
"practice what it preaches." At the end of the historic meeting, the STJ
issued a proclamation demanding the protection of "Negro womanhood"
and decrying black women's "second-class" status, which "denies us dignity and honor."[134]

As part of the campaign to protect black womanhood, the STJ called
for the immediate freedom of Rosa Lee Ingram, a black sharecropper
widow and mother of twelve who was convicted and sentenced to death
in the self-defense slaying of a white man in Ellaville, Georgia, on November 4, 1947.[135] John Stratford, a sixty-four-year-old white sharecropper
who lived on the same property as Ingram and her family, harassed Ingram
for years. She finally fought back after he tried to force her into a shed to
have sex with him. "He never tried to rape me," she told a reporter,
" . . . he just tried to compel me."[136] Angered by her repeated rejections,
Stratford lashed out. Cursing her out, he grabbed his gun and used the
butt as a bludgeon. "I grappled with him," she remembered, "and he
dropped the gun. He choked me and nearly tore off my sweater."

Rosa Lee Ingram, a sharecropper and mother of twelve,
was sentenced to death for the self-defense slaying of a
white man in Ellaville, Georgia, on November 4, 1947.
The NAACP raised thousands of dollars to challenge the
conviction. Ingram was finally released from prison on
August 26, 1959. Ingram (seated) with sons Sammie
(center) and Wallace (standing) in an Albany, Georgia,
jail cell, 1948.

When Ingram's sixteen-year-old son, Wallace, heard the scuffle, he ran
to his mother's aid. "Please stop beating mama," he begged.[137] Stratford
persisted, and Wallace picked up the gun. Wallace rammed the gun into
Stratford's head, knocking him to the ground. Rosa Lee and her son left
Stratford lying in the grass and ran home, unaware that he was dead.
Within two months, she was on death row for murder.[138]

The Sojourners for Truth and Justice rallied to free Rosa Lee Ingram from
prison and praised her for "defending the honor of all womanhood." They
argued that her willingness to fight back against a white man's sexual and
physical advances was not a crime but instead was "the first step in ending
the indignities heaped upon Negro women everywhere in our land." "WE
SHALL NOT BE TRAMPLED UPON ANY LONGER," the women declared.[139]

·   ·   ·

Black women in Montgomery, especially those in the Women's Political Council, could have adopted the Sojourners' rallying cry as their own. When members of the WPC, Rufus Lewis's Citizens Committee, and the Federation of Negro Women's Clubs marched into another meeting with the city commission in March 1954 and demanded better treatment on the buses, city leaders again refused to budge. Jo Ann Robinson was furious. As she heard more "stories of unhappy experiences" on the buses, she decided to give Mayor W. A. "Tacky" Gayle a piece of her mind. Robinson fumed, Gayle recalled later; she said "they would just show me," he claimed. "They [said] they were going in the front door and sitting wherever they pleased."[140]

Lest Gayle misunderstand the threat, Robinson sent him a letter on May 21, 1954, just four days after the momentous Supreme Court decision in *Brown v. Board of Education* that banned segregation in public schools. In the letter, Robinson spelled out exactly what would happen should Gayle and the other city commissioners ignore the WPC's demands. Since "three-fourths of the riders of those public conveyances are Negroes," Robinson warned, "they could not possibly operate . . . if Negroes did not patronize them." "More and more of our people are already arranging with neighbors and friends," she asserted, "to ride to keep from being insulted and humiliated by bus drivers." In addition, Robinson pointed out, more than twenty-five local organizations had begun talking about a "city-wide boycott of the buses," and plans were already "being made to ride less or not at all, on our buses."

Perhaps the earth-shattering Supreme Court ruling gave Robinson the courage to issue such a forceful warning. After all, it appeared that Jim Crow was beginning to die a slow but sure death. Maybe she was inspired by the spirit of the Sojourners for Truth and Justice. More likely, however, she had simply had enough. Threatening a boycott was perhaps the only option remaining after requests to be treated with dignity fell on deaf ears for more than a decade.

Ten years earlier Thurgood Marshall had warned that the abuse and mistreatment of black women on public conveyances was "dynamite." Just after Robinson sent her letter to Mayor Gayle, a news report hit the black community like a "bombshell." Claudette Colvin, a fifteen-year-old high school girl, had been manhandled, arrested, and indicted for refusing to relinquish her seat to a white man.[141]

CHAPTER 3

"Walking in Pride and Dignity"

CLAUDETTE COLVIN, A SPIRITED and studious tenth grader at Booker T. Washington High School, boarded the Highland Gardens bus near Dexter Avenue Baptist Church after school on March 2, 1955. She had spent the school day studying Harriet Tubman and Sojourner Truth, "black heroes and how they broke down Jim Crow laws," as she put it. Each student brought in articles about racial violence and discrimination. Her class spent the afternoon talking about the bleak racial conditions in Montgomery. By the time she boarded the bus, Colvin was filled with resentment over the city's double standard of justice. She plopped down in the rear section reserved for "colored" passengers.[1]

At the next stop, passengers climbed aboard and filled the remaining seats—the first ten rows reserved for whites, blacks in the back. Mrs. Ruth Hamilton, visibly pregnant, sat down next to Colvin. A white couple squeezed into the last two seats directly across from them. When the bus driver, Robert W. Cleere, saw that the color line had been breached—black and white people could not sit across from one another—he ordered Colvin and Hamilton to stand in the aisle to preserve segregation. Hamilton refused to give up her seat. Placing her hands on her protruding belly, Hamilton told Cleere that she "was not going to get up," because, she said, she "didn't feel like it."[2]

Uncomfortable asking a pregnant woman to relinquish her seat, the driver turned to Colvin and threatened to call the police unless she moved. Colvin did not budge. Furious, Cleere pulled the bus to the curb in the middle of the downtown business district, locked the passengers in, and walked away. He soon returned with two policemen. The officers lumbered onto the bus and stood over Hamilton and Colvin, staring down at the stubborn women. "Move," ordered one of the officers. A black man seated behind Hamilton interrupted the standoff and offered Hamilton his seat, which she accepted, leaving Colvin alone. The police demanded to know why she ignored the driver's direct order.

"It's against the law here," an officer reminded her.

"I didn't know that it was a law," Colvin shot back, "that a colored person had to get up and give a white person a seat when there were not any more vacant seats and colored people were standing up."

Colvin had a point—the city law required passengers to move only if another seat was available. Since all the seats were taken, Colvin had every right to stay put. The officers seemed genuinely stumped until she sat up and with righteous indignation said, "I [am] just as good as any white person."

A hush fell over the crowded bus. The driver and the two officers stepped outside to consider their options. "We just sat there," Gloria Hardin, another passenger, recalled. "We didn't know what was going to happen but we knew something would happen." Colvin waited quietly for Cleere and the police. "I thought he would stop and shout and then drive on," Colvin said later. "That's what they usually did."[3] Colvin's assertion of equality seemed to have pushed Cleere over the line. He told the police to arrest her. Clambering back onto the bus, Cleere pointed at Colvin. "I have had trouble out of *that thing* before," he said.[4] The police slowly walked over to Colvin, grabbed her arms, and jerked her toward the aisle. She began to sob and pulled against the officers, trying to remain in her seat. "I wasn't getting up," she said later. "I couldn't. I had it in my mind that it was wrong."[5]

"You black whore," an officer shouted, then yanked her from the seat and kicked her down the aisle toward the front of the bus. The other officer dragged the weeping teenager down the steps and pushed her into their patrol car.[6] Colvin was terrified. "You just didn't know what white people might do at that time," she recalled later. "I didn't know if they were crazy or if they were going to take me to a Klan meeting." When she heard one of the officers make a joke about her breasts and bra size, she feared the worst. Stories of ordeals like the one Gertrude Perkins endured at the hands of the Montgomery police were common currency in the black South. "I started protecting my crotch," she remembered. "I was afraid they might rape me."[7]

Deep history and day-to-day life in Montgomery gave her plenty of reasons to be afraid. Away from the public glare and in the backseat of a white man's car, anything could happen. They could take Colvin wherever they wanted and do whatever they pleased without fear of punishment. It was the worst possible situation for a young black woman—something generations of mothers had warned their daughters to avoid at all costs.

Colvin tried to remain calm as the police drove her to the jail and booked her for violating the city's segregation laws. Furious that the teenager had defied them, they also charged her with assault and resisting arrest. To drown out the horror of being in jail, Colvin recited poetry and scripture. "I recited Edgar Allan Poe," she recalled, " 'Annabel Lee,' the characters in *Midsummer Night's Dream,* the Lord's Prayer, and the Twenty-third Psalm."[8]

Colvin may have asked the Lord to be her shepherd, but the local trinity of Fred Gray, E. D. Nixon, and Jo Ann Robinson planned her deliverance. News of Colvin's stand against segregation and subsequent detention spread quickly through town. "In a few hours every Negro youngster on the streets discussed Colvin's arrest," Jo Ann Robinson remembered. "Telephones rang, clubs called special meetings . . . mothers expressed concern . . . [and] men instructed their wives to walk or to share rides."[9] Almost immediately, blacks formed the Citizens Coordinating Committee, led by Robinson, Rufus Lewis, and Fred Gray, Montgomery's newest and youngest black attorney. They sent out an appeal to "Friends of Justice and Human Rights." They requested financial assistance and called for an "unconditional acquittal of Miss Claudette Colvin."[10] Martin Luther King, Jr., the baby-faced Baptist preacher who had only been in town for a few months, called the situation an "atrocity" that "seemed to arouse the Negro community." He remembered later: "There was talk of boycotting the buses in protest."[11] In fact, there had been an explicit threat to boycott the buses by the Women's Political Council nearly a year earlier. But fighting the city was risky, if not dangerous. "People had everything to lose," Jo Ann Robinson noted, "and nothing to gain."[12] Committee members shelved the boycott and decided to appeal to city and bus officials directly, and if that failed, they reasoned, then they would go to court.

The first meeting the Citizens Coordinating Committee had with police commissioner Dave Birmingham and J. H. Bagley, the manager of the bus company, went relatively well. Birmingham, an amiable if demagogic populist, frequently met with black constituents and often responded to their complaints. In 1953, for example, Birmingham acknowledged widespread police brutality in black neighborhoods and appointed the city's first seven black police officers—four men and three women—the most in the state. Birmingham expressed deep concern over what happened to Colvin and conceded that the driver acted improperly. He and Bagley agreed that bus drivers ought to treat all passengers with courtesy and promised to take a look at the "Mobile plan," a seating scheme used in Mobile, Alabama, in which there was no firm color line. Blacks filled seats from the back of the bus forward and whites from the front to the back until they met somewhere in the middle.[13] With assurances that Birmingham and Bagley would consider changing some of the most humiliating practices on the buses, Jo Ann Robinson and King left the meeting feeling optimistic. But within a few days, as King recalled, "the same old patterns of humiliation continued."[14]

The second meeting was more confrontational. Backed by a crowd of black women from the WPC and the Federation of Negro Women's Clubs, Rufus Lewis and Fred Gray presented petitions that demanded an end to mistreatment on the buses to Mayor Gayle and a cadre of city and corporate attorneys. Nixon had invited Rosa Parks, but she refused to attend. The race pride that she had learned from her Garveyite grandparents drew limits. "I had decided," she said, "that I would not go anywhere with a piece of paper in my hand asking white folks for any favors."[15]

Parks's instincts proved correct. At the meeting, Robinson urged complacent city commissioners to again accept the "Mobile plan," but Jack Crenshaw, the attorney for the bus company, quickly quashed the idea, claiming it would violate the city's segregation laws. City attorneys backed Crenshaw. The meeting ended in stalemate. Since the city's leaders stubbornly sided with segregation, Attorney Gray decided to take Colvin's case to court. Instead of asking for a kinder, gentler Jim Crow on the buses, he would challenge its constitutionality.[16]

On March 18, 1955, Fred Gray, the twenty-four-year-old attorney, stood before Judge Wiley C. Hill, whose first cousin was U.S. senator J. Lister Hill, and defended Colvin, who pleaded not guilty to all charges. A native of Montgomery and a former student of Jo Ann Robinson at Alabama State University, Gray returned to the Cradle of Confederacy after law school to "destroy everything segregated that [he] could find."[17] He wasted no time. Segregation ordinances on the city buses violated the equal protection clause of the Fourteenth Amendment, Gray asserted. Judge Hill quickly overruled Gray's claim, swatting it away as if it were a pesky fly. Gray pushed ahead. Colvin was innocent, he insisted, because it was a crime to disobey a bus driver's order to relinquish a seat only if there were other seats available in the colored section.[18] Since more than a dozen witnesses testified that no other seats were available, Gray claimed Colvin had not violated the law.

Gray also produced witnesses who testified that Colvin was calm and well behaved, rather than unruly and wild, as the officers claimed. Under cross-examination, the bus driver, Robert Cleere, admitted that Colvin was "not talking in a rage" and was not "disturbing anybody on the bus." When asked if Colvin ever hit the officers, Cleere had to admit he "didn't see her hit them."[19] When circuit solicitor William F. Thetford asked one of the police officers if Colvin "hit or strike [sic] or scratched" him, the officer said simply, "No, sir." Thetford seemed surprised by his witness's answer. When he asked the officer again if Colvin caused a commotion, the policeman could only say "She started crying." But, he added, he "didn't hear her scream too loud" and didn't remember her swearing.[20] Although Gray proved Colvin did not violate any laws and was not unruly or abusive, Judge Hill found her guilty of assault and battery and charged her with violating the *state* rather than city segregation laws, something Thetford had thrown in at the last minute. Hill sentenced Colvin to indefinite probation.[21]

When Gray appealed the decision in circuit court on May 6, 1955, Thetford dropped the state segregation charge, a sly move that destroyed Gray's plan to use Colvin's case to test the constitutionality of bus segregation. Despite the solicitor's backpedaling and the lack of evidence, circuit court judge Eugene Carter found Colvin guilty of assault and battery, assessed a small fine, and declared her a juvenile delinquent.[22]

Stunned by the harsh decision, Colvin burst into tears. Spectators and supporters who filled the courtroom, Jo Ann Robinson recalled, "brushed away their own tears" as her "agonized sobs penetrated the atmosphere of the courthouse."[23] African Americans in Montgomery, Robinson remembered, "were as near a breaking point as they had ever been. Resentment, rebellion, and unrest were evident in all Negro circles." The unexpected verdict hit the black community, she said, "like a bombshell."[24]

.   .   .

Colvin was not the first woman to be arrested for violating Montgomery's segregation code. She was, however, the first to plead innocent and challenge the city in court. And she had the support of all three hundred members of the Women's Political Council. "Bless her heart, she fought like a little tigress," said Irene West, an influential WPC member and widow of a prominent black dentist.[25] Virginia Durr, a well-known white liberal in Montgomery, told a friend that Colvin's case "created tremendous interest in the Negro community." African Americans were "fighting mad," she said, adding that Colvin's arrest "may help give them the courage to put up a real fight on the bus segregation issue."[26]

Jo Ann Robinson had been itching for a boycott for over a year, and now she began laying the groundwork. The timing seemed right; after Colvin's second trial, Robinson recalled, "large numbers [of women] refused to use the buses . . . for a few days." These private protests convinced her that the community was ready for action, but she had to convince E. D. Nixon, whose connections and expertise would be necessary for any successful mass movement.

With Mary Fair Burks, her colleague from Alabama State, and two carloads of women, Robinson led a caravan to E. D. Nixon's house to sketch out plans for a citywide boycott.[27] Robinson and Burks told Nixon that they had found a "victim around whom they could rally community support for a general protest" and assured him they were ready to mobilize the masses. Robinson told Nixon that they "had already planned for fifty thousand notices calling people to boycott the buses; only the specifics of the time and place had to be added."[28] The women asked Nixon for his support.[29]

Nixon hesitated to endorse a general boycott before meeting with Colvin and her parents. He asked Robinson to give him some time. Nixon had followed Colvin's case. In fact, the seasoned labor union operative had already contacted Virginia Durr's husband, Clifford, a local white attorney and former New Deal "brain-truster," to discuss legal and political options. Still, he worried about using Colvin as a symbol for the fight. A visit to Colvin's home made his decision easy. Nixon arrived at Colvin's house in the King Hill section of Montgomery, a lower-class black enclave with tumbledown houses, unpaved streets, and outdoor privies. When Colvin answered the door, Nixon saw that she was pregnant. "My daughter," Colvin's mother explained, "done took a tumble."[30] Nixon decided that Colvin could not possibly serve as the community's standard-bearer, nor be a good litigant.

For starters, an unwed pregnant teenager might be a divisive symbol for a community where fissures of class, religion, and color already presented tough challenges. Her stomach was beginning to swell, Nixon argued, and her mother was ashamed to have her appear in public.[31] But it was more than Colvin's pregnancy and her parents' shame that concerned Nixon. Colvin's dark skin color and working-class status made her a political liability in certain parts of the black community. Colvin's mother was a maid, and her father did yard work. They lived in one of the poorest sections of town, where juke joints rocked until dawn and, Nixon acknowledged, "men would drink too much and get into a fight." "It wasn't a bad area," Colvin said years later, "but it had a bad reputation."[32]

In some ways, Colvin's roots in King Hill could have made her the perfect symbol for a bus boycott, since she was one of thousands of working-class black women who suffered humiliation and mistreatment daily on the buses. Though Jo Ann Robinson was firmly rooted in the middle class, she saw Colvin as a kind of black everywoman who would inspire others. But Nixon refused. "She's just not the kind we can win a case with," he said.[33] Robinson fumed. She "liked to have a fit," Nixon recalled. "She jumped all over me." But he was resolute: "I'm not going to go out on a limb with it."[34] "I've handled so many cases that I know when a man would stand up and when he wouldn't," Nixon argued. "You've got to think about the newspapers, you got to think about public opinion, you got to think policies and so forth, and intimidation."[35] His point was not easily dismissed.

Despite her support for Colvin, who was a straight-A student and a member of the NAACP Youth Council, Rosa Parks believed that Nixon was right. Parks knew that Colvin had stepped outside the bounds of respectable behavior for a young woman in the 1950s.[36] "If the white press got hold of that information," Parks feared, "they would have [had] a field day . . . They'd call her a bad girl and her case wouldn't have a chance."[37] And Parks knew Montgomery. Even if African Americans there were, as the historian Taylor Branch put it, "willing to rally behind an unwed pregnant teenager—which they were not—her circumstances would make her an extremely vulnerable standard-bearer."[38] Without Nixon's support, Robinson and her colleagues on the Women's Political Council would have to wait for another arrest.

It did not take long. On October 21, 1955, police arrested and fined Mary Louise Smith, an eighteen-year-old maid, for refusing to give up her seat and stand in the colored section so that a white woman could sit down.

"I am not going to move," she declared when the driver asked her to stand. "I got the privilege to sit here like anybody else."[39] After meeting Smith and her family, Nixon decided that she could not be the boycott's symbolic heroine, because her father had a tendency to drink too much and she lived in a "low type of home" in Washington Park, a poor section of town similar to King Hill.[40] A few days after her arrest, Smith's father paid the fine, making a legal challenge impossible.

Colvin and Smith were victims of time, place, and circumstance. By late 1955, black leaders in Montgomery had little choice but to embrace the "politics of respectability" amid the growing white backlash sparked by the 1954 *Brown v. Board of Education* decision.[41] Just four days after the landmark Supreme Court ruling, Thomas P. Brady, a circuit court judge in Brookhaven, Mississippi, and author of the segregationist manifesto *Black Monday,* called on state legislators to build an organization that would protect white supremacy by any means necessary. Their response was the White Citizens' Council (WCC), an organization designed to "counteract the NAACP and other left-wing organizations."[42] The WCC quickly spread throughout Mississippi and the Deep South, especially areas where African Americans pressed for desegregation of schools or public accommodations. In Mississippi alone, the WCC counted twenty-five thousand members in 1955 and nearly eighty thousand in 1956.[43] The WCC recruited supporters by relying heavily on sexual scare tactics and the paranoia that *Brown* would lead to "racial amalgamation." Headlines in the *Citizens' Council,* the organization's newsletter, warned that "mixed marriage," "sex orgies," and black men raping white girls were "typical of stories filtering back from areas where racial integration is proceeding 'with all deliberate speed.' "[44]

In this environment, political respectability required middle-class decorum. Shining a spotlight on a pregnant black teenager would only fuel white stereotypes of black women's uninhibited sexuality. Colvin's swollen stomach could have become a stark reminder that desegregation would lead to sexual debauchery. Smith's shaky social status could raise the question of whether black citizens merited equal treatment in the minds of whites and might divide African Americans along class lines. If Nixon and the WPC supported Colvin and Mary Louise Smith, they risked evoking black stereotypes that could ultimately smother any movement for change.

Respectability had been a staple of African-American politics since Reconstruction, when whites used racist violence and sexual abuse to shore up white supremacy.[45] Silence and secrecy among black clubwomen at the turn of the century helped counter slanderous images and kept the inner lives of African Americans hidden from white people. This self-imposed reticence, Darlene Clark Hine argues, "implied that those [African-American women] who spoke out provided grist for detractors' mills and, even more ominously, tore the protective cloaks from their inner selves."[46] In the wake of *Brown,* testimony and openness were temporarily replaced with silence.

Testimony triumphed throughout the 1940s as African Americans rallied around black women who had been sexually abused, no matter their class status. Recy Taylor was a struggling sharecropper, yet her case served as the catalyst for a national campaign. In 1947 the NAACP and the National Council of Negro Women—both solid, middle-class organizations—stood by Rosa Lee Ingram despite the fact that she was poor and had a dozen children.[47] Gertrude Perkins was hardly a model of respectable womanhood, but Montgomery's middle-class black ministers rallied to her defense, risking their livelihoods, if not their lives, to help preserve her dignity and bodily integrity.

Five years later, amid rising white opposition to *Brown* and growing anti-Communism at home and abroad, African Americans found themselves hemmed in politically. As Southern McCarthyites equated black self-assertion with a Marxist plot to destroy America, the WCC and the KKK claimed desegregation efforts would lead to "mongrelization" and "amalgamation." The powerful cocktail of anti-Communism, white supremacy, and sexualized propaganda and paranoia enabled whites to push aside or even kill African Americans who asserted their humanity. By February 1956, forty thousand white Alabamians, many from Montgomery, joined the Citizens' Council crusade, helping to launch the "massive resistance" movement.[48] Mayor Gayle and other city commissioners, not to mention state senators, proudly proclaimed solidarity and allegiance to the WCC as it became the "mouthpiece of southern defiance."[49] E. D. Nixon undoubtedly sensed this hysteria when he refused to raise a pregnant teenager up as the symbol of the integration struggle. In mid-1950s Alabama, he had to find someone whose class background, moral reputation, and public record could withstand withering white scrutiny and inspire African-American unity.

Because she was so perfect for the role, it is tempting to think that Rosa Parks's famous stand against segregation was a planned protest. She was,

Rosa Parks at a desegregation workshop at Highlander Folk
School in July 1955, five months before the Montgomery bus
boycott began. Seated to her right is Frederick Douglass
Patterson, former president of Tuskegee University, founder of
the United Negro College Fund, and supporter of the 1944–45
Recy Taylor campaign.

as historian J. Mills Thornton argues, "more actively involved in the struggle against racial discrimination, and more knowledgeable about efforts
being made to eliminate it, than all but a tiny handful of the city's forty-five
thousand black citizens." She knew Nixon was searching for a "plaintiff
who was beyond reproach" and was certain he would support her, since she
fit his qualifications of respectability.[50] But it is unlikely that she planned
a protest. Instead, when Rosa Parks had an opportunity to resist, she seized
it. Her decision to stay put that fateful day was rooted in her history as a
radical activist and years of witnessing injustice—from Recy Taylor to
Gertrude Perkins to Jeremiah Reeves.[51] She had grown up in the Garvey
movement. She and her husband had labored in the Scottsboro struggle as
a young married couple. In 1944 her investigation of the Recy Taylor case
launched a national crusade. For more than a decade, her work with the
NAACP, the Brotherhood of Sleeping Car Porters, and other groups placed
her at the center of Montgomery's black freedom struggle. Her decision to
keep her seat on December 1, 1955, was less a mystery than a moment.

Rosa Parks boarded the Cleveland Avenue bus on December 1, 1955, and
slipped into a seat near the middle of the bus—an area passengers referred
to as "no-man's-land" because it was not designated white or black. When

the ruddy-faced bus driver saw her seated there, he yelled, "Let me have those front seats." Parks sat still. "Make it light on yourself," he shouted, "and let me have those seats!" Parks recognized the driver immediately. It was James F. Blake, the same operator who had mistreated her in 1943. She turned to look out the window and ignored Blake's order. "I couldn't see how standing up was going to 'make it light' for me," she said later. "The more we gave in and complied, the worse they treated us."[52]

When Blake stepped off the bus to call the police, Rosa Parks remained calm, though she knew better than anyone what kind of danger she faced. She had twelve years of notes on nearly every case of racial brutality in and around Montgomery. There was no way to be without fear, but she held herself steady. As she waited, perhaps she conjured up the spirit of her grandfather, who sat up many nights with a double-barreled shotgun to protect their little home from the Klan in Pine Level, Alabama.[53]

Parks also recalled the ten days she had spent in the company of the South's most active reformers at the Highlander Folk School, a training center for labor and civil rights activists in Tennessee.[54] Her experience at Highlander in the summer of 1955 was a highlight in her career as an activist and one of the first times she said she did not "feel hostility from white people." She had been reluctant to leave that interracial island, and now she found herself stranded on a city bus, about to be arrested—or worse.[55]

Two white police officers, F. B. Day and D. W. Mixon, climbed onto the bus and ambled toward Parks.[56] One asked why she refused to give up her seat. "Why do you all push us around?" she shot back.

"I do not know," the officer replied, "but the law is the law and you're under arrest."[57] The officers picked up her purse and shopping bags, escorted her to their squad car, and drove her to the city jail.

News that her daughter was in jail must have sent shivers down Leona McCauley's spine. Rosa's mother had been a member of the NAACP since 1943 and had worked with her daughter on the Recy Taylor case in 1944; she must have known about Gertrude Perkins, Flossie Hardman, and the other women who were abused in and around Montgomery.[58] Parks was vulnerable every minute she was in jail. When she finally called home, her mother immediately asked, "Did they beat you?"[59] That these were her first words speaks volumes about the context of Parks's protest.

If E. D. Nixon shared Leona McCauley's fears, he kept them hidden. Instead, he seemed positively jubilant. "That's it!" Nixon shouted after he heard about the arrest, then picked up the telephone to spread the good news. Johnnie Carr, Parks's childhood friend and fellow NAACP member, was one of the first people on Nixon's list. "Mrs. Carr," Nixon said gravely, "they have arrested the wrong woman."

"Who have they arrested?" she asked.

"Rosa Parks!" Nixon replied, barely able to contain his glee.

"You're kidding," Carr said.

"No," he chuckled, "they arrested Rosa Parks. They arrested the wrong woman!"[60]

Unlike Claudette Colvin or Mary Louise Smith, Parks was the *perfect* woman to rally around. "She was secretary for everything I had going," Nixon told reporters, "the Brotherhood of Sleeping Car Porters, the NAACP, Alabama Voters' League, all those things." Plus, he said, she could "stand on her feet, she was honest, she was clean, she had integrity. The press couldn't go out and dig up something she did last year, or last month, or five years ago. They couldn't hang nothing like that on Rosa Parks."[61] As long as Nixon could persuade Parks to press charges, she could serve as the symbol of segregation in court, and Nixon and attorney Fred Gray could use her arrest to strike a blow at Jim Crow.

Only her husband stood in the way. In the 1950s this was no small obstacle. Raymond Parks begged his wife to turn Nixon down. "Oh Rosa, Rosa, don't do it, don't do it," he pleaded. "The white folks will kill you."[62] Though his days as a defender of the Scottsboro boys had passed and he no longer held secret, armed meetings in the middle of the night, he knew something about the risks entailed in protesting white supremacy. He was certainly not ready to sacrifice his wife.

When Jo Ann Robinson heard that Parks had been arrested, she did not wait for Nixon's approval to launch a boycott; nor did she ask Rosa and Raymond Parks what they thought. Instead, she planned the kind of protest that members of the Women's Political Council had been demanding. "The Women's Political Council will not wait for Mrs. Parks's consent to call for a boycott of city buses," Robinson scribbled on the back of an envelope as soon as she heard the news. "On Friday, December 2, 1955, the women of Montgomery will call for a boycott to take place on Monday, December 5."[63]

Robinson quickly drafted a more detailed announcement, called John Cannon, her colleague at Alabama State University, and asked for access to the college's mimeograph machines. Cannon agreed, adding that he had been mistreated on the buses one too many times.[64] As darkness fell across campus, Cannon, Robinson, and two student assistants met in a basement office. There they copied, cut, and bundled 52,500 flyers. Only the rising sun and the fear of being caught chased them home.

The flyers announced the boycott, promoting it as an effort to protect black womanhood:

Another Negro woman has been arrested and thrown in jail because she refused to get up out of her seat on the bus for a white person to sit down. It is the second time since the Claudette Colvin case that a Negro woman has been arrested for the same thing. This has to be stopped. Negroes have rights, too, for if Negroes did not ride the buses, they could not operate. Three-fourths of the riders are Negroes, yet we are arrested, or have to stand over empty seats. If we do not do something to stop these arrests, they will continue. *The next time it may be you, or your daughter or mother.* This woman's case will come up on Monday. We are, therefore, asking every Negro to stay off the buses Monday in protest of the arrest and trial. Don't ride the buses to work, to town, to school, or anywhere on Monday . . . Please stay off all buses Monday.[65]

In the early morning hours, Robinson called her foot soldiers in the WPC and told them it was time for their long-planned protest. She explained the distribution routes they had sketched out for delivering the announcement. Before breakfast on Friday, December 2, Dr. Mary Fair Burks, Mrs. Mary Cross, Mrs. Elizabeth Arrington, Mrs. Josie Lawrence, Mrs. Geraldine Nesbitt, Mrs. Catherine N. Johnson, and a dozen other women waited on street corners for Robinson and her student helpers to hand over the huge stacks of flyers. The women delivered the notices to schools and storefronts, beauty parlors and beer halls, barbershops and businesses. By midafternoon, "practically every black man, woman, and child in Montgomery knew the plan and was passing the word along," Robinson said. "No one knew where the notices had come from or who had arranged them and no one cared."[66] Just before she rallied her troops, Robinson called Nixon to let him in on the news. This time he could not say no. Of course, he had no such intention.

Neither did Rosa Parks. Despite her husband's pleas, she decided that the benefits of a legal battle and a boycott outweighed any personal risks. "There had to be a stopping place," she said, "and this seemed to be the place for me to stop being pushed around. I had decided that I would have to know once and for all what rights I had as a human being and a citizen, even in Montgomery, Alabama."[67] Parks told her husband about her decision and gave Nixon permission to go ahead with the legal case, both defying gender roles as a dutiful wife, and defining them by agreeing to serve as a model of dignified womanhood in court.

From that moment forward, Rosa Parks's history as an activist and defiant race woman disappeared from public view. Nixon and others promoted her as a model of the middle-class ideals of "chastity, Godliness, family responsibility, and proper womanly conduct and demeanor."[68] She was the kind of woman around whom all African Americans in Montgomery could unite. She was "humble enough to be claimed by the common folk," Taylor Branch notes, and "dignified enough in manner, speech, and dress to command the respect of the leading classes." Though Parks was far from a bruised blossom in need of chivalry, her role as a symbol of virtuous black womanhood was decisive in Montgomery as even the most reluctant middle-class ministers rallied to her defense.

The day after Parks was arrested, more than fifty black activists and community leaders gathered in the basement of Dexter Avenue Baptist Church to hash out conflicting ideas about Jo Ann Robinson's call for a boycott.[69] The debate was fierce, with some ministers refusing to be part of the boycott. But Parks's presence and her moving appeal to the ministers to do something about the long-standing abuse of black women in Montgomery brought unity. Undoubtedly, members of the Women's Political Council echoed her sentiments. Many of the ministers and political leaders, according to the historian Douglas Brinkley, "did not want to be on record as abandoning a good Christian woman in need." They decided to put aside their differences to "embrace 'Sister Rosa'" by "promising to promote the one-day boycott in their Sunday sermons."[70] Parks's iconic role as the respectable, even saintly heroine played a role in the wider political world and was crucial at the birth of the boycott. Because it was the first Sunday of the month, parishioners filled almost all the pews in Montgomery's black churches. Ministers decried the arrest of Rosa Parks and urged congregants to join in the one-day boycott on Monday, December 5, and assemble afterward at the Holt Street Baptist Church for further instructions.

Monday December 5, 1955, was a rainy, bone-cold day. Robinson and others worried that the downpour would dampen the one-day protest, but those fears quickly dissipated as empty buses began rolling through Montgomery's rain-soaked streets. Rosa Parks awoke early and watched the normally packed Cleveland Avenue bus whiz past her house without a single passenger. Parks felt vindicated. "I could feel that whatever my individual desires were to be free," she said later, "I was not alone. There were many others who felt the same way."[71] Like Parks, Johnnie Carr watched with satisfaction as the empty buses splashed through intersections. She even decided to trail one in her car. They "didn't pick up a single soul," she remembered with glee. "They were just moving down the street empty."[72] When Parks and Carr saw the sidewalks clogged with black women under dark umbrellas walking to work or waiting for a ride, they were elated.

Montgomery officials, who did not share the excitement, inadvertently boosted boycott participation. Surely, they reasoned, the near-universal abandonment of the buses by their happy Negroes must reflect coercion by agitators. The city assigned police escorts to bus routes in black neighborhoods in order to "protect Negro riders" from potential "goon squads."[73] If any black women were tempted to get on the bus that miserable Monday morning, the sight of police with shotguns surrounding the buses can only have strengthened their resolve.

Confident that the one-day boycott was going to be successful, Parks readied to play her part in court. "I knew what I had to do," she recalled. "I remember very clearly that I wore a straight, long-sleeved black dress with a white collar and cuffs, a small black velvet hat with pearls across the top, and a charcoal-gray coat. I carried a black purse and wore white gloves."[74] Her conservative, Puritan-like clothing—and her memory of exactly what she wore forty years later—indicated a keen understanding of the importance of the politics of respectability.

Flanked by E. D. Nixon and her two attorneys, Fred Gray and Charles Langford, Rosa Parks ascended the courthouse steps with confidence and grace. Her elegant deportment made quite an impression on the five hundred supporters who crowded the steps of Montgomery's city hall, many of whom were her charges in the NAACP Youth Council.[75] Mary Frances, one of the girls in the crowd, saw Parks and shouted, "Oh, she's so sweet! They've messed with the wrong one now."[76] Frances and others began to chant "They've messed with the wrong one now" as Nixon, Parks, and her attorneys, both in their best Sunday suits, waded through the throng of supporters and disappeared into the crowded courtroom.

The trial lasted no more than five minutes. Judge John B. Scott quickly found Parks guilty of violating the state segregation law, despite the fact that she had been arrested for violating the *city's* segregation ordinance.[77] He then gave her a suspended sentence and fined her fourteen dollars. As Parks turned and walked briskly out of the courtroom, two policemen scurried to her side. She and Nixon walked down a long hallway to the city clerk's office to sign an appeal bond. Gray and Langford stayed behind to file an appeal. The sight of police officers escorting Parks sent the crowd into hysterics. They surged, crowding around Parks so she could hardly move. "It was the first time I had seen so much courage among our people," Nixon recalled. Despite his excitement, he urged calm. "Everything is all right," he said, gesturing toward the heavily armed policemen who suddenly lined the hall. "Keep calm because we don't want to do anything to make that man use the shotgun." After Nixon signed the bond and handed Parks to her husband, he turned to the angry crowd and told them to go home. "Don't hang around," he urged, "because all they want is some excuse to kill somebody."[78]

Parks asked her husband to drop her off at Fred Gray's office to work the phones for the rest of the afternoon. Meanwhile, Gray, E. D. Nixon, Ralph Abernathy, Reverend E. N. French, and a handful of other ministers assembled in the basement of the Mt. Zion AME Zion Church to hammer out a plan for that evening's mass meeting. They needed a name and a president for their new organization. Nixon suggested the Citizens Coordinating Committee, a kind of amalgam of titles from previous campaigns to protect black women like Recy Taylor and Gertrude Perkins. Ralph Abernathy, the young Baptist minister in town, wrinkled his nose at the suggestion. "No, I don't like that," he said. "What about the Montgomery Improvement Association?" "That sounds good," Reverend French, pastor of the Hilliard AME Zion Church, said. "I believe I can go along with that." Abernathy then turned to Nixon. "Brother Nixon, you going to serve as president, ain't you?" Nixon smiled. "Not unlessen you don't accept the man I got in mind."[79]

Reverend Martin Luther King, Jr., was only twenty-six years old, virtually unknown outside his upper-crust congregation at Dexter Avenue Baptist. But everyone who met him knew he was good-looking, intelligent, and eloquent. To Nixon, however, the crucial fact was that King was not beholden to anyone, white or black. "He didn't have to bow to the power structure," Nixon recalled. "So many ministers accept a handout, and then they owe their soul."[80] King had not even had the opportunity to sell out. "He had not been here long enough for the city fathers to put their hands on him," as Nixon put it.[81]

Although historians would later argue that Nixon wanted to be president of the MIA and that Rufus Lewis, Nixon's chief political rival, engineered King's nomination, Nixon and other established leaders in Montgomery were not eager to take on what in all likelihood would be a short-lived and dangerous exercise. After all, their plans called only for a one-day boycott. No one knew what would happen next, but most were confident it would not include glory or fame.[82] Though they all knew a moment had come, no one suspected that *the* moment had come.

Though Nixon was happy to let King head the MIA, he did not shrink from bold leadership. When some ministers suggested that their names remain secret to protect themselves and their families from white retribution, Nixon exploded in anger. "They was talking about slipping around, didn't want the white folks to know," Nixon recalled. "How you going to run a bus boycott in secret?" he demanded. Then, using language that, as Nixon put it, "wasn't in the Sunday school books," he chastised the timid preachers. "How the hell you going to have a protest without letting the white folks know? What's the matter with you people?" he asked, flabbergasted by their cowardice. "Here you have been living off the sweat of these washwomen all these years, and you have never done anything for them. Now you have a chance to pay them back. And you're too damn scared to stand on your feet and be counted."[83] Scolding the black ministers for shirking their manly duties, he dared them to rise up in defense of black womanhood. "We've worn aprons all our lives," he said. "It's time to take the aprons off . . . If we gonna be mens, now's the time to be mens."[84]

Nixon's tirade may have convinced the ministers to stand up for black women, but it did not mean they planned to share leadership with them. Indeed, Jo Ann Robinson and Rosa Parks, the two women who made the boycott possible, were not at the meeting where the Montgomery Improvement Association was born and Martin Luther King, Jr., was chosen as its president. Whether Nixon and others simply forgot to include Robinson and Parks or explicitly excluded them is not known. It was not until the mass meeting that night that Robinson realized her leadership had been subverted. "The men took it over," she said. They had "definitely decided to assume leadership."[85]

That night, December 5, 1955, more than five thousand African Americans squeezed into the sanctuary, the balcony, and the basement annex at the Holt Street Baptist Church. A wave of bodies spilled out the double doors and clogged six blocks of city sidewalks outside. Cars jammed the streets surrounding the modest church, unable to move even an inch. Volunteers set up loudspeakers so that the throngs of people clamoring unsuccessfully for a seat could stand outside and hear Nixon, Ralph Abernathy, Martin Luther King, Jr., and other ministers make their debut as "mens." The moment was electrifying.

King started slowly, speaking about the murky nature of segregation laws, then began to rock the crowd with his incredible oratory, bringing a steady stream of "yeses" and "amens." When King praised Parks, the audience applauded and cheered on their new heroine. "And since it had to happen," King declared, "I'm happy that it happened to a person like Mrs. Parks."

"Yes," the crowd shouted.

"Nobody can doubt the boundless outreach of her integrity," King said.

"Sure enough," someone in the audience yelled.

"Nobody can doubt the height of her character; nobody can doubt the depth of her Christian commitment and devotion to the teachings of Jesus."

"Yes!" roared the crowd.

"Nobody can call [Rosa Parks] a disturbing factor in the community . . . She is a fine Christian person, unassuming, and yet there is integrity and character there."

The crowd, undulating in call and response, shouted, "All right!"[86]

Then, in the gospel tradition of turning one person's burden into a shared experience, King spoke to everyone who had been mistreated on the buses or humiliated by segregation. "There comes a time," he began, his voice steady and even, then rising, "when people get tired of being trampled over by the iron feet of oppression." A roar of approval rolled over the crowd. "There comes a time, my friends, when people get tired of being plunged across the abyss of humiliation, where they experience the bleakness of nagging despair." As emotions swelled and the applause shook the rafters of the old church, King reached a crescendo: "There comes a time when people get tired of being pushed out of the glittering sunlight of life's July and left standing amid the piercing chill of an alpine November."[87] The amazing thunder of sound—clapping, screaming, and foot stomping, drowned King out.

He had touched a nerve. In those few sentences, King captured the soul-deep sense of humiliation and degradation that the mostly working-class audience of maids, cooks, teachers, and day laborers undoubtedly felt. The language King employed to describe the effect of mistreatment on the buses—"abyss of humiliation" and "nagging despair"—speaks to the way racial and sexual subjugation conspire to steal a person's humanity. It is no surprise that the audience erupted in raw emotion. King then skillfully moved to control the anger and enthusiasm, to remind the audience that they had the power—through Christian love, faith, and unity—to over-throw the system that had oppressed them for so long.

After King's momentous speech, Reverend E. N. French stepped onto the pulpit and presented Rosa Parks to the crowd. If there was one woman in Montgomery who could testify to the decades of injustice under Jim Crow, it was Rosa Parks. Not only could she speak about her own mis-treatment and abuse on the buses—something that so many of the women assembled together shared—she could also place her arrest in the long his-tory of crimes committed by whites against blacks, something of which she had intimate knowledge.

Just before Reverend French presented Rosa Parks to the crowd, she asked him if the men in charge that night wanted her to say a few words. French told her that she had "had enough and [had] said enough and you don't have to speak." She nodded and they walked toward the front of the church. "I have the responsibility," Reverend French proclaimed to the pulsating crowd, "to present to you the victim of this gross injustice, almost inhumanity, and absolute undemocratic principle, Mrs. Rosa Parks."[88] The audience erupted in applause as she stood silent before them.

We can only wonder what Rosa Parks might have said that night in front of throngs of supporters and fellow sufferers. Perhaps she would have spoken about the abuses suffered by Recy Taylor, Gertrude Perkins, Flossie Hardman, Claudette Colvin, and so many of the women present that night, conjuring up a collective spirit of defiance and self-defense. She might have called on her decades of experience defending ordinary black Alabamians from white terror and her long struggle for human rights to remind her peers of their long and continuing struggle for justice and to push for mass action. Her testimony could have changed the way she was received and forever remembered.

Because Reverend French and the ministers leading the mass meeting that night silenced Parks, they turned her into the kind of woman she wasn't: a quiet victim and solemn symbol. From that moment forward Parks was sainted and celebrated for her quiet dignity, prim demeanor, and middle-class propriety, her radicalism all but erased as she became the

Madonna of Montgomery. She "looked like a symbol of Mother's Day," L. D. Reddick, a history professor at Alabama State, proclaimed, though Parks was neither a mother nor, at just forty-two years old, matronly.[89] The deliberate construction of Rosa Parks as a symbol of virtuous black womanhood began that evening. Reverend Abernathy said as much: "Mrs. Rosa Parks was presented to the mass meeting because we wanted her to become symbolic of our protest meeting."[90]

Unlike Claudette Colvin and Mary Louise Smith, Parks's respectability gave credibility to the nascent Montgomery Improvement Association, minimized controversy, and allowed African Americans to claim the moral high ground in what would become an all-out war against white supremacy. At the same time, they protected themselves and Parks by playing down her radicalism, which would have encouraged opposition, if not outright violence, in an environment poisoned by anti-Communist paranoia and the racist rhetoric of White Citizens' Councils.

The presentation of Parks as a woman worthy of protection enabled African-American ministers and male leaders, most of whom had been resistant to the WPC's calls for a boycott, to take credit for and assume leadership of the boycott. By stepping forward, they could fulfill their manly duty to defend black womanhood, a role that white supremacy had denied them for centuries. Jo Ann Robinson, who complained in her memoir about black men's inability or unwillingness to protect black women from abuse and mistreatment on the buses, understood the enormous symbolism displayed at the Holt Street Baptist Church that night when the leading black men of the community claimed leadership and, as Nixon put it, removed their "aprons." The ministers, Robinson noted, were finally "catching up with their congregations."[91]

If the ministers caught up with their congregations by assuming the leadership of the MIA, black women, who filled the majority of the pews that evening and every mass meeting thereafter, kept the MIA and the bus boycott running. Although newspapers focused on King as the leader and ministers' names lined the MIA's letterhead, Robinson made sure that she, along with Mrs. A. W. West, a wealthy eighty-year-old widow and WPC member, and Rosa Parks served on the executive committee. In fact, it was Robinson, "more than any other person," according to King, who "was active on every level of protest."[92] As long as WPC members handled the day-to-day business of the boycott, Jo Ann Robinson did not challenge the MIA's male leadership. "We felt it would be better," Robinson said, "if the ministers held the most visible leadership positions."[93]

Robinson stacked the MIA staff with her own WPC members, guaranteeing control of the boycott's daily operations. She chose each woman carefully. Mrs. Erna Dungee, a "sophisticated, socially involved woman," was the MIA's financial secretary and worked for the boycott full time. Mrs. Maude Ballou became Martin Luther King's personal secretary. Ballou, a quiet and dedicated worker, earned King's trust, Robinson recalled, by "never remembering" any of his business. Mrs. Martha Johnson was the MIA's secretary clerk. She assisted all the other leaders of the MIA and "never got two persons' business mixed up." Mrs. Hazel Gregory served as the general overseer of the MIA. She knew "where everything was, never got anything mixed up, and could get what was needed immediately," Robinson remembered fondly. Gregory's position also included "managing the business and taking care of the building where the MIA was housed."[94] Only at the podium did women take a backseat in the boycott.

The public face of the boycott belied the crucial role Jo Ann Robinson played in making it a success. During an interview with Rufus Lewis on January 20, 1956, Donald T. Ferron, an oral historian from Fisk University, questioned the leadership of the boycott in his notes. "The public recognizes Reverend King as *the* leader," he wrote, "but I wonder if Mrs. Robinson may be of equal importance. The organizational process is being kept secret, as well as the organizers."[95]

It was Jo Ann Robinson, not Martin Luther King, Jr., who served as the chief strategist for the Montgomery Improvement Association. She negotiated with city leaders and bus company officials, edited the MIA newsletter, and ferried African Americans to and from work for nearly 381 days, all while holding down a full-time teaching job at Alabama State. "Few realize how much Jo Ann did," Fred Gray recalled. Hardly anyone knew, for example, that "much of the activity . . . occurred at Jo Ann Robinson's house."

The enormous spotlight that focused on King, combined with the construction of Rosa Parks as a saintly symbol, hid the women's long struggle in the dimly lit background, obscuring the origins of the MIA and erasing women from the movement. For decades, the Montgomery bus boycott has been told as a story triggered by Rosa Parks's spontaneous refusal to give up her seat followed by the triumphant leadership of men like Fred Gray, Martin Luther King, Jr., E. D. Nixon, and Ralph Abernathy. While these men had a major impact on the emerging protest

African-American women were the backbone of the Montgomery bus boycott.
Here black women walk to work in February 1956.

movement, it was black women's decade-long struggle against mistreatment and abuse by white bus drivers and police officers that launched the
boycott. Without an appreciation for the particular predicaments of black
women in the Jim Crow South, it is nearly impossible to understand *why*
thousands of working-class and hundreds of middle-class black women
chose to walk rather than ride the bus for 381 days.

Women walked, Parks claimed in an interview in April 1956, not merely in support of her but because she "was not the only person who had been mistreated and humiliated . . . Other women had gone through similarly shameful experiences," Parks said, "some even worse than mine."[96] These experiences propelled African-American women into every conceivable aspect of the boycott. African-American women of means, professional women like Jo Ann Robinson, and society women like Irene West brought their own gifts to the boycott, even though many did not ride the buses. Erna Dungee, MIA financial secretary, said women "really were the ones who carried out the actions . . . We organized the parking lot pick-ups . . . drove the cars," and did "the little day-to-day things, taking care of the finances, things like that. When all the dust settled," she told an interviewer, "the women were there when it cleared. They were there in the positions to hold the MIA together."[97]

Class status did not dictate women's roles. More than any single individual, the city's domestic workers put the Montgomery City Lines out of business. "The maids, the cooks, they were the ones that really and truly kept the buses running," Georgia Gilmore recalled. "And after the maids and the cooks stopped riding the bus," she added, "well, the bus didn't have any need to run."[98]

During the first few months of the boycott, Willie M. Lee, a researcher from Fisk University, went to Montgomery to figure out why so many domestic workers were determined to stay off the buses. "I'll crawl on my knees 'fo I get back on dem buses," one woman said while waiting at a carpool dispatch center. Her friend agreed, "I ain't 'bout to get on dem buses . . . I'll walk twenty miles 'fo I ride 'em."[99] Irene Stovall, a mother and domestic servant, told Lee that she was "never gon git back on dem ole buses" because the bus drivers sexually harassed her. They "say nasty thangs and dey talk under folks' clothes," Stovall said. "They ain't gittin no more of my dimes."[100]

A tall, stately maid named Mrs. Beatrice Charles told Lee a long story about why she refused to ride the buses. She said she was staying off the buses because the abuse black women suffered had "been happening since [she] came here before the war."[101] Bus drivers "make you get up so white men could sit down," she testified. "But we are sure fixing 'em now and I hope we don't ever start back riding. It'll teach them how to treat us," she said. "We people, we are not dogs or cats." Then she told Lee about a recent dispute with her white employer, Mrs. Prentiss. When Prentiss asked her if she rode the bus, Mrs. Charles replied, "I sure didn't."

Prentiss seemed shocked at the woman's brazen response. "Why, Beatrice, they haven't done anything to you," she said.

"Listen, Mrs. Prentiss," Charles replied, "you don't ride the bus, you
don't know how those ole nasty drivers treat us and further when you do
something to my people you do it to me too . . . I don't have anything in
my heart but hatred for those bus drivers."[102]

Mrs. Prentiss attempted to mitigate her employee's anger by arguing
that she had "always been nice" and then added, "I just can't see white and
colored riding together on the buses." "It just wouldn't come to a good
end," Prentiss proclaimed. Prentiss hinted at the underlying fears white
Southerners harbored after the *Brown* decision. Many worried that bus
integration was merely an entrée to "social equality" or interracial sex. For
example, Sam Englehardt, the local leader of the Citizens' Council, warned
whites in February 1956 that the bus boycott was "piddling stuff." What

Three police officers watch a group of African-
American women waiting at a carpool pick-up
location. The Montgomery Improvement
Association set up an alternate transportation
system that utilized more than three hundred
private cars to carry thousands of passengers to
and from work each day.

protesters are really after, he insisted, was "complete integration, even to intermarriage."[103]

Beatrice Charles set Mrs. Prentiss straight about who wanted to sleep with whom. "You people started it way back in slavery," she said. "If you hadn't wanted segregation, you shouldn't got us all mixed up in color . . . Right now I can sit on my porch and when it starts getting dark, I can look down the street by those trees and see colored women get in the cars with policemen. And what about that colored boy who had to leave town 'cause that white woman out here was going crazy about him? So you can't tell me that it's over."[104] By bringing up the issue of white men prowling around black neighborhoods searching for black women, and the double standard applied to black men caught with white women, Mrs. Charles gave voice to the sexual and racial components of the protest movement.

When Mrs. Prentiss threatened to participate in the White Citizens' Council's plan to starve the maids for a month, her maid laughed. "I sure won't starve. You see, my husband is a railroad man, my son and daughter have good jobs, and my daddy keep plenty of food on his farm. So I'm not worried at all, 'cause I was eating before I started working for you."[105]

Beatrice Charles spoke for many women who beamed with a new sense of what Martin Luther King, Jr., called "*somebodyness.*" Jo Ann Robinson articulated that newfound sense of power and pride at a mass meeting in late March 1956. "The whole world is watching the boycott," she said with glee. "The whole world respects us . . . You go downtown now and people show respect. Negroes are proud now, they hold their heads high and strut," Robinson said. "I have never been so proud to be a Negro." Martin Luther King, Jr., often rhapsodized about a "New Negro" emerging out of the black freedom movement who replaced self-pity with self-respect and self-doubt with dignity. "In Montgomery," he boasted, "we walk in a new way. We hold our heads in a new way."[106]

The fear that had immobilized African Americans for so long seemed to disappear as the boycott continued into its second month. This sentiment was audible at the many carpool pick-up locations around Montgomery, where domestics gathered to wait for rides from black volunteers. Willie Lee listened in on many of these conversations, recording them for posterity. "We got these white folks where we want 'em," Dealy Cooksey, a forty-year-old domestic servant, said. "Dere ain't nothing dey can do but try to scare us. But we ain't rabbit no more," she warned, "we done turned coon . . . It's just as many of us as the white folks and dey better watch out what they do."[107]

Mrs. Allen Wright, a forty-five-year-old cook, agreed. "They bit off more than they can chew when they put one of our fine ladies in jail," she proclaimed. "Clyde Sellers [the new police commissioner] might as well give up," she said, "'cause we ain't gonna be pushed down no more. Our eyes is open and dey gonna stay open."[108]

At least one woman in the group threatened to meet white resistance with violence. Whites "think they bad 'cause they got guns," Willie May Wallace, a store maid, argued, "but I sho hope they know how to use 'em, 'cause if they don't, I'll eat 'em up with my razor." A white man "bet not come up on me and hit me 'cause . . . he'll be in pieces so fast he won't know what hit him."[109] Then Wallace told Lee a story about her confrontation with a white female co-worker. When Wallace told her colleague that she was never going to ride the buses again, the white woman "bristled all up lack she wanted to hit me," the maid said. But "I told her . . . a white woman ain't been born that would hit me and live." Even though the police may come, she boasted, "when they do you'll be three D: Dead, Damned and Delivered." The maid was proud to note that "that huzzy ain't did nothing but spoke to me since den. When they fine you ain't scared of 'em," she chortled, "they leave you 'lone. Son-of-a-bitches."[110]

At the weekly mass meetings, hundreds of African Americans gathered to renew spirits and reenergize tired bodies. Photographs of the crowds invariably reveal large female majorities. Here they shared their stories of defiance and testified about their degradation, transforming bitter memories and shame into weapons of protest. Reverend Robert Graetz, a white minister who became active in the bus boycott, recalled that when women told their stories, the "people would cheer" for their new heroines. The "maids were the soldiers," he said. "They rallied the leaders."[111]

At an evening assembly in March 1956, one woman stood up and said she was with the protest because she had been called a "nigger" on the bus. Worse, she argued, "I was asked to give a white *man* a seat," she said. "I am filled up to my bones, in this, it's way down in my bones and when there ain't no protest," she said, offering a profound defense of her humanity, "I'm still gonna have it. I'm still gonna have my protest."[112] After

African-American women filled the pews at weekly mass meetings.

her moving testimony, the congregation sang the Negro spiritual "Nobody Knows the Trouble I've Seen," translating the troubles they had all seen into "Glory, Hallelujah."

Women at the mass meetings demanded that they be treated like human beings, worthy of protection and respect. The male leaders of the boycott made sure that women's actions were celebrated in the community. One minister praised a group of women whom he saw "walking in pride and dignity." They "would do justice to any queen," he declared.[113] Another preacher honored the "ancient" Mother Pollard, a well-known elderly black woman, who refused to accept a ride or an exemption from the boycott because of her frailty. "My feets is tired," she said, "but my soul is rested."[114] These weekly testimonies gave boycotters a sense of worth and agency and united the "walking city" as individual burdens were universalized and spread out over the whole.

The mass meetings fostered a sense of community that did not exist before the boycott. "Everybody walked together. We rode together," Zelia Evans, a teacher at Alabama State and WPC member, recalled. "There was a togetherness that I hadn't seen before. We had suffered and sacrificed so long," she added, "we were ready . . . to support a movement."[115] "It was the first time in the history of Montgomery," Robert Nesbitt, the secretary for the Dexter Avenue Baptist Church, recalled, "that all the ministers threw away their little egos . . . and united."[116]

In order to fund the daily operations of the Montgomery Improvement Association and finance the expensive alternative transportation system,

Montgomery's African Americans had to raise enormous amounts of money. A fleet of nearly three hundred private automobiles picked up passengers at forty-two locations and ferried the former bus riders around town. The city's black social clubs held dances and sponsored activities to raise funds. Black churches took up a collection every Sunday. The Federated Women's Clubs threw parties to raise needed cash, and women went door to door, canvassing neighborhoods for donations. Their efforts paid off. Within the first few months of the boycott, when donations from outside organizations like the national NAACP were rare, members of the MIA raised a quarter of a million dollars, primarily from local blacks.[117]

The most consistent local fund-raiser was Mrs. Georgia Gilmore, a nurse, midwife, and defiant mother of six, who used her experience as a cook to raise money. Gilmore was a "pretty, smooth-complexioned black woman as large in kindness as she [was] in body," said B. J. Simms, leader of the MIA's transportation system. But, he warned, "don't rub her the wrong way. Would you believe that this charming woman once beat up a white man who had mistreated one of her children?" he asked. "He owned a grocery store and Mrs. Gilmore marched into his place and wrung him out!"[118]

Gilmore had a long history of standing up for herself and fighting for justice. She refused to follow bus drivers' demands and insisted on being treated with dignity. A Montgomery minister recalled Gilmore's reputation: "Even the white police officers let her be," he said. "The word was 'Don't mess with Georgia Gilmore, she might cut you.' " "But Lord," he reminisced, "that woman could cook."[119] When the MIA announced its plan to boycott the buses for one day, Gilmore immediately called her friends and enlisted their talents for the boycott.

"What we could do best," Gilmore proudly declared, "was cook." That day, Gilmore recalled, she and a handful of her friends "collected fourteen dollars amongst ourselves and bought chickens, bread and lettuce and started cooking . . . We made a bundle of sandwiches," she said, to sell at the mass meetings at Holt Street Baptist Church.[120] From there Gilmore and her fellow chefs began preparing and selling full dinners, pies, and cakes. They called themselves the Club from Nowhere.

The ambiguous club name was strategic: it helped safeguard the women from "the police and laws" who, Gilmore complained, "go around trailing our members and giving them traffic tickets the way they were doing with so many colored folk." And it provided anonymity when selling their wares. Each day the women sold their savory sandwiches and chicken dinners door to door and to hungry downtown workers, black and white. "When we'd raise as much as three hundred dollars for a Monday night rally," Gilmore explained, "then we knowed we was on our way for five hundred on Thursday night."[121]

When the call for collections came at weekly mass meetings, Gilmore would stand up and shout, "We're the Club from Nowhere!" and walk the women's profits up to the front of the church. Gilmore's proud strolls to the collection plate became one of the most anticipated weekly rituals. As Gilmore strutted back to her seat, boycotters rattled the church rafters with "dignified applause, foot stomping, and exclamations of 'Aaaamen, Amen!' "[122] The excitement and support for the Club from Nowhere, Gilmore explained, encouraged "other ordinary folks" to do "the same thing in their neighborhoods—competing with us to raise more than us."[123]

It was hard to compete with the Club from Nowhere. They raised "maybe a hundred and fifty or two hundred dollars or more a week," Gilmore recalled. Inez Ricks, a black woman who lived on the other side of town, was up for the challenge. When she set up a competing women's club, the Friendly Club, the rivalry heated up. The collegial competition enlivened the meetings while inspiring other women.

Gilmore and her Club from Nowhere "represented more than the actual cash they contributed each week," B. J. Simms insisted. "This fine woman and her team represented the grass-roots type of support and enthusiasm that launched the boycott and kept it moving to the very end."[124] Without support from working-class women like Gilmore, the bus boycott would have failed. And yet Gilmore, like all the women who risked their lives and livelihoods to make the thirteen-month protest possible, has been relegated to the footnotes of history. "We made the world take notice of black folks in Montgomery," Gilmore said, but now "we're all in the Club from Nowhere." Simms agreed. "Most of the people who made indispensable contributions" to the boycott, he argued, "were soon forgotten and today are ignored as nobodies from nowhere."[125]

Those "nobodies" made the Montgomery movement possible by finding "ingenious ways to keep the boycott alive."[126] Though ministers like Martin Luther King and Ralph Abernathy filled public leadership positions, black women were "the power behind the throne," as Erna Dungee, WPC secretary and MIA finance manager, put it. "We really were the ones who carried out the actions," she insisted.[127] Like Dungee, Hazel Gregory insisted that it was working-class women whose collective refusal to ride the buses "made it work." "If you hadn't had those people, you would not have been able to [succeed]," she said.[128]

Besides serving as the boycott's foot soldiers, handling the day-to-day business of the MIA, and leading local fund-raising drives, black women helped keep the carpool running. At least twenty-nine women worked as regular carpool drivers or dispatchers. Ann Smith Pratt, a hairdresser, was the chief dispatcher. She worked the ham radio "directing taxi drivers and the church station wagon crew to urgent pickups at thirty-two designated sites."[129] After Rosa Parks lost her job as a seamstress at the Montgomery Fair on January 7, 1956, she often filled in as a dispatcher, sometimes working from sunup to sundown.[130] And Alberta James was, according to her peers, "unquestionably the best driver employed by the MIA transportation committee."[131]

Middle-class women who had their own cars, mostly black but some white women, used their vehicles and their free time to transport their less affluent neighbors. One of the boycott's classic sights was when Mrs. A. W. West, an eighty-year-old widow, rambled down the streets in her green Cadillac limousine every morning between seven and eleven in the morning "to chauffeur people about."[132] "And that's why," Virginia Durr, a white activist, noted, "Mrs. West was called a queen." Mrs. West was regaled by other women for her daily contributions. She was the kind of woman "who did not have to do it," Durr said. "Because she could have stayed at home and said that she was, you know, elderly."[133]

Since black women provided the backbone of the boycott, they were also the primary targets of white retaliation. Aside from getting fired from their jobs, which was the most common reprisal, African-American women walking to work remained vulnerable to physical and sexual harassment. Whites in passing cars pelted pedestrians with "water balloons and containers of urine . . . rotten eggs, potatoes and apples."[134] Jo Ann Robinson was terrified when two white men threw a brick through her window. Shortly thereafter she saw two policemen pour acid on the hood of her car. The next morning the car "had holes as large as a dollar" all over its hood and roof, she said.[135] Armed whites stood on street corners and jeered at the walking women. "Look at dem red bastards over der watching us," a domestic protested. "Dey got dem guns, but us aint skered." "I don't mind dying," she said, "but I sho take one of dem with me."[136]

African-American women were constant targets of physical and sexual assaults during the modern civil rights movement. Here, armed white men attack two black women after a desegregation attempt in Montgomery, Alabama.

The fact that white men with guns could not force black women back into their "place" indicated the sense of power and pride the boycott aroused among African Americans.[137] King argued that this new sense of pride and power was a crucial component of the movement. One "can not understand the bus protest," King said later, "without understanding that there is a new Negro in the South, with a new sense of dignity and destiny."[138]

Segregationists, however, had little interest in Negroes, old or new. City commissioners, angered by the success of the boycott and their inability to quell it, launched a city-sponsored intimidation campaign on January 23, 1956. Mayor Gayle called it his "get tough" policy. Denouncing the MIA as a "group of Negro radicals," Gayle claimed he was "tired of pussy-footing around" and ordered police to "break up Negro car pools by diligent enforcement . . . of all traffic regulations" and to charge African Americans waiting for rides at dispatch stations with loitering.[139] "Every black person would get a traffic ticket two and three times a week . . , There was no need arguing with police," Georgia Gilmore recalled. Gilmore alone received more than thirty tickets. "We just took [them]" she stated. "Policemen would give hundreds and hundreds of tickets every day to black people."[140] One day after Gayle's "get tough" announcement, he and Commissioner Frank Parks publicly declared their support for and membership in the White Citizens' Council.[141]

The official announcement, Clifford Durr pointed out, "was quite naturally taken by the denizens of the woodwork and the underside of rocks to be a signal to come out and do their worst."[142] Those "denizens" dynamited Martin Luther King's home on January 30 and bombed E. D. Nixon's house two days later. At an MIA meeting on February 2, members of the executive committee decided to employ armed guards for the homes of key individuals thought to be the most vulnerable to attack. A number of women were at the top of the list, including Rosa Parks, Erna Dungee, Jo Ann Robinson, Euretta Adair, and Maude Ballou. Parks was especially worried. "Some strange men have been coming into my neighborhood inquiring about this woman who caused all this trouble," she reported. Parks then asked for the MIA to provide night watchmen.[143]

She had reason to be afraid. On February 10, just over a week after Rosa Parks helped Nixon's wife clean up the mess made by the bomb, more than ten thousand whites attended what they billed as the "biggest prosegregation rally in the United States since the Civil War." There Mississippi senator James Eastland, a rabid racist, told the cheering crowd that the prescription for a segregationist victory was to "organize and be militant."[144] Other speakers, surrounded by hundreds of Confederate flags, boasted that they would "give the niggers a whipping" and teach Rosa Parks a "harsh lesson."[145] By singling Parks out for special punishment, Citizens' Council members implied that they wanted to do more than physically abuse her. Ironically, after they threatened her, Mayor Gayle and Commissioners Sellers and Frank Parks promised to "hold the line against Negro integration."[146] Gayle did everything he could to hold that line, including turning a blind eye to the Citizens' Council's public declaration of its intent to "abolish the Negro race" with "guns, bows and arrows, sling shots and knives."[147]

While the WCC did Gayle's dirty work, the mayor harnessed the city's institutional power to harass boycotters and shut down the carpool system. On February 13 local prosecutors summoned more than two hundred African Americans to testify about who was behind the boycott. The special grand jury, impaneled by Judge Eugene Carter, who had sentenced Claudette Colvin nearly a year earlier, was charged with investigating whether African Americans violated a 1921 statute outlawing boycotts "without just cause or legal excuse."[148] On February 21 the grand jury returned indictments against Rosa Parks, Reverend King, and eighty-seven others, more than a dozen of whom were women.[149] It was, accord-

Mayor Gayle's "get tough" policy backfired when scores of African Americans turned themselves in for voluntary arrest. Rosa Parks.

Mrs. A. W. West   Jo Ann Robinson

ing to Taylor Branch, "the largest wholesale indictment in the history of the country."[150]

Mayor Gayle's attempt to frighten boycotters with the threat of arrest and jail time—something African Americans had special reason to fear—backfired when a fearless E. D. Nixon marched to the courthouse and turned himself in. "Are you looking for me?" Nixon asked the sheriff. "Well, I am here."[151] Parks followed Nixon's example, and soon hundreds gathered around the courthouse applauding and celebrating the bravery and courage of those arrested. "We took the news as a joke, a pretense, an excitement for the moment," Jo Ann Robinson noted. Outside the courthouse, she remembered, "Negroes laughed, determined to stand their ground. They were defiant, willing to go to jail, ready to let Americans and the world know that they could not and would not take any more."

Jail could not possibly be worse than death, many reasoned, and African Americans were, according to Robinson, ready "to die for justice and freedom."[152] The crowd grew larger and more celebratory as more and more blacks voluntarily turned themselves in, transforming the jailhouse, a place to be feared and avoided at all costs, into a place of honor. Sheriff Butler, clearly peeved by the "perversion of the penal spirit," demanded silence. "This is no vaudeville show," he shouted to no effect.[153]

Euretta Adair   E. D. Nixon

Watching the crowd mock the police, Jo Ann Robinson realized the world she had always known had somehow changed. The fear that had held black people down had begun to evaporate. "If there was any nervousness or uneasiness," she argued, "it was on the part of the whites."[154] Whites seemed especially tense when scores of black domestics descended upon the courthouse. "From the alleys they came," B. J. Simms gleefully recalled. "Black women with bandannas on, wearing men's hats with their dresses rolled up. This is what scared white people." When a policeman tried to get control of the crowd, the women surged forward. "All right, you women get back," the officer shouted as he reached for his billy club. Then "these great big old women with their dresses rolled up," Simms recalled, "told [the officer], 'Us ain't going nowhere. You done arrested us preachers and we ain't moving.' " When the officer reached for his gun, the fearless women dared him to use them. "I don't care what you got," one woman said. "If you hit one of us, you'll not leave here alive."[155]

The public confrontation between black women and the police in Montgomery was a long time coming. That night black women served notice that they were no longer going to be violated by or pushed around by white police officers. They put their bodies on the line in defense of their humanity, something anyone watching could see. The standoff, the

Reverend Solomon Seay, Sr.   Reverend Ralph Abernathy

editor of *The Christian Century* argued in 1956, "marked the first fateful assertion of their full dignity as human beings."[156]

On March 19 twenty-eight black women asserted their full dignity and their right to protest abuse on the buses at the only trial held after the mass arrests. Prosecutors tried Martin Luther King, Jr., for conspiracy and held the other eighty-eight indictments in abeyance. They believed that if they could remove King as leader of the boycott, it would quickly fall apart. At first the defense played dumb. Most witnesses feigned ignorance of King's role in the boycott and some acted as if the boycott were simply a figment of the prosecutor's imagination. Gladys Moore seemed to take offense at the suggestion that King started the protest. "Wasn't no one man started it," she insisted. "We all started it overnight."[157] Estella Brooks testified that King had nothing to do with her decision to stay off the buses. She told the judge she had not been on a bus since August 12, 1950, the day a policeman shot and killed her husband for arguing with a bus driver. "No one told me to stop riding the buses," Gladys Moore said after prosecutors tried to get her to blame King. "I stopped because we had been treated so bad down through the years that we decided we

Reverend E. N. French   Reverend Martin Luther King, Jr.

wouldn't ride the buses no more."[158] Finally, in what seemed like an effort
to shame the judge into ruling for the defense, King's attorneys "sum-
mon[ed] a stream of Negro women to the stand to testify about cruelties
they had seen and endured on the buses."[159]

Time magazine reported that the women eagerly testified, often without any prompts. The black women, *Time* noted, "began talking before
defense lawyers asked their names; others could hardly be stopped."[160]
By detailing one insulting experience after another, a group of core women
activists denounced the system that denied their humanity on a daily basis.
Almost all of them testified that they had stopped riding the buses because
white drivers had humiliated them or abused them.

Martha K. Walker said she stopped riding because drivers constantly
heaped abuse upon her and her blind husband, who was a veteran of World
War II. Gladys Moore testified that bus drivers treated women "just as
rough as could be . . . like we are [not] human." Bus drivers, Georgia
Gilmore declared, mistreated people "positively for nothing."[161]

Henrietta Brinson said the mistreatment was too much: "I am just fed
up with these bus drivers . . . just fed up to my neck." They "don't want
to treat us the right way," she said. Referencing one particularly mean
operator, she told the court that he said, "All you niggers are pushing

Fred Gray

like a passel of cows." She stared at the judge. "Cow," she said, "that's what he called us." [162]

Judge Carter sat in stony silence, completely unmoved. At the end of the trial, he pronounced King guilty of conspiracy to violate the 1921 law and ordered him to pay a five-hundred-dollar fine or serve a year at hard labor. [163] Like Judge Carter, the national newspaper and magazine reporters waiting outside for the ruling ignored the black women's testimonies that detailed decades of mistreatment and denied King's leadership in the boycott. Instead, the media turned King into an apostle of civil rights. A reporter for *The New York Times* recorded the time, down to the exact minute, that King emerged from the courthouse. It was 4:39 P.M. A throng of supporters erupted in cheers when King emerged, many of them shouting, "Behold the King!" and "Hail the King!" as though he really were "Alabama's Modern Moses," as *Jet* magazine called him. [164]

At Holt Street Baptist Church, where thousands of African Americans gathered that night, ministers presented Reverend King as a Christlike figure sent to Montgomery to deliver blacks from their misery. "Here is the man," one minister proclaimed when introducing King to the mass meeting, "who today was nailed to the cross for you and me." [165] While the exaltation of King fit into a distinctly black Christian tradition,

African Americans gather outside the courthouse as Reverend Martin
Luther King, Jr., stands trial for conspiracy.

it obscured other leaders. "From that day onward," Rufus Lewis recalled
later, "Rosa Parks became a secondary figure."[166]

It was not just Rosa Parks, the radical activist, who was written out of
the story of the Montgomery bus boycott. Jo Ann Robinson and her army
of women in the WPC, as well as the thousands of working-class women
who made Montgomery "the Walking City," were reduced to the footnotes
of history. While the media were partly to blame in framing the story
around King, other civil rights organizations, in an effort to use Montgomery's success to spark similar civil rights campaigns throughout the
South, recast the bus protest as a movement led by ministers.

Shortly after the boycott ended on December 21, 1956, nine months after
the trial that turned Martin Luther King, Jr., into a modern Moses, the
Fellowship of Reconciliation (FOR) published a comic book that cast King
as a fearless freedom fighter and experienced organizer who had led his
people out of bondage. In FOR's retelling of the bus protest, Reverend
King and his cavalry of militant ministers came to the rescue of Rosa
Parks, who refused to move from her seat "because she was tired and her
feet ached." The cartoon features a nervous King, worried sick about
Parks's arrest, who stays up all night planning a response. "Something
ought to be done," King, visibly upset, says to his wife. "Rosa is a good
woman and not a trouble maker. They had no right arresting her." A help-

Rosa Parks speaks with an interviewer as she arrives at court
with E. D. Nixon (center) and eighty-nine other African
Americans on trial for violating a 1921 antiboycott law.

less Coretta, seated next to King, asks, "But what can we do?" The next
frame portrays King as an organizer, standing in front of a roomful of men
demanding a public response. "We ought to *protest*," he says, pointing at
the men, "and not ride the buses for a day." In the next image, King stands
over a mimeograph machine with his shirtsleeves rolled up. He and
another man run off "a few hundred" copies of the announcement calling
for a one-day boycott. And the rest, as they say, is history.[167]

Unfortunately, this King-centric and male-dominated version of events
obscures the real history of the Montgomery bus boycott as a women's
movement for dignity. The focus on King is so absolute that even today
many historians overlook the fact that it was four female plaintiffs,
Claudette Colvin, Mary Louise Smith, Mrs. Aurelia Browder, and Mrs.
Susie McDonald, who filed the lawsuit that finally ended segregation on
public transportation and put teeth into the *Brown* decision.

On December 17, 1956, the United States Supreme Court affirmed the
U.S. district court's decision in *Browder v. Gayle* that segregation, even outside public schools, violated the due process and equal protection clause
of the Fourteenth Amendment. The ruling signaled the death knell of the
"separate but equal" doctrine established by the Supreme Court in the
1896 *Plessy v. Ferguson* decision. But it also heralded something signifi-
cantly more important. The *Browder* decision determined more than where
one could sit on a bus. It was an affirmation of African Americans' human-

This Fellowship of Reconciliation comic book, published circa 1957, gave rise to the myth of Rosa Parks's "tired feet" and Martin Luther King, Jr.'s, heroic leadership of the Montgomery bus boycott.

ity. The Supreme Court, as Ralph Abernathy and Martin Luther King, Jr., put it, "ruled that we have the right to sit with dignity."[168]

Response to the decision indicated its powerful emotional impact. At an enormous mass meeting in Montgomery that night, Reverend Solomon S. Seay, Sr., burst into tears at the pulpit when he cried out, "God is on our side." A hush fell over the ecstatic crowd when Reverend Graetz, the lone white minister in the movement, walked to the front of the church and began to read from Corinthians I: "When I was a child, I spake as a child," he recited, "I understood as a child, I thought as a child; but when I became a man I put away childish things." The passage struck a nerve. Before Graetz could finish his reading, the mostly female crowd rose to their feet and cheered. "Several women," according to the *Montgomery Advertiser,* "screamed with what appeared to be religious ecstasy."[169]

Graetz captured the essence of the Supreme Court victory. Though even the biblical language was gendered, the women in the audience that night understood that the *Browder* decision signaled African Americans' arrival as full human beings, as men and women worthy of recognition and respect. While the legal ruling made segregation on public conveyances unconstitutional, the boycott was never just about integration. It was about what Martin Luther King, Jr., later called the "thingification" of white supremacy.[170] By walking hundreds of miles to protest humiliation and testifying publicly about physical and sexual abuse, African Americans—mostly women—reclaimed their bodies and demanded the right to be treated with dignity and respect.

The legal and moral victory over white supremacy in Montgomery gave African Americans around the country a sense of hope for the future, an inspirational and powerful figurehead in Martin Luther King, Jr., and an organizing model—nonviolent direct action, which they hoped to use throughout the South to dismantle Jim Crow. Segregationists intent on thwarting black advances launched their own war to retain their position of power in the South. A swirling storm of white resistance had been gathering since the 1954 *Brown v. Board of Education* decision. As African Americans in Montgomery returned to the buses and some Southern schools took baby steps toward compliance with the *Brown* decision, the "massive resistance" movement thundered through the South. Drawing on whites' deepest fears about integration and interracial sexuality, Citizens' Council members and other die-hard segregationists used economic intimidation, sexualized violence, and terror to derail desegregation and destroy the developing black freedom movement. Between the Montgomery bus boycott and the student sit-in movement in 1960, African Americans hoping to re-create the Montgomery experience faced the forces of Jim Crow, sparking some of the fiercest battles for manhood and womanhood of the modern civil rights movement.

CHAPTER 4

"There's Open Season on Negroes Now"

THE SEVENTH-GRADE TEACHER AT Dunbar Junior High School in Little Rock, Arkansas, dismissed her students early on May 17, 1954. News of the historic Supreme Court decision striking down segregation in public schools had just hit the airwaves, and she feared a violent white response. As students streamed out of the all-black school, she urged them to "pay attention to where you're walking. Walk in groups, don't walk alone." "Hurry," she added. Melba Patillo, a twelve-year-old African-American student at Dunbar, wondered what all the fuss was about. Still, Melba was happy to have the afternoon free. She gathered her books and started on the route she had taken home for nearly six years. According to her autobiography, published several decades later, she meandered through a grassy stretch of blooming persimmon trees and daydreamed about becoming a movie star and moving to New York or California.

The sound of rustling leaves snapped her back to reality. She stopped and listened carefully, straining to see through the thick flora. Suddenly a deep voice sliced through the brush. "You want a ride, girl?" She could not see anyone. Then it came again. "Want a ride?"

"Who is it?" she asked nervously.

"I got candy in the car," a man's gravelly voice sang out. "Lots of candy." Patillo inched forward and saw a burly white man coming toward her. She turned and fled in the opposite direction, screaming for help and running

Melba Patillo

as fast as her black-and-white saddle shoes could carry her. "You better come and take a ride home," he growled. "You hear me, girl?"[1]

He was a "huge" man, Patillo recalled later, built "like a wrestler." He chased Patillo through the wooded path, screaming about "niggers wanting to go to school with his children and how he wasn't going to stand for it." Suddenly Patillo tripped on her shoelaces and fell. As she struggled to stand, he grabbed her shoulders, thrust her to the ground, and flipped her over on her back. "He slapped me hard across the face," she said in her memoir, then pinned her down and began fumbling with his belt buckle.[2] "I'll show you niggers the Supreme Court can't run my life," he said as he reached under Patillo's dress and ripped off her underwear. In her account, she scrambled out from underneath him and started to run.[3]

Melba Patillo arrived home, shaken and disheveled. She told her grandmother that a white man attempted to rape her. Patillo's grandmother, who loved to garden and read Shakespeare and Langston Hughes, listened and then quietly shuttled Melba to the bathroom and started a bath. "You soak a while, child. When the water goes down the drain, it will take all that white man's evil with it."[4] Melba sat in the tub for what seemed like hours, listening to the muffled voices of her parents and grandmother arguing about whether they should call the police. When she finally emerged, her family encouraged her not to feel ashamed about the attack. Her father, Howell Patillo, an enormous man who worked as a hostler's assistant on the Missouri Pacific Railroad, reached for Melba and pulled her close. "We ain't gonna call the law," he said. "Those white police are liable to do something worse to her than what already happened."[5] Survival sometimes required that silence surround sexual violence, especially in an environment poisoned by the fierce backlash to *Brown.* Eventually Melba would tell her story of the struggle in Little Rock for students across the country, but silence was not the only choice. Between 1956 and 1959, sex and sexual violence sat at the center of the freedom struggle, and African Americans deployed different strategies to carry the movement through a crucial and difficult transition, including testimony, armed self-defense, and international pressure.

In the decade before *Brown,* African Americans in Little Rock, Arkansas, and throughout the South had testified openly about white attacks on black women. In the 1940s, for example, Daisy Bates, the acclaimed free-

Daisy and L. C. Bates and two police investigators examine a Ku Klux Klan cross left in their front yard in October 1956. Bates and her husband were targets of the Klan years before the Little Rock crisis began because of their vocal support for equality and justice for African-American rape victims in their newspaper, the *Arkansas State Press.*

dom fighter and leader of the Little Rock Nine, used the power of the
Arkansas State Press, the newspaper she and her husband, L. C. Bates,
owned, to call attention to the long history of white-on-black rape. Like
Rosa Parks, Bates was a militant activist long before she orchestrated a
showdown between Governor Orval Faubus and the federal government
over the integration of Central High School in 1957. Her newspaper
became a thorn in the sides of Little Rock's white and black leaders, whom
she pilloried regularly for failing to remedy the injustices of Jim Crow,
especially police brutality and the abuse of black women. For Bates, rape
was not just a political and legal issue that required state and community action, it was personal.

When Daisy Bates was just was seven years old, three white men brutally raped and murdered her mother. Bates's father blamed the attack
on the "timeworn lust of the white man." She was "not the kind to submit," he explained to his daughter, "so they took her."[6] Overwhelmed by
guilt and pain, he abandoned Daisy at a young age. She vowed revenge.
"Young as I was, strange as it may seem," Daisy Bates wrote in her memoir years later, "my life now had a secret goal—to find the men who had
done this horrible thing to my mother." The whole ordeal left her feeling like a "little sapling, which, after a violent storm, puts out only
gnarled and twisted branches."[7] When she became older, Bates decided to
transform her hatred and anger into positive action and "make it count for
something."[8] Over time the "little sapling" became a towering oak: Bates
became a fierce freedom fighter and leader of the Little Rock NAACP and
in 1952 president of the Arkansas State Conference of NAACP branches.[9]

As an outspoken advocate for African Americans, Bates, like Rosa
Parks, became known as the go-to person for victims of racial and sexual
violence in Little Rock. She listened to them and scribbled notes, then
placed their stories on the front page of her newspaper. The *State Press*
became Bates's personal bullhorn, which she used to amplify demands
for justice and voting rights and call for an end to the wanton sexual abuse
of black women. Banner headlines between 1941 and 1955 made the
crime public, helped to mobilize the black community, and alerted white
officials that crimes against black women would not go unnoticed. For
example, on July 17, 1942, the *State Press* published photographs of
two white Little Rock police officers who raped Rosa Lee Cherry, a
nineteen-year-old African-American student at Dunbar High School.
Daisy Bates even printed a transcript of Cherry's grand jury testimony.
This helped secure public support for an indictment. Bates then argued

that a conviction was necessary to save the "great state of Arkansas." Although the white policemen walked free after their case ended in a mistrial, Bates's vigilance on the Cherry case and others like it made it impossible for white authorities to ignore crimes against African-American women.[10] Her outspoken attacks on rape and other forms of sexualized violence helped secure trials and, in some instances, even rare convictions of white assailants who attacked black women in Arkansas during the 1940s and early 1950s.[11]

By 1954, however, a veil of secrecy had descended among African-American activists. In the years after *Brown,* more than half a million people opposed to integration and dedicated to white supremacy joined organizations like the White Citizens' Councils, the Ku Klux Klan, and the American States Rights Association, and launched an all-out war against the burgeoning freedom struggle. Death threats and dynamite blasts shook civil rights advocates across the region. The Patillos understood that the swirling storm of resistance that segregationists unleashed after *Brown* made silence about sexual violence a political imperative.

Segregationist leaders throughout the South urged "massive resistance" to *Brown.* They recruited supporters by denigrating the "traitorous" Supreme Court, while exploiting whites' fears about integration and interracial sexuality. *U.S. News & World Report* announced that many white Southerners opposed *Brown* because they feared "eventual amalgamation of the races—meaning miscegenation, intermarriage or whatever you want to call it." Judge Leander Perez, a political heavyweight in Louisiana, told supporters that the goal of integration was "miscegenation." "You make a Negro believe he is equal to the white people," he said, "and the first thing he wants is a white woman. And that's why there are so many criminal assaults and rapes." In a pamphlet titled *You and Segregation,* Georgia senator Herman Talmadge argued that the Almighty "Advocates Segregation," and warned that the "ultimate aim and goal of NAACP leaders . . . is the complete intermingling of the races in housing, schools, churches, public parks, public swimming pools and even in marriage."[12] The *Brown* decision, he said, was "judicial tyranny" and "the greatest single blow ever . . . struck against constitutional government." "Resistance to tyranny," Mississippi senator James O. Eastland told white supporters, "is obedience to God."[13] Walter Givhan, an Alabama state senator and ardent supporter of the White Citizens' Council, argued that desegregation was simply a ruse to "open the bedroom doors of our white women to Negro men."[14]

Alabama state senator Samuel Englehardt, Jr.,
an ardent segregationist and member of the
White Citizens' Council, promotes a "white
only" anti-integration rally.

Demagoguery of "miscegenation" fanned followers' fears to red-hot
rage. Most did not explicitly advocate violence, but their extremist
rhetoric undoubtedly encouraged it.[15] Some politicians could not hold
back. "A few killings now," a Mississippi legislator boasted, could "save
a lot of bloodshed then." At a massive Citizens' Council rally in Alabama,
Senator Eastland cheered on the white mob that blocked Autherine Lucy,
an African-American woman, from attending the University of Alabama
in February 1956. He praised them for not letting the "NAACP run your
schools." Southern whites, he told the audience, were "obligated to defy"
Brown.[16] When some whites responded by launching campaigns of violence and terror, many of those legislators stood silent, offering tacit
approval while protecting themselves from blame.

Other political leaders fully supported the White Citizens' Council and
its goals but worried that violence could hurt the segregationists' cause.
J. P. Coleman, the pragmatic governor who led Mississippi between 1956
and 1960, feared that defiance of federal law would hurt the state's standing in the national Democratic Party or provoke federal intervention. Coleman hoped to achieve the same goals as Eastland and other radicals
through what he called "practical segregation."[17] He pushed for the creation of a state agency that would mirror the FBI's investigative prowess
and function as a public relations bureau. His goal was to "keep racial conflict out of the press while quietly and effectively managing the state's fight

against integration."[18] Coleman tested the effectiveness of the newly formed State Sovereignty Commission in May 1956, when four white men from Tylertown, a small village in the Piney section of Mississippi, kidnapped a young black woman on the eve of her wedding and gang-raped her.

It was just before dawn on May 13, 1956—Mother's Day—when Ernest Dillon, a twenty-nine-year-old siding salesman; his brother Ollie, a middle-aged construction worker; and Olen and Durora Duncan, twenty-one-year-old cousins, went looking for "some colored women." Wielding a shotgun, Ernest Dillon approached Stennis Butler, a thirty-year-old black sharecropper who was outside preparing for the day's work. Dillon ordered him to take him and his friends to a home with black women inside. Annette Butler, a sixteen-year-old high school student, was in bed with her mother when she heard someone pounding on the front door of their two-bedroom home. Ernest Dillon introduced himself as a policeman. "You're under arrest," he said to the girl, for "sacking up with your boy-friend." When her mother objected, Dillon raised the shotgun, grabbed the teenager, and pulled her outside. He kept the shotgun trained on the girl's mother as his brother pushed her into the backseat of the car. Olen Duncan revved the engine and drove away, leaving Butler's mother alone in the front yard.[19]

The four white men drove Butler deep into the Bogue Chitto swamp, where they took turns raping her. Olen Duncan threatened to "cut her neck off" if she resisted. "I followed his instructions," she testified at the trial. When they finished, the four white men piled into the car and left Annette stranded in the woods. Wandering through the swamp half naked, she stumbled upon a group of black fishermen and ran to them for help. They led her out of the woods and delivered her to the police. Sheriff A. E. (Bill) Andrews took her complaint and then drove her home to get dressed.[20] Later that day Sheriff Andrews brought Olen Duncan in for questioning, and he willingly signed a statement testifying that he had had "intimate relations" with Annette Butler. "It was done with every safe-guard for the right of the defendant," Sheriff Andrews said, "after [Dun-can] had been repeatedly advised that anything he might say could be used against him."[21] A few days later District Attorney Michael Carr charged all four men with "forcible ravishment and kidnap" and sent them to the Magnolia jail to await trial.[22]

Judge Tom Brady, a fierce white supremacist and one of the fathers of the White Citizens' Councils, presided over four separate trials in Pike

County Circuit Court four months after the attack. The assailants must have wondered what kind of punishment Brady would impose since his public pronouncements against interracial mixing were already legendary. *Time* magazine called Brady the "prophet" of segregation and his manifesto, *Black Monday,* the "Bible of the White Citizens' Council movement."[23] When confronted with real interracial mixing and actual rapists, not the fictional black rapists he saw lurking behind every school-desegregation case, Brady buckled under the weight of his own racial prejudices. He appointed the "finest lawyers in Mississippi" to defend the four white assailants.[24]

Ernest Dillon may not have understood Brady's gesture, since he pleaded guilty on March 26, 1957, to the lesser charge of "assault with intent to rape." It was a risky plea that left his co-conspirators vulnerable. On the other hand, the plea bargain released him from trial and from the threat of the death penalty or life imprisonment—the state's only punishments for rape.[25] It also freed the jurors from having to declare a white man guilty of raping a black woman and defused any complaints of unequal justice or outside criticism of the state. It is likely that Dillon believed he would receive a minor sentence or even a suspended sentence. Politically, the plea deal worked for everyone—except, of course, Annette Butler.

On April 4 Olen Duncan, described by the *McComb Enterprise Journal* as a "slender man with facial skin paled to a dead white," surprised the packed courtroom by pleading not guilty despite his previously signed admission.[26] His declaration of innocence fueled a day of intense testimony. Annette Butler took the stand and provided what the newspaper called "lurid details" of the attack. She easily identified Duncan as the driver and told the jury he was the second man to rape her.

In an effort to portray Butler as a prostitute or at least a juvenile delinquent, Duncan's attorneys grilled her about her whereabouts the night before the attack. Butler told the jury that she had accompanied her mother and cousin to a juke joint called Willie's Penthouse and stayed out past midnight. Defense attorneys then called George W. Wingo, a local white man, to testify about the "general reputation" of Butler. "It is not good," he said without hesitation. They did not bother asking any African Americans about Butler's standing in the community—even though they trotted out a number of white men who testified that Olen Duncan's stature was impressive.[27]

Michael Carr, the district attorney, urged the jury to consider Duncan's signed confession above all else. The girl submitted to the four men not because she was easy, he argued, but because the assailants "placed [her] in such fear of severe personal injury and for her very life." Despite Duncan's admission of intercourse and his friend's guilty plea a week earlier, the all-white, all-male jury unanimously acquitted Olen Duncan of rape.[28] On April 5, Judge Brady declared a mistrial when Olen's cousin, Durora Duncan, also pleaded not guilty and the jury deadlocked.

News of the acquittal and mistrial infuriated a group of African-American women, who wrote an anonymous letter to the *McComb Enterprise Journal.* They criticized the jurors for acquitting "confessed rapists" and argued that "an alleged 'bad-reputation' " did not "excuse the criminal act which was committed." "We feel that no Negro Woman is safe within the bounds of her own home," they said, "despite the fact that she is a law-abiding citizen."[29] A group of black ministers made a similar argument in a statement submitted to the newspaper: "It is a dreadful thing to think our widows and their children have no protection, that their homes can be invaded by men of other races and that all the security of democracy is denied them."[30]

On April 5, 1957, Judge Brady sentenced Ernest Dillon to twenty years of hard labor. Brady castigated Dillon for bringing "bitter condemnation upon his community and state and the entire South" for attacking Annette Butler. His actions, Judge Brady told Dillon, "will bring further vitriolic attacks on our region from those who hate the South." Brady then scolded Dillon for integrating and declared him unfit for membership in the white race. "No action could be more in contrast with the beliefs of the segregationist," he argued. Dillon had the "good fortune," Brady said, sounding disappointed, "of having able counsel . . . and prosecuting attorneys who were willing to show leniency . . ."[31] It was a harsh way of telling Dillon that he would be a sacrificial lamb.

The twenty-year sentence was nothing to sneeze at. It was highly unusual, if not unheard of, in the Magnolia State. And yet it served a political purpose. The trials and the lengthy sentence blunted outside criticism of the state's long history of racial terror. White leaders could point to Dillon as proof that Mississippi did not discriminate. At the same time, state senator Mayes McGehee, the chairman of the general legislative investigating committee of the State Sovereignty Commission, argued that the state's rape laws tied the jury's hands—they simply had no choice but to acquit most of the men. "There wasn't necessarily any prejudice involved," he said. "Whether that had been a white girl involved or a colored girl, a jury is very reluctant to pass a death sentence or life imprisonment for that charge upon a man." The sheriff, the district attorney, and the county attorney, McGehee added, "made every possible effort to get a conviction in that case."[32] Oliver Emmerich, the editor of the *McComb Enterprise Journal,* echoed McGehee's sentiments and argued that the people of Mississippi think "such crimes are repugnant." "As with all heinous crimes," he said, "it leaves broken, bleeding hearts in its wake." "The world must know, and our people must know," he argued, "that the law enforcement officers of this area were alert and dutiful and that the evidence was taken on the spot, without delay, and to the credit of the people of Pike and Walthall Counties and Mississippi as well."[33] By giving Dillon twenty years, Judge Brady and the Sovereignty Commission sent a message: even the most vehement segregationists still believed in law and order.

Except when they didn't. The lengthy jail sentence did not stop whites from terrorizing blacks in Mississippi or elsewhere. Citizens' Council members, Klansmen, and their ilk harassed African Americans over the phone, on the streets, and in public places. Hate mail peppered black activists, and threatening calls kept their phones ringing through the night. Rosa Parks, for example, constantly received calls from angry whites who yelled "Die, nigger!" whenever she or her husband picked up the phone.[34] Like other blacks committed to the freedom struggle, Rosa Parks lost her job and was blacklisted in Montgomery, as were her husband and mother. After an especially vicious death threat in the summer of 1957, Parks called her cousin in Detroit sobbing. "Rosie, get the hell out of Montgomery," he urged. "Raymond's right; Whitey is going to kill you."[35]

Parks knew that harassment and economic intimidation were not the outer limits of white terror. She packed up her things and moved her family to Detroit in the summer of 1957, just as white vigilantes started bombing black homes, churches, and businesses in Montgomery. Dynamite damaged or destroyed the homes and churches of prominent ministers and bus boycott leaders like Ralph Abernathy, Robert Graetz, and Martin Luther King, Jr. In Birmingham at least twenty-one bombings directed at blacks between 1955 and 1958 turned the "Magic City" into "Bombingham." In small towns and cities throughout the South, white mobs beat and sometimes killed African Americans—especially those who advocated desegregation or voting rights—with baseball bats, brass knuckles, tire irons, rusty chains, and other implements of torture. In the Mississippi Delta white men murdered three black males in 1955: In May whites murdered the Reverend George Lee for registering voters. In

August, Lamar Smith, a sixty-year-old farmer, was killed in broad day-light, apparently for voting in a primary and teaching other blacks how to register.[36] Later that month, on August 28, 1955, J. W. Milam and Roy Bryant murdered fourteen-year-old Emmett Till in Money, Mississippi.

Till, a Chicago native in Mississippi to visit his uncle, Mose Wright, accompanied a group of black teens and children to Bryant's Grocery and Meat Market to purchase candy. Unaware of the strict racial etiquette governing interracial interactions, the black youngster allegedly flirted with Bryant's young wife after purchasing some bubble gum. Four nights later Roy Bryant and J. W. Milam kidnapped Emmett Till, brutally beat him, and then shot him in the head. They tied a metal cotton gin fan around his neck with barbed wire and pushed him into the Tallahatchie River. A fisherman spotted Till's body, and investigators pulled the mutilated corpse from the river three days later. *Jet* magazine printed photos of the gruesome remains, exposing the savage and murderous side of segregation to the nation and the world, and the NAACP launched a national campaign for justice. Still, an all-white jury acquitted Bryant and Milam of murder on September 23. Four months later they admitted guilt to the journalist William Bradford Huie for an article in *Look* magazine. Bryant justified his actions and accused Till of wanting more than bubble gum that August afternoon. "When a nigger gets close to mentioning sex with a white woman," Bryant argued, "he's tired o' livin.' "[37] The response to the article was immediate. "There's open season on the Negroes now," one Mississippi man said. "They've got no protection and any peckerwood who wants can go out and shoot himself one and we'll free him." The NAACP demanded punishment for the shocking deaths. It issued a pamphlet, titled *M Is for Mississippi and Murder,* to publicize the killings.[38]

Besides murder, whites also used sexual violence as a weapon of terror—and not always against black women. In Union Springs, Alabama, about forty miles southeast of Montgomery, Klansmen attacked Edward Judge Aaron, a thirty-four-year-old African American, while he and his wife walked along a country road on September 2, 1957. Klan members berated Aaron, known among whites as a "white folks' nigger," before they pistol-whipped him. "You think any nigger is as good as a white man? You think nigger kids should go to school with my kids?" they shouted. As the men pummeled Aaron to the ground, one of them managed to tear off Aaron's pants. Then he flashed a shiny razor blade and grabbed Aaron's scrotum and pressed the blade into his flesh, severing his testicles.[39]

·　　·　　·

The castration of Edward Judge Aaron vividly illustrated white fears that *Brown* would unleash the black beast rapist of Reconstruction lore. The fear was so great that an unsubstantiated rumor or an innocent glance, a misconstrued gesture or an informal greeting between a black man and a white woman, could end in murder. In Montgomery, for example, a group of Klansmen heard a vague rumor that a black truck driver was intimately involved with a white woman. On a cold January night in 1957, three dedicated Klan members randomly attacked Willie Edwards, Jr., a delivery truck driver who happened to be in the wrong place at the wrong time. The Klansmen walked Edwards to the edge of a bridge that stretched across the Alabama River. Edwards swore he was innocent and denied any interest or involvement in an interracial tryst, but his speech fell on deaf ears. The Klansmen forced Edwards to the edge of the bridge and made him jump to his death.[40]

African Americans were not always victims. In Richmond, Virginia, on July 27, 1956, Rudolph Valentino Henry, a thirty-one-year-old combat veteran, stabbed a white man for harassing his wife. Henry and his wife, Carrie, were walking home from a downtown movie theater when John Morgan, a white city employee, whistled and honked his horn at the couple as they passed in front of his parked car. "Who are you whistling at," Henry asked. "Don't you know that's my wife?"

"I don't give a damn if it is your wife," Morgan shot back. "If I want to make a date with her I will." Morgan reached for what appeared to be a gun, jumped out of the car, and a fight ensued.

"They began to scuffle," Carrie Henry told the newspaper, "and the white man had a grip on my husband and was getting the best of him." In order to break loose, she said, her husband "stabbed [Morgan] with a little clasp knife." "He had to do something," she insisted. "It was his life or the other man's." Finally Morgan backed off and turned and walked away. "We thought he was going to get some help," Henry said, "so we ran across the parking lot and went home . . . We didn't know that he was dead until we read about it in the papers."[41]

The murder may have been a mistake, but the clash between Rudolph Henry and John Morgan was part of a larger struggle that had been brewing all summer. "It happens every night," Rufus Wells, a writer for the *Richmond Afro-American,* argued in an article titled "Mashers Molest Women, Police Look Other Way." "After sundown," Wells said, "certain colored neighborhoods in Richmond become a happy hunting ground for white men on the prowl for illicit romance." White men in "limousines and Tin Lizzies," Wells reported, "cruise slowly around the block and leer and whistle" at black women. The bolder ones simply parked their cars and waited, he said, "ready to proposition any woman who chances by." Wells argued that these "wolves, mashers and sex perverts" roam the streets and assault women with impunity. "They're getting worse and worse," an older black woman argued. "One night last week, a car containing three white men drove slowly past the house three or four times. Finally they parked a few doors away and two of them started toward my house. I got up and went inside and locked the door," she said. "They're getting so they'll snatch you from your own porch."[42]

She was one of many residents who argued that violence would flare if police refused to protect black women. To be sure, John Morgan was not the first white man to pay a price for "molesting" black women that summer. Local African Americans killed a thirty-one-year-old white man earlier in the summer and severely beat another man in late August for "accosting women in the vicinity." "They [the police] are not going to protect our women," a local black man stated, "so we have to do it ourselves. Every time we catch a man molesting women we try to beat his brains out."[43]

When Rudolph Valentino Henry stood trial for the "Wolf Whistle" murder of John Morgan in front of an overflowing courtroom on November 10, 1956, he pleaded guilty to involuntary manslaughter. He did not intend to kill Morgan, he said; he simply tried to defend his wife from attack. Henry's lawyer, Martin A. Martin, a prominent attorney and NAACP leader, placed the case in the long history of white-on-black assault and argued that Henry had a right to protect his family. A white police officer served as the key witness. Detective Sergeant F. S. Wakefield of the Richmond Police Department testified that he had received "numerous complaints of white men molesting colored women in that neighborhood." The judge must have recognized the volatility of the situation and decided to suspend Henry's sentence. "I'm mighty happy to be back," the former vet declared after the judge issued his ruling. "I've been around the world," he said, "but there is no place like home."[44]

The public exposure of Southern white men's proclivity for "nighttime integration" did not stop the usual suspects from railing against perceived threats posed by desegregation. Citizens' Councilors and Klansmen busied themselves by educating their progeny and protecting them from the threat of race mixing. Though their children were not yet afflicted by puberty or the hysterical fear of black men as rapists—what W. J. Cash called the "southern rape complex"—adults seemed to feel it necessary to spell out the unwritten rules of white supremacy.[45] "The racist," Southern poet and essayist Wendell Berry wrote, "fears that a child's honesty empowered by sex might turn in real and open affection toward members of the oppressed race, and so destroy the myth of that race's inferiority."[46] They created a pamphlet for young whites called the *Manual for Southerners,* which claimed that "if boys and girls share the school room, lunch room, dances, sports, rest rooms and playgrounds, then the boys and girls will want to date each other." Worse, the booklet warned, "integration always leads the races to marry one another."[47]

Segregationists fought to keep their children insulated in lily-white schools, but they could not control the growing affection for African-American music among their youth. Many whites greeted rock and roll as if it were "a guided missile," as Eldridge Cleaver remembered, "launched from the ghetto into the very heart of suburbia. It succeeded, as politics, religion, and law could never do, in writing in the heart and soul what the Supreme Court could only write on the books."[48] Chuck Berry, Fats Domino, LaVern Baker, Little Richard, and their interracial bands belted out blues, ballads, and bebop over integrated airwaves, effectively launching a revolution that rattled and roused teenagers and shook up segregationists, who bristled at the idea of their offspring listening to the new "jungle music." Dancing was worse since, in their opinion, it would inevitably lead to race mixing, juvenile delinquency, and sexual immorality.[49]

Because black musicians performed in front of segregated but sold-out crowds of screaming, ecstatic teenagers, it became impossible to maintain a strict color line in the South. As a result, many concerts inadvertently became interracial dance parties, where black and white fans found themselves pressed against one another. For example, in the mid-1950s, black and white teenagers mobbed concerts given by Fats Domino, whose songs "Ain't That a Shame" and "Blueberry Hill" propelled him to the head of the Top 40 charts. The petrified parents of white teens picketed these concerts with signs that read "Rock and Roll Breeds Integration" and "Ask Your Preacher about Jungle Music."[50] One worried parent summed up their complaint in a letter to Sam Phillips, the producer and owner of Sun Records, which launched the careers of Elvis Presley, Johnny Cash, Roy Orbison, and Jerry Lee Lewis. Rock and roll, the parent informed Phillips, was "ruining our children. These little kids are falling in love with niggers!"[51] Similar complaints forced many venues to ban interracial dancing. In 1956 the Louisiana legislature outlawed mixed-race dancing entirely.[52]

Asa Carter, a notorious anti-Semite and racial terrorist who served as head of the North Alabama White Citizens' Council and later became Governor George Wallace's speechwriter, railed against "sensuous Negro music" in his magazine *The Southerner*.[53] Rock and roll, he said, appealed to the "base in man" and encouraged "animalism and vulgarity." It was part of an NAACP plan, he warned, to "mongrelize America."[54] Carter fanned the flames of interracial fear and sexual paranoia around Birmingham in the weeks before Nat "King" Cole was scheduled to give a concert at the Municipal Auditorium on April 10, 1956. He printed pictures of Cole standing next to adoring white females in *The Southerner* above captions like "Cole and His White Women" and "Cole and Your Daughter." In an accompanying article, Carter insinuated that Cole had ulterior motives that any self-respecting segregationist would recognize. "You have seen it," he said, "the fleeting leer, the look that stays an instant longer . . . the savagery."[55]

No one had to stretch his or her imagination to understand what Carter was getting at. Indeed, the whole world witnessed white reaction to the "fleeting leer" when whites murdered Emmett Till in Mississippi the year before. The Till slaying cast a pall over every interracial exchange, but Nat "King" Cole did not expect to be attacked simply for singing his songs, especially in front of a segregated audience. Still, he went out of his way to remove any hints of sexuality from his show and presented himself as nonthreatening in style and demeanor. When the footlights burst open and illuminated the stage, Nat "King" Cole bounded forward and sailed through two songs. Suddenly, a group of white thugs scurried to the platform, leaped over the footlights, and knocked Cole to the ground. Their goal was to push Cole out of the way and "take control of the microphone and lecture the audience about integration."[56]

While Asa Carter's low-life allies literally attacked Nat "King" Cole, more sophisticated segregationists pressed the issue. James J. Kilpatrick, the elegant and conservative editor of the *Richmond News-Leader,* told James Baldwin that he regarded the Negro writer as a citizen, but that did not mean he wanted Baldwin to marry his daughter. "You're not worried about me marrying *your* daughter," Baldwin shot back. "You're worried about me marrying *your wife's* daughter. I've been marrying *your* daughter since the days of slavery."[57] Baldwin's comment brilliantly captured the cruel conundrums of interracial sex and sexual violence between white men and black women in the South.

These fears gripped whites in the small town of Monroe, North Carolina, in 1958, when an innocent kissing game between black and white children became front-page news around the world as hysterical adults cried rape and demanded revenge. This single event reinforced Gunnar Myrdal's observation a decade earlier that sex was "the principle around which the whole structure of segregation . . . is organized."[58] Indeed, the "Kissing Case," as it became known, exposed the power of sex in maintaining the South's racial hierarchy and underscored the extent to which whites would fight to preserve it.

Sissy Sutton, a seven-year-old white girl, and her two friends must not have read the *Manual for Southerners*. If they had, they would have known that playing a kissing game in a ditch on an autumn afternoon with David Ezell "Fuzzy" Simpson and James Hanover Grissom Thompson, eight- and ten-year-old African-American boys, was strictly prohibited. The three girls had been minding their own business, watching a group of black and white boys play cowboys and Indians on October 28. "At first it was just boys playing," Thompson later recalled. "We was just running through the water with our feet first, acting crazy like kids." Sutton and her friends joined the fun, and after a few boys drifted off toward home, a white boy suggested they play a kissing game.

According to the rules, one of the boys said, each girl would have to sit on a boy's lap and kiss him, "like on TV or in the movies."[59] Though nobody knows exactly who kissed whom, somebody seems to have kissed somebody.

Sutton told her mother about the game when she returned home that evening. When Mrs. Sutton realized her daughter had actually touched a black boy, she was furious. Hysterical, she called the police and reported that Simpson and Thompson had attempted to rape her little girl. Mr. Sutton grabbed his gun, gathered up some friends, and went searching for the prepubescent assailants. The growing mob of angry men first went to Thompson's home, where they threatened "not only [to] kill the boys but to lynch the mothers." Mrs. Sutton insisted that she "would have killed Hanover myself if I had the chance."[60]

Later that afternoon police officers spotted the boys tugging a red wagon down the street, completely oblivious to the growing mob of men searching for them. The officers jumped out of the car "with their guns drawn," grabbed the boys, and shoved them into the car. "We'll teach you little niggers not to kiss white girls," one of the officers snapped. When they arrived at the jail, Thompson recalled, the policemen "threw us down and then started beating us." They "hit us hard in the chest, call[ed] us all kind of names . . . and talked about how they was going to lynch us." The police put the boys behind bars and held them there for six days as the Klan clamored for blood outside. No one contacted their parents.[61] Even if the police wanted to call the boys' mothers, they would have had a hard time finding them. Both women had holed up with neighbors after their homes became targets of terrorist attacks. Evelyn Thompson fled after a carload of angry whites sprayed her windows with bullets and masked men burned a cross on her front lawn. The final straw may have been when someone shot the family's dog and left it dead in the front yard.[62]

News reports of the illicit kissing game hewed closely to the politics and prejudices of the color line. Some white reporters detailed an attempted rape in which one of the boys held Sutton down until the other could extract a kiss or more. White officials argued that the boys were guilty of "molesting three white girls." Even Governor Luther Hodges insisted that Thompson and Simpson "had assaulted" the girls. The *Carolina Times,* on the other hand, a black newspaper, argued that the "crisis in Monroe . . . had nothing to do with assault or delinquency." According to Louis Austin, the editor, the racial hubbub was the product of white angst and shame, and that Thompson and Simpson had not yet learned the "unwritten law of white supremacy" that "white is right and God . . . has made one race of men superior to another." "No one but a bunch of numbskulls," he fumed, "with hearts full of the filthiest kind of dirt would attach any significance to what children of six to ten years of age do at play."[63]

At a hearing on November 4, 1958, J. Hampton Price, a juvenile court judge, found Hanover Thompson and Fuzzy Simpson guilty of molestation and sentenced them to the Morrison Training School for Negroes in Hoffman, North Carolina, for "indeterminate terms."[64] The ridiculousness of the charge and the harshness of the sentence, not to mention the fact that Judge Price referred to the boys twice as "niggers," convinced Robert F. Williams, the militant leader of the Monroe, North Carolina, NAACP, to launch a major publicity campaign. Williams organized the Committee to Combat Racial Injustice (CCRI) with assistance from Conrad Lynn and George Weisman, activists in New York who had connections to the Socialist Workers Party; C. K. Steele, president of the Talla-hassee, Florida, NAACP and head of the successful 1956 Tallahassee bus boycott; and Carl Braden, co-founder, with his wife, Anne, of the liberal Southern Conference Education Fund. Their plan was to remove the story from the narrow confines of Monroe, North Carolina, and place it on a world stage, shaming the state and ultimately the entire nation.

It was not difficult to sell the story outside the South. The *London News-Chronicle* gobbled up the "Kissing Case" and prominently placed it on the front page on December 15, 1958. With the paper's circulation of more than one million, the story quickly spread. In Italy newspapers ran sympathetic photos of Thompson and Simpson in juvenile detention on the front page under headlines bemoaning the excessive punishment: "He Will Grow Up in Jail." Similar stories appeared throughout Europe; even the Soviet Union and China ran the story, presenting it as a mockery of American democracy. The CCRI hoped the "lever of worldwide public-ity and the fulcrum of Cold War politics would lift them to victory."[65] At the very least, they knew it would expose the South's growing racial and sexual hysteria. But what they really desired was enough global pres-sure to prod President Eisenhower or Congress to take action. After two months of negative publicity at home and abroad, Governor Hodges finally issued the order to release Fuzzy Simpson and Hanover Thompson. The two boys reunited with their mothers on February 13, 1959, nearly four months after their arrest.[66]

Domestic racial politics had vexed America's cold warriors for many years, forcing the federal government at times to intervene on behalf of African Americans in order to avoid international embarrassment. For example, when Arkansas governor Orval Faubus activated the National Guard to block nine African-American children, including Melba Patillo, from inte-grating Little Rock's Central High School in 1957, and then removed them as an angry mob converged on the school, the whole world took notice.[67] Televised images of well-dressed black children surrounded by straight-faced soldiers and angry, screaming whites transported Jim Crow into homes around the country and the globe, making Little Rock the "foremost international symbol of American racism."[68]

President Dwight Eisenhower, furious that Faubus had defied both fed-eral law and tolerated, if not encouraged, mob violence in the streets of Little Rock, decided to let the governor know that, as David Halberstam put it, he did not "look kindly on frontal challenges by junior officers."[69] On September 24, Eisenhower sent one thousand paratroopers from the 101st Airborne Division into Little Rock, becoming the first president since Reconstruction to use the military to defend African Americans' constitutional rights. In a televised address that night explaining his decision, Eisenhower told the nation that the Little Rock crisis had threatened America's position in the Cold War. "It would be difficult to exaggerate the harm that is being done to the prestige and influence, and indeed to the safety of our nation around the world," Eisenhower argued. "Our enemies are gloating over this incident and using it everywhere to misrepresent our whole nation. We are portrayed as a violator of those standards of conduct which the peoples of the world unite to proclaim in the charter of the UN."[70] By the next day the fierce and flinty paratroopers, from the unit that had stood up to the Nazi Wehrmacht and the Chinese People's Liberation Army, stared down the segregationists and escorted Melba Patillo and eight others to class.[71]

Federal intervention finally forced Governor Faubus to integrate Central High School, but it did not stop demagogues in Dixie from flirting with secession, passing resolutions of interposition, and terrorizing African Americans. On the contrary, the sight of federal troops on Southern soil fueled massive resistance. That year Alabama, Mississippi, Georgia, and Florida "nullified" *Brown*.[72] Overall, eleven Southern states passed more than 450 acts and resolutions in the decade after the controversial Supreme Court decision in order to maintain "lily-white" schools.[73] Southerners' deep-seated fear of interracial sexuality trumped their enthusiasm for anti-Communism. Not even the threat of international embarrassment stopped some segregationists from enforcing their beliefs and biases with violence and terror. The Southern Regional Council, a liberal organization, reported more than 530 acts of segregationist violence and economic intimidation against African Americans between 1954 and 1959.[74]

Because of this backlash, direct action campaigns like the Montgomery bus boycott waned, prompting the historian Adam Fairclough to call the period between 1956 and 1960 the "fallow years."[75] Even Martin Luther King, Jr., found himself in a tactical conundrum. "No matter how many cheers he received or how many tear streaked faces assured him that lives were transformed," Taylor Branch notes, "tomorrow's newspapers still read pretty much like today's. Segregation didn't disappear."[76] The NAACP, legally banned from operation in Alabama and starkly curtailed in Texas and Arkansas, avoided confrontation with white authority and instead sponsored legal cases, which slowly crept through the courts.[77] The Southern Christian Leadership Conference (SCLC), created in 1957 to parlay the Montgomery success into a national movement, and the Congress of Racial Equality (CORE), a mostly Northern organization formed in 1948 to protest racial segregation, had yet to come up with a strategy that would mobilize the masses. Roy Wilkins, the head of the national NAACP, recognized the threat posed by massive resistance. "The race," Wilkins said, "is in a life and death struggle for all the ground it has won since Reconstruction. Between the ruthlessness of the South and the what-the-hell attitude of the North, we could lose."[78]

Although civil rights organizations confronted increasingly hard sledding in the years after Montgomery, the "fallow period" actually yielded a fertile crop of campaigns. As Montgomery had in the 1940s and 1950s, these struggles focused national attention on sexualized violence toward African Americans and the sexual exploitation of black women at the hands of white men. Reaction to the *Brown* decision was sexually charged and it unfolded in a Cold War context that confined civil rights movements, yet made "sex cases" especially useful for organizing purposes. Federal sensitivity to world opinion, and the existence of a left-wing media that spotlighted black women's testimony, brought the issue of white-on-black rape to the forefront of the freedom struggle. Indeed, Montgomery, Alabama, and Little Rock, Arkansas, were not the only places in which attacks on black women fueled protests against white supremacy.

Often ignored by historians, a number of these campaigns led to trials and even convictions throughout the South. For perhaps the first time since Reconstruction, Southern black communities could imagine state power being deployed in defense of their safety and respectability as men and women. This was clear in Tallahassee, Florida, where Betty Jean Owens, an African-American college student, stood in front of an all-white jury in 1959 and testified about being kidnapped and gang-raped by four white men. "All eyes," Roy Wilkins argued, "will be upon the state of Florida."[79]

CHAPTER 5

"It Was Like All of Us Had Been Raped"

ON MAY 2, 1959, FOUR WHITE men in Tallahassee made a pact (as one of their friends testified in court later) to "go out and get a nigger girl" and have an "all night party." They armed themselves with shotguns and switchblades and crept up behind a car parked alongside a lonely stand of scrub pines and blackjack oaks near Jake Gaither Park. When they reached the car, Patrick Scarborough pressed his sixteen-gauge shotgun against the driver's nose and ordered Richard Brown and his companions out. Dressed in formal gowns and tuxedos, the four African Americans reluctantly stepped out of the car. All were students at Florida A&M University (FAMU), where R&B crooner Roy Hamilton had sent a "capacity audience . . . into musical bliss" at the Orange and Green Ball that night.

Scarborough forced the two black men to kneel, while his friend David Beagles held the two black women at knifepoint.[1] When Betty Jean Owens began to cry, Beagles slapped her and told her to "shut up or she would never get back home." Waving his gun, Scarborough ordered Richard Brown and his friend Thomas Butterfield back into the car and told them to leave. As Brown and Butterfield moved toward the car and then slowly drove away, Edna Richardson broke free and ran to a nearby park, leaving Betty Jean Owens alone with their attackers.

Beagles pressed the switchblade to Owens's throat and said, "We'll let you go if you do what we want," then forced her to her knees, slapped her as she sobbed, pushed her into the backseat of their blue Chevrolet, and drove to the edge of town, where he and his friends raped her seven times.[2]

When the four armed white men in Tallahassee forced Thomas Butterfield and Richard Brown to drive away, leaving Betty Jean Owens at the mercy of their assailants, the two black freshmen drove around the corner and waited. As the blue Chevrolet disappeared down the street, Brown and Butterfield hurried back to the scene. Edna Richardson, the black woman who was able to get away, saw her friends from her hiding spot, called out to them, and then ran to the car. Hoping to save Owens, the FAMU students rushed to the local police station to report the crime.[3]

Similar situations in other Southern towns had often left African Americans without police aid. Although the Tallahassee police were not known for repression and brutality, they were hardly friendly toward African Americans, who made up nearly 40 percent of the city's population. Frank Stoutamire, the chief of police, was a genial if temperamental man who sold eggs out of the trunk of his patrol car to blacks and whites and often ignored violations of the county's ban on liquor. Russell Anderson, a minister at FAMU, remembered that Stoutamire "stayed in power by playing the races against each other." He would "act like he was a friend of the blacks when he was around them," Anderson said, but he "let it be definitely known that he was a white man's man."[4]

In 1937, for example, investigators implicated Stoutamire, then the

Scene of the crime where four white men from Tallahassee, Florida, kidnapped and raped an African-American college student.

Joe D. Cooke, Jr., an intern from Florida State University, defied racial conventions when he agreed to search for the white assailants of an African-American college student.

Leon County sheriff, in a gruesome double lynching. Police arrested Richard Ponder and Ernest Hawkins, two black teenagers, for robbing a downtown business and threatening an officer with a knife. They were in the county jail no more than a few hours when four men with paper bags over their heads kidnapped the youths at gunpoint. They drove them three miles outside of town and riddled their bodies with bullets, then left the scene littered with hand-painted signs warning blacks to "stay in your place." Only Stoutamire and the police chief knew who held the keys to the county jail, but the investigation was quickly shelved.[5] By the time Stoutamire became the chief in 1953, he relied more on threats than on violence, but his policemen never hesitated to enforce white supremacy. They issued bogus tickets when it served their own interests, sent detectives to spy on and infiltrate black organizations, and harassed African Americans relentlessly.[6]

Stoutamire and his officers were off the night Betty Jean Owens was attacked. The officer on duty in Florida's capital city that evening was Joe D. Cooke, Jr., an energetic nineteen-year-old intern from Tallahassee who was majoring in criminology at Florida State, the all-white local university. Much to the surprise of the three black students, he called for backup and eagerly agreed to look for Owens and her assailants.

After a lengthy search, one of the students finally spotted the blue

Chevrolet and shouted, "That's it!" It was just after four A.M. Deputy Cooke turned on his flashers and drove alongside the car. Attempting to escape, the kidnappers led Cooke "twisting and turning" through the dark, tree-lined streets of Tallahassee "at speeds up to 100 miles per hour." One of the white men suggested "dumping the nigger," but William Collinsworth, a twenty-four-year-old married telephone lineman, said, "We can't now, he's on our tail." Finally, Collinsworth pulled his car to the curb, grabbed his shotgun, and got out of the car. The young deputy drew his pistol and ordered all four to line up against the car or, he threatened, "I will shoot to kill."[7]

As they waited for assistance from Cooke's supervisor, they heard muffled screams coming from the car. Richard Brown and Deputy Cooke peered through the rear window and saw Betty Jean Owens bound and gagged, lying on the backseat floorboards. Brown tried to help her out of the car, but as her feet touched the ground, she collapsed. Cooke drove Betty Jean Owens and her friends to the local colored hospital, while Deputy Sheriff W. W. Slappey arrested the four white men and drove them to the jailhouse.[8]

Laughing and joking on the way to the police station, the four white men apparently did not take their arrest seriously nor think they had done anything wrong. Collinsworth, for example, worried less about the charges against him than about the safety of his car. Deputy Sheriff Slappey revealed his disgust when he handed the men over to Sheriff Raymond Hamlin, Jr. "They all admitted it," Slappey said. "They didn't say why they did it, and that's all I'm going to say about this dirty business." William Collinsworth, Ollie Stoutamire (the sixteen-year-old cousin of police chief Frank Stoutamire), Patrick Scarborough, and David Beagles, whom the *Pittsburgh Courier* called the "element which sports duck-bill haircuts," confessed in writing to abducting Owens at gunpoint and having "sexual relations" with her. When Sheriff Hamlin asked the men to look over their statements and make any necessary corrections, Beagles, a high school senior and part-time service station attendant, smiled and bent over the table. He made one minor adjustment before he and his friends were hustled off to jail.[9]

If the four white men did not take their arrests seriously, students at FAMU, a historically black university that anchored middle-class black life in Tallahassee, did. Many of them were veterans of the Tallahassee bus boycott in 1956, a Montgomery-inspired campaign that highlighted both students' preference for direct action and their willingness to rally

behind the protection of black womanhood rather than the plodding litigation favored by the NAACP.[10] White authorities had charged Carrie
Patterson and Wilhelmina Jakes, roommates at FAMU, with "inciting a
riot" after they refused to move to the colored section of a city bus on
May 26, 1956. As in Montgomery, the women who fueled the boycott
fought for the dignity of their personhood. They were "real upset," Jakes
said later, that bus drivers "were treating us like criminals . . . like we
weren't human beings."[11]

A burning cross on the front lawn of their home baptized them into the
struggle and galvanized the black community into action. A student-led
boycott forced the city bus company to shut down, five months faster than
the boycott in Montgomery. Despite economic intimidation, constant
police harassment, and violence, African Americans stayed off the buses.
At a mass meeting in June, C. K. Steele, a Baptist minister who helped
lead the boycott, said that blacks would rather "walk in dignity than ride
in humiliation."[12] Steele had preached at Hall Street Baptist Church in
Montgomery, Alabama, during the 1940s, when the Recy Taylor and
Gertrude Perkins cases shook up the ministers and mobilized community
action. He arrived in Tallahassee in 1952 and quickly became a community leader. Steele's experience in Montgomery and strong relationship
with civil rights advocates in Florida and throughout the South made him
a natural mentor for the FAMU students. "Without the students," he
insisted, "there would be no movement." "They are the militants—they're
your soldiers." The buses were finally integrated in the spring of 1957,
two years before the four white men armed themselves to kidnap and rape
Betty Jean Owens.[13]

When FAMU students heard news of the attack on Owens and the subsequent arrest of four white men, a small group planned an armed march
to city hall to let city officials know that they were willing to protect black
womanhood the same way whites "protected" white womanhood—with
guns. Mainstream student leaders persuaded them that an armed march
was "the wrong thing to do" and patched together a "Unity" demonstration only twelve hours after Betty Jean Owens was admitted to the local
colored hospital.[14]

As the four white men sat in jail, fifteen hundred students filled Lee
Auditorium, where Clifford Taylor, president of FAMU's Student Government Association, said he "would not sit idly by and see our sisters,

On May 4, 1959, more than one thousand Florida A&M University students gathered on the university's quadrangle to demand justice for Betty Jean Owens, who was brutally raped by four white men two nights before.

wives, and mothers desecrated." Using language white men in power could understand, student leaders professed their "belief in the dignity, respect, and protection of womanhood" and announced that they would petition the governor and other authorities for a "speedy and impartial trial."[15]

Early the next day more than a thousand students gathered in the university's grassy quadrangle with signs, hymns, and prayers aimed at the national news media, which sent out stories of the attack across the country. The students planned to show Tallahassee and the rest of the nation that white men could no longer attack black women without consequence. Student protesters held signs that declared, "It could have been YOUR sister, wife, or mother." Some students linked the attack in Tallahassee to larger issues related to the black freedom struggle: two students held up a poster depicting scenes from Little Rock, Arkansas, that read, "My God How Much More of This Can We Take."[16]

It was the deeply personal issue of rape, however, that gave the students their focus. Patricia Stephens Due, a Miami native and student at FAMU, remembered feeling helpless and unsafe. "We all felt violated, male and female," she recalled. "It was like all of us had been raped." Student leader Buford Gibson, speaking to a crowd, universalized the attack when he said,

From left to right: Patrick Scarborough, David Beagles, Ollie Stoutamire, and William Ted Collinsworth.

"You must remember it wasn't just one Negro girl that was raped—it was all of Negro womanhood in the South."[17] By using Betty Jean Owens as a black everywoman, Gibson challenged male students to rise up in protest and then placed the protection of black womanhood in their hands. Unlike white men who historically used the protection of white womanhood to inspire mob violence, Gibson's speech inspired students at Florida A&M to maintain their nonviolent demonstration.

At about the same time, white men in Poplarville, Mississippi, used the "protection of womanhood" as justification for the lynching of Mack Charles Parker, a black man who was charged with the kidnapping and rape of a twenty-four-year-old white woman who could barely identify him in a police lineup. Two days before his trial, a group of eight to ten white men obtained keys to Parker's unguarded jail cell, savagely beat him, and then dragged him screaming down three flights of stairs. FBI agents located Parker's bloated body floating in the Pearl River on May 4, 1959, just two days after four white men gang-raped Betty Jean Owens. The Parker lynching cast a shadow over Tallahassee, brutally reminding the black community that white women's bodies were off limits, while the bodies of black women were fair game.[18]

The accelerating media coverage, student-led protests, and a threat to boycott classes at Florida A&M forced circuit court judge W. May Walker, a white-haired former firefighter, to call members of the grand jury into special session in Tallahassee on May 6, 1959. More than two hundred black spectators, mostly students, squeezed into the segregated balcony at the Leon County Courthouse to catch a glimpse of Betty Jean Owens and her attackers before they retreated into the secret hearing. Still undergoing hospital treatment for injuries inflicted during the attack and for "severe depression," Owens was accompanied to the courthouse by a nurse, the hospital administrator, and her mother.[19]

Gasps and moans sounded from the balcony when, after two hours behind closed doors, Collinsworth, Beagles, Scarborough, and Ollie Stoutamire emerged and calmly faced the judge. When they all pleaded innocent, making a jury trial mandatory, African Americans roared with disapproval. Dr. M. C. Williams, a local black leader, shouted, "Four colored men would be dead if the situation had been reversed. It looks like an open and shut case." Defense attorneys for Collinsworth and Scarborough argued for a delay, insisting that public excitement threatened a fair trial, but Judge Walker ignored their objections. For the first time in Florida history, a judge sent the white defendants charged with raping an African-American woman back to jail to await their trial. Echoing the sentiments of the people around him, a young boy traced "we want justice" in the dust on the railing of the segregated balcony.[20]

Justice was the last thing the black community expected. In the thirty-four years since Florida began sending convicted rapists to the electric chair instead of the gallows, the state had electrocuted thirty-seven African Americans charged with raping white women. Before this, Florida had led the country in per capita lynchings, surpassing notoriously violent states like Mississippi, Georgia, and Louisiana. From 1900 to 1930 white Floridians lynched 281 people, 256 of whom were African American. Throughout its history, Florida had never executed or lynched a white man for raping a black woman.

Florida's violent history included the "little Scottsboro" case, involving Samuel Shepard, Walter Irvin, and Charles Greenlee, black men accused of raping a white woman in Groveland, Florida, in 1949. After the U.S. Supreme Court overturned their guilty verdicts in 1951, Sheriff Willis McCall picked up Shepard and Irvin from Raiford State Prison to transfer them back to the county. On the way there, McCall pulled to the side of the road and asked the two handcuffed men to change the tire, then shot them both in the chest. "I got rid of them," he told his boss over the radio, "killed the sons of bitches." Walter Irvin survived the shooting, but Samuel Shepard died that day.[21]

In Tallahassee, memories of the "little Scottsboro" case hung over the African-American community in 1954 when the state electrocuted Abraham Beard, a seventeen-year-old black youth accused of raping a white woman. Apart from the race of the accused, the Beard case featured an almost identical cast of characters as the Tallahassee case four years later: an all-white jury had tried and convicted Beard in the same courtroom where Betty Jean Owens faced her attackers. Judge W. May Walker presided and William D. Hopkins served as the state prosecutor. Harry Michaels, Patrick Scarborough's attorney in 1959, served as Beard's court-appointed attorney in 1954. Both the "little Scottsboro" and the Beard cases revealed the extent to which the protection of white women served as the ultimate symbol of white male power and the foundation of white supremacy. When African Americans in Tallahassee demanded equal justice for Betty Jean Owens, that foundation began to crumble.[22]

News that four white men would actually face prosecution for raping a black woman plunged both whites and blacks into largely unfamiliar territory. It not only highlighted the bitter ironies of segregation and "social equality" but allowed African Americans to make political use of them. According to the *Pittsburgh Courier,* the rape case "is the worst headache the Dixiecrats have ever suffered." All of their "arguments for white supremacy, racial discrimination, and segregation fall by the wayside," the *Courier* argued, and the arguments against school desegregation seem "childishly futile." "Time and again," another newspaper editor argued, "Southern spokesmen have protested that they oppose integration in the schools only because it foreshadows a total 'mingling of the races.' The implication is that Negroes are hell-bent for intimacy, while whites shrink back in horror." "Perhaps," the writer argued, "as Lillian Smith and other maverick Southerners have suggested, it is not quite that simple."[23]

While prominent members of Tallahassee's conservative white community expressed their shock and horror at the rape, they continued to stumble into old narratives about race and sex. The indictment helped incite age-old fears of miscegenation and stereotypes of the "black beast rapist." The historian William H. Chafe argues that "merely evoking the image of 'miscegenation' could often suffice to ring the alarm bells that would mobilize a solid phalanx of white resistance to change."[24] For exam-

State prosecutor William Hopkins   Judge W. May Walker

ple, white women around Tallahassee began to speak openly about their
"fear of retaliation," while young couples avoided parking "in the country moonlight," as one said, "lest some Negroes should be out hunting
in a retaliatory mood." Reflecting this fear, as well as the larger concern
with "social equality," Florida legislators, like other lawmakers throughout the South, passed a series of racist bills designed to segregate children by sex in order to circumvent the *Brown* decision and "reduce the
chances of interracial marriage."[25] The extent to which the myth of the
"black beast rapist" was a projection of white fears was never clearer than
when the gang rape of a black woman conjured up terror of *black-on-white*
rape. The fact that the black community rallied around Betty Jean Owens
threatened white male power—making the myth of the black savage a
timely political tool.

Black leaders from all over the country eagerly used the rape case for
their own political purposes as well. Most focused on the lynching of black
men in similar cases, placing the crime against Betty Jean Owens into a
larger dialogue about the power struggle between black and white men.
As A. D. Williams, a black businessman in Tallahassee, put it, "The white
men are on the spot." Reverend Dennis H. Jamison felt that the indictment of four white men indicated a "better chance at Justice than any

involving the races in the South," but added, "still no white men have ever been executed." Elijah Muhammad, leader of the Nation of Islam, used almost the exact same language as white supremacists, accusing the "four devil rapists" of destroying the "virginity of our daughters." "Appeals for justice," he fumed, "will avail us nothing . . . We know there is no justice under the American flag."[26] Nearly all the editorials in major black newspapers echoed his sentiments.

Ella Baker, the spirited director of the Southern Christian Leadership Conference (SCLC) and perhaps the most important grassroots organizer in the South, felt that the evidence in the Tallahassee case was so strong that "not even an all-white Florida jury could fail to convict." Reminding whites of their tendency to mete out unequal justice toward black men, she warned, "With memories of Negroes who have been lynched and executed on far less evidence, Negro leaders from all over the South will certainly examine every development in this case . . . What will Florida's answer be?" The *New York Amsterdam News* called for equal justice, noting that the "law which calls for the death sentence does not say that Negro rapists should be punished by death and white rapists should be allowed to live." The *Pittsburgh Courier* bet on acquittal, despite the fact that the case "is as open and shut as a case can be."[27]

At the annual SCLC meeting in Tallahassee a few days after the indictment, Martin Luther King, Jr., praised the student protesters for giving "hope to all of us who struggle for human dignity and equal justice." But he tempered his optimism with political savvy, calling on the federal government to force the country to practice what it preached in its Cold War rivalry with the Soviet Union. "Violence in the South can not be deplored or ignored," King declared, directing his criticism at President Dwight Eisenhower; "without effective action, the situation will worsen." King exploited a political context in which America's racial problems were increasingly an international issue. The BBC broadcast segments of the FAMU student speeches condemning the rape and racial injustice, while newspapers throughout Europe watched the case closely. A black soldier stationed in Germany winced when a German man mocked American rhetoric of democracy. "It is funny that you are over here to protect us from the Russians," he said, "when there is no one to protect your people from the KKK and white Americans."[28]

King exploited the chasm between rhetoric and reality to highlight the injustice of Jim Crow. "It is ironical that these un-American outrages occur as our representatives confer in Geneva to expand democratic principles . . . It might well be necessary and expedient," King threatened, "to appeal to the conscience of the world through the Commission on Human Rights of the United Nations." This international angle was a strategy shared by mainstream integrationists, leftist radicals, and black nationalists alike. Audley "Queen Mother" Moore, leader of the Universal Association of Ethiopian Women, petitioned the United Nations Human Rights Commission in person to end the "planned lynch terror and willful destruction of our people." She tied issues of race, gender, sex, and citizenship together by demanding Justice Department assistance for Betty Jean Owens's rape case, an FBI investigation of the Mack Charles Parker lynching, and basic voting rights.[29]

Robert F. Williams, militant president of the Monroe, North Carolina, chapter of the NAACP and leader of the defense in the 1958 "Kissing Case," insisted that African Americans stand their ground and defend themselves. The Parker lynching, the Tallahassee rape case, and two local cases where white men stood accused of attacking black women inspired Williams to defend racial pride and black womanhood. On May 5, 1959, Williams and a group of angry black women converged on the Union County Courthouse to hear testimony in two trials. Georgia Davis White, a maid at the Hotel Monroe, accused Brodus F. Shaw, a white railroad engineer, of beating and kicking her down a flight of stairs after she allegedly disturbed his sleep. The judge dismissed the charges against Shaw, even though he did not show up for court. That same day white jurors giggled while Mrs. Mary Ruth Reed, a pregnant black sharecropper, testified that Lewis Medlin, a white mechanic, attempted to rape her in front of her five children. In an effort to get help, she scooped up her youngest child and ran across a field. Medlin knocked her down and pummeled her until a neighbor finally heard her screams and called the police. In court, Medlin's attorney argued that he had been drinking and was "just having a little fun." Then, turning to the white jurors, the attorney pointed to the woman sitting next to Medlin. "You see this pure white woman, this pure flower of life?" he said. ". . . This is Medlin's wife . . . Do you think he would have left this pure flower, God's greatest gift," he asked, "for *that*?" Reed burst into tears as the jury broke for deliberation. Less than ten minutes later they returned a not guilty verdict.[30]

The black women with Williams were furious. Before the trial, they had wanted to "go and machine gun [Medlin's] house," but Williams had urged them to let the courts handle it. "We would be as bad as the white people if we resorted to violence," he told them. Since the judge and jury had virtually laughed Reed out of court, the women blamed Williams. "I had kept the black men in the community from killing this man," Williams said bitterly. The shocking indifference of the verdict enraged Williams. "We didn't have as much protection as a dog down there," he said later, "and the Government didn't care about us." Turning to the reporters left in the courtroom, Williams demanded a response. "We cannot rely on the law," he said. "We get no justice under the present system. If we feel that injustice is done, we must right then and there on the spot be prepared to inflict punishment on these people. . . . If it's necessary to stop lynching with lynching," he argued, "then we must be willing to resort to this method."[31] Williams's exhortation set off a national controversy, culminating at the 1959 national NAACP convention where the executive secretary, Roy Wilkins, suspended Williams for his stance. Williams defended his position by citing the tragedy in Tallahassee. "The young prom escorts of the co-ed who was kidnapped and raped at gunpoint by four white men in Tallahassee," he insisted, "would have been justified in defending the girl had they had weapons." "We as men," he stated to the delegates, "should stand up as men and protect our women and children."[32]

Roy Wilkins shared Williams's gender and race politics but not his methods for achieving justice. In a letter to Florida governor LeRoy Collins, a moderate segregationist with national political ambitions, he invoked the lynchings of Mack Charles Parker and Emmett Till, noting that the victims' skin color alone kept them from receiving a fair trial and that their deaths created political embarrassment at home and abroad. "Full punishment has been certain and swift in cases involving a white victim and a Negro accused," he said, "but the penalty has neither been certain nor heavy in cases involving a Negro victim and a white accused . . . For these reasons," Wilkins threatened, "all eyes will be upon the state of Florida."[33]

On June 12, 1959, at least four hundred people witnessed Betty Jean Owens face her attackers and testify on her own behalf. Owens approached the witness box with her head bowed. She wore a white embroidered blouse and a black-and-salmon-checked skirt. Gold earrings drew attention to her close haircut and sharp cheekbones. The African-American press cast her into the role of respectable ladyhood by characterizing her as a middle-class coed "raised in a hard-working Christian household" with parents devoted to the "simple verities of life that make up the backbone of our democracy." Unlike white women, who were often able to play the role of "fair maiden" before a lynch mob worked its will on their alleged attackers, Betty Jean Owens had to tell her story in front of hundreds of white people in a segregated institution. She knew that the four white men who raped her might go unpunished.[34]

Rain pattered against the courtroom windows as state prosecutor William Hopkins asked Owens to detail the attack from the moment she and her friends left the Florida A&M dance. "We were only parked near Jake Gaither Park for fifteen minutes," she said, when "four white men pulled up in a 1959 blue Chevrolet." She identified Patrick Scarborough as the man who yelled, "Get out and get out now," as he poked the shotgun into her date's face. When Owens began to cry, David Beagles pressed a "wicked looking foot long knife" to her throat and forced her down to the ground. He then pulled her up, slapped her, and said, "you haven't anything to worry about." Owens testified that Beagles pushed her "into the car and the boy with the knife then pushed my head down in his lap and yelled at me to be quiet or I would never get home." "I knew I couldn't get away," she said. "I thought they would kill me if I didn't do what they wanted me to do."[35]

She continued with the horrible details. As the car pulled off the highway and into the woods, "the one with the knife pulled me out of the car and laid me on the ground." Owens was still wearing the gold and white evening gown; they tugged at her dress and, she testified, "pulled my panties off." She then told how each one raped her while she was "begging them to let me go." "I was so scared," she said, "but there was nothing I could do with four men, a knife, and a gun . . . I couldn't do anything but what they said." Owens testified that the men eagerly watched one another have intercourse with her the first time around but lost interest during the second round. "Two of them were working on taking the car's license plate off," she said, "while the oldest one" offered her some whiskey. "I never had a chance to get away," she said quietly. "I was on the ground for two or three hours before the one with the knife pushed me back into the car."

After the men collectively raped her seven times, Owens continued, Stoutamire and Beagles blindfolded her with a baby's diaper, pushed her onto the floorboards of the car, and drove away. When she heard the police sirens and felt the car stop, she pulled the blindfold down and began yelling for help. After police ordered the men out of the car, Owens recalled, "I was so scared and weak and nervous that I just fell on the ground and that is the last thing I remember."[36]

Betty Jean Owens then described the physical injuries she sustained from the attack. "One arm and one leg," she said, "were practically useless" to her for several days while she was at the FAMU hospital. A nurse had to accompany her to the grand jury hearing a few days after the attack, and she needed medication for severe depression. She also had a large bruise on her breast where the bodice stay from her dress dug into her skin as the four men pressed their bodies into hers. Asking her to identify some of the exhibits, her lawyer William Hopkins flipped open the switchblade used the night of the attack, startling some of the jurors. Immediately the three defense attorneys jumped up and called for a mistrial. "By flashing the knife," they argued, "Mr. Hopkins tried to inflame the jury and this prejudiced their clients' constitutional rights to a fair trial." Judge Walker denied their motion, signaling Hopkins to continue.

When asked whether she consented, Owens clearly told Hopkins and the jury, "No sir, I did not."

"Was it against your will?" Hopkins asked.

"Definitely," she replied.[37]

Defense attorneys grilled Owens for more than an hour, trying to prove she consented because she never struggled to get away, and that she actually enjoyed the sexual encounter. "Didn't you derive any pleasure from that? . . . Didn't you?" attorney Howard Williams yelled repeatedly. Williams kept pressing her, "Why didn't you yell or scream out?"

"I was afraid they would kill me," Owens said quietly.

She showed signs of anger when Williams repeatedly asked if she was a virgin, attempting to characterize her as a stereotypical black jezebel. Owens retained her composure, refused to answer questions about her chastity, and resisted efforts to shame her. The defense made a last-ditch effort to discredit Owens by arguing that if the young men had actually raped her and threatened her life, she would have sustained more severe injuries.[38]

Proceeding with the state's case, attorney Hopkins called the doctors, both black and white, who had examined Owens after the attack. They told the jury that they found her in a terrible condition and that she "definitely had sexual relations" that caused injuries that required a five-day hospital stay. Richard Brown, Thomas Butterfield, and Edna Richardson took the stand next. They all corroborated Owens's testimony, adding that after the attack, Owens was "crying, hysterical, and jerking all over." Brown testified that Scarborough pointed the shotgun into his car window and ordered him and Butterfield to kneel in front of its headlights. Defense attorney John Rudd, a city judge who had been especially rough on African Americans during the 1956 bus boycott, asked Brown on cross-examination whether it was a "single or double barrel shotgun they pointed into your car?"

Brown replied, "I only saw one barrel, sir."

Laughter rolled down from the balcony, upsetting Rudd. "I cannot work with this duress and disorder at my back, a boy's life is at stake here!" Judge Walker called for order and reprimanded the spectators.[39]

When the prosecution finally rested its case at eight-thirty P.M., defense attorneys moved for a directed verdict of acquittal, claiming the state failed to prove anything except sexual intercourse. Judge Walker denied the motion and insisted the defense return the next day to present their case.

Amid a sea of people in the tiny courtroom, David Beagles, a towheaded eighteen-year-old high school student with a crew cut, sat rigidly on the stand, pushing a ring back and forth on his finger as he answered questions from his attorney. His mother buried her head in her arms as she listened to her son tell the jury his side of the story. Beagles testified that he had a knife and Collinsworth had a shotgun. The four of them, he said, were out "looking around for Negroes who had been parking near Collinsworth's neighborhood and bothering them." When they came upon the Florida A&M students, Beagles admitted holding the switchblade, but then said he put it away when he saw they were dressed in formal wear. He admitted that they ordered Brown and Butterfield to drive away, but insisted that he "*asked* the girls to get into the car." He denied the rape, arguing that Owens consented and even asked them to take her "back to school to change her dress."

Under cross-examination, Beagles admitted that he "pushed her, just once . . . not hard," into the car; that he said, "If you do what we want you to, we'll let you go," and then blindfolded her with a diaper after the attack. Defense attorney Howard Williams then asked Judge Walker to remove the jury, as Beagles detailed the confession he made the night of the crime. Williams argued that when police officers arrested the young men, they "were still groggy from a night of drinking," making their taped confessions inadmissible. Under Hopkins's cross-examination, however, Beagles admitted that his confession was entirely voluntary and that he actually looked over the written statement and made an adjustment.[40]

Patrick Scarborough, a twenty-year-old who was AWOL from the air force, admitted that he was married to a woman in Texas and testified that he had intercourse with Owens twice. He emphatically denied using force, despite the fact that he acknowledged that there was one shell in the barrel of his shotgun and two in the magazine. When Hopkins questioned him, Scarborough admitted that Owens pleaded, "Please don't hurt me," but insisted that she offered "no resistance." He denied kissing her at first, and then said he kissed her on the neck while he had sex with her.[41]

Defense attorneys tried a series of contradictory approaches to win over the jury. First, they focused on discrediting Owens instead of defending their clients, because the prosecution repeatedly drew self-incriminating information from them. Then they tried to use each man's ignorance to prove his innocence, highlighting their low IQs and poor educations. When that failed, they detailed the dysfunctional histories of each defendant. Attorney Harry Michaels told the jury that Patrick Scarborough's juvenile record was the result of a sorry childhood. His mother died when he was born, Michaels told the jury, his father committed suicide shortly thereafter, and his grandparents reared him.

Similarly, character witnesses for William Collinsworth described his sordid home life and drinking problem. Nearly every member of Collinsworth's family took the stand, spilling sorrowful stories about their poverty and dysfunction. His sister, Maudine Reeves, broke down on the stand and had to be taken to the hospital. His wife, Pearlie, told the jury through sobs and tears that he was "not himself when he was drunk," but when he was sober, "you couldn't ask for a better husband." She failed to mention on the stand what her letter to the judge made explicit: that her husband regularly beat her.

Unable to achieve any real sympathy, defense attorneys switched gears and attempted to portray their clients as reputable young men who were incapable of rape. Friends and family members lined up to testify that these young men "were good boys" and that defendant Ollie Stoutamire in particular had dropped out of school after the sixth grade, but had "nothing but pure and moral intentions."[42]

Finally, the defense appealed to the jury's prejudices in both more and less predictable ways. Owens was a jezebel, they insisted, and could not have been raped. But attorneys for Collinsworth blamed his actions on the "Indian blood" pulsing through his veins. Pensacola psychiatrist Dr. W. M. C. Wilhoit backed him up when he argued that "it is a known fact that individuals of the Indian race react violently and primitively when psychotic or intoxicated." When Collinsworth added alcohol to his "Indian blood," Wilhoit argued, "he was unable to discern the nature and quality of the crime in question."

The attorney for Stoutamire, City Judge John Rudd, blamed "outside agitators." The defendants are "being publicized and ridiculed to satisfy sadists and people in other places," Rudd yelled during closing arguments. "Look at that little skinny, long legged sixteen-year-old boy. Does he look like a mad rapist who should die . . . Should we kill or incarcerate that little boy because he happened to be in the wrong place at the wrong time?"[43]

In their summations to the jury, defense attorneys S. Gunter Toney and Harry Michaels followed Rudd's lead. "The crime here is insignificant," they said. " . . . The pressure, clamor, and furor are completely out of proportion." Pointing to Scarborough, Michaels told the jury "his motives, intentions, and designs that night were wholesome, innocent and decent." The fact that Owens could "have easily walked ten feet into the woods where nobody could find her," Michaels said, proved that she consented. Waving her gold-and-white gown in front of the jury, he pointed out that it was "not soiled or torn," which he said proved no brutality was involved. Finally, he called for an acquittal, arguing that the jury could not possibly convict on the basis of "only one witness—the victim, and confessions that admitted only one fact—sexual intercourse." Sitting in the segregated balcony, Charles U. Smith, a sociologist at Florida A&M University, gasped when he heard Williams yell, "Are you going to believe this nigger wench over these four boys?"[44]

In his closing argument, prosecuting attorney William Hopkins grabbed the shotgun and Betty Jean Owens's prom dress and appealed to the jury for a conviction. "Suppose two colored boys and their moron friends attacked Mrs. Beagles' daughter . . . had taken her at gunpoint from a car and forced her into a secluded place and regardless of whether they secured her consent or not, had intercourse with her seven times, leaving her in such a condition that she collapsed and had to be hospitalized?" Betty Jean Owens, he said, "didn't have a chance in the world with four big boys, a loaded gun and a knife. She was within an inch of losing her life . . . she was gang-raped SEVEN times." "When you get to the question of mercy," he told the jury, "consider that they wouldn't even let that little girl whimper."[45]

Restless spectators, squeezed into every corner of the segregated courthouse, crowded back into their seats when jurors emerged after three hours of deliberation with a decision. An additional three hundred African

African Americans and whites outside the Leon County Courthouse in Tallahassee eagerly await the verdict of four white men accused of raping Betty Jean Owens, a black college student.

Americans held a silent vigil outside. A. H. King, the jury foreman and a local plantation owner, slowly read aloud the jury's decision for all four defendants: "guilty with a recommendation for mercy." The recommendation for mercy saved the four men from the electric chair and, according to the *Baltimore Afro-American,* "made it inescapably clear that the death penalty for rape is only for colored men accused by white women." A. H. King defended the mercy ruling by arguing that "there was no brutality involved" and insisted, implausibly, that the decision would have been the same "if the defendants had been four Negroes."[46] Judge Walker deferred sentencing for fifteen days, cleared the courtroom, and sent the four white men to Raiford prison.

African Americans who attended the trial quietly made their way home after the bittersweet verdict. The *Pittsburgh Courier* reported that "throughout Negro Tallahassee, there was resentment that the rapists had not been given the death sentence." The verdict cast a pall of gloom, the article continued, "thick enough to be cut with a knife." Betty Jean Owens's mother told reporters that she was "just happy that the jury upheld my daughter's womanhood." Reverend A. J. Reddick, former head of the Florida NAACP, snapped, "If it had been Negroes, they would have gotten the death penalty." "Florida," he said, "has maintained an excellent record of not veering from its pattern of never executing a white man for the rape of a Negro," but he acknowledged that the conviction was "a step forward." Owens showed a similar ambivalence in an interview by the *Amsterdam News*. "It is something," she said. "I'm grateful that twelve white men believed the truth, but I still wonder what they would have done if one of our boys raped a white girl."[47]

Florida A&M students, who had criticized Butterfield and Brown for failing to protect black womanhood a week earlier, were visibly upset after the trial. In fact, letters to the editors of many African-American newspapers condemned the two men and all black men for failing to protect "their" women. Mrs. C.A.C. in New York City felt that all Negro men were "mice" and not worthy of respect because "they stand by and let the white men do anything they want to our women." She then warned all black men that they "would never have freedom until [they] learn to stand up and fight." In a letter to the *Baltimore Afro-American,* a black man accepted her challenge: "Unless we decide to protect our own women," he argued, "none of them will be safe." Some African-American women felt they should protect themselves. A white woman sent her black maid home one day after she came to work with a knife, "in case any white man came after her," reported the *Tallahassee Democrat*. Still, many felt that "someone should have burned."[48]

Despite their anger at the unequal justice meted out, some African Americans in the community considered the guilty verdict a victory. The Reverend C. K. Steele, Jr., head of the Tallahassee chapter of the SCLC, reminded others that four white men "wouldn't have even been arrested twenty years ago." The Reverend Lowery, state president of the Florida NAACP, saw a strategy in the mercy recommendation. He thought that it could help "Negroes more in the long run" by setting a precedent for equal justice in future rape cases. Later that summer, for example, Leon A. Lowery and others helped launch a successful campaign to highlight the unequal justice meted out for black men accused of raping white women. They asked Governor LeRoy Collins to commute the sentences of four black men who lingered on death row.[49] A white jury sentenced Ralph Williams to death for having a consensual relationship with a white woman; John Edward Paul confessed to raping a white woman after police tortured him and shot him in the foot; an all-white jury sentenced Sam Wiley Odum to death after only six minutes, despite the fact that he had an alibi and was nowhere near the alleged rape victim; and Jimmie Lee Clark was sentenced to the electric chair for attempted rape, though police beat a confession out of him.[50]

After Judge Walker handed down a stern lecture and life sentences to the four white men on June 21, 1959, some African Americans in Tallahassee applauded what they felt was a significant step in the right direction. Betty Jean Owens's mother argued that the conviction and life sentence were "open vindication for my daughter." Her daughter told the *Baltimore Afro-American,* "I feel better now for the first time since it happened." "For the first time I feel safe," Owens said. "After the jury recommended mercy," she continued, "I thought that one or two of them might have been turned loose and that the others would get short terms. And that was why I was afraid . . . I felt they would come back and do something to me."[51] Owens's intuition would prove correct. According to the *Chicago Defender,* when David Beagles was paroled in 1965, he sought retribution. Four years after his release, he allegedly tracked down and murdered a thirty-year-old black woman and buried her body in a shallow grave. He thought it was Owens. Instead, it was Betty Jean Robinson Houston, an entirely different woman.[52]

Unlike Owens and her family, many others exhibited outrage at the verdict. Roy Wilkins praised it as a move toward equal justice, but acknowledged in a private letter the "glaring contrast that was furnished by the Tallahassee verdict." In light of the recent lynching of Mack Charles Parker, no one really had to wonder what would have happened had the attackers been black. Editors of the *Louisiana Weekly* called the trial a "figment and a farce" and insisted that anyone who praised the verdict "confesses that he sees nothing wrong with exacting one punishment for white offenders and another, more severe for others." The editors of the *New York Amsterdam News* were "outraged" by the verdict. "We are not going to place ourselves in the ludicrous position of saying that we're satisfied. The verdict of guilty was the very least we expected," the editors wrote. "It was obvious they were guilty from the start . . . They were caught at the scene, made confessions, and the victim clearly identified them." Anyone who said the "half-loaf they got represents progress," they argued, "is simply making a virtue out of the vice of appeasement and laying the groundwork for the same unjust system to continue for the next one hundred years."[53]

The simple fact of the conviction was too much for some whites, who felt that sending four white men to jail for raping a black woman upset the entire foundation of white dominion. Many believed the guilty verdict was the result of a "Communist-inspired" NAACP conspiracy, which would ultimately lead to "miscegenation." Letters to Judge Walker fea-

Another Sample of Separate But Unequal?

FOUR ADMITTED ATTACKERS OF FLA. COED

SOUTH'S HISTORY OF NEVER CONDEMNING A WHITE MAN FOR RAPING A COLORED WOMAN

AMERICAN PROMISE OF EQUAL JUSTICE

This cartoon, featured in an African-American newspaper, places sexual violence at the center of the civil rights campaign for equal justice. It also demonstrates African Americans' belief that historically, Southern white men went unpunished for sexually assaulting black women, even when they admitted to the crime. May 16, 1959.

tured a host of common fears and racist stereotypes of black men and women. One man reminded the judge that a conviction "would play into the hands of the Warren Court, the NAACP, and all other radical enemies of the South . . . even though the nigger wench probably had been with a dozen men before." Mrs. Laura Cox told Judge Walker in a letter that she feared this case would strengthen desegregation efforts, posing a direct threat to white children who might attend integrated schools. "If the South is integrated," she argued, "white children will be in danger because the Negroes carry knives, razors, ice picks, and guns practically all the time." Petitioning Judge Walker for leniency, Bill Arens reminded him that "Negro women like to be raped by the white men" and that "something like this will help the Supreme Court force this low bred race ahead, making whites live and eat with him and allow his children to associate with the little apes, grow up and marry them."[54]

It is ironic that a rape case involving a black woman and four white men would conjure up images of the black brute chasing white women with the intent to mongrelize the white race. The Tallahassee case attests to the persistence of such images decades after Reconstruction, when the mythological incubus took flight, justifying mob violence and a reign of terror throughout the South.[55] To be sure, anxieties about the black beast rapist and fears of "miscegenation" conveniently surfaced when white men feared losing their monopoly on power.

Despite segregationists' efforts to maintain the status quo, the conviction signaled an enormous break with the past. While the verdict was due largely to the confluence of localized issues—a politically mobilized middle-class African-American community; the lower-class status of the defendants, who were politically expendable; Florida's status as a "moderate" Southern state dependent on outside tourism; and media pressure— the case itself was rooted in a decades-long struggle for black women's bodily integrity that had far-reaching consequences.[56] Like the Recy Taylor case, the Tallahassee case focused national attention on the sexual exploitation of black women by white men. The life sentences helped secure convictions elsewhere that summer. In Montgomery, Alabama, Grady F. Smith, a retired air force colonel, was sentenced to fourteen months of hard labor for raping a seventeen-year-old African-American girl. In Raleigh, North Carolina, Ralph Lee Betts, a white thirty-six-year-old ex-convict, was sentenced to life imprisonment for kidnapping and molesting an eleven-year-old African-American girl. And in Beaufort, South Carolina, an all-white jury sentenced a white marine named Fred G. Davis to the electric chair—a first in the history of the South—for raping a forty-seven-year-old African-American woman.[57]

Betty Jean Owens's grandmother recognized the historic and political significance of the verdicts. "I've lived to see the day," she said, "where white men would really be brought to trial for what they did."[58] The *Louisiana Weekly* argued that the verdict "indicates that the South is, after one hundred years, moving toward equal justice." For nearly a century, the editors argued, "the white South has excused the white man involved in the ugly crime of rape of a Negro woman, but became incensed like wild men if it was the other way around. Just take a look at the complexion of the 'darker' race in the South and you'll find that amalgamation is not something that is about to start, but what started one hundred years ago."[59]

John McCray, the editor of the South Carolina *Lighthouse and Informer,* realized the importance of guilty verdicts. "From personal observation and civil work," McCray noted, "our women have been molested and their defilers allowed to go free for the last quarter of a century. This forced intimacy," he said "goes back to the days of slavery when our women were the chattel property of white men." For McCray, the life sentences indicated a new day: "Are we now witnessing the arrival of our women?" he asked. "Are they at long last gaining the emancipation they've needed?" James Booker, a writer for the *Amsterdam News,* took it a step further: the Tallahassee case, he said, "will go down in history as the turning point in the struggle of Negroes for equal justice."[60]

It is not a coincidence that black college students sparked the sit-in movement soon after Betty Jean Owens was brutally raped. Patricia Stephens Due, who felt that the rape symbolized an attack on the dignity of all African Americans, organized Tallahassee's first Congress of Racial Equality (CORE) chapter just six weeks after Owens's trial. Florida A&M CORE members launched an uneventful sit-in campaign that fall. A year later, in the spring of 1960, they successfully desegregated local lunch counters, theaters, and department stores, as did black college students throughout the South.[61]

The sit-in movement spread rapidly across the South after four North Carolina A&T students demanded service at Woolworth's lunch counter in Greensboro on February 1, 1960. By the end of the week, hundreds of black college students jammed Greensboro's segregated lunch counters and restaurants, quietly demanding service and stubbornly refusing to leave, even when angry whites poured ketchup on their heads, put cigarettes out on their necks, and pummeled them with their fists. Although the students targeted restaurants, their goals were, according to activist Ella Baker, "bigger than a hamburger or a giant-sized Coke."[62] The students carried signs condemning the "lack of dignity and respect" shown to them and demanded universal human rights. "I felt as though I had gained my manhood," Franklin McCain, one of the four pioneers, said later. By the end of February, black college students had launched sit-ins in thirty-one cities and eight states across the South.[63]

During the next three years, the nation and the world witnessed African Americans risking their lives for human rights during the Freedom Rides in 1961; watched "Bull" Connor unleash snarling police dogs on black children during the Birmingham movement in 1963; heard about Martin Luther King, Jr.'s, dream at the Lincoln Memorial; and saw investigators pull the bodies of three voter registration workers out of an earthen dam in Philadelphia, Mississippi, in 1964.

Despite the almost unlimited media focus on racial violence, inter-

African-American women made up the bulk of the 257 Florida A&M University students who were arrested for protesting segregated movie theaters in Tallahassee in the spring of 1963.

racial rape cases no longer made national headlines. A cursory glance at newspapers in the early 1960s might suggest that white-on-black rape had abated and that black women were relatively safe from white racial and sexual violence.[64] But the "Second Reconstruction" was nearly as violent and dangerous for black women as the first, when white Southerners had used rape as a "weapon of terror" to reclaim their power after the Civil War.[65]

The Tallahassee verdict proved that a new day had dawned in the South, but it was not yet a new world. During the 1960s black women, particularly voting-rights activists, remained vulnerable to rape and sexualized violence, especially in places where television crews and NAACP organizers could not go: private homes and prison cells. Nowhere was this clearer than in Mississippi, where white supremacy was backed by state leaders and legislators, protected in the courts, and reinforced on the local level by police, the White Citizens' Councils, and the Ku Klux Klan. It was a "closed society," as James W. Silver put it, "as near to . . . a police state as anything we have yet seen in America."[66] And yet even in the most intransigent part of the country, where sexual violence against black women was endemic, there was a slow transformation taking place.

CHAPTER 6

"A Black Woman's Body
Was Never Hers Alone"

FANNIE LOU HAMER, A forty-three-year-old sharecropper and freedom fighter from the Mississippi Delta, knew that sexual terror was common in the history of the South. Hamer's grandmother, Liza Bramlett, spoke often of the "horrors of slavery," including stories about "how the white folks would do her." Bramlett's daughter, Hamer's mother, remembered that "this man would keep her as long as he want to and then he would trade her off for a little heifer calf. Then the other man would get her and keep her as long as he want—she was steady having babies—and trade her off for a little sow pig." Twenty of the twenty-three children Bramlett gave birth to were products of rape. At some point, Hamer's mother must have decided death—hers or someone else's—was preferable to her own mother's experience. Fannie Lou Hamer remembered her mother packing a nine-millimeter Luger into their covered lunch bucket, just in case a white man decided to attack her or her children in the cotton fields.[1]

Hamer's mother and grandmother taught her the painful truth that in the Mississippi Delta, if not the entire South, a "black woman's body was never hers alone."[2] If she was at all unclear about this lesson, the forced hysterectomy she received in 1961 when she went to the hospital to have a small cyst removed from her stomach left little room for confusion. "I went to the doctor who did that to me," she said, "and I asked him, 'Why? Why had he done that to me?' He didn't have to say nothing—and he

Fannie Lou Hamer

didn't." "He should have told me," she said. "I would have loved to have had children." The practice was so common that blacks often called it a "Mississippi appendectomy."[3] Hamer, like other black women who received the same procedure, had little recourse. If she had called a lawyer, she said, "I would have been taking my hands and screwing tacks into my casket."[4] The brutal beating Hamer received in the Winona, Mississippi, jail only reinforced these lessons.

On June 9, 1963, Fannie Lou Hamer and a group of Student Nonviolent Coordinating Committee (SNCC) volunteers returned to Mississippi from a citizenship training school in Charleston, South Carolina. At a rest stop in Winona, Mississippi, just thirty miles from the Delta town of Greenwood, police arrested Hamer and her companions for attempting to desegregate the bus terminal's lunch counter and drove them to the local jail. The county sheriff met the black women at the door. "I been hearing about you black sons of bitches over in Greenwood, raising all that hell," he said. "You come over here to Winona, you'll get the hell whipped out of you."[5] He was not kidding. Once in custody, each activist received a savage and sexually abusive beating by the Winona police.

Officers first assaulted and sexually humiliated June Johnson, a beautiful and statuesque sixteen-year-old. Everyone in the jail must have heard Johnson's screams and the thump of fists and boots hitting flesh as policemen yelled, "We're going to teach you how to say 'yes, sir' to a Mississippi white man." According to Hamer, the officers "tore off most of her clothes" and then forced her to strip off the rest as they watched.[6] Johnson's co-workers gasped when they saw her naked, bloody body and "bulging" eye as she stumbled back to her cell.

Officers then brutalized Annelle Ponder, a coordinator for the Southern Christian Leadership Conference and organizer of the trip. Three policemen took turns viciously beating her with a "blackjack . . . belt, fists and open palms," while berating her for not showing racial deference. "I want to hear you say 'Yes Sir,' nigger," one officer yelled repeatedly.[7] "They really wanted to make me say 'yes, sir,' " Ponder recalled, "and that is the one thing I wouldn't say."[8] When the police finished pounding Ponder, they directed their fury at Fannie Lou Hamer.

Hamer, a stocky, churchgoing woman with a powerful singing voice, had worked as a field secretary for SNCC since B. D. Marlowe, her former employer and plantation owner in Sunflower County, fired her for registering to vote in the fall of 1962. Sunflower was home to both Parchman penitentiary and Senator James O. Eastland, both notorious symbols of white supremacy. Hamer and her husband, "Pap," had worked on Marlowe's plantation for eighteen years, but once she stepped outside the narrow confines of Jim Crow, Marlowe kicked her off his land and notified the local White Citizens' Council, which harassed her and Pap relentlessly. Unable to find a job, she became an organizer for SNCC.

For over a year, Mrs. Hamer had been traveling around the Mississippi Delta rousing local blacks with her witty and bold speeches, soul-stirring songs, and fervid commitment to the plight of the poor. Robert Jackall, a Georgetown professor who volunteered in Sunflower County in 1967, was struck by Hamer's charisma. It was "her unvarnished, earthy forcefulness, devoid of all pretense," he said; "her unshakeable conviction in the justness of her cause, proved by her personal sufferings and the risks she continued to take; her ennobling vision of racial harmony and of personal redemption for those who seek it; and her ability to articulate her ideas with a powerful religious rhetoric that had deep resonance for her audience but that had no trace of practiced cant."[9] Hamer concentrated her efforts in Greenwood, home of the White Citizens' Council and the center of SNCC's Delta activities. Her leadership inspired working people scarred by poverty and racism, but it also made her a constant target of intimidation, harassment, and sexualized violence.

"You bitch," one officer yelled, "we going to make you wish you was dead." He ordered two black inmates to beat Hamer with a "long wide blackjack," while other patrolmen battered "her head and other parts of her body." As they ruthlessly beat her, Hamer felt them repeatedly, "pull my dress over my head and try to feel under my clothes."[10] When she attempted to pull her dress down in order to, as she put it, "preserve some respectability through the horror and disgrace," a white officer "walked over, took my dress, pulled it up over my shoulders, leaving my body exposed to five men."[11]

Hamer found out later that Lawrence Guyot, a civil rights activist who came to the Winona jail to inquire about the women's status, was arrested and sexually tortured as well. "They forced me to take off my pants," Guyot remembered, "and they threatened my testicles with burning sticks."[12] Hamer was sure her attackers were sadists. She remembered their facial expressions during her beating and believed they "displayed pleasure that was sexual in nature."[13]

Like many of her foremothers, Hamer did not shy away from detailing the sexual aspects of her beating. She told her story on national television at the Democratic National Convention in 1964, and to congressmen investigating civil rights abuses in June 1964, and she continued to tell it "until the day she died," offering up her testimony as a form of resistance to the sexual and racial injustice of segregation.[14] Hamer's testimony, like that of other black female civil rights activists abused in Mississippi, Georgia, and Alabama in the early 1960s, countered white supremacist narratives of miscegenation, put segregationists on the defensive, and helped convince President Lyndon B. Johnson to use the power of the federal government to protect civil rights activists.

Fannie Lou Hamer was not the only woman willing to speak out publicly against sexualized violence in Southern jails. On June 6, 1963, three days before the Winona incident, Dorothy Height, president of the National Council of Negro Women (NCNW), and Jeanne Noble, president of Delta Sigma Theta, went on WNEW, one of New York City's most popular radio stations, to announce an exclusive report documenting "indignities to girl freedom demonstrators in Southern prisons."[15] Dorothy Height revealed that the leaders of twenty-four women's groups had met a month earlier to hear firsthand accounts of "brutality and sexual abuse" from civil rights demonstrators in the South. Respectability and reticence, hallmarks of the black clubwomen's movement in the early twentieth century, gave way to stark testimony as Height told thousands of people lis-

Two trustees carry an African-American woman to the paddy wagon in
Jackson, Mississippi, 1963. African-American female activists were often
sexually harassed and abused in prisons.

tening to the radio that day that black and white female activists in Jackson, Mississippi, "were raped by attendants at the jails."[16] According to
Height, the young women who were arrested in Jackson in the spring and
summer of 1963 "had been subjected to internal exams at the hands of
attendants there and under very unsanitary conditions." One young
woman told Jeanne Noble that she was "asked to strip naked and stand
before male prisoners in the yard of the jail" and was one of many women
forced to undergo "unsanitary and unmedical [sic] vaginal exams."[17]

The incidents Height and Noble recounted for the radio audience
reflected common practices in prisons throughout the South during the
civil rights years, though they were rarely documented at the time. When
the Freedom Riders poured into Jackson, Mississippi, in the summer of
1961, they were immediately arrested and delivered to Parchman penitentiary, a twenty-thousand-acre prison farm in the middle of the Delta
and the most fearsome prison in the South.[18] Officers herded the demonstrators into exam rooms with cattle prods, where both men and women
"were ordered to strip naked for thorough body searches." The women
endured "rough, painful vaginal searches," by prison guards who used
gloves dipped in Lysol.[19]

In Clarksdale, Mississippi, police arrested Miss Bessie Turner for
allegedly stealing money and then viciously flogged her. Turner told
SNCC officials later that police made her "pull up [her] dress and pull

down [her] panties" and then began to whip her with a "wide leather strap." When that failed to coerce an admission out of her, the officer told Turner to "turn over an [sic] open your legs and let me see how you look down there." He then took the leather strap and hit her "between [her] legs." Not quite satisfied, the officer made Turner stand up and expose her breasts. "He said he was looking for the money in my bra," she testified later.[20]

Unita Blackwell, a SNCC activist from Mayersville, Mississippi, remembered how dangerous it was to organize in rural areas. "Every time I drove down the highway, I knew I might be arrested," she said. "One time I was coming from Yazoo City and met the police. I had on pants and he made me take them off." He stared for a bit, then turned to another officer, and according to Blackwell, said, "You want some of this?"[21]

Mississippi police did not hold a monopoly on the sexual humiliation and abuse of black women. According to a SNCC report, some of the worst incidents occurred in jails in southwest Georgia in the fall of 1962 and spring of 1963. Faith Holsaert, a SNCC field secretary in Albany, Georgia, was "obscenely questioned" by the police and "fondled by officers during her booking." She was also sexually intimidated, she said, when officers "propositioned" her. Other SNCC workers were, she said, "forced to strip to their panties," and at least one girl was sexually assaulted. LaVette Christian, a local teenager from a movement family, woke up in the middle of the night to find a prison official "standing over her." According to SNCC documents, he "started rubbing her arms and legs" and she kept telling him "No, no."[22] Police threw Mrs. Marion King in the Albany jail in July 1962 when she was seven months pregnant. "Police officers shoved her, kicked her and punched her in the face," the SNCC report said, "causing her to fall to the ground and lose consciousness." One month later King gave birth to a stillborn baby.[23]

A report issued by the Medical Committee for Human Rights, an organization of physicians designed to provide medical assistance during Freedom Summer, showed that Georgia was not alone in its deployment of sexual abuse. The report documented "extreme sexual brutality" in Jackson, Mississippi, where police hit male activists' testicles with clubs, pulled women's dresses up, fondled their breasts, and ogled them while they were given vaginal exams.[24]

"As a woman," Jeanne Noble exclaimed on WNEW, "I can think of no greater indignity than rape . . . or sexual exposure . . . or unsanitary conditions." Height agreed and said that was why she called a special con-

Police crammed a group of teenage girls into a filthy stockade without beds, toilets, or running water in Leesburg, Georgia, after they were arrested for protesting segregation at a movie theater.

ference. The women's organizations that attended, Height said, "came away . . . determined that this is one thing we could do as women . . . We could speak out and work toward the elimination of these horrible atrocities that seem to be vented against women and girls."[25] These abuses, which often occurred behind closed doors and were exposed only months later, garnered neither the media coverage nor the organizational support necessary to stop them from happening. Height and Noble deviated from their own organizations' historic silence surrounding sexual violence by exposing the reality of rape and sexual abuse in Southern prisons. The National Council of Negro Women and Delta Sigma Theta embraced the tradition of testimony and used their institutional voices as weapons in the war against white supremacy.

They also organized. On October 4, 1963, Dorothy Height; Shirley Smith, executive director of the National Women's Committee for Civil Rights; Polly Cowan of the Citizens Committee for Children in New York; and Dr. Dorothy Ferebee, director of health services at Howard University, flew to Selma to bear witness and hear testimony from sixty-five young women and their parents about "police brutality and hideous jail conditions" in Dallas County.[26] Young women from Selma had called Height, "begging her to come see accounts firsthand and make an effort to have women's organizations come to [their] aid."[27]

That night sixty-five teenagers and their parents assembled at First Baptist Church, where they testified about their experiences in Selma's jails. According to Polly Cowan, who recorded the meeting, Dorothy Height skillfully elicited the girls' stories. "The teenagers had been tossed into cells without room for them all to sit on the floor," Cowan recalled. "They were given no blankets, insufficient drinking water. They had no toilet facilities. There was sawdust in the small amount of food they were served. Salt was substituted for sugar in their coffee." There were numerous threats of sexual assault on the girls by local police. The black teenagers told Cowan and Height that the warden threatened them constantly. "If you don't behave," he allegedly said, "the men prisoners will be let into your cells."[28] In order to protect themselves, the female freedom fighters "huddled together at night, taking turns staying awake in case the guards came in to harass them."[29]

As if to underline the point, about fifty policemen surrounded the church as the clubwomen streamed out. "They stood in clumps," Cowan reported. "It was dark with only one street light," she said, but she could see their weapons: "clubs, pistols . . . and cattle prods. The yellow helmets and arm bands added to the impression that this was an invasion." Walking out of the meeting into the cluster of police was "frightening," Cowan said. "One hardly dared to look up from the red dirt of the church parking lot." As she walked past one of the state troopers, she noticed his cattle prod dangling from his belt and recalled a story she had heard from a local woman: pointing to one of the electric cattle prods, the mayor of Selma boasted that he could "make a nigger jump three feet with one of these."[30] The social standing of Dorothy Height and the Northern professional women who accompanied her did not exempt them from the threats described in the testimony of the young black women of Selma, Alabama.

In March 1964 Dorothy Height convened an "off the record" meeting in Atlanta with the NCNW, the YWCA, the National Council of Catholic Women, the National Council of Jewish Women, and the Church Women United to "discuss police brutality and the treatment of women and girls who had been arrested for civil disobedience in the seven most troubled cities."[31] In preparation for the meeting, each organization sent delegates to Southern movement towns to document local conditions. At that meeting, the leading clubwomen, whom Polly Cowan called the "Cadillac Crowd," formed an interracial organization that sent teams of women to

Mississippi in 1964 to establish ties among white and black women, observe civil rights projects, and bear witness to atrocities.[32]

"Wednesdays in Mississippi" helped bring outside resources and much-needed institutional attention to the stark conditions in the Deep South. Unfortunately, the integrated teams of middle-class women spent only one day a week in different towns in Mississippi observing work in Freedom Schools and community service projects. They seemed to be more comfortable doing traditional clubwomen's work, like community service and moral uplift, than documenting sexual abuse on the front lines of the freedom struggle. This strategy ignored black women's struggles with sexual discrimination and sexualized violence, despite the fact that it was an historic and ongoing issue.[33] Though the clubwomen made good connections with local activists, Wednesdays in Mississippi did not translate into an effective program to protect black women from sexual violence.

Stories of sexual abuse and violence in Southern jails rarely reached a mass audience during the 1960s. If they received any press at all, it paled in comparison to the national and international attention given to the major civil rights campaigns under way throughout the South. African Americans' victory over Eugene "Bull" Connor in Birmingham, Alabama, in the spring of 1963, followed by the successful March on Washington later that summer and the signing of the Civil Rights Act into law on July 2, 1964, mortally wounded Jim Crow and began to dismantle the social and legal underpinnings of segregation.[34] But blacks remained vulnerable to white attacks and were still denied the franchise in many places throughout the South. In Alabama and Mississippi, for example, segregationists were on the defensive, and they dug in—their opposition to black equality became further entrenched, making change difficult and dangerous.

Still, the ability to simply *survive* white intransigence and federal indifference gave blacks a new sense of empowerment that enabled them to slowly overcome their fears.[35] Endesha Ida Mae Holland, an eighteen-year-old African-American woman, gained a sense of pride and self-worth when SNCC started organizing voter-registration drives in Greenwood in 1962. By pushing aside fears of white violence and joining the local movement, she began to understand what Martin Luther King, Jr., called "somebodyness." "People started looking up into my face, into my eyes," Holland remembered. "Whereas the whole town, to me, was looking down its nose at me," she said, "the movement said I was *somebody;* I was *somebody,* they

"The movement said I was *somebody*." Endesha Ida Mae Holland (far left) with SNCC voting-rights activists.

said."[36] It was a message that transformed her life. Just seven years earlier Holland had been the victim of a terrible sexual assault.

On August 29, 1955, a day after J. W. Milam and Roy Bryant kidnapped Emmett Till, a wealthy white woman named Mrs. Lawrence asked Holland if she would babysit her granddaughter for the day. "Ida Mae," as she was known then, frequently did babysitting and domestic work to help her mother, who spent her days ironing white folks' clothes inside their tiny tarpaper shack. Since it was Ida Mae's eleventh birthday, Mrs. Lawrence promised her two dollars and a "birthday bonus" if she would come by their big plantation-style home later that afternoon.[37] After Ida Mae played with the child for a bit, Mrs. Lawrence summoned her upstairs. "Mr. Lawrence wants to see you and wish you a happy birthday," she said. Mrs. Lawrence called her into the bedroom where her husband, a wizened old man, lay beneath crumpled blankets. Mrs. Lawrence tore back the sheets, exposing what Holland called "his old shriveled *thing*—a slimy white penis asleep on his pasty leg."[38]

Then she scooped Holland up, placed her on top of the bed, and quickly left the room. The old man reached for Holland, "pulled down [her] shorts and snapped down [her] panties," and began to fondle her. She was terrified. Her mother, she said in her memoir, had repeatedly told her to never allow anyone to "touch [her] down there." Holland screamed and "beat [her] hands against the wall, grabbing and pushing at the same time, looking for something to hold on to." Lawrence asked the child if she was enjoying herself, as if she were a grown woman engaged in a consensual act. "Nawsir," Holland replied, "it hurts." The rape lasted for what Holland said "seemed like a lifetime." "I began to think I was dying," she remembered.[39] When Lawrence finished, he handed Holland a five-dollar bill and told her to go downstairs. When Holland opened the door and walked out, Mrs. Lawrence looked at her, as Holland put it, "without expression, as if she'd gone somewhere else." "But I knew," Holland said, "that *she* knew the bull had thrown me."[40]

Holland's experience was a common one for many African-American girls and women working in white households. Indeed, she suspected the "bull" had thrown plenty of other girls her age. Through "sly innuendo, knowing glances, and telling silences," Holland said, she figured about half the girls in Greenwood—maybe even the whole Delta—lived without "daddies who knew the score about white men and kept their daughters safe by refusing to let them work in white households."[41] Of those, she estimated that approximately three-fourths were victims of rape. "Folks used to tell how, in the South no white man wanted to die without having sex with a black woman," Holland said. "It was just seen as part of life and if you . . . were black, you were always at the mercy of white people."[42] "You didn't need to be sitting babies or cleaning houses to fall victim to the white man's lust," she remembered. "We could just as easily be picking cotton or walking to the store or spending money in the white man's store when the mood would take him and he'd take us— just like that, like lightning striking." Like Fannie Lou Hamer, Holland understood that black women's bodies did not belong to themselves. They "belonged to everyone," she said.[43]

By the time SNCC organizers came to Greenwood in 1962, Holland was a high school dropout and a prostitute. One day she saw a well-dressed young black man walking through town and decided to follow him, hoping to turn a trick. "I got it—come an' get it," she sang. "Come and get you some." She strutted and sashayed behind him until they reached the local SNCC headquarters. He turned around and asked if she was going to "help get all these people signed up?" It was Bob Parris Moses, a twenty-six-year-old, Harlem-born, Harvard-educated math whiz who came to Mississippi in the summer of 1961 as a SNCC organizer to register black voters.[44] Moses introduced Holland to the other volunteers, and before she knew it, she was sitting in front of a typewriter, helping local sharecroppers fill out voter-registration forms. By the end of the day, she felt different. "Being treated with respect was something wholly new for me," she said in her memoir.[45] Holland quit selling sex and joined the freedom movement, eventually becoming a field secretary for SNCC. "Being around the SNCC people," she said later, "had turned my narrow space into a country bigger than I'd ever imagined."[46]

Organizing helped local people regain a sense of humanity, but they remained vulnerable to white retaliation and physical harm. Bob Moses and other SNCC leaders eventually came to believe that federal indifference would fade only when *white* bodies and lives were threatened.[47] SNCC proposed a summer project that would recruit hundreds of white students from Northern states to help register Mississippi blacks. The presence of Northern whites, Bob Moses believed, would shine a bright light on the state so the rest of the country could see "what was really happening."[48] Moses made this clear at an orientation session for volunteers. "When you come South," Sally Belfrage, a white volunteer-journalist in Greenwood, remembered Moses saying, "you bring with you the concern of the country—because the people of the country don't identify with Negroes." After requesting federal protection for three years; after the harassment and murder of so many African Americans in Mississippi, the FBI finally responded to black demands and sent in a "crack team" to Mississippi on the eve of Freedom Summer. "Now [that] the federal government is concerned," Moses told the volunteers, "there will be more protection for us, and hopefully for the Negroes who live there."[49]

As Northern volunteers flooded into the state in June 1964, white Mississippians braced themselves for what they considered a military—and sexual—invasion. According to the historian John Dittmer, white Mississippians "made interracial sex a centerpiece of their attack on the summer project itself."[50] The presence of Northern whites, unaccustomed to Jim Crow and uninterested in maintaining Mississippi's white power structure, threatened to undermine the state's racial hegemony and expose white Mississippians to other ways of thinking about race. In order to discredit the goals of Freedom Summer and shore up white solidarity, state and local officials acted as if the student volunteers were an army of amalgamation hell-bent on forcing the state to allow interracial sex and marriage. The arrival of these sex-crazed white "beatniks" and "black rapists" disguised as civil rights activists propelled whites to rise up in defense of the so-called "Southern way of life."[51] White fears bordered on hysteria. According to *Newsweek,* many "believed interracial bands were com-

Ready to meet the "Army of Amalgamation." Allen Thompson (front, center), mayor of Jackson, Mississippi, poses with his police force and armored tank as the city prepares for the arrival of black and white voting-rights volunteers in the summer of 1964.

ing . . . to start violence" and assault white women.[52] Some were even convinced that "black men wearing white bandages on their throats had been designated to rape white women."[53] Local newspapers and public officials, *The New York Times* reported, "did little to discourage these ideas."[54]

To protect themselves, white Mississippians prepared for war. They stocked up on guns, ammunition, and dynamite and renewed their membership in, or joined, the local Ku Klux Klan.[55] Allen Thompson, the mayor of Jackson, Mississippi, felt that "Armageddon [was] just around the corner."[56] *Newsweek* reported that Mayor Thompson planned to save his state from these interracial incubi with his "impressive—and expensive— deterrent force of men and military power." Thompson hoped that 450 riot police, 220 new shotguns, six dogs, and a "13,000 pound armored tank . . . abristle with shotguns, tear-gas guns and a sub-machine gun," would stop the integrated infantry from advancing. "We're ready for them," Thompson told *Newsweek.* "They won't have a chance."[57]

That hundreds of white women were coming to Mississippi to work for the movement must have made Thompson and his segregationist soldiers seethe with rage. The mere presence of white women in the black community helped make the summer of 1964, according to John Dittmer, "the most violent since Reconstruction."[58] In addition to the tragic murders of Northern volunteer Andrew Goodman and CORE organizers Michael Schwerner and James Chaney in Neshoba County on June 21, 1964, there were at least three other homicides that summer.[59] Additionally, organizers reported more than thirty-five shootings and sixty-five cases of arson at individual homes and movement offices. Klansmen and their allies burned thirty-five black churches to the ground; while police arrested one thousand movement people and eighty activists suffered beatings.[60] Shocking as these numbers are, they do not account for subtle forms of personal abuse and sexual attacks that often went unreported.

Summer volunteers were keenly aware of the fact that white women working alongside black men and sharing conversation or contact with them violated the South's most sacred taboo. If they did not understand this, they quickly learned the rules. Most African-American SNCC workers came of age in the 1950s, when white men had brutally murdered Emmett Till for talking fresh to a white woman; they did not want to subject local blacks to any danger if they could help it.[61] Organizers instructed the white volunteers to abide by local custom and maintain strict separation. This is why so many white female volunteers were confined to office jobs instead of community organizing; it was not simply because of sexism, as some argued later.[62] Still, white women and black men were often seen working together and enjoying one another's company.[63] "It's one thing to have white women work in the office," Chuck McDew, a SNCC worker, remembered. "It's another [for a black man] to be driving around in rural areas with a white woman sitting by your side. Whites can't handle that. Imaginations just went wild."[64] The sight of white women mingling with African Americans, especially black men, constituted the "ultimate white supremacist nightmare."[65] Worse, the sight of interracial couples—whether they were romantic partners or not—"only added to the rage and sense of impotence of white segregationists," Karl Fleming, a correspondent for *Newsweek,* remembered. "That is what it was *all* about, *all* the time, everywhere," Fleming said. "It was the great underpinning of the whole damn thing—just pure sexual fear."[66]

Sally Belfrage, a white volunteer whose astute memoir provides one of the most vivid accounts of Freedom Summer, knew that whites' overblown orations about interracial sex masked an all-out effort to defend their position atop the political, economic, and social hierarchy. Integration, she insisted, was nothing new in Mississippi. "For generations," Belfrage argued, whites had been crossing the color line to indulge in what African Americans called "nighttime integration." Belfrage dismissed arguments against "race mixing" and the "mongrelization of the white race" among opponents of civil rights, since "the principle was one-sided depending upon the color of the man involved."[67] "It's too late for the white man to start worrying about integration," she said, quoting an African-American woman, "because [he] has already mongrelized the white race and the black one too. The only thing [he] hasn't done," she argued, "is claim [his] children." The "light-skinned products of the sinful doctrine of racial amalgamation," Belfrage said, "were everywhere, and those of us who got up early met the not infrequent sight of white men driving out of the Negro neighborhood at dawn."[68]

Belfrage's stark analysis of and witness to white men's appetite for "nighttime integration" while feigning disgust for it during the day captured the long history of the racial and sexual subjugation of African Americans and the political maneuvering required to maintain the racial status quo. Like Belfrage's analysis, black women's testimonies concerning the actualities of interracial sexual violence consistently challenged the white supremacist narrative of miscegenation. One story from Grenada, a segregationist stronghold on the eastern edge of the Delta, illustrates this perfectly.

When police charged L. J. Loden, a married white man, with raping a sixteen-year-old African-American girl in the summer of 1960, it did not make headlines. Loden's actions were not all that unusual. But when he was forced to stand trial and then convicted of rape on July 27, his world—and that of white men in the Delta—seemed upside down.[69] The victim testified that Loden picked her up on the pretense of hiring her as a housemaid, but when she got into his car, he attacked her. She did not consent, she said at the trial, but actively "resisted his advances." She testified that she struggled to escape and repeatedly stabbed him with a penknife during the assault. When a jury of twelve white men delivered a guilty verdict without recommending mercy, Loden was, by default, sentenced to death.[70]

The ruling could have had profound implications throughout the state—no white man had ever been sentenced to death for raping a black woman in Mississippi, or in the South for that matter. Between 1940 and 1965, only ten white men were convicted of raping black women or girls in Mississippi despite the fact that it happened regularly. Besides Loden, Clyde Johnson, an Adams County white man, received fifteen years for assault with intent to rape. In Jones County, Laverne Yarbrough was convicted of raping a seven-year-old black child and sentenced to life. He was paroled shortly after sentencing. Bennett Austin and Charles Wiggins were convicted of raping a black teenager and received a paltry two-year sentence. In Brookhaven, Ernest Dillon received twenty years in prison, having confessed to raping a black woman on the eve of her wedding. Robert Hamblin of Union County and Abraham Sloan of Washington County each received one year for attempted rape. And in Yazoo County, the "gateway to the Delta," Bobby Smith received five years for assault with intent to rape a black middle-aged woman.[71] Ten cases scattered over fifteen years and hundreds of miles hardly qualified as justice for a crime that happened as routinely as white-on-black rape.

A death sentence in the Loden case would have fundamentally reordered the infrastructure of white supremacy that had been in place since slavery and shattered the unspoken rule that reserved the state's electric chair for black men. No Mississippi white man, certainly not Circuit Judge Henry Lee Rogers, was going to set *that* precedent. Rogers recalled the jurors and told them to reconsider. Surely, he chided, they did not "mean the verdict to read that way." Rogers reasoned that the jurors "did not realize that the 'guilty as charged' verdict made execution mandatory" and insisted they "modify [their] verdict."[72] As instructed, the white jurors changed their verdict and recommended mercy for Loden. He was finally sentenced to life in prison with the possibility for parole in ten years.[73] In the end, it was both an incredible victory and a stunning loss. It would take an additional five years before Mississippi sentenced a white man, guilty of raping a black teenager, to life in prison without parole.[74] And never, not once, would a white man pay with his life for raping a black woman.[75]

When President Lyndon B. Johnson signed the Civil Rights Act on July 2, 1964, segregation suffered a serious blow but survived.[76] African Americans could now theoretically receive equal treatment in restaurants, hotels, and theaters, but they could not count on access to the ballot nor on the federal government to protect them from physical harm. Southern segregationists remained firmly ensconced in positions of power. However, by the time fall breezes swept Freedom Summer into the past, thousands of black children had attended Freedom Schools; even more African Americans overcame their fears and survived white terror in an effort to be treated like human beings and citizens; and more than eighty thousand African Americans participated in the "freedom vote," a series of mock elections organized by the Council of Federated Organizations (COFO) to dramatize black disfranchisement.[77] COFO's efforts culminated in the organization of the Mississippi Freedom Democratic Party (MFDP), which protested black exclusion from the political process in Mississippi and challenged the state's lily-white delegates at the Democratic National Convention in Atlantic City in August.

Beneath red, white, and blue bunting, among Democrats from all over the country, Fannie Lou Hamer testified in Atlantic City about the savage beating she received in Winona, providing painful details and stark evidence of white reprisals for voter registration. Her emotional testimony challenged the Democratic Party's commitment to civil rights in front of a national television audience. "Is this America?" she asked. "The land of the free and the home of the brave, where we have to sleep with our telephones off the hooks," she said, her voice shaking, "because our lives be threatened daily, because we want to live as decent human beings, in America?" Hamer's testimony helped push President Johnson to offer the MFDP two at-large seats at the convention, but they refused, arguing that, as Hamer put it, "we didn't come all this way for no two seats."[78] Johnson's meager offer at least proved that Mississippi was no longer a place where whites could torment blacks with complete impunity. African Americans in Mississippi, many of them women who testified about sexual violence, had finally forced federal intervention and congressional action on behalf of their humanity. It was perhaps the most dangerous threat to white hierarchy yet.

.   .   .

Die-hard segregationists responded by mobilizing an army of Klansmen and other rigid racists to discredit and disrupt the freedom struggle. In Selma, Alabama, in 1965, they used the age-old fear of interracial sex and black-on-white rape to unleash a campaign of terror that began with the beatings on the Edmund Pettus Bridge during the Selma-to-Montgomery march and culminated in the murder of Viola Liuzzo. Liuzzo, a white housewife from Detroit, embraced the civil rights movement and died in a hail of gunfire while ferrying demonstrators in her automobile. Her detractors, of course, accused her of embracing black men.

CHAPTER 7

Sex and Civil Rights

ON MARCH 25, 1965, more than ten thousand civil rights activists and supporters spilled into downtown Montgomery, Alabama, and assembled where Jefferson Davis had once taken the oath of office as president of the Confederacy and where George Wallace had recently declared, "Segregation now, segregation tomorrow, segregation forever!" The interracial throng had passed four hard days and four harrowing nights on the lonely highway that connects Selma to the state's capital. They braved a pounding rain and slept in strangers' fields to demand voting rights and federal protection from violence.[1] The normally bustling downtown was nearly empty since Governor George Wallace declared a "danger holiday for female state employees," ostensibly to protect them from the sexual threat posed by black marchers.[2] The empty streets did not seem to bother the weary but jubilant crowd. "Segregation is on its deathbed in Alabama," Martin Luther King declared to the cheering audience. "The only uncertain thing," King added, "is how costly the segregationists and [Governor George] Wallace will make the funeral."[3]

Segregation would not die gracefully. During the Selma-to-Montgomery march, Alabama's staunchest segregationists used a kind of sexual McCarthyism in order to defame the demonstrators and to derail the new legislation that Lyndon Johnson had sent to Congress guaranteeing the right of African Americans to vote. The appeal to whites' baser instincts, and fears about sex and race, indicates how desperate the diehards had become. It also underscored the importance of sex and sexualized violence to the maintenance of white supremacy. They no longer smeared civil rights activists as mere Communists or outside agitators; now they were purely sex fiends, intent on spreading a culture of depravity throughout the country. But by 1965, these tactics were increasingly less effective.

Situated in the center of Alabama's Black Belt, an area known for its rich, inky soil and grinding poverty, Selma mirrored the Mississippi Delta in its history of near-feudal oppression of African Americans. By the 1960s, the White Citizens' Council (WCC) held dominion over the rolling pastures and cotton fields that surrounded the riverfront town.[4] The mayor of Selma and the county probate judge chose its leadership; the presidents of Selma's banks sat on the council's executive committee; both editors of Selma's newspapers were "zealous adherents" to the dictates of the WCC; Selma's two radio stations and lone television outlet aired Citizens' Council propaganda as a public service; and white preachers presented their ideology as the gospel truth during Sunday services. State senator Walter Givhan, whose sprawling plantation sat in the western corner of the county, was in the WCC's pocket. He served as chairman of the Dallas County chapter until 1958 and then led the statewide Association of Alabama White Citizens' Councils for four years.[5] In Selma, there was no room for opposition to the councils' rigid racial and sexual ideology, even among whites.

James Clark, the bellicose county sheriff who wore a "Never" (integrate) button pinned to his uniform, enforced white supremacy with an iron fist. Standing more than six feet tall and weighing 220 pounds, Clark strode through Selma as if he were General Patton. He wore a hard helmet and had a .38-caliber pistol strapped to his side and a swagger stick and an electric cattle prod dangling from his belt. Clark policed white conformity and terrorized African Americans by parading through town with a mounted posse made up of Citizens' Council and Klan members. When SNCC organizers arrived in 1962 to help register blacks to vote—less than one percent were registered in Dallas County—Sheriff Clark stood at the top of the courthouse steps, blocking the entrance.[6]

The most polite request to enter the registrar's office could set off Clark's notorious temper, prompting beatings, mass arrests, and other violent outbursts. For example, in mid-January 1965 Clark snatched Mrs. Amelia

Dallas County sheriff Jim Clark uses a billy club and an electric cattle prod to push voting-rights activists away from the courthouse.

Boynton, a prominent member of the black community and head of the Dallas County Voters League, from a long line of people waiting to register. He grabbed her coat lapels, pulled her toward his fleshy, scowling face, then shoved her down the sidewalk toward a patrol car. He arrested Boynton for "criminal provocation." The next month Clark beat James Bevel, an organizer for SCLC, with a nightstick and threw him in jail. Each night police hosed down Bevel with cold water until he was shaking with viral pneumonia. When a group of black schoolchildren held a silent demonstration outside the courthouse in mid-February, Clark lined them up and forced them to march three miles out of town to a gravel pit, shocking them with his electric cattle prod along the way.

Clark's "primitive itch to attack Negroes," as Taylor Branch put it, drove him thirty miles outside Dallas County to Marion, Alabama, on February 18, 1965, where local activists planned a nighttime march. Clark stood among state troopers who amassed outside Zion's Chapel Methodist Church, waiting for the five hundred protesters inside to file out. When the doors to the chapel opened, police shot out the streetlights, sprayed black paint on the lenses of reporters' cameras, and charged into the crowd. "Negroes could be heard screaming," *The New York Times* reported, "and

Jim Clark ordered hundreds of schoolchildren arrested after they held a silent demonstration outside the Dallas County Courthouse on February 3, 1965. He forced them to march three miles out of town to a detention center.

loud whacks rang through the square."[7] State trooper James Bonard Fowler and a handful of other policemen chased a group of activists into Mack's Café, then overturned tables and lunged at patrons. When Jimmie Lee Jackson, a young black laborer, saw an officer beating his mother, he rushed to her defense, thrusting himself between the police and her crumpled body. Fowler responded by pumping two bullets into Jackson's stomach. He died eight days later.[8]

The brazen murder of Jimmie Lee Jackson by an Alabama state trooper and the police brutality on display in Marion that cold winter night infuriated African Americans around Selma. Many felt the federal government was responsible since it had promoted voter registration but refused to protect black lives. "He was murdered," Martin Luther King, Jr., said at Jackson's funeral, "by the irresponsibility of every politician from governors on down who has fed his constituents the stale bread of hatred and the spoiled meat of racism." Jackson, King continued, "was murdered by the timidity of a federal government that can spend millions of dollars a day to keep troops in South Vietnam and cannot protect the lives of its own citizens seeking the right to vote."[9] King and the SCLC proposed a symbolic march from Selma to Montgomery. "We wanted to carry Jimmie's body to George Wallace and dump it on the steps of the capitol," Albert Turner, the leader of the Marion movement, said later. "We had decided that we were going to be killed or we was going to be free."[10]

The goal of the march was to force federal action by focusing national media attention on Selma as Sheriff Clark and his gang of Klansmen committed acts of brutality. This had been the SCLC's strategy in Birmingham in 1963, where the irascible and intemperate "Bull" Connor, who hailed from Selma, reacted to nonviolent black activism with violence. His decision to unleash ferocious police dogs and fire hoses on African-American children protesting segregation in 1963 was met by national and international outrage and, as civil rights leaders predicted, federal action.[11] Sheriff Clark proved to be as helpfully hot-tempered as Connor: "We should put him on the staff," one SCLC organizer cracked.[12] King announced that the Selma-to-Montgomery march would begin on March 7, 1965.

Ordered by Governor Wallace a day earlier to prevent the march to Montgomery, state troopers and local policemen in riot gear amassed at the foot of Edmund Pettus Bridge and spread out across Highway 80. As Colonel Al Lingo oversaw his team of troopers, and Jim Clark's men saddled up their horses and dispersed gas masks, a line of African Americans, two abreast, made their way slowly across the Alabama River. After crossing the bridge, they came face-to-face with a human barricade.[13] "When we got to the apex of the bridge, and started down," F. D. Reese, president of the Dallas County Voters League, said, "you saw nothing but a sea of blue. Helmets, state trooper cars, saw masks on the belt of the state troopers, billy clubs and so forth."[14]

Like the silence that settles in before an enormous storm, all was quiet as the well-dressed black men and women paused to consider their options. Major John Cloud, Lingo's deputy, picked up a bullhorn and ordered the crowd to disperse. "This is an unlawful assembly . . . Go home or go to your church," he bellowed. "This march will not continue. Is that clear?" Hosea Williams, an SCLC leader who stood at the front of the line, managed to squeak out a request to talk to Cloud, but the major quickly shut him up. "There is no word to be had," Cloud declared. Then he turned to his troopers and ordered them to advance.[15]

With their clubs thrust out like bayonets, the line of police slowly moved forward until they stood nose to nose with the marchers, who had not budged. Sounds of gunfire broke the silence when Sheriff Jim Clark discharged a canister of tear gas. Others quickly followed his lead. Amid the billowing gas, state troopers and the mounted posse charged into the line of protesters, mercilessly beating them with nightsticks and rubber hoses laced with spikes.[16] Horses trampled on the fallen, and the dense crack of hard wood on human bones could be heard over the din.[17]

Bloody Sunday. An Alabama state trooper accosts Annie Cooper, an African-American woman, as members of Jim Clark's mounted posse rally in the background.

That evening ABC interrupted the forty-eight million Americans who were watching the television premiere of *Judgment at Nuremberg,* an Academy Award–winning film about Nazi war crimes, to broadcast scenes from the wanton attack on African Americans in Selma.[18] Images of policemen clubbing women as they struggled to stand and mounted officers flattening children shocked sympathetic Americans and sent a powerful message about the brutality of Jim Crow. When Martin Luther King, Jr., called for another march to protest what they now called "Bloody Sunday," thousands of supporters streamed into Selma.

Though Sheriff Clark and Al Lingo had been exposed as brutal bullies to the entire nation, local whites hailed them as heroes. As civil rights workers planned their response to Bloody Sunday, Clark and his men believed they had gotten the best of King and his allies. After a federal injunction stymied a second demonstration on March 9, scores of students, sharecroppers, seminarians, and civil rights sympathizers from all walks of life poured into the town. When they finally braced for the long walk to Montgomery on March 21, they did so under federal protection.[19] Segregationists responded by defaming the demonstrators as sexual fiends.

The Alabama state legislature fired the opening salvo on March 23, 1965, by printing Act 159 in the *Montgomery Advertiser.* The act accused civil rights activists of leading the "innocent people of Alabama" into a den of corruption and sin. "There is evidence of much fornication," the resolution stated, "and young women are returning to their respective states apparently as unwed expectant mothers."[20] A few days later William Dickinson, the freshman congressman from Alabama, denounced the marchers as perverts on the floor of the United States House of Representatives. "Drunkenness and sex orgies were the order of the day," he fumed. "Negro and white freedom marchers invaded a Negro church in Montgomery and engaged in an all night session of debauchery within the church itself."[21]

Dickinson dismissed any notion that activists volunteered to go to Selma. He had proof, he said, that they were actually "hired to march for ten dollars a day, free room and board and all the sex they wanted." When civil rights activists were not engaging in "instances of public sexual intercourse," Dickinson proclaimed, they spent their time "in a hotel in Montgomery" engaged in group sex. [22] "Free love," the congressman continued, "is not only condoned, it is encouraged . . . Only by the ultimate sex act with one of another color can they demonstrate they have no prejudice." Dickinson promised skeptical legislators and constituents sworn affidavits from eyewitnesses, photographs, and "motion picture proof" showing that "this bunch of Godless riff-raff engaged in acts of indecency." Dickinson would only allow House members to view his "proof" privately, however, as it was "too obscene for public showing."[23]

Dickinson could not resist the opportunity to make money and political hay from the salacious stories. Indeed, the affidavits and photos were not too obscene to publicize in a magazine, written and distributed to the public by Albert C. Persons, a stringer for *Life*. Hired by Congressman Dickinson to investigate the demonstrations in Selma, Persons's "findings" appeared in his voyeuristic and somewhat pornographic glossy, *Sex and Civil Rights: The True Selma Story*. The propaganda piece sold for one dollar and quickly became one of the best-selling books that season.[24] *Sex and Civil Rights* documented alleged "eyewitness" accounts of white female volunteers who "had no underpants on" and of public "smooching and lovemaking between Negroes and whites." Persons spared no details in describing the so-called "sex acts" between James Forman, executive director of SNCC, and a "red-haired girl whose name is Rachel." Apparently, an anonymous African-American mole saw Forman and "Rachel" engaging in "an abnormal sex act which consisted of each of the two manipulating the other's private parts with their mouths simultaneously."[25]

Most of the so-called eyewitness accounts and affidavits came from state troopers and reflected segregationists' salacious interracial fantasies.[26] Walter L. Allen, one of Colonel Lingo's key deputies, claimed he "lost count of the times I saw Negro and Caucasian males fondling the breasts of black and white girls." He also alleged that he saw "one white girl holding a Negro's penis through his trousers." Captain John Williams swore that he saw "white girls and Negro boys laying under blankets on the grass . . . From their movement," he said, "it is my best judgment that they were having intercourse."[27] Interestingly, nearly all the accounts detailed behavior that occurred over a week *before* the march began—before most white volunteers had arrived in Selma. And most of the affidavits offered different variations of the same story, as if each witness simply repeated official talking points.

Many of the photos offered up as irrefutable proof of interracial impropriety consisted of cleverly doctored images.[28] One in particular shows three men, two black and one white, wrestling with one another, the white man's hand thrust between the legs of a black man. The caption, three question marks, suggested the strange positioning was a sign of homosexuality.[29] Another photo focuses in on a white woman and black man standing arm in arm—and completely out of proportion—amid a number of African Americans sitting on the ground.[30] The pictures that do not look doctored feature leading captions. For example, one photo of a trash can full of 7-Up bottles pretends to offer evidence of excessive drunkenness by asking, "No Booze?"[31]

Other sections of the magazine portray the leading ministers of the movement, Martin Luther King, Jr., and Ralph Abernathy, as sexual deviants by linking them to Bayard Rustin, a master strategist who organized the March on Washington in 1963 and who was openly gay at a time when it was despised and criminalized.[32] While the section, entitled "Bayard and Ralph, Just a Couple of the Boys," claims to "not be concerned with a person's private sex life," it goes to enormous lengths to detail their sexual misadventures. Included is a 1953 police report detailing Rustin's arrest for "sex perversion" and a partial transcript from a 1958 trial in which details of Ralph Abernathy's extramarital affair were exposed.

Persons viewed leaking this information as a public service that would be instructive, he said, "to any who are interested in knowing what direction the civil rights movement may be moving."[33] *Sex and Civil Rights* gave credibility to the outrageous rumors swirling around the Selma march. Its professional veneer and glossy photographs, sworn affidavits by well-known state officials, and facsimiles of official documents made the propaganda piece a politically useful tool. Coming on the heels of Dickinson's speech to the House of Representatives, the book bolstered the congressman's claims and helped disseminate them among the broader public.

African Americans protested the rumors, which to them seemed utterly ridiculous. "These white folks must think we're supermen to be able to march all day in the rain," one marcher said, " . . . and make whoopee all night and then get up the next morning and march all day."[34] Virginia Durr, a white civil rights supporter from Montgomery, worried that society was losing "all sense of reality." The stories about "sexual orgies," she said with exasperation, "are quoted and believed all over town."[35] One story particularly irked Durr. In a letter to fellow activists Carl and Anne Braden on May 3, 1965, she said that according to rumors, "SNCC Kids (Negroes) raped a white girl in the Ben Moore Hotel forty-seven times, and was taken to St. Margaret's, where she died." Durr called St. Margaret's to verify the rumor and found that it contained "not a word of truth."[36] Still, the whole town, Durr complained, "BELIEVES THE CHARGES AND REPEATS THEM OVER AND OVER. And whether the girl was raped forty-three times or forty-seven times is a matter of great debate."[37]

Some enterprising reporters tried to debunk Dickinson's claims and other rumors of sexual debauchery, but many preferred to let their readers decide what to believe.[38] "Did Martin Luther King's organization recruit civil rights mercenaries with offers of money plus food and sex?" Al Kuettner, a reporter for the United Press, asked. "A substantial segment of southern society believes the answer is yes." As for the most commonly repeated charge of wild orgies under the tents each night, Kuettner said, the truth "depends on your definition of an orgy."[39]

The *New York Times* offered a more balanced analysis that allowed the participants some space for rebuttal. It accused Dickinson of "spreading slanderous falsehoods" in an effort to "defame and debunk the whole civil rights movement with a new type of McCarthyism."[40] John Lewis, chairman of SNCC, told the *Times* that Dickinson and Persons's smears were nothing new. "Segregationists are preoccupied with interracial sex," he argued. "Which is why you see so many shades of brown on the march."[41] Virginia Durr seconded Lewis's assessment. "All of the cesspool of sickness connected with sex guilt comes out in these stories," she said. Segregationists' fear of interracial sex and corresponding paranoia, she said, "came from the fact that white men of the South had had so many sexual affairs with black women. And they just turned it around. It's the only thing I can figure out that made them so crazy on the subject."[42]

But it was not just the "crazies," as Durr put it, who were afflicted by sexual paranoia that summer.[43] Congressman Dickinson's efforts were part of a broader campaign run out of Governor George Wallace's office to discredit the civil rights movement. Wallace commissioned a film that purported to document "the inflammatory activity . . . by beatniks, pinkos, misguided do-gooders, and out and out communist sympathizers" that occurred on the Selma-to-Montgomery march. A press release issued by the cigar-chomping Wallace promised that the film would "Stand Up for Alabama." Since "the left-wingers spend millions of dollars to promote their causes," he said, "certainly we, as independent, freedom-loving Alabamians, can do as much."[44] Mainstream magazines like *Time, Newsweek,* and *U.S. News* "stood up for Alabama" without any prodding from Wallace. They provided a national platform and some measure of respectability for the rumors in articles entitled "Kiss and Tell," "Charges of Interracial Sex," and "Orgies on the Rights March."[45]

A few months later Sheriff Jim Clark hurled the final and what was perhaps the crudest accusation. *I Saw Selma Raped,* Clark's personal account of events that spring, portrayed civil rights activists and the federal government as sexual vampires, eager to attack an innocent and defenseless city.[46] "Make no mistake about it," Clark argued in the book, "sex and civil rights go together in the most licentious ways possible to imagine."[47] Nationwide repetition of state propaganda contributed greatly to the racial and sexual hysteria that swirled around Selma that spring and summer. It was within this storm—and perhaps as a result of it—that four Klansmen murdered white Detroit housewife Viola Liuzzo.

Shuttling tired marchers back and forth from Montgomery to Selma on the night of March 25, Liuzzo and Leroy Moton, a nineteen-year-old African American, knew they had to be on the lookout for hostile Klan members waiting to attack them on the dark and lonely stretches of Highway 80. What they didn't know was that a carload of Klan members, whipped into a frenzy by the wild rumors of interracial sex, spotted them at a stoplight in Selma shortly before their final trip of the day. "Well, I'll be damned," a Klansman exclaimed when he saw Liuzzo sitting next to Moton in the front seat of her Oldsmobile. Eager to send a powerful message about interracial mixing, they trailed the volunteers as they drove toward Montgomery, speculating about all the "lewd acts the racially mixed couple must have in mind."[48] When they had gotten far enough out of town and into a desolate stretch of highway through Lowndes County, the car carrying the four Klan members overtook Liuzzo's vehi-

Viola Liuzzo

cle. With their guns poking out of the rolled-down windows, the Klansmen fired into Liuzzo's speeding car, killing her instantly. She slumped over the steering wheel while Moton frantically steered the car into a ditch. Moton remained absolutely still as the men got out of their car and inspected their work. With blood splattered all over Liuzzo and Moton, the Klansmen drove off believing they had killed both passengers. Deeply shaken but alive, Moton crawled out of the car, flagged down a passing truck full of freedom marchers, and told them about the brutal murder.[49]

When FBI director J. Edgar Hoover found out about the murder from Gary Thomas Rowe, a paid informant who received permission from the FBI to ride along with the Klan that night, he immediately began damage control.[50] Jack Anderson, a reporter for *The Washington Post,* speculated that, in an effort to protect himself and the FBI from any appearance of complicity, Hoover "marshaled the bureau's resources to blacken the dead woman's reputation."[51] Anderson's use of the term "blacken" is particularly apt. Within twenty-four hours after Klansmen killed Liuzzo, the director of the FBI portrayed her as a traitor to her race, a prostitute, and a derelict mother—what Klan lawyer Matt Murphy later called a "white nigger"—who got what she deserved.[52]

In an internal memo sent to President Lyndon Johnson the next morning, Hoover deflected any bureau responsibility in the murder by echoing the Klan's justification for killing Liuzzo. Hoover advised President Johnson, who was under pressure to call Liuzzo's husband and offer condolences, to hold back, arguing that she was not a respectable woman worthy

An Alabama state trooper's car is parked near the site where the Ku Klux
Klan fatally shot Viola Liuzzo and injured Leroy Moton.

of presidential sympathy. By riding around with a black man after dark,
Hoover argued, she was outside the bounds of white womanhood. Liuzzo,
he said, had "indications of needle marks in her arms where she had been
taking dope." And, he added, she had been "sitting very, very close to the
Negro in the car; it had the appearance of a necking party."[53] Hoover then
instructed staffers to "leak his speculations to Klan informants," who in
turn sent them to their press contacts.[54] The media blitz successfully
changed the subject from FBI complicity in a killing to questions about
Liuzzo's morality and fitness as a mother.[55]

Despite Hoover's personal biases and beliefs, the FBI apprehended the
culprits and assembled a legal case against them. At the state murder trial
in Haynesville, Alabama, which began on May 6, 1965, Klan attorney
Matt H. Murphy defended his clients and his organization by claiming
to protect white supremacy. "I am proud to be a white man," Murphy
declared in a studied drawl. "I am proud to stand on my feet," he said,
pumping his fist into the air, "and say that I am for white supremacy."
"This white woman," he said, then paused and turned toward the jurors
with a grin. "White woman?" he sneered, "Hah! Where's that N.A.A.C.P.
card?" Digging into his breast pocket, he pulled out Liuzzo's bloodied
membership card. He had found it earlier that day while rummaging
through Liuzzo's purse.[56] Murphy's defense relied upon denouncing Liuzzo
as a "white nigger" and repeated innuendos suggesting she and Moton
"were linked in a sexual relationship." It did not seem to matter to either

An all-white jury found Klansmen Collie Leroy Wilkins (in hat), Eugene Thomas (center stairs), and William Eaton (top) not guilty for the murder of Viola Liuzzo. On December 3, 1965, Wilkins, Thomas, and Eaton were found guilty of conspiracy to violate Liuzzo's civil rights, a federal charge.

Murphy or the jury that the state toxicologist, Dr. Paul Shoffelt, found absolutely "no evidence of recent sexual relations" when he performed Liuzzo's autopsy.[57]

The attacks on Liuzzo's character were worse than most newspapers indicated. Virginia Durr could barely stomach Murphy's repeated aspersions in court. "The three days at the trial made me sick, literally," she said in a letter to friends. "The poor dead woman was on trial and the Counsel for the KKK asked the most vile and obscene questions about the state of her underwear and her dead body." They tried to turn her into "some kind of sex fiend as well as a dope fiend." Murphy, she said, piled "vileness upon vileness," all in the name of "Southern White Tradition and Pure White Southern Womanhood."[58] The venomous attacks terrified Durr: "I get both sick and frightened by [the Klan]," she said.[59]

The Klan made no effort to hide its presence at the trial; Klansmen strutted around the courtroom as if they owned it. Robert Shelton, the Imperial Wizard of the Knights of the Ku Klux Klan in Alabama, weaved through the aisles, shaking hands and chatting with white spectators. He advised the defendants, offered himself up for news interviews, and disparaged Liuzzo mercilessly. Liuzzo was not a "mother of five lovely children and a community worker," he said to a reporter; she was a "fat slob with crud that looked like rust all over her body." Worse, he added, she was frequently "bra-less."[60] He also assured anyone who would listen that he had eyewitnesses who "saw Liuzzo behaving like a whore."[61] Defense attorneys used the same strategy to justify Liuzzo's murder: "Klonsel" Murphy argued that "acquittal is certain." Integration, he said to the journalist William Bradford Huie, "breaks every moral law God wrote . . . All I need to use is the fact that Mrs. Liuzzo was in the car with a nigger man and she wore no underpants."[62]

Prosecuting attorneys at the trial did nothing to defend Liuzzo's dignity; nor did they try to rebut attacks launched by the defense. "No one, prosecutor or defense lawyer, had a kind word for the dead woman during the four day trial," *The New York Times* reported.[63] Even her personal items retrieved from the crime scene were treated with disrespect. Instead of receiving protection as state's evidence, the bloodstained objects found in her car were thrown into a bunch of cardboard boxes and were made available to reporters and Klansmen, who rustled through them at will.[64] The only attempt prosecution made to humanize Liuzzo was by presenting her as a mother of five children.[65] Surprisingly, ten jurors voted for a conviction of manslaughter, which carried a ten-year sentence, while two held out for an acquittal. The deadlock forced the judge to declare a mistrial.[66]

Although most jurors believed the Klansmen were guilty of manslaughter, many felt Liuzzo was just as culpable for violating the gender and racial norms of the day. One woman who sat in on the trial told reporters that she didn't "know why they kept calling Mrs. Liuzzo a 'mother of five children.' " "A mother wouldn't have gone off," she said, "and left her children and come here."[67] "I have five children, too," Sheriff Clark told a reporter, "but the night this happened, my wife was at home with the children where she belongs."[68] Clark's statements reflected popular opinion about women's roles at the time. A survey in *Ladies' Home Journal* showed that a majority of American women felt that Liuzzo did the wrong thing by leaving her children to risk her life for a social cause. Fifty-five percent "felt strongly" that she "should have stayed home" while only twenty-six percent said she "had a right" to go.[69] For most of the women surveyed, Liuzzo's decision to go to Selma defied acceptable maternal and feminine behavior.

While civil rights activists viewed Viola Liuzzo as a martyr who gave her life for equal justice and African-American dignity, many whites viewed her as an abject mother, guilty of the most reprehensible crime: abandoning her children in favor of cavorting with black men. The truth—that Liuzzo had help at home and did not abandon her children, that she did not use drugs or engage in extramarital sex with African Americans—did not seem to matter. Rumors about her fitness as a mother and lack of sexual and racial restraint only added to the belief that by traveling to Selma to help with civil rights, she had ventured far outside the bounds of respectable white womanhood. When J. Edgar Hoover fanned the flames of these rumors in order to protect his own secrets, he did not just "blacken" her character; he treated her the way white men had historically treated black women.

The attacks on Viola Liuzzo foreshadowed the criticism heaped on black women and families in a report issued by the Department of Labor at the end of that summer.[70] Named after the assistant secretary of labor, Daniel Patrick Moynihan, the "Moynihan Report" blamed decades of matriarchy for the "crisis" of black family pathology and degeneration, instead of the legacy of white supremacy, laws banning interracial marriage, and the historic rape of black women by white men.[71] Stokely Carmichael, the charismatic proponent of "Black Power" who became the head of SNCC in 1966, pointed to the history of sexualized violence and argued that matriarchy was not the problem. "The reason we are in this bag isn't because of my mamma," he said, "it's because of what they did to my mamma."[72] Other comments from prominent black leaders echoed Carmichael's concerns. "For two centuries," Bayard Rustin said, "black families had been denied human status in order to safeguard the property rights and breeding prerogatives of slave owners." Martin Luther King, Jr., agreed. The problem of black poverty was rooted in a past too "ghastly" to discuss, he said. "No one in all history had to fight against so many psychological and physical horrors to have a family life," King noted. "Our children and our families are maimed a little every day of their lives."[73] News outlets did not focus on the legacy of segregation and sexualized violence on the black family. Instead, reporters pointed to black pathology as the reason for poverty and rising crime rates in Northern and Western cities.

The riots in the Watts section of Los Angeles were used to bolster those claims. On August 11, 1965, five days after Lyndon Johnson signed the Voting Rights Act into law, Watts exploded in a race riot. The five-day firestorm exposed the powder keg of racial tension and economic instability in American urban centers and destroyed any myths about the North and West as "the promised land." As the locus of racial turbulence shifted from the rural South to Northern cities, the nation turned its sympathy and attention away from civil rights. Urban riots, increased American involvement in Vietnam, a nascent antiwar movement, and a growing belief that the Voting Rights Act completed African Americans' campaign for civil rights made it easy for many Americans to ignore ongoing struggles for dignity and justice in the South as the sweltering summer of 1965 gave way to the crisp days of fall.

On November 11, 1965, however, African Americans in Hattiesburg, Mississippi, won one of the most important legal cases in the civil rights movement. As in Selma, white segregationists in Hattiesburg were on the defensive, but their response to the abduction and rape of an African-American teenager shocked the nation. The story has been largely forgotten.

Hattiesburg was the only city in the southern half of Mississippi where SNCC made inroads organizing the local black community before 1963. Nestled in the Piney Woods section of the state and home to the University of Southern Mississippi, Hattiesburg was somewhat less violent than the Delta towns, though it was equally repressive in denying African Americans the right to vote.[74] Theron Lynd, the Forrest County circuit clerk, disfranchised so many African Americans that, as John Dittmer noted, he "put his Delta counterparts to shame."[75] Lynd was "totally uncooperative; totally hostile; and very rude," Victoria Gray Adams, a local black businesswoman active in voter-registration campaigns, said. "He just did everything possible to discourage you aside from saying 'get out of here.' "[76] To curtail fear and build confidence, Victoria Gray Adams and Vernon Dahmer, a businessman, voting-rights activist, and two-term head of the local NAACP, worked with local people to organize citizenship schools and voter-registration drives. Over time their efforts helped make Hattiesburg what historians later called the "Mecca of the Freedom School" movement.[77]

Like the men and women who defied white supremacy in the Delta and Alabama's Black Belt, African Americans in the Piney Woods region faced immediate economic and physical reprisals by hostile whites. Hattiesburg was only thirty miles away from Poplarville, where a white mob kidnapped and lynched Mack Charles Parker in 1959. That same year white officials from Hattiesburg with ties to the State Sovereignty Commission framed and imprisoned Clyde Kennard, a thirty-five-year-old native of Forrest County and World War II vet, who tried to desegregate the University of Southern Mississippi. Judge Stanton Hall sentenced him to seven years in Parchman penitentiary for allegedly masterminding a plot to steal twenty-five dollars' worth of chicken feed. Ignoring Kennard's advanced cancer, prison officials forced him to do backbreaking labor in Parchman's fields each day.[78]

Despite federal intervention in Mississippi during Freedom Summer, by the end of 1964 a Ku Klux Klan resurgence threatened black activists throughout the state.[79] In Laurel, Mississippi, a small town just outside Hattiesburg, Sam Bowers, the forty-year-old Imperial Wizard of the White Knights of the Ku Klux Klan, declared that his mission "was the destruction of the Mississippi civil rights movement." Since the White Citizens' Council had been unable to crush the freedom movement, the White Knights felt it was their turn to try. According to the *Hattiesburg American,* the White Knights were known as the "most secretive and violent of the Klan groups in Mississippi."[80] Bowers ordered members and like-minded supporters to stockpile weapons and ammunition, practice military drills, and study "counterattack maps, plans and information" to prepare for the coming racial Armageddon. His appetite for violence was well known. Though most suspected his involvement in the kidnapping and murder of James Chaney, Andrew Goodman, and Michael Schwerner in the summer of 1964, he was not convicted until 1967, and then only for violating their civil rights.[81] The revival of the Klan, especially one focused on racial terrorism, worried moderate segregationists who preferred to intimidate blacks without physical brutality, which tended to draw media and federal attention.

Victoria Gray Adams and other Hattiesburg blacks hoped to draw the federal government into the fray. In the spring of 1965, Adams and Dahmer invited white clergy from the National Council of Churches to join "Freedom Day," a massive voter-registration campaign designed to highlight Theron Lynd's defiance of the new Voting Rights Act. Adams and others thought that the presence of white clergy, like Northern students' involvement in Freedom Summer, would surely inflame Bowers and other segregationists who would act foolishly enough to draw national interest. Local police, however, bucked Bowers and the Klan and adopted a nonviolent approach toward the activists. It was the same strategy that Laurie Pritchett, the chief of police in Albany, Georgia, effectively used to stymie an SCLC campaign in 1961. Instead of beating blacks who sought the franchise, police quietly and gently arrested them, denying them the media attention they needed. Even stubborn Theron Lynd grudgingly allowed more than 150 African Americans to complete the registration test.[82]

Though media coverage failed to materialize, the successful registration campaign nonetheless strengthened the movement in Hattiesburg. At the same time it strained relationships between the "moderate" and radical forces of white supremacy. With the federal government more willing to intervene and the legal structures of Jim Crow nearly destroyed, whites in Mississippi struggled to maintain their unity as well as their power. These tensions were on display in Hattiesburg in the fall of 1965, when a white man stood before a white judge and jury for kidnapping and raping an African-American teenager.

On July 13, 1965, Norman Cannon, a slim, bushy-haired young man, pulled his old-model red-and-white Chevrolet up to Mrs. Lillie Beal's little shotgun house in a Negro neighborhood in Hattiesburg. He told the older woman he was "looking for a babysitter." He had spoken to one of Mrs. Beal's neighbors, he said, who suggested there was "a young girl living here who sought work." Cannon told Beal that he lived across town and that he would be happy to drive her fifteen-year-old granddaughter, Rosa Lee Coates, to his house to "keep the children while he and his wife were away."[83] Lois Miles, a neighbor, recalled that Cannon's visit was not uncommon. "Whites came by a lot," she said, "to sell their wares—greens, fish, cookies." She said that it was not unusual for white men and women to come searching for day workers and babysitters, either.[84] Rosa Lee Coates agreed to babysit and got into Cannon's car. When it was clear he was not driving across town, but out of town, the young girl protested. After traveling about fifteen miles, past Rawls Spring Road and over the Big Creek Bridge, Cannon pulled onto a heavily shaded gravel road used by a logging company. Wielding a yellow-handled knife, he pushed the girl out of his car and threatened to cut her head off unless she submitted. Beneath a canopy of towering pines and atop a mound of fire ants, Cannon raped Coates at knifepoint and then quickly drove away, leaving her stranded in the woods.[85]

Not long after the attack, a passing motorist found the teenager wandering dazedly along Highway 49. He picked her up and rushed her to the hospital, where she told local police and her grandmother what happened.[86] Within forty-eight hours, police held Cannon in custody, and Coates easily identified him out of an eight-man lineup. Police notified district attorney James Finch and James Dukes, the young county prosecutor, about the crime. Finch was a gray-haired courthouse hand, Dukes a newly minted lawyer with a blond buzz cut, but they both knew they faced a dilemma. If they brought a case against Cannon, it would be the first time in Forrest County history that a white man was charged with raping a black woman. If he were acquitted, it could arouse and anger local African-American leaders, who were well organized and feeling stronger after their successful Freedom Day registration drive. Yet both men, as members of the town's white elite, were also well aware of the state's desire to avoid federal attention and bolster Mississippi's reputation after the atrocities committed during Freedom Summer. Even the State Sovereignty Commission, once considered the "watchdog of segregation," was now engaged in a public relations campaign. The new goal, as a press release put it, was to "project Mississippi outside the state, as a good place to be, as a good place to work [and] as a good place to settle down."[87]

Aware of the potential public relations disaster, Finch, Dukes, and other white city officials met for several hours the night of the attack and chewed over the political implications of the case.[88] "This was not a pleasant case," Dukes said later. "In prior years," he said, "when whites committed acts like this they just swept them under the rug." After much debate, Finch and Dukes decided to file rape charges against Cannon—a first for Forrest County and a highly unusual step in Mississippi. Four days after the attack, the Forrest County grand jury indicted Norman Cannon and sent him to the county jail to await his trial.[89]

Dressed in a dark suit and polished loafers, Cannon pleaded innocent on November 9, 1965, the first day of his trial.[90] Cannon admitted he was not married and had had sexual relations with the African-American girl, but he denied using any force. He then spun a long story designed to exculpate himself from any guilt. Cannon told the judge and jury that three days before he picked up Rosa Lee Coates, he saw her standing near a bus stop with a white boy "all hugged-up together." When the bus pulled to the curb and the white boy got on, Cannon approached the heavyset teenager, he said, and asked her "if she liked to go out with white boys." When the teenager said yes, Cannon said, he asked her out on a date. He testified that Coates told him "he could take her out . . . any day, just to come by her house and say he needed a babysitter."[91] When asked by the prosecution why he wanted to date an African-American girl, Can-

County prosecutor James Dukes (left) and district attorney James Finch outside the Forrest County Courthouse.

non told the jury he became interested in having an interracial affair after "watching television programs which showed Negroes and whites dating."[92] Finch and Dukes, the *Hattiesburg American* reported, "snorted with disgust" at the outlandish excuse. "He was not the sharpest knife in the box," Dukes said later.[93]

On the stand, Cannon continued to spin his yarn. He claimed he used the agreed-upon code word on July 13 and drove the girl outside town, where she readily had sex with him. Cannon's description of their "romp" in the woods and his attorney's portrayal of Coates as a prostitute became "so rugged," according to the *Hattiesburg American,* that the court reporter, Betty Hamil, threw her pen down and excused herself from the courtroom. "The whole damn jury wanted to walk out," Dukes said. "It was the most disgusting thing." "We had to get a male reporter out of Vicksburg just to continue," Dukes recalled. "Betty Hamil said she was just not going to do it. She had been court reporter for gruesome murder cases. Klan cases. But that case? Well," Dukes said, "she couldn't do it."[94]

Cannon's story may have sounded plausible to whites inclined to believe that all black women were sexually promiscuous, but Finch and Dukes quickly destroyed his argument. Cannon sat "impassively" as the two attorneys took turns picking apart his story. Dr. Willis Walker, a white physician who examined the victim after the attack, testified for the prosecution that Coates had been a virgin and had sustained internal injuries consistent with rape. Police officers told the jury that they found pieces of the victim's clothing at the crime scene. They also testified that Cannon signed a statement when he was arrested denying any relationship with Rosa Lee Coates and that he had admitted he had just met her. Mary Louise Wade, a friend and neighbor of the victim, corroborated police statements. Cannon was "driving around the Negro neighborhood," she said, looking for a girl to hire. When Cannon asked Wade if she would babysit for him, she said no and suggested he go to Beal's house. "Twenty minutes later," Wade recalled, she "saw Cannon drive by her house with Rosa Lee Coates in the front seat with him." Wade identified Cannon in the courtroom.

Mrs. Lillie Beal did not hesitate, either. According to the *Hattiesburg American*, Beal "arose from the witness stand, walked across the room in front of the bench and pointed a long, brown finger at the defendant." "That's him," she said confidently, "right there." Beal testified that Cannon lured her granddaughter into his car on the pretense that he needed a babysitter. She recounted the events that led to the assault and told the jury that her granddaughter would not have consented. When she finally saw Rosa Lee at the hospital, Beal said, she was crying and was as "nervous as a wretch." "The child's brassiere was gone," Beal testified. "And her slip—all she had on was her outside dress." [95]

Cannon's counsel was the well-known Klan attorney Lawrence Arrington. A short, portly man who had represented Sam Bowers, Arrington did his best to discredit the victim. First he insinuated that Coates was sexually active by asking her grandmother if she were "fully developed." [96] Then he argued that the "hymenal laceration" the victim suffered could have "been made by most any means." When Dr. Walker said he didn't know "of any other means which deposits sperm," Arrington backed off. [97] "He thought all of this would be cute before a white jury," James Dukes said later in a slow drawl. "But it was totally repugnant. Whether it's white or black, an older white man and a young girl with her menstrual period," he said shaking his head in disgust, "it was bad." [98] When attacks on the victim seemed to fail, Arrington argued that his client was illiterate and that the jury should take pity on him because he did not have much education. [99]

Finally, the trial turned on the testimony of the victim herself. Dressed in a starched white cotton blouse, a purple skirt, yellow tennis shoes and white socks, Rosa Lee Coates presented herself as a respectable and dignified young lady. Speaking from the witness stand, she spoke in a low, steady voice. She used "fifteen-year-old words," Dukes said. "She was very subdued." Coates denied having met Cannon prior to July 13, tactfully challenged attempts by the defense to portray her as promiscuous, and described her courageous attempts to escape. Once she realized Cannon had no intention of using her as a babysitter, she said, she did everything she could to get away. When Cannon stopped the car at an intersection, she testified that she "opened the door on her side of the car and tried to jump out." But Cannon caught her, she said, and he "slammed the door on [my] right foot." Coates attempted to escape again when Cannon stopped the car on the gravel road. She told the jury that she "tried to run," but when she "slipped down in the mud," Cannon "caught the back of her dress and hit her on the side of her face." "I tried to fight," she said softly. "I was crying and asking him to leave me alone when he pulled out a knife and held it to the side of my neck." Cannon then "ripped off her clothing," she said, and in the newspaper's parlance, "ravished her." When Cannon finished, he made Coates "lie on [her] stomach, face against the ground." Then he drove away.[100]

The *Hattiesburg American,* the local white daily, was impressed with the victim's "clear and simple" testimony and reported that it was "impossible on cross-questioning to trip her up." Cannon's testimony, the newspaper reported, was "full of contradictions." [101] The jury must have agreed. After deliberating for five and a half hours, jurors emerged from isolation and delivered their verdict: guilty as charged. Because jurors believed that Cannon did not inflict brutality on the victim, they recommended mercy. As a result, he received a life sentence instead of the death penalty.[102] Still, the shocking verdict was the first of its kind in the history of Forrest County and, according to *The New York Times,* represented a "major breakthrough for the state of Mississippi."[103] The ruling, the *Jackson Advocate* reported, represented the "first time since Reconstruction that a white man had been convicted [and sentenced to life in prison] for raping a Negro."[104]

Strangely, the legal victory seemed to go unnoticed by local civil rights activists.[105] By the fall of 1965, the organizational infrastructure that existed during Freedom Summer had been disassembled. Many veteran organizers had moved away. Those who remained suffered severe "battle fatigue" or were busy waging their own small-scale wars against white supremacy.[106] Years of harassment and brutality, layered atop the murders

Cannon found guilty of rape, jury gives him life
Verdict is first of its kind in history of Forrest County; defense will appeal

The front page of the November 12, 1965, *Hattiesburg American* highlights the historic verdict.

of Goodman, Schwerner, and Chaney, and the failure of the Democratic Party to seat delegates from the Mississippi Freedom Democratic Party at the national convention in Atlantic City in the summer of 1964, left many civil rights workers worn out and disillusioned. Even the black press seemed to ignore the groundbreaking verdict.[107] The muted response at the time was unusual; historically, similar cases had served as catalysts for community mobilization.

Perhaps it was because, unlike officials in Selma, Mississippians had done everything right—there was nothing to protest and therefore no reason to organize. White police officers in Hattiesburg arrested Cannon less than forty-eight hours after the attack; prosecutors indicted him two days later and then mounted a serious case against him. Even though Cannon employed a Klan lawyer who repeatedly tried to appeal to segregationist sentiment among white jurors at the trial, Dukes and Finch—certainly no supporters of civil rights—easily deflected his racial arguments. The prosecution destroyed Cannon's flimsy justification for the heinous crime. When the defense tried to sully the victim's character, prosecutors did not stand silent, as they had in the Liuzzo case; instead, they successfully defended Coates's chastity and respectability.

"It wasn't a black and white thing," Dukes insisted years later. "Once they saw that we indicted him and we were going to prosecute him and bring him to trial—it didn't have racial overtones. It was just an unsavory character who took advantage of a fifteen-year-old."[108] Time and distance may have blunted Dukes's memory of the racial implications of the case, but their strategy worked to keep local African-American activists and the federal government at bay.

The night before the jury sentenced Cannon to life in prison, Mississippi senator John Stennis warned members of the State Farm Bureau Federation that the federal government would "assume jurisdiction" over Southern states if they failed to enforce their own laws. "We can make friends and allies," he said, "and help our own cause more by prosecuting assault, arson, bombings and like crimes." Failure to do so, Stennis argued, "would create a curtain of misunderstanding."[109] Since Mississippi could not afford any more "misunderstandings," the State Sovereignty Commission prepared to rebut outside criticism of the Cannon case.

Prior to Cannon's trial, Earle Johnston, Jr., the director of the State Sovereignty Commission, ordered a review of all the white inmates who had been sent to Parchman penitentiary for statutory rape in the past thirty years. Johnston planned to report the findings, which would then debunk any Northern arguments purporting to claim that, in his words, "Mississippi and the South in general never punish a white person who commits a crime against a Negro."[110] Tom Scarbrough, the Sovereignty Commission's best investigator, told Johnston that his research found "a number of white men have been sent to the penitentiary for various crimes committed against Negroes," but, he said, he would have clerks double-check the "race of the victims" so that "we may compile an absolute record for the good of Mississippi."[111] Instead of carping about Cannon's conviction, as they surely would have done in earlier years, Mississippi's most strident segregationists held it up as an example of the state's racial rebirth. Even the Mississippi Supreme Court upheld Cannon's conviction and life sentence a year later.[112] By punishing Cannon, state officials could bolster Mississippi's reputation outside the South and fend off further federal intrusions.

The verdict could not have come at a better time. On November 15 the *Hattiesburg American* reported that the U.S. Civil Rights Commission issued a report that "called for new laws to permit prosecution of racial violence in federal courts when local officials fail to act."[113] At the White House the next day, President Johnson told civil rights advocates that the Justice Department would act on the commission's recommendations and "introduce new civil rights legislation to attack discrimination in the justice system." "We intend to make the jury box, in both state and federal courts," he declared, "the sacred domain of justice under the law."[114] It is possible that Cannon's life sentence served as a defensive measure— a metaphorical finger in the dike, holding back federal intervention in Mississippi's courts.

Even if Senator Stennis and the Sovereignty Commission thought Cannon's conviction would shore up segregation, it had broad implications for the civil rights movement and the nation as a whole. The life sentence was recognized nationally as a major win for the African-American freedom struggle. While the legal victory flew under the radar of local civil rights activists, it made the front page of the nation's top newspapers, including *The New York Times,* the *Los Angeles Times,* and *The Washington Post.*[115] Correspondent Jack Nelson of the *Los Angeles Times* hailed the verdict as a sign of a "new respect for the Negro as a person." Until recently, he argued, "a white man could rape a Negro in Hattiesburg with virtual impunity, but . . . feelings have been changing." For example, Nelson said, "the conviction rested solely on the testimony of the Negro girl. The fact that the jury would believe [her] over [a white man] is as significant as the verdict itself."[116] And yet the story has not received the historical attention it deserves.

This is due, in part, to the jury's decision to keep Cannon from the electric chair. The life sentence fueled criticism of the South's unequal sentencing practices, breathing new life into the NAACP's campaign to end the "racial double standard" in rape cases.[117] In the spring of 1966 the NAACP Legal Defense Fund (LDF) sent its army of lawyers to court on behalf of hundreds of African-American men languishing on death row for rape. Armed with sociological studies and statistics documenting discrimination in sentencing for rape cases, its representatives demanded equal justice. Newspapers documented the LDF's new campaign and followed the organization's legal maneuvering in a number of cases, some of which reached the Supreme Court. Over time the issue became a crusade to end the death penalty.[118]

By focusing on men convicted of rape rather than the female survivors of sexual violence, the LDF's efforts steered attention away from the larger meanings of the Cannon conviction. The guilty verdict was the result of decades of black women's testimony of rape and years of campaigns to protect black women from sexual attack—from Recy Taylor to Betty Jean Owens to Rosa Lee Coates. It also came after black Mississippians' long struggle to open the "closed society" and indicated that the state of Mississippi had finally recognized black women's right to bodily integrity. Even if the life sentence served the state's political purposes, Cannon could have easily been acquitted or, more typically, could have served a minimum sentence. The attorneys' decision to take a black woman's complaint seriously, the willingness of the all-white, all-male jury to sentence Can-

Mildred and Richard Loving (sitting center) share a laugh with friends
during an outing in Virginia in 1965. In 1967 the U.S. Supreme Court
unanimously ruled that Virginia's antimiscegenation statute, which had
resulted in the couple's arrest shortly after their 1958 marriage, was
unconstitutional.

non to life in prison, and state officials' determination to let him rot in
Parchman penitentiary for many years indicated, at least symbolically, the
full arrival of African Americans as human beings. Because it destroyed a
pillar of white supremacy that was rooted in slavery—the ability of white
men to rape black women without legal consequence—the Cannon decision ought to be considered a significant milestone in the modern civil
rights movement.[119]

One of the last legal barriers to black women's bodily integrity and
respectability fell in 1967, when the Supreme Court banned laws prohibiting interracial marriage in the landmark *Loving v. Virginia* decision.
Rooted in colonial rules regulating interracial relationships, these laws
served as a foundation for slavery and white supremacy. In 1691 Virginia
legislators made "miscegenation" illegal and criminalized those who trans-
gressed this racial boundary. Designed to "prevent that abominable mix-
ture of negroes, mulattoes, and Indians intermarrying with English, or
other white women," the antimiscegenation laws awarded white men
exclusive sexual access to white women and preserved racial "purity" in
property and inheritance rights.[120] At the same time white slave masters'
stolen access to black women's bodies strengthened their political, social,

and economic power, partly because other colonial laws made the offspring of slave women the property of their masters.[121] Together, these laws denied black women the rights granted by a legal relationship by restricting and punishing marriage but not fornication or childbirth out of wedlock. They also created a system that allowed white men to use black women as concubines and sexually abuse them with impunity. By policing white women and black men's sexual and marital choices while retaining power over black women's bodies, white men maintained their position on top of the racial and sexual hierarchy. The Thirteenth Amendment abolished slavery in 1865, but the antimiscegenation laws remained.

The sixteen states that still prohibited interracial marriage in 1967 were, with one exception, all former slave states.[122] When Richard Loving, a twenty-four-year-old white bricklayer from Caroline County, Virginia, and Mildred Jeter, an eighteen-year-old black woman who was his childhood sweetheart, exchanged vows in Washington, D.C., on June 11, 1958, they avoided the 1691 law rooted in Virginia's slave past but risked arrest each time they returned to their home state.[123] When the newlyweds visited their in-laws just one month after their wedding, three policemen barged into their bedroom in the middle of the night, dragged them out of bed, and arrested them for violating the state's antimiscegenation laws.[124] The Lovings pleaded guilty in court a few months later and received a one-year prison sentence, which the judge suspended provided the interracial couple left the state and did not return as husband and wife for twenty-five years.[125] They moved to Washington, D.C., where they were safe from prosecution but were otherwise miserable. They longed for the day when they could return to Virginia to be near their families.

In 1963, at the height of the civil rights movement, Mrs. Loving sought assistance from the Justice Department. In a letter to Attorney General Robert F. Kennedy, she asked if "there was any way he could help us."[126] Kennedy suggested she contact the American Civil Liberties Union (ACLU) since it had been involved in litigation for many years to overturn laws banning interracial marriage.[127] Bernard S. Cohen, a lawyer and ACLU member from Virginia, eagerly embraced the Lovings' case. With assistance from the NAACP Legal Defense Fund, the Lovings carried their argument all the way to the Supreme Court. Cohen and members of the Legal Defense Fund argued that the law was rooted in an unconstitutional slave system and that they had a "right" to marry whomever they wanted without fear of being terrorized or treated like criminals.

On June 12, 1967, Chief Justice Earl Warren delivered the unanimous decision of the Supreme Court and declared that "the racial classifications in these statutes [are] repugnant to the Fourteenth Amendment." The Fourteenth Amendment, Warren said, required "that the freedom of choice to marry not be restricted by invidious racial discriminations."[128] The Lovings cheered the decision at a press conference later that day. Richard Loving told reporters that he and his wife were "just really overjoyed" and that they planned to "go ahead and build a new house" in Caroline County, Virginia. Mildred Loving offered a more telling analysis of what the victory meant. "I feel free now," she said.

Issued just two years after Norman Cannon was sentenced to life in prison for raping an African-American teenager, *Loving v. Virginia* signaled the emancipation of black women and constituted another nail in Jim Crow's coffin. Along with the NAACP's legal challenges to Southern jury discrimination and unequal sentencing, and passage of the 1968 Civil Rights Act granting bodily protection for civil rights workers, the Cannon and Loving verdicts ushered in the "new day of justice" for black women that John McCray had wondered about after the Tallahassee case in 1959.[129] *State v. Cannon* and *Loving v. Virginia* helped dismantle the legal infrastructure that denied black women dignity, respectability, and bodily integrity. These cases destroyed the racial and sexual argument for segregation and white supremacy. The century-long struggle to protect African-American women from white sexual violence, built upon the testimonies of black women like Ida B. Wells, Recy Taylor, Gertrude Perkins, and Betty Jean Owens, had laid the groundwork for this victory. African-American women's willingness to speak out against sexual violence, to publicly testify about interracial rape in the segregated South, and to organize campaigns to demand full legal and social rights slowly destroyed these legacies of slavery.

But would these victories last? The right of black women to defend themselves from sexual violence was tested in 1975, when Joan Little, an African-American woman from Washington, North Carolina, stood trial in the ice-pick slaying of a white jailer.

CHAPTER 8

"Power to the Ice Pick!"

IN THE QUIET DARKNESS just before daybreak on August 27, 1974, Sergeant Jerry Helms ambled into the Beaufort County Jail in Washington, North Carolina. Escorting a drunken prisoner, he walked through the double doors, down the carpeted stairs to the basement, and turned left toward the women's section of the small but clean jailhouse. Poking out of the cell of the sole female prisoner was a pair of shoeless feet in brown socks. Moving closer, Helms saw that the feet belonged to the burly, sixty-two-year-old white jailer, Clarence Alligood, whose lifeless torso slumped over his thighs. Except for the socks, Alligood was naked from the waist down. His yellow-and-white plaid shirt was caked with blood, and a thin line of semen stretched down his leg. His right hand loosely held an ice pick, and his left arm, dangling toward the floor, clutched his pants. Blood pooled on the linoleum tiles next to a woman's nightgown. A bra hung on the cell door. The petite twenty-year-old black woman who had occupied that cell for two months was gone.[1]

Helms and the Beaufort County police immediately began a search for Joan Little, who they believed had murdered Alligood as part of an elaborate plan to escape. After the state declared Little an armed and dangerous outlaw, local police issued orders to shoot her on sight. Armed with service dogs and "high-powered rifles," police combed through the dusty

In hiding for over a week after killing Clarence Alligood and escaping from the Beaufort jail, Joan Little surrenders to the North Carolina State Bureau of Investigation on September 7, 1975. She is accompanied by her attorney Jerry Paul.

streets of "Back of Town," the black community in Washington, going door to door inquiring about Little's whereabouts.

Few knew where she had been hiding. Ernest "Pops" Barnes, an aged and nearly blind man, had granted Little shelter in his tiny run-down shack that was notorious among neighbors as a "liquor house." Pops agreed to provide a safe sanctuary for Little after she told him that Alligood forced her to strip. He "tried to make me suck him," she said. She told Pops she killed him with an ice pick in self-defense.[2] Squeezed between a couple of old feather mattresses, Little managed to elude police during four nerve-wracking searches of the house. When an officer sat down on Pops's bed during one investigation, Little remained still as a stone, barely able to breathe.[3]

After nearly a week in hiding, the fear and tension finally forced Little out. She sent word to Marjorie Wright, a childhood friend and sympathetic ally. Wright called Jerry Paul, a local attorney who worked on civil rights cases, who was known among whites and blacks as an eccentric nonconformist. Together they spirited Little out of the county in the middle of the night and helped her surrender to the State Bureau of Investigation (SBI) in Chapel Hill.[4] On September 7, Charles Dunn, head of the SBI, arrested Joan Little for first-degree murder. Two days later a grand jury indicted her. If found guilty, Little would die in the state's gas chamber.[5]

.   .   .

Much had changed since 1947, when the NAACP, the Civil Rights Congress, and the Sojourners for Truth and Justice had launched a national and international campaign to free Rosa Lee Ingram. That year an all-white jury sentenced Ingram, a black sharecropper and mother of twelve, to death in the self-defense slaying of a white man in Ellaville, Georgia.[6] In the 1940s it was nearly impossible for black victims of sexualized violence to receive justice in the courts. In 1944 a grand jury in Henry County, Alabama, refused to indict Recy Taylor's assailants despite their admissions, a gubernatorial intervention, and a national campaign for her defense. In 1949 the Montgomery police department would not even hold a lineup for Gertrude Perkins, who charged two officers with kidnapping and rape. After a citywide protest, Perkins had her day in court, but the grand jury refused to indict anyone for the crime. Black women had achieved small victories in their fight for bodily integrity throughout the 1950s, but they were few and far between. It was not until 1959 that an all-white jury in Tallahassee, Florida, sentenced four white men to prison for life in the brutal gang rape of Betty Jean Owens. It took another six years before Mississippi, the most unreconstructed Southern state, followed suit. In 1965 an all-white jury in Hattiesburg sent Norman Cannon to prison for life for kidnapping and raping Rosa Lee Coates.

Victories of the mid-1960s rested on decades of black women's organizing and personal testimony. Courage and persistence had dramatically altered the political and legal landscape for black women raped or sexually abused by white men. Despite the threat of life sentences, some white men still believed black women's bodies belonged to them. As a result, African-American women continued to organize and use their public voices to demand safety from sexual abuse. In 1974 Joan Little became the symbol of a campaign to defend black womanhood and to call attention to the sexualized racial violence that still existed ten years after Congress passed the 1965 Voting Rights Act.

The Free Joan Little campaign brought disparate activists and organizations, each with their own resources and agendas, into a loose but powerful coalition. Feminists and women's liberation organizations spoke out against sexual violence and advocated a woman's right to self-defense; civil rights and Black Power groups saw the Little case as another example of police brutality and Southern injustice; opponents of the death penalty and prison reformers hoped the case would draw attention to their emerging campaigns. Ultimately, the Joan Little case became a test of whether an African-American woman, as Karen Galloway, one of Little's attorneys, put it, "finally had a right to defend herself against a white man's sexual assault."[7]

Although African-American voter registration and political participation surged in the years after the Selma campaign, political rights did not guarantee full equality or economic opportunity.[8] In 1966 Martin Luther King, Jr., agued that a "tragic gulf" existed between the promises of civil rights legislation and their fulfillment.[9] The Civil Rights Act of 1964 and the Voting Rights Act of 1965, for example, did little to remedy the de facto segregation, squalid housing conditions, chronic unemployment, police brutality, and lack of educational opportunity that blacks still faced throughout the country. The 1965 assassination of Malcolm X, the leading black critic of nonviolence, only fueled the movement toward black nationalism and Black Power and away from the "beloved community," splitting the civil rights coalition. Riots engulfed cities throughout the country for three searing summers after the Selma-to-Montgomery march. The uprisings exposed and expressed the betrayal many African Americans felt in the failure of the civil rights movement and the federal government to remedy racial and economic oppression. In 1966 alone thirty-eight riots erupted in cities from San Francisco to Providence, Rhode Island. In 1967 Detroit exploded: forty-three people were killed, two thousand were wounded, and more than five thousand were burned out of their homes.[10] By the end of the decade, a half-million blacks in more than three hundred cities witnessed violent uprisings in which 250 people died, eight thousand were injured, and more than fifty thousand were arrested.[11]

As younger black activists began to move toward organizations that advocated Black Power, white activists used the lessons of the civil rights movement to challenge the social and political inequalities of power in new, predominantly white organizations. The New Left, a mostly student-led movement that emerged in the early 1960s and was critical of Cold War brinkmanship and committed to participatory democracy, direct action, and mass mobilization, gained power as the Vietnam War escalated. By the end of the decade, New Left activists were the leading antiwar protesters and were convinced that the United States was "the leading enemy of peace and justice on the planet."[12] Instead of working within the existing political system, young radicals advocated a wholesale transformation.

At the same time, a rising white backlash spread throughout the nation, undermining support for civil rights advances. In the 1968 presidential election, George Wallace captured 13.5 percent of the popular vote by appealing to white anger and fears of unrestrained civil rights activists and antiwar demonstrators. The small number obscures the fact that more than 30 percent of Democratic voters in Wisconsin and Indiana, and 43 percent of Democrats in Maryland, chose the unabashed racist for president, indicating significant support outside the Deep South.[13] Though not as overtly racist as Wallace, Richard Nixon appealed to the "silent majority" by opposing "forced busing" for school desegregation, criticizing social disorder, and promising to restore "law and order."[14] Nixon's language was softer than Wallace's, but the message was equally harsh.

In an atmosphere of increased racial polarization, Martin Luther King, Jr., and the SCLC struggled to revive the spirit of the beloved community and to wed continuing struggles for racial and economic justice to Lyndon Johnson's War on Poverty. For a brief moment in the spring of 1968, during the Memphis sanitation workers' strike, the old civil rights coalition rallied together.[15] Strikers asserted their personhood, demanded dignity and respect, and called for economic justice. Carrying signs that declared "I AM A Man," the Memphis garbage workers placed their protest in the long struggle for freedom and human rights.

The assassination of King on April 4, 1968, shattered the Memphis movement and killed any hopes for a renewed freedom movement. Racial violence flared in 125 cities in twenty-nine states, leaving thirty-nine dead, thousands injured, and millions reeling with sadness and disbelief.[16] Amid the riots, Black Panthers in Oakland, California, engaged in a ninety-minute shoot-out with city police that left co-founder Eldridge Cleaver wounded and seventeen-year-old Bobby Hutton dead.[17] The murder of Martin Luther King, Jr., combined with FBI surveillance, leadership upheavals, internal violence, incarceration, and gender problems among civil rights and Black Power organizations, signaled the end of an era.[18]

The Little case unfolded amid murderous violence as African Americans in North Carolina fought to integrate public schools and gain full citizenship. Events in two cities provide the most gripping examples. In May 1970 African Americans in Oxford torched the town's tobacco warehouses after three white men brutally murdered Henry Marrow in broad daylight. Marrow, an African-American soldier and young father, allegedly talked fresh to a white woman. The historian Timothy Tyson, who was a child at the time, remembered living in an "atmosphere of war." After the riot, a siege mentality set in among whites who defended the murderers and targeted blacks for violent reprisal.[19] In the spring of 1971 Wilmington, like Oxford, "hovered on the edge of racial cataclysm," as Tyson put it. The controversies over school desegregation—busing, discrimination toward black students, the closure of all-black schools, and the dismissals of beloved black teachers and administrators—left many African Americans angry and resentful.[20]

Fueling this rancor in Wilmington, the Rights of White People, a white supremacist organization, terrorized blacks and incited violence.[21] White racists and black militants exchanged gunfire, while black snipers fired at police officers, many of whom were members of the Ku Klux Klan. The National Guard patrolled the streets, and storefronts and businesses regularly went up in flames.[22] Accused of arson but primarily guilty of leading a boisterous movement for Black Power, Ben Chavis, a field organizer for the United Church of Christ's Commission for Racial Justice, was sentenced to prison along with nine others implicated in the racial conflagration. They became known as the "Wilmington Ten."[23] Angela Davis, an outspoken prison reform activist and an icon of the Black Power movement, used her organization, the National Alliance Against Racist and Political Repression, to launch a campaign for their defense.[24] It was through her work on the Wilmington Ten case that she heard about Joan Little's plight in Washington, North Carolina.

Race relations were as volatile in the small towns and hamlets of Beaufort County as they were in Wilmington. Police killings, Klan burnings, and bomb threats met African-American integration efforts.[25] When Sheriff Otis "Red" Davis bragged to a Northern reporter about the "racial harmony" that existed in eastern North Carolina "since integration was forced on us in 1965," he was painting a picture of a New South that did not yet exist. In fact, many clung to the past; 70 percent of voters in Beaufort County supported Wallace in the 1972 presidential primary. "If time had not exactly stood still in eastern North Carolina until the late 1960s," the journalist Mark Pinsky noted, "it was dragging its feet. And nowhere did it dig in its heels more than in Beaufort County—in matters of voting rights, jury service, public accommodations, school desegregation, and police brutality."[26] When a federal court ordered Beaufort County to desegregate its public schools in 1965—more than a decade after *Brown*—whites responded with violence and intimidation. The Ku Klux Klan enjoyed a resurgence and night riders terrorized African Americans who supported desegregation. The next year the NAACP Legal Defense and Educational Fund filed a lawsuit alleging that the "intimidation of black students . . . had made school desegregation impossible without federal intervention."[27]

When the *Washington Daily News* broke the story about the murder of jailer Clarence Alligood and the missing black female inmate, calling it the "most brutal ever to happen in this county," it practically invited reprisal against Little. As if he were a soldier killed in action in Vietnam, the paper eulogized Alligood's service to the county and said he "gave his life in the line of duty."[28] The newspaper failed to report that Alligood had been found naked from the waist down. Once word got out that the medical examiner had found semen on his thighs and that his "urethral fluid was loaded with spermatozoa," evidence that he died at the moment of sexual climax, Joan Little's claim that he sexually assaulted her gained credibility. However, since many whites still could not believe that a black woman could be raped, they fell back on old stereotypes to explain the unusual circumstances of Alligood's death.

Casual conversations among whites in Washington pegged Little as a stereotypical jezebel, and rumors about her respectability, or lack thereof, spread throughout town. Joan Little, some whites argued, seduced Alligood, lured him into her cell, and killed him so she could escape. For the local car dealer, this excuse made perfect sense—only the murder was a strange turn of events. "Hell, to them fucking is like saying good morning, or having a Pepsi-Cola," he snorted. Henry Hardy, a textile executive, agreed. "I'll tell you one thing," he said, "she didn't lose her honor in that cell. She lost that years ago at Camp Lejeune," a marine base outside town. Hardy obviously believed the rumor that Little was a budding madam, who "ferried her girlfriends to the base for prostitution."[29] The plant manager at Coca-Cola, who claimed to know Alligood well, found it hard to believe he had a sexual encounter with a black woman. Alligood, he said, "was so racially biased that he wouldn't want a colored woman." Sheriff Jack O. Harris sided with the plant manager but wondered why, if Alligood was going to break down and integrate, he would choose Little, "all eat up with syphilis like she was."[30]

Jerry Paul, Little's long-haired, heavy-lidded, shambling primary defense attorney, knew that many white men in and around Washington still believed black women existed, as he put it, "somewhere between the animal and the human."[31] A husky former East Carolina football player

Native son. Attorney Jerry Paul, a former East Carolina football player, defied the state's racial status quo by representing African Americans and working on civil rights cases.

who was born and raised in Washington, North Carolina, Paul reveled in bucking the small town's strict racial codes by befriending African Americans and working on civil rights causes. Local people told reporters he was not a native son but was adopted. "That's what my daddy always used to say," Paul told *The New York Times*. "Always said that I must have some nigger blood or some Jewish blood as much as I love the niggers."[32] Racial politics aside, he knew that liaisons between white men and black women, whether coerced or consensual, had a long history. Among white men, he said, they were "completely accepted." "I used to hear 'em in the workplaces," Paul explained, "bragging about how they got some pussy the night before, and always the question would come up, 'Was it white or black?' " Invariably, he said, someone would say, "Oh, it was black . . . I picked up this nigger walking on the road."

Local whites sympathized with Clarence Alligood, Paul explained. "They're programmed to believe that she lured him in there," he said. "And if she didn't . . . then he went back there to have a little fun [and] that's okay too. That's expected." Most whites believed that the mistake Alligood made, Paul said, was "*getting caught* back there."[33] With no eye-witnesses and only circumstantial evidence available to pin a first-degree murder charge on the young black woman, Paul expected the prosecution to fall back on these time-worn stereotypes to win its case. He also expected them to call up Joan Little's dysfunctional family history and her criminal record, which was long, to paint a picture of a sexually deviant delinquent who murdered Alligood in cold blood.

Little was no Rosa Parks. She was the oldest of nine children. Her mother had been married twice and had four children with Little's father, and five children with her stepfather. Little's father abandoned the family and moved to New York when she was still a child, and her new stepfather had a tendency to drink too much. Little had her first sexual encounter when she was fourteen and contracted syphilis the following year. As a teenager, Little often ran away from home, earning a reputation among family and friends as an "escape artist." She dropped out of high school at fifteen, but her mother had a judge declare her a truant and sent her to Dobbs Farm Training School in Kinston, North Carolina. When she ran away from Dobbs Farm, Little's mother sent her to live with relatives in Philadelphia. There Little developed a thyroid problem and came home for surgery three weeks before she was supposed to graduate from high school. Without a diploma and no real job prospects, Little worked sporadically until 1973, when at age eighteen she went to work as a Sheetrock finisher and got romantically involved with Julius Rogers, a man twenty years her senior. Toward the end of the year, she began to get in trouble with the law as well.

In Jacksonville, North Carolina, police charged Little with possession of stolen goods and a sawed-off shotgun; on January 3, 1974, police in Washington, North Carolina, arrested her for shoplifting, but the charge was dismissed. Six days later police arrested her again for shoplifting, and this time she drew a suspended sentence. Less than a week passed before Little was arrested again. This time police charged her with three separate felonies: breaking, entering, and larceny. A grand jury indicted Little on March 15, 1974, and on June 4, 1974, she received a seven-to-ten-year jail sentence.[34]

Little's attorneys knew that her criminal record would make it easy for the prosecution to present her as a calculating killer. Such an argument would play well locally—and not just among whites. Many African Americans in Washington did not think Joan Little was a respectable young woman either. Maggie Buck, a white beautician at the Cinderella Beauty Salon, told a reporter that even "my black maid didn't sympathize with Joan Little." Little was so mean, Buck recalled, "she stole her own aunt's color TV." Buck's maid may not have been completely forthright with her employer on issues regarding race, but other African Americans expressed

Joan Little, February 3, 1975.

similar opinions. Golden Frinks, perhaps the most well-known civil rights leader in North Carolina, argued that prominent members of the black community in Washington had "ostracized" Little because she was a "wayward girl" who had "led a fast life." Little's behavior, he said, "was not up to the general moral standard of the community." After hearing about Little's escape and subsequent arrest, Frinks went to Mount Hebron Baptist Church, where Little's family were registered members, hoping to organize a campaign for her defense. They turned him away. "You see,"

Frinks recalled, "the community had moved thumbs down on Little because of her previous record [and] her breaking and entering into a mobile home of a black person."[35]

Respectability mattered, but not as much as it had in previous decades. The year 1975 was not 1955, when respectability had been the defining issue that made Rosa Parks—and not Claudette Colvin—the symbol of wronged black womanhood in Montgomery, Alabama. The two decades between the Montgomery bus boycott and Joan Little's trial witnessed enormous social, political, and economic changes that permanently altered the American landscape. The civil rights movement and the women's movement helped free African Americans and women from the strict racial and sexual codes that had been inscribed in the social and legal bedrock of the United States for centuries. Certainly the national exposure of police brutality, institutional racism, and the violent practices of white supremacists in the 1960s and early 1970s—especially the murder of Viola Liuzzo and the kidnapping and rape of Rosa Lee Coates in 1965—undermined arguments linking race and sex and played a role in challenging the importance of the victim's respectability and innocence.

By the mid-1970s the National Organization for Women had made tremendous legal and political inroads, partly because of the legacy of the civil rights movement and African-American activism on sexual violence. The Equal Rights Amendment was debated fiercely across the country and had been ratified by more than thirty states. In 1973 the Supreme Court gave women power over their own reproductive choices in the landmark *Roe v. Wade* decision. Women's liberation groups challenged conventional definitions of rape and domestic violence and pressured police and other law enforcement officials to stop blaming the victim.[36] White feminists in New York finally caught up with their African-American sisters by testifying publicly about rape in 1971.[37] In 1973 the National Organization for Women formed the NOW Rape Task Force to investigate rape laws around the country. Over the next few years, rape crisis centers and rape hotlines sprouted up throughout the country; radical feminists held conferences dedicated to discussing sexual violence; and a wave of public speak-outs put rape on the national political agenda.[38]

Maggie Buck, the white beautician in Washington, seemed to grasp these historic changes when she told a reporter that "even if a girl has loose morals, she should be able to pick the man she wants to be raped by."[39] Buck's bizarre phrasing of the right of women to choose their sexual partners—and even their assailants—indicated that Little might garner more sympathy among all women, regardless of race or political position, whose views on gender and sexuality had been influenced by the women's rights movement.

However, Joan Little was not going to be the only one on trial. If the prosecution drew on racial stereotypes of wanton women and blacks' tendency toward criminality, then Little's defense attorneys would paint a picture of North Carolina mired in a Tobacco Road past, where ignorant "rednecks" lorded over innocent and defenseless blacks.[40] This strategy would hurt the state's image and, given the still-contested great social changes, maybe even lead to an acquittal. Indeed, the violent clashes over school desegregation made North Carolina the focal point of national news stories throughout the 1970s and seriously damaged the state's "progressive mystique."[41] *The New York Times* reported the "growing concern" of state officials, who feared losing tourists and industry to other "sunbelt" states in the South. They worried that "national attention . . . [will hurt] the state's already battered image of racial moderation." Governor James E. Holshouser, the *Times* noted, was especially "sensitive to the critical publicity the state has been receiving lately."[42] "They know they're racists," attorney Jerry Paul quipped, "but in 1975, it may not be a good thing to admit you're a racist—they think that the nation comes down on you if you're that way and you won't get industry in your town."[43]

In the year leading up to Little's trial, Jerry Paul presented her to the public as a poor but brave black woman who had defended her dignity from a lecherous racist and was being railroaded into the gas chamber by a Jim Crow justice system. Paul pounced on state prosecutors every time they said or did something that hinted of racial prejudice as proof that they were stuck in an Old South mind-set. David Milligan, the editor of the *Beaufort-Hyde News,* resented Paul's strategy because, he complained, the Northern press eagerly lapped it up and spat it out in caricature: "This is the South. Here's a rinky-dink town with its shacks and shanties. You've got this old redneck sheriff and this old redneck jailer and this pore little ole colored gal. She's there in jail, so defenseless, so innocent, and she gets raped and ravaged by this gross jailer and all of a sudden, out of nowhere, she struck out, trying to defend herself. She had to kill the jailer and now those ignorant rednecks are gonna get their revenge on her. They're gonna make her pay for it with her life."[44]

Paul couldn't have said it better himself. He and a coterie of supporters spent ten months repeating that story, or versions of it, at rallies and media events, whipping up support for Little throughout the country. More than a canny legal strategy, Little's story would resonate with feminist and antirape organizations, Paul realized, as well as large swaths of the black public. Civil rights and Black Power activists, who had intimate knowledge of Jim Crow justice, would rally to her defense. He teamed up with Karen Galloway, the first African-American woman to graduate from Duke Law School, who signed on as Little's co-counsel the same day she passed her bar exam.[45] Together the novice and the native son traveled to Washington, D.C., to speak to women's organizations. We "sold the Joan Little case," Paul said later, "and all the women's groups started to pick it up."[46]

Movement magazines and newsletters, like the feminist periodical *Off Our Backs,* helped spread Little's story through feminist circles before the mainstream media picked it up.[47] Angela Davis's article in *Ms.* magazine brought national attention to the trial and introduced thousands of activists and institutions across the nation not only to Joan Little's plight but to black women's long battle against sexual violence. "All people who see themselves as members of the existing community of struggle for justice, equality, and progress," Davis argued, "have a responsibility to fulfill toward Joan Little."[48] The Southern Poverty Law Center, with former SNCC leader Julian Bond at the helm, signed on early as well. They used Morris Dees's direct mail expertise to solicit funds from people across the nation for Little's defense. The letter they mailed to a quarter of a million people claimed Little's case represented the "most shocking and outrageous example of injustice against women on record."[49]

As word of Little's defiant stand against sexual violence spread, national feminist groups and civil rights organizations rallied behind her. The Women's Legal Defense Fund, the Feminist Alliance Against Rape, the Rape Crisis Center, the National Black Feminist Organization, and the National Organization for Women, which was struggling to appeal to women of color, joined the fund-raising effort and mobilized nationwide support.[50] The national NAACP maintained its historic reluctance to embrace "sex cases" and did not get involved; however, local chapters helped raise money.[51]

In an article for *The Black Scholar,* Maulana Ron Karenga, a Black Power advocate, cultural nationalist, founder of the US Organization, and inventor of Kwanzaa, called on African Americans to "accept and support [Little's] account of what actually happened and to reject . . . the version offered by the oppressor." Karenga placed the attack on Little into a long history of "personal and political terrorism directed against black women and the black community since slavery." Her willingness to resist Alligood's advances, Karenga argued, proved that even though "the movement was at a lull, our people were still in motion, still resisting."[52] Little's decision to fight back became a catalyst for a much larger struggle.

Rosa Parks, who had been an antirape activist since she helped organize the campaign to defend Recy Taylor in the early 1940s, helped found a local branch of the Joan Little Legal Defense Committee in Detroit, where she had fled two years after the Montgomery bus boycott. In a press release issued on March 12, 1975, the committee announced a student rally at the University of Detroit, a march to be held April 18, and a massive fundraising drive to defend Little "all the way to the Supreme Court if necessary." They hoped that "Miss Little will be acquitted of the charge of first degree murder," the press release stated, "but, also, that the question, 'should a woman defend herself against a rapist?' will be decided in the affirmative." Within a month the Detroit committee had secured local speakers and entertainment for the April rally, sent five hundred solicitations for donations, and appeared on local television and radio programs to call on Detroit citizens to rally to Little's defense.[53] Similar chapters emerged throughout the country.

Bernice Johnson Reagon, founder of the a cappella group Sweet Honey in the Rock, and a former SNCC activist who worked closely with Fannie Lou Hamer the summer after she was assaulted in the Winona, Mississippi, jail, saw Joan Little as a kind of everywoman trapped by a racist and sexist society. Her song, "Joanne Little," became the anthem for what became the "Free Joan Little" movement. The song's refrain, "Joanne is you, Joanne is me, our prison is this whole society," rallied Little's diverse supporters.[54]

The Southern Christian Leadership Conference, the organization founded by Martin Luther King, Jr., supported Little and demanded protection for black womanhood. The Reverend Ralph Abernathy, King's hand-picked successor and Montgomery bus boycott veteran, joined Golden Frinks to headline a protest at the Beaufort County Courthouse. "Here is a young Black woman locked in jail," Abernathy shouted, "sexually assaulted [and] charged with first degree murder, simply because she protected herself from being raped by a white barbarian."[55] It was perhaps the SCLC's most outspoken statement in defense of black women's bodily integrity.

At the grassroots level, African-American women in North Carolina who had labored for human dignity without recognition or celebration began organizing on Little's behalf. They drew from deep wells of experience fighting racial injustice and sexual abuse. In 1975 a number of them joined hands across the state to form Concerned Women for Justice and Fairness to Joan Little (later known as the Concerned Women for Justice or CWJ).[56] Mrs. Christine Strudwick, veteran of the Durham, North Carolina, freedom struggle, who became CWJ's second vice president, recalled that she "felt like Joan could have been one of my daughters and was caught up in a situation [in which] she really had no control."[57] Strudwick cultivated local support and introduced Little's attorneys to black churchwomen at the Union Baptist Church in Durham, which served as the organizational base for local civil rights activists in the 1950s and 1960s. By calling on the churchwomen at Union Baptist, Strudwick placed Little's case in the hands of experienced activists who understood the long history of sexual abuse of black women. Together they helped raise money, provided moral support, and offered assistance to Little's mother.[58]

The Durham branch of the Joan Little Defense Fund served as the home base for state and national organizing. It was originally founded by Little's attorneys to help raise funds for her defense but was primarily run by black female college students. According to a press release, Yvonne Davis, a student at the University of North Carolina, Chapel Hill, "traveled, making talks and arranging publicity . . . for little or no pay." She was also responsible for keeping in contact with groups around the country. Alexis Randolph "kept [the Joan Little Defense Fund] going almost single-handed." Vivian Grimes, a secretary in Jerry Paul's law firm, "spent numerous hours working on the case, on and off the job." Tyree Barnes, a student at Guildford College, was in charge of a survey for jury selection and, according to a committee newsletter, "has on many occasions taken it upon herself to carry out many of the things that needed doing." Nancy Mills helped set up the first rally in Washington, D.C. Celene Chernier, a prison reform activist and representative of the North Carolina Alliance Against Racial and Political Repression, helped nurture relationships with like-minded organizations. Larry Little, head of the Winston-Salem Black Panther Party, secured support from Black Power advocates. Their efforts, along with the direct mail efforts of Julian Bond and Morris Dees at the Southern Poverty Law Center, raised approximately $250,000 for Little's defense.[59] Months before Joan Little's trial began, her supporters had already decided she was innocent.

Little still had to face a North Carolina judge and jury. Her attorneys hoped it would not be in Beaufort County, where too many people knew Little's criminal history and hard reputation. In April 1975, Jerry Paul and Karen Galloway petitioned Superior Court Judge Henry A. McKinnon for a change of venue, arguing that Beaufort County's jury-selection process was racially biased. Paul and Galloway spent $38,992 on social scientists who helped develop an "attitude profile survey" designed to detect patterns of prejudice. They wanted to know if African Americans and young people were purposely excluded from the local jury pool—a tactic used by white Southerners for many years to deny blacks equal justice. A diverse jury would render a different verdict than an all-white jury, they reasoned, because the attitudes of blacks, women, and the young significantly diverged from average white male jurors. "If it could be shown that attitudes were different, and the three groups were underrepresented," Courtney J. Mullin, the social psychologist who headed the survey, said, "then Joan Little would receive . . . not a jury of her peers . . . but rather the justice of a middle-class, middle-aged white male segment only."[60]

On April 22 Judge McKinnon granted the change of venue, not because of systematic racial discrimination, he argued, but "because it would be almost impossible to select an impartial jury . . . because of extensive pretrial publicity."[61] Little and her attorneys won a double victory that day. Despite McKinnon's denials, Paul and Galloway succeeded in portraying racism as the reason for the change of venue. By moving the trial to Raleigh, the state capital, Little could count on a jury drawn from a more urban and liberal population, who knew virtually nothing about her disreputable past.

The "trial of the decade," as the *Chicago Tribune* put it, began on July 15, 1975. Five hundred supporters rallied outside the Wake County Courthouse, a white cement behemoth in downtown Raleigh. They hoisted placards demanding the court "Free Joan Little" and "Defend Black Womanhood," and loud chants could be heard over the din of traffic and conversation. "One, two, three. Joan must be set free!" the crowd sang. "Four, five, six. Power to the ice pick!"[62] Inside, Little sat quietly in a modest pink and blue dress as her attorneys and the prosecutors tested competing narratives and argued over potential jurors. William Griffin, the boyish thirty-one-year-old prosecutor, presented Little as a seductive and calculating killer who murdered Alligood as part of a plot to escape. She deserved

Demonstrators demand "Justice for Joanne" outside the Wake County
Courthouse.

the death penalty, he claimed, and looked for potential jurors who supported it.[63]

The defense, *The New York Times* reported, "made clear today that they
were putting the Southern system of justice on trial as much as defending
a young black woman accused of first-degree murder."[64] When assistant
prosecutor Lester Chalmers dismissed the first black prospective juror, Jerry
Paul, hewing to this strategy, yelled, "I object! He's excusing them because
they're black." Chalmers was an easy target—he had defended the Imperial Wizard of the Ku Klux Klan in front of the House Un-American Activities Committee a few years earlier—and the defense eagerly exploited it.
Chalmers "bristled" at the charge and told Judge Hamilton Hobgood, the
sixty-four-year-old jurist with a reputation for fairness and a knack for
country humor, that he "objected to the objection." "I'd expect the Klan
to object to that statement," Jerry Paul quickly shot back.[65] Paul goaded
Chalmers about his past association with the bedsheet brigade for the nearly
two weeks it took to pick a jury, setting the stage for a courtroom brawl
between the South's legacy of racial and sexual violence and Joan Little.
In the end, the jury consisted of six African Americans and six whites. Nine
of the twelve were women, and all but five were under forty years old.[66]

As prosecutors struggled to present a case based on circumstantial evidence, defense attorneys placed the case in its historical context. They

argued that Southern police officers had a long history of assaulting and
sexually harassing black women in their custody.[67] In the Beaufort County
Jail, they said, black women were wholly unprotected. Officers kept a cam-
era trained on female prisoners at all times, watching them—or "peep-
ing at them," as Paul put it—while they showered, changed clothes, and
used the toilet. Little testified that when she tried to "tie up a blanket to
block the TV monitor" and protect her privacy when she was naked, officers took her blanket away. She also described how, when she wanted to
take a shower, she "had to call the jailer and have him turn the water on."
Then he would stand outside her cell and watch, she said.[68]

Karen Galloway told the jury that Little was not the only victim of sexual abuse in the Beaufort County Jail but was one of many black women
harassed by Alligood and other white officers who routinely attacked black
women. Galloway summoned a stream of black women to the stand to testify about their experiences. Rosa Ida Mae Roberson, described by the
Los Angeles Times as a "hefty black woman who was jailed for twenty-one
days for making threatening phone calls," told the jury that Alligood
propositioned her about "seven to ten times" while she was incarcerated.
Alligood, she said, teased her about being "confined so long [she] needed
sex." When Roberson warned the wizened jailer that she "would kill him
if he entered her cell," he backed off. Phyllis Ann Moore, a nineteen-year-
old black woman, testified that during her short stay in the Beaufort
County Jail, she witnessed Alligood sexually harass Little by repeatedly
asking her if she "missed her man." Little ignored the sexual innuendo,

An eclectic group of protesters join forces to "Free Joan Little," July 14, 1975.

"Power to the Ice Pick"—an African-American woman pickets outside the Wake County Courthouse in Raleigh, July 21, 1975.

Moore said, and once "turned away in disgust and muttered that she'd report the jailer if he said it again." But it was the last witness, who, according to the *Los Angeles Times,* "seemed to command the closest attention of the jury." [69]

Jurors listened with rapt attention as Galloway questioned Anne Marie Gardner, a twenty-six-year-old black woman, who said Alligood made repeated sexual advances toward her. "Alligood came to the female section just about every night," Gardner told the jury. When she scrubbed the floors, she said, Alligood shuffled along behind her, attempting to pinch and fondle her breasts. "I'd knock his hand away," she said. [70] When Lester Chalmers asked Gardner on cross-examination why she did not report the behavior, someone in the audience said, "Come on, mister." "I wanted to forget it," Gardner snapped back. [71]

By presenting multiple victims of Alligood's predatory lust, the defense readied the jurors for Little's testimony. Paul and Galloway had prepared her for this moment; they spent months training Joan Little in the art of respectability. She had to assert her dignity and personhood without being too brash and appear reputable without being too demure. It was a difficult task since Little had what Paul called a "negative side" that her attorneys did not want to slip out. "She's not an honest person," Paul admitted later. "She's not a kind person. She's a violent person. That doesn't mean she committed this crime," he explained, "it only means she's a product

Outside the Wake County
Courthouse, Raleigh, July 14, 1975

Black and white women assert their
right to self-defense outside the
Joan Little trial, August 17, 1975.

of her environment."[72] If she had said, " 'I did a brave thing, I killed the old lecher and I'm glad of it,' " Paul argued, "she would have blown it."[73] Paul and Galloway taught Little how to behave in a way that made the jury believe she was an honorable and decent young woman and that any allusions by the prosecution to her criminal or sexual history were signs of their racism, not her moral shortcomings.

Jerry Paul helped create an image of respectability by pairing Little with Galloway, who was middle-class, educated, poised, well spoken, and respectable. "To be really good on the stand," Paul told a journalist later, "the client must be an extension of her lawyer. The client literally must *be* her lawyer." Paul saw that Galloway commanded respect when she spoke to the jurors. White women in particular responded to her grace and self-assurance. "I figure if they'll accept Karen," Paul said, "she'll drag Joan along with her. They'll never look at Joan." Galloway's presence, Paul explained, provided jurors with "an image of what Joan can be . . . and maybe is."[74]

By the time Little testified on her own behalf, almost a month after the trial began, the prosecution's case was severely weakened. On August 6 Judge Hobgood reduced the charge against her to second-degree murder because, he said, the "state had failed to offer sufficient evidence that she had planned the killing."[75] As prosecutors lost legal ground, they increasingly relied on racial and sexual stereotypes to make their case. This was most clear when Little, after sitting expressionless for nearly three weeks, finally took the stand.

Wearing a peach pullover and checkered pants, the petite woman testified that she killed Clarence Alligood in self-defense after he forced his way into her cell. She spoke so softly at times that jurors and spectators leaned forward, straining to hear the details of what happened almost a year earlier.[76] Choking back tears, Little told the jury how Alligood brought her sandwiches and snacks, often after midnight, without her asking. After about three weeks in jail, she said, Alligood started making passes at her, "talking about how nice I looked in my gown and that he wanted me to you know, have sex with him."

"Well, what did you say?" Paul asked.

"I told him to leave and that if he didn't I was gonna tell."[77]

On cross-examination, prosecutor William Griffin asked her why she did not follow through on the threat to report Alligood.

"Coming up as a black woman," Little told the jury, "it's a difficult thing . . . it's a question of your word against a white person."[78]

All of Alligood's late-night visits with snacks and sandwiches were a ploy, the defense claimed, to manipulate Little into having sex with him. When he walked into her cell in the early-morning hours of August 27, 1974, he had a "silly grin on his face, a weird look," Little testified. "He said that he had been nice to me and it was time I be nice to him." Holding back tears, Little told the jury that she rebuffed Alligood and told him that she "wasn't gonna be nice to him."[79] Alligood was unmoved, she said; he slipped his shoes off, walked into the cell, and started to fondle her breasts. "You might as well [tell]," Little claimed Alligood said as he "started to feel all over me." The other police officers, he said, "aren't going to believe you anyway." With a tiny voice barely audible in the courtroom, Little told the jury that she began to cry when Alligood stepped closer, pulled her nightgown up over her head, and "stuck his left hand in between my legs." With his right hand, she said, he grabbed her neck and said, "Give me some pussy."[80] "I was scared," she said, "so I just let him do that."[81]

Little continued with her raw testimony. She described how the jailer removed his pants, then forced her to her knees and, ice pick in hand, pushed her head down between his legs and told her to "suck him." "I didn't know whether he was going to kill me or what," she said, trembling. She wept as she described how she grabbed the ice pick when his grip loosened. "I reached for it and it fell," she said. "He grabbed for it . . . I grabbed for it," she said, burying her face into a handkerchief. She looked at the jury, her eyes puffy from crying, and told them that she "got to the ice pick first [and] struck at him each time he came at me." In the struggle, she said, she lashed out at Alligood after he grabbed her wrists and ran when he finally fell down.[82] Little's testimony touched a raw nerve among the black women jurors, especially Cora Judkins and Pecola Jones, who wept softly as Little dried her eyes and prepared for more of Griffin's cross-examination.

Three hours of "wheedling and battering" by Griffin, *The New York Times* reported, "failed to evoke any anger from the young black woman." Griffin's cross-examination followed what Wayne King, the *Times* reporter, called "the classic courtroom pattern where allegations of rape are made—an attempt to impeach the accuser's reputation and/or force her into a contradiction through anger or simple repetition of the facts."[83] On the latter point, Griffin and his assistant prosecutors failed miserably. By making Little repeat answers to their questions and retell the more brutal aspects of her struggle, they appeared insensitive.

"You never screamed?" Griffin asked.

"No, I just stood there," Little said quietly.

"You just stood there," Griffin said with incredulity. "You didn't slap his hands away from you, you didn't push him away from you?"

"No sir," Little replied.

"Did you strike him, hit him, push him?"

"No," she said. "I just stood there."

"You just stood there."

Clearly exasperated, Griffin raised his voice. "You never hollered, shouted, pushed him away, struck him or anything?"

"I was scared and I didn't know whether to scream or what, because he could have killed me right then and there."

"He had not threatened you at that point, had he?" Griffin argued.

"He was bigger than me," she said, pointing out that the jailer was over two hundred pounds and she was half that size.

"But you didn't fight him off, is that right?"

"May I say something?" Little asked.

"No I want you to answer my question," Griffin replied.

"No I did not," Little said. "But if you had been a woman," Little added, "you wouldn't have known what to do either, you probably wouldn't have screamed either because you wouldn't have known what he would have done to you."[84]

When prosecutors could not rattle Little, they attacked her credibility and portrayed her as a prostitute. Griffin asked Little if she gave a bondsman sexual favors in return for a loan to get out of jail; if another woman was her lover while she awaited trial in the women's prison; if she had a venereal disease; and if she ferried women to Jacksonville, North Carolina, as part of a prostitution ring. To all but one question, Paul objected, and Judge Hobgood overruled. Little calmly defended herself, maintaining her composure and her dignity.[85] Griffin and his fellow prosecutors continued their strategy during their closing arguments.

Just because there was "sexual activity under way," Griffin argued, did not "give her the right to kill this man." He suggested that not only did Little have consensual sex with the jailer, *she* seduced *him*. What else could explain Alligood's erection, Griffin asked. "[It's] strange to me that a man with rape on his mind would go in with an erection?" Griffin said. "That's strange to me. Does that make any sense at all? A man with rape on his mind?" Finally, Griffin described Little as a "calculating criminal, who, bent on escape, lured the jailer into her cell with a promise of sexual favors" and then, "at the moment of ecstasy, she let him have it." She "stabbed a man all over his body," Griffin told the jury. She directed the blows at his heart, he said. "How else would a man sit there and take those kind of wounds? How else?"[86]

Defense attorneys painted a different picture in their closing statements. Wearing the same color and sporting a similar, short Afro as her client, Karen Galloway taped off a four-by-seven-foot box on the courtroom floor and stood inside it, inviting the jurors to put themselves in Joan Little's shoes. Galloway skillfully transported the jurors to the Beaufort County Jail the night of the crime. Imagine a "young black woman whose white jailer had come to her cell demanding sex," she said. "Imagine Alligood's power and Miss Little's sense of fear."[87] Here is a "two hundred pound man sitting on the bunk; you on your knees on the floor," Galloway said, adroitly re-creating the sense of physical powerlessness Little must have felt. *The New York Times* reported that the young attorney then "described in stark language the sexual assault, weaving into the account over and over again, the power of the jailer." Alligood was a "man of position, of authority," she argued. Little ran, Galloway said, because "white men in the South could do anything to black women and get away with it. She ran to save her own life." Pointing to the white male prosecutors as if they were guilty too, Galloway said, "They suggest that she enjoyed it."[88] As a respectable black woman, Galloway's condemnation of white men's lawlessness and indifference toward black women's humanity was a powerful indictment. Her ability to make Alligood's power and perversion real enabled the jury to gain a sense of what she called Little's "defenselessness, paralysis, [and] violation." Her performance reduced the jurors to tears.[89]

The defense team could have easily rested after Galloway's wrenching closing argument, but Paul wanted the jury to understand that Little's story fit into a long and painful history. Taking the jury back to Jim Crow, Paul opened his dog-eared copy of Gerda Lerner's *Black Women in White America* and read a long passage written in 1902 by an anonymous African-American woman. The essay denounced white men for defiling black women while simultaneously proclaiming, "No Negro women are virtuous." The author hoped that "someone will arise who will champion [black women's] cause and compel the world to see that we deserve justice, as other heroes compelled it to see that we deserved freedom."[90] Paul argued that that someone was Joan Little.

"God chose Joan Little," Paul insisted, "like he chose Rosa Parks" to end the "domination of southern black women by white males."[91] "And that is what this case is all about. This case compels the world to see that women, black women, deserve justice; that women are victims of rape and that rape is not a sex crime and that they do not lure men into raping them. It is a crime of violence, of hatred, of humiliation." He then put the entire history of the South's racial and sexual subjugation on trial and asked the jury to decide whether it wanted to continue to live in a world dominated by white supremacy. "Whose word do you believe?" he asked. "The history of whiteness on a pedestal, white southern womanhood on the pedestal, righteousness, purity, or do you believe the black woman who has a history of being lower than the prostitute?"[92]

After deliberating for seventy-eight minutes, the jury unanimously voted to acquit Joan Little.[93] As Mark Neilson, the jury foreman, read the verdict, Little's attorneys clustered around her as she broke into sobs. Wiping the tears away, she said, "It feels good to be free."[94] News of the victory quickly spread to the crowd of one hundred supporters outside. When Little emerged, the throng erupted into cheers and chanted, "Freedom! Freedom! Freedom!"[95] At a press conference later that day in the green-and-yellow lobby of the Lemon Tree Inn, Little told reporters that she "always had confidence in the people." She believed she received a fair trial, Little said, despite the fact that prosecutors were, as she put it, more "interested in sending black women to the gas chamber than the truth."

Joan Little (left) and Karen Galloway, July 14, 1975. Galloway was the first
African-American woman to graduate Duke Law School.

Standing next to Galloway, Little told the crowd of television reporters
and journalists that she hoped her experience might help women who "go
through the same kinds of abuse."[96]

Michael Coakley, a reporter for the *Chicago Tribune* who sat through the
five-week trial, argued that Little's case provided a national airing for issues
that plagued the country, particularly "racism, sexism, and prison reform"
and "the whole question of self-defense against rape."[97] The case helped
fuel a public debate about the prosecution of sex crimes and aided feminist efforts to redefine rape as a crime of violence, aggression, and humiliation that had little, if anything, to do with sex. Additionally, by
constantly challenging prosecutors' implied arguments that Little could
not have been raped because she was not respectable, she and her attorneys
helped dispel stereotypes of black women as promiscuous jezebels who
could not be legitimate victims of rape. The fact that these characteriza-
tions were seen as racist attempts to smear the victim indicated that a New
South could emerge from the ruins of the old. "I like to think we at least
made a beginning," Galloway said later. "Maybe now rape victims won't
have to take the witness stand and become the defendant."[98]

The Joan Little case proved that respectability still mattered, but only
to a degree. Despite the fact that Paul compared Little to Rosa Parks, she
was *nothing* like the heroine of the Montgomery bus boycott. By 1975,
respectability was no longer the defining trait supporters looked for before
rallying to the cause. Everyone knew that Little had been incarcerated, but

that did not stop supporters from insisting that she still had a right to her own body and deserved to be treated with respect. Certainly the modern civil rights movement, which forced the nation to recognize African Americans as citizens and human beings, created the conditions for the change. When Paul told the jury that "there is no human being on the face of the earth" who has the right to violate or abuse another person, "no matter who you are or where you think you come from or whatever possession or control you have," he expressed those changes.[99]

While the verdict in the Little case highlighted these breaks with the past, there was much continuity with it. The trial drew national and international attention, and a broad coalition of supporters rallied in defense of Little's womanhood and her right to self-defense. The widespread support for Little among disparate leftist and liberal organizations resembled the nationwide coalitions that formed to demand justice for Recy Taylor in 1944 and Rosa Lee Ingram in 1947. Like the Committee for Equal Justice for Mrs. Recy Taylor and the Sojourners for Truth and Justice, the Free Joan Little campaign, led primarily by African-American women, helped mobilize support on behalf of black womanhood and served as a catalyst for larger struggles.

The Free Joan Little campaign is often portrayed as the product of second-wave feminism, which finally enabled women to break the code of silence surrounding sexual violence and "speak out" against rape. While this may be true for white, middle-class feminists who became active in the antirape movement in the early 1970s, African-American women had been speaking out and organizing politically against sexual violence and rape for more than a century.[100] When Jerry Paul read to the jury an African-American woman's essay from 1902 decrying the lack of protection for black womanhood, he bore witness to not only the decades of abuse black women faced during slavery and Jim Crow but also to their long history of speaking out against it. While Paul highlighted this history and helped it find a broader audience, it was African-American women who bore the ultimate burden of testimony.

Speaking out was never easy. Joan Little told reporters shortly after her trial ended that the "toughest thing" about her entire ordeal was testifying. "I spent many months trying to force it from the bottom of me, to try to tell people what happened. I knew people would think that I must have enticed him," she said. "I don't think any woman enjoys talking about being sexually attacked."[101] For African-American women who were raped or sexually harassed in the segregated South, or anywhere their bod-

In this cartoon, published in the
Baltimore Afro-American, Joan Little is
portrayed as a champion prizefighter
who knocked out Jim Crow,
August 19–23, 1975.

ies were not their own, speaking out was downright dangerous. As a result,
testimony must be seen as a form of direct action and radical protest
against the racial and sexual status quo. Indeed, the willingness of African-
American women to testify about the crimes committed against their personhood took enormous courage and strength and indicated that even
decades before the women's movement, they understood that the "personal
is political."

In 1959 John McCray wondered if African-American women had
finally been emancipated after an all-white jury in Florida found four white
men guilty of raping Betty Jean Owens. Fourteen years later, a cartoon
published in the *Baltimore Afro-American* provided an answer. Portrayed as
a champion boxer, Joan Little stands atop a battered and bruised Jim Crow.
With stars swirling around his head, looking tired and overweight in his
Confederate flag shorts, old Jim Crow is down for the count. Hoisting Little's gloved fists up into the air, "trainers" Jerry Paul and Karen Galloway
proclaim victory for their champ and a triumph over "Dixie Racism."[102]

EPILOGUE

"We All Lived in Fear for Years"

RECY TAYLOR TURNED EIGHTY-NINE on December 31, 2008. I met
her and her youngest brother at his tidy ranch house just down the street
from the Rock Hill Holiness Church in Abbeville, Alabama. We came
together on the same day that one million Americans gathered in Washington, D.C., to witness the inauguration of the country's first black president. I talked with the slight, spry woman whose courage and testimony
in 1944 helped inspire the modern civil rights movement. Recy, Robert
Corbitt, and I watched the inaugural events on television in a sunroom
filled with family photos and lush houseplants. The little cabin where Recy
and Robert's father, Benny Corbitt, lived out his final days was visible
through the windows, reminding us, as William Faulkner put it, that "the
past is never dead, it isn't even past."[1]

This seems especially true in Abbeville, where Taylor's family and the
families of her assailants have lived nearly side by side for decades. On
the night before the inauguration, fifteen family members crowded into
the living room to talk about what had happened to Recy. Corbitt, a lean
man with a warm smile, said, "You'd be surprised at how close they lived.
We were very segregated—but we were neighbors. It's just that we were
in the gray houses and they were in the nicer houses."[2]

Hugo Wilson's house is within sight of Lewey Corbitt's sprawling bungalow. The sagging ranch that Billy Howerton grew up in is right across the street from Will Cook's old place. Joe Culpepper's peeling two-story colonial is around the corner from Three Points. Although the cow pastures surrounding Abbeville lie fallow and the sharecropping shacks gave way to modern apartments and fast-food restaurants, the physical layout and population of the tiny rural outpost remain nearly the same as they were in 1944.

For the Corbitt family, those county roads and old homes surrounding Abbeville will always be crime scenes—there has been no resolution or reconciliation, no justice. The violence resonates through generations.

"I used to watch for them," Robert said, referring to the assailants, most of whom stayed in Abbeville until they died. Many of their children and grandchildren are still there. Corbitt used to drive past their houses whenever he was in town and kept an eye on their comings and goings.

"I didn't do anything," he said, "but I was angry."

At seventy-two, he is still haunted by what happened to his oldest sister more than six decades ago. When he returned to Abbeville in 2001, after living most of his adult life in New York City, he spent days searching through microfilmed copies of the local newspaper and pestering locals about what they remembered. Not surprisingly, most whites denied it ever happened, while blacks remembered it well.

"For sixty-five years I've been thinking about it," Corbitt said, his voice even softer than usual. "A whole week didn't go by without me thinking about it. She was like a mother to me," he said, recalling how their mother died when Recy was seventeen and he was one. "She raised me and took care of all six of us, so when I came back here, I tried to dig up something on it."[3]

Recy's other brother, R.J., the oldest son in the family, now an octogenarian, had clear memories of the day he found out about the assault. He had been out of town, "putting down pipe" for Hennison, Black and Green, a construction company, and heard about the rape from migrant farmworkers passing through town. He rushed home and asked his father to name the men so he could find them and retaliate.

"He sat me down and talked to me," R.J. recalled.

"Now listen," Benny Corbitt said to his son, "you know how these folks is here. She's safe. Just be quiet on it for a while. Don't try to do anything or see anybody. You ask them that done it, you might get in trouble. Somebody could put you up. Best be cool and let me handle it."

R.J. remembered that his father would often go to the police station and ask Deputy Lewey Corbitt if they had made any progress on the case, but he was always turned away.

"On things like that," R.J. said, "you didn't go and get into they [white folks'] business. You stay out of it. See, back then if you say anything or do anything and if you weren't a good worker or something they'll send you to prison. They wouldn't even think nothin' about it. So you had to be very quiet. 'Cause they didn't take no chances on you. When they come on ya, they come on ya with a cry. Daddy always talked to me. He said, 'Recy all right. Just stay out of it.' "[4]

Arthur, a stocky, strong-jawed nephew, shook his head slowly. According to the family, he is the spitting image of Benny Corbitt.

"You got to remember," he said, squinting at me, "at that time, black men were lynched. They held back because if they got lynched they couldn't protect the family. If you dead, you can't protect anyone."[5]

Another sister, Mary Murry, agreed. "Daddy wasn't scared, but he couldn't do what he wanted to do because he had no money, no transportation, didn't have an education. It handicapped him."[6]

"It affected him emotionally," Robert said to a chorus of "mm—hmms."[7]

Recy's sister, Alma Daniels, a feisty woman with a sharp tongue and a sparkle in her eye, nodded. "But Daddy stayed mad at them [the police] for a long time," she said. "He always got back at them."

A few years after the attack, Lewey Corbitt's wife asked Benny to kill some chickens for her. "He said okay," Alma said, as she started to giggle. "Daddy had a whole case of chickens. He took every one of those chickens and snatched their heads off and threw them down on Lewey Corbitt's front yard." Lewey Corbitt just stood there, bewildered by Benny's behavior. "There were chickens *everywhere*," she said, laughing.[8]

For a few years after the attack, Recy Taylor stayed close to home and surrounded herself with family and friends. "I was so afraid they were going to hurt me," she said. "They did tell me they were going to kill me if I told." She and her sisters only went out during the day, stayed away from Will Cook's store, and never walked at night. She did not have any other children.

It wasn't until most of the assailants left town and joined the army that Taylor finally felt safe. "I felt like I was back with my good friends and wouldn't be bothered anymore," she said. But local whites treated her poorly; most wouldn't talk to her or looked the other way when they saw her. The police continued to deny the crime ever happened.

"Lewey Corbitt just laughed at me," she said. "He denied he was there."[9]

"The city let her down so bad," said Robert.[10]

In 1965 Recy Taylor, her husband Willie Guy Taylor, and their daughter Joyce Lee moved to a small town in central Florida, where they had been picking oranges for many years. In 1967 Joyce Lee died in a car accident; she left behind one child. Recy's husband died shortly thereafter.[11]

"Recy had a hard life," Robert said. "When our mother died, everyone fell in her hands. She had to take care of all the children. The school she went to was tiny—the teacher went no higher than sixth grade. It was a tough life livin' in the gray house." She is still "very hurt," he said. "I didn't realize the effect rape took on people until it happened to my sister. After all that," he said with a sigh, "she lost her only daughter."[12]

"I never had nothin'," Taylor recalled, her gray hair tied up with a shiny red wrap. "I still don't have nothin'."[13]

The next morning Recy, Robert, and I gathered together to watch the inauguration before they took me on a tour retracing Recy's steps that late summer night in Abbeville, 1944. The past and the present, normally so incongruent, seemed to merge when Michelle Obama, the great-great-granddaughter of slaves and slave owners, cradled Abraham Lincoln's Bible in her palms and extended her hands toward her husband for his oath of office. I turned to Taylor and asked if she ever believed an African-American woman would become the First Lady. "Not in my lifetime," she said.[14]

Growing up in the Jim Crow South, Taylor knew that black women were not even considered *ladies*. From slavery through most of the twentieth century, white Americans denied African-American women the most basic citizenship and human rights, especially the right to ownership and control of their own bodies.

To see Michelle Obama take her place among a pantheon of distinguished American women was to bear witness to African-American women's centuries-long struggle for dignity and respect. Understanding that struggle, Michelle Obama told *The Washington Post* before the 2008 election, "is a process of uncovering the shame, digging out the pride that is part of that story—so that other folks feel comfortable about embracing the beauty and the tangled nature of the history of this country."[15]

The brutal rape of Recy Taylor in 1944, and the sexual exploitation of thousands of other black women in the United States before and after the Civil War, is a central part of our history that has been grossly understated and unacknowledged for far too long. Though it may seem unnecessary, even lurid, to examine the details of sexual violence, it is crucial that we hear the testimonies black women offered at the time. Recy Taylor's willingness, for example, to identify those who attacked her and to testify against them in two grand juries broke the institutional silence surrounding the long history of white men's violation of black women, countered efforts to shame or stereotype her as unchaste, and made white Southern leaders, including the governor of Alabama, recognize her personhood. As a result, her testimony, like so many others, was a momentous event that deserves our recognition. Until we come to terms with our history—even its most shameful secrets and their legacies—we can neither really understand the past nor appreciate the present.

Acknowledgments

When I first thought about becoming a historian, leaders in the field warned me that research and writing is a lonely endeavor. In order to succeed, they cautioned, I would have to endure a long and isolated journey through musty archives, dark microfilm rooms, and silent library stacks. They never told me about all the warm, joyful, and generous people I would meet along the way. This book would not be possible without them.

A hearty thanks goes out to all the archivists, librarians, and fellow historians whose knowledge, good humor, and patience guided my research at institutions around the country. Thanks especially to Curtis Austin and Patricia Buzzard Boyett at the University of Southern Mississippi; Karen Jean Hunt of the John Hope Franklin Collection at Duke; the amazing folks at the Southern Historical Collection at the University of North Carolina, Chapel Hill; William LeFevre at the Walter P. Reuther Library in Detroit; Cornelia Taylor at the S. H. Coleman Library at Florida A & M University; Kenneth Chandler at the Mary McLeod Bethune Council House; and the staffs at Cayuga Community College Library, the Alabama Department of Archives and History, the Schomburg Center for Research in Black Culture, Emory University, and the Wisconsin Historical Society.

Financial and moral support for the initial research came from the Department of History at Rutgers University, where I completed my Ph.D. During my time there, Steven Lawson and Nancy Hewitt treated me like family. They opened their home to me, shared meals and conversation, taught me how to be a better scholar and teacher, and spilled gallons of ink on draft chapters. Deborah Gray White, Jennifer Morgan, Jan Lewis, Ann Fabian, Herman Bennett, and Paul Clemens embraced my project early on and provided encouragement and support when I needed it most. My classmates rescued me from the loneliness of archival research, and provided inspiration, friendship, and dark chocolate when necessary.

During my "spare time," I taught tenth-grade history at the Horace Mann School in New York City alongside some of the finest historians, teachers, and students. Barry Bienstock, Peter Sheehy, Andy Trees, and Elisa Milkes made every day a pleasure.

When it came time to revise my dissertation into a book, I had the great luck to receive a one-year fellowship from the Center for the Study of the American South in Chapel Hill, North Carolina. It was a luxury to devote myself full-time to writing in such a beautiful and collegial environment, where Harry Watson, Jacquelyn Dowd Hall, William Ferris, Barb Call, Nancy Gray Schoonmaker, and Stephen Inrig offered fellowship and fun in equal measure. Tim Tyson, Perri Morgan, and Hope and Sam opened their home and their hearts to me that year. I am forever grateful for their love and friendship. My new colleagues at Wayne State University welcomed me into a lively intellectual environment in 2008 and have provided substantial financial and moral support for this book. Thanks especially to Marc Kruman, Denver Brunsman, Jose Cuello, Liette Gidlow, Marsha Richmond, Fran Shor, Kidada Williams, and Sandra Van-Burkleo, who took time out of their busy schedules to read early drafts. Their ideas and insights undoubtedly made this a better book.

For thirteen years Tim Tyson and Craig Werner have offered unwavering support, encouragement, and faith in this book and its author. Tyson once told me that "ink is love" and they *must* love me because they read and reworked every page of every draft I gave them. Their insight and artistry as scholars and storytellers are evident throughout. If there is anything poetic in this book, it is because of them. The mistakes are mine alone. I hope someday I can repay them for welcoming me into, and showing me how to build and sustain, a beloved community.

That beloved community is made up of some of the best folks around and they have enriched this book and my life in innumerable ways. Thank you to Davarian Baldwin, Rebecca Bortner, Martha Bouyer, Lance Broumand, Sean Cassidy, David Cecelski, Bill Chafe, Katherine Charron, Heesun Choi, Robert Corbitt and family, John Dittmer, Crystal Feimster, Gillian Brown-Fink, Krystal Frazier, Marisa Fuentes, Glenda Gilmore, Ed and Carmen Gitre, David Goldberg, Robin Goldstein, Francina Graef, Christina Greene, Matt and Kathy Grossman, Lori Henn, Darlene Clark Hine, Charles Hughes, Melody Ivins, Hassan Jeffries, Steve Kantrowitz, Jenny Kelly, Carmen Khair, Shirley Kramer, Peter Lau, Rhonda Lee, Bill Levy, Phil and Gina Levy, Steve Levy, Andy Lewis, the Mattheis family, Rob McCreanor, Grace and Richard McGuire, Janice Min, Richard

Mizelle, Perri Morgan, Sarah and Brett Mountain, Danielle Olekszyk, Marcia, Karl, Jen, and Felicia Rosh and their families, Karen Routledge, Erandy Pacheco Salazar, Rebecca Scales, Adriane Lentz-Smith, Lisa and Pete St. John, Heather Thompson, Hope and Sam Tyson, and the Zenner/Azzolina family.

Charlotte Sheedy is my real-life fairy godmother. Her lifelong commitment to women's rights and the African-American freedom struggle is an inspiration to me and I feel incredibly lucky and grateful to have her as an agent and friend. She immediately saw the possibilities and promise of this project and has skillfully shepherded me through the publication process. Not only has she taught me how to be a better writer, she inspires me to be a better woman. She is whip-smart and witty, gracious and nurturing, and full of love and joy. Thank you, Charlotte.

Every good writer has a good editor and I am fortunate to have Vicky Wilson in my corner. She fought to publish this book while it was still a dissertation and has championed it throughout the editing and production process at Knopf. Her sharp eye and creativity freshened the manuscript, and her patience and good humor throughout were indispensable.

My family's unconditional love and support make everything possible. Thank you to Phyllis St. Michael and Tim and Dee McGuire for giving me the world. I met Adam Rosh in 1998 at the University of Wisconsin. For the past twelve years, he has been my inspiration, my best friend, and biggest advocate. I love him more each day. In July 2008, we welcomed our first child, Ruby, into the world. She is my light and my joy and I hope we can give her everything that has been given to us. This book is dedicated to her.

It is also dedicated to Recy Taylor and all the survivors of sexual violence. Their silent resistance and sometimes bold testimonies are examples of human dignity and hope.

Notes

Note on abbreviations and citations: Names of archival collections, most newspapers, and a few magazines and journals are abbreviated, as are some oral interviews. See the bibliography for full citations.

PROLOGUE

1. "Report" and "Supplemental Report," submitted by N. W. Kimbrough and J. V. Kitchens, December 14 and 27, 1944, folder 1, CS. Hereafter cited as "Report" and "Supplemental Report" respectively. See also Earl Conrad, Eugene Gordon, and Henrietta Buckmaster, "Equal Justice Under Law," pamphlet prepared by the Committee for Equal Justice for Mrs. Recy Taylor, n.d., in folder 3, ibid. The Rockhill Holiness Church is still there but is now called the Church of God in Christ. Thanks to Robert Corbitt and Josephine Baker for a tour of the church.
2. I-Corbitt 3, I-Corbitt, and I-RTC. Corbitt, Recy's youngest brother who was a witness to the events that followed the attack, corroborated nearly every detail in the governor's report.
3. "Report," 7. According to reports, seven men were in the car but only six participated in the gang rape. Billy Howerton claims he did not have sex with her. The other assailants corroborated Howerton's testimony. See "Report," 9–10.
4. I-RTC, I-Corbitt 8.
5. Gerda Lerner, *Black Women in White America: A Documentary History* (New York, 1972). See also Jacqueline Dowd Hall, "The Mind That Burns in Each Body: Women, Rape and Racial Violence," in Ann Snitow, Christine Stansell, and Sharon Thompson, eds., *Powers of Desire: the Politics of Sexuality* (New York, 1983), 328–49; Leslie Schwalm, *A Hard Fight For We: Women's Transition from Slavery to Freedom in South Carolina* (Chicago, 1997), 37, 44–45, 119–21; Tera Hunter, *To 'Joy My Freedom* (Cambridge, Mass., 1997), 10–11; Leon Litwack, *Trouble in Mind* (New York, 1998), 342–43; and Sharon Block, "Lines of Color, Sex and Service: Comparative Sexual Coercion in Early America," in Martha Hodes, ed., *Sex, Love, Race: Crossing Boundaries in North American History* (New York, 1999), 141–63.
6. Hall, "Mind That Burns," 330.
7. Ida B. Wells-Barnett, "Southern Horrors: Lynch Law in All Its Phases," in Wells-Barnett, *On Lynchings: Southern Horrors, A Red Record, Mob Rule in New Orleans* (Salem, Mass., 1991), 65, 30.
8. Chana Kai Lee, *For Freedom's Sake: The Life of Fannie Lou Hamer* (Urbana, Ill., 1999), 9–10.

9. Maria Bevacqua, *Rape on the Public Agenda: Feminism and the Politics of Sexual Assault* (Boston, 2000), 21.

10. Linda Brent, "Incidents in the Life of a Slave Girl," in Henry Louis Gates, Jr., ed., *The Classic Slave Narratives* (New York, 1987), 335.

11. Bevacqua, *Rape,* 24.

12. Paula Giddings, *When and Where I Enter: The Impact of Black Women on Race and Sex in America* (New York, 1984), 31.

13. Ibid., 86–87.

CHAPTER 1. "THEY'D KILL ME IF I TOLD"

1. Rosa Parks with Jim Haskins, *Rosa Parks: My Story* (New York, 1992). The population estimate for Abbeville in 1940 was 2,080 people, about 30 percent of whom were African American; see *The WPA Guide to 1930s Alabama* (Tuscaloosa, Ala., 1941), 343. Professional genealogists at ProGenealogists Family Research and Ancestry Research charted Rosa Parks's family lineage using census records and death certificates. They put their findings, which parallel historical and autobiographical accounts, online. See http://www.progenealogists.com/parks/aqwn01.htm (accessed October 22, 2007).

2. Parks with Haskins, *My Story,* 8.

3. For more on the "New South," see Edward L. Ayers, *The Promise of the New South: Life After Reconstruction* (New York, 1992).

4. Parks with Haskins, *My Story,* 9.

5. C. Vann Woodward, *The Strange Career of Jim Crow* (New York, 1966), 67–109 passim.

6. Parks with Haskins, *My Story,* 15.

7. Ibid., 12–18; "belligerent attitude," 16.

8. Douglas Brinkley, *Rosa Parks* (New York, 2000), 16.

9. Leona stayed behind, Parks with Haskins, *My Story,* 9; "don't put up with bad treatment," ibid., 15.

10. The description of Abbeville comes from Earl Conrad, *Jim Crow America* (New York, 1947), 5–6.

11. I-Corbitt 3, I-RTC.

12. Petitions and letters signed by Parks in folder 4, CS.

13. Statement of Recy Taylor, in "Report," 8. Recy and her brother Robert remember events differently. In interviews conducted in 2008 and 2009, they both say that Will Cook did not pick up their father and did not search for the assailants. Instead, they say that Benny Corbitt went searching for his daughter on his own and met her on the roadside near the intersection of Elm Street and East Alabama. Given Will Cook's reputation among blacks as a brutal racist and his dishonesty in the report itself, I tend to believe Corbitt and Taylor's account. Cook had a vested interest in portraying himself as a respectable policeman who followed standard procedures when the governor's investigators interviewed him in 1944. See I-RTC, I-Corbitt.

14. I-Corbitt 3.

15. Statement of West Daniel, in "Report," 11–13; statement of Fannie Daniel, ibid., 9–11; statement of Recy Taylor, ibid., 8; statement of George H. Gamble, ibid., 2–3.

16. Statement of George H. Gamble, ibid., 3.

17. John Dollard, *Caste and Class in a Southern Town* (Madison, Wis., 1988), 139.

18. "Supplemental Report," folder 1, CS.

19. "New World of Black Men," in Brinkley, *Rosa,* 23. For more on Garvey and the UNIA, see Mary G. Robinson, *Grassroots Garveyism: The Universal Negro Improvement Association*

in the Rural South, 1920–1927 (Chapel Hill, N.C., 2007); Colin Grant, *Negro with a Hat: The Rise and Fall of Marcus Garvey* (New York, 2008).

20. Glenn Feldman, *Politics, Society and the Klan in Alabama, 1915–1949* (Tuscaloosa, Ala., 1999), 16.

21. Parks with Haskins, *My Story,* 30.

22. Feldman, *Politics,* 54–55.

23. Parks with Haskins, *My Story,* 31.

24. Ibid., 48.

25. Brinkley, *Rosa,* 27.

26. Parks with Haskins, *My Story,* 55–60.

27. Robin D. G. Kelley, *Hammer and Hoe: Alabama Communists During the Great Depression* (Chapel Hill, N.C., 1990), 84–85.

28. Dan Carter, *Scottsboro: A Tragedy of the American South* (Baton Rouge, La., 1979), 7–8.

29. Brinkley, *Rosa,* 38.

30. "Nigger rape case," in Carter, *Scottsboro,* 12; stunning rapidity and harsh sentence, ibid., 50; "cold blooded 'illegal' lynching," ibid., 49; "synonymous with," ibid., 50.

31. For the best summary of African-American activism in Alabama in the 1930s and early 1940s, see Kelley, *Hammer and Hoe.*

32. Parks with Haskins, *My Story,* 75.

33. Brinkley, *Rosa,* 58; Parks with Haskins, *My Story,* 79.

34. Johnnie Carr was the first female member of the Montgomery branch. Parks was the second. See Steven M. Millner, "The Emergence and Career of a Social Movement," in David Garrow, ed., *The Walking City: The Montgomery Bus Boycott, 1955–1956* (New York, 1989), 445; J. Mills Thornton, *Dividing Lines: Municipal Politics and the Struggle for Civil Rights in Montgomery, Birmingham and Selma* (Tuscaloosa, Ala., 2002), 58–59. See also Brinkley, *Rosa.*

35. Brinkley, *Rosa,* 48, 68. Brinkley notes that these early records were permanently lost when a friend inadvertently threw them away while cleaning out the shed where they were stored; Parks with Haskins, *My Story,* 49.

36. Brinkley, *Rosa,* 70; Parks with Haskins, *My Story,* 84–85.

37. Petitions and letters signed by Parks in folder 4, CS.

38. Fred Atwater, "$600 to Rape Wife? Alabama Whites Make Offer to Recy Taylor Mate!", *CD,* January 27, 1945, 1.

39. "Report," 3.

40. See witness list, "Report," 14. For more on Bill Baxley, see Diane McWhorter, *Carry Me Home: Birmingham Alabama and the Climactic Battle of the Civil Rights Revolution* (New York, 2001), 573–75.

41. Earl Conrad, "Death Threat Made Against Rape Victim," *CD,* March 17, 1945, 9; I-RTC 30.

42. I-Corbitt 3.

43. For more on Alabama's "Popular Front" politics, see Kelley, *Hammer and Hoe,* 152–92 passim. Biondi calls the coalition between radical or leftist black organizations, labor unions, and more middle-class, traditional organizations like the NAACP, the "Black Popular Front." Martha Biondi, *To Stand and Fight: The Struggle for Civil Rights in Postwar New York City* (Cambridge, Mass., 2003), 9.

44. More than thirty national labor unions and many more locals supported Recy Taylor. See "Press Release," February 3, 1945, folder 4, box 430, ECC. Other organizations that played an active role in Taylor's defense include the National Council of Negro Women, the International Labor Defense, and the Montgomery branch of the NAACP: "Partial Sponsor List," December 28, 1944, ibid.

45. SNYC held its first conference in Richmond, Virginia, in 1937, and more than five hundred delegates from thirteen states attended. While many leaders in SNYC were members of the Communist Party, its advisory committee was staffed by prominent, respectable middle-class leaders like Mary McLeod Bethune, Charlotte Hawkins Brown, and sociologist Charles Johnson. The conference helped SNYC members lead a campaign to organize five thousand tobacco workers into the Tobacco Stemmers and Laborers Industrial Union, netting them a 20–33 percent wage increase. The third annual SNYC conference, held in Birmingham in 1940, was the "largest to date" and drew 650 delegates and much praise throughout the South as a beacon of hope and light amid white repression. See Kelley, *Hammer and Hoe*, 201, 202.

46. Ibid., 222.

47. Ibid., 203.

48. Erik S. McDuffie, *Long Journeys: Four Black Women and the Communist Party, USA, 1930–1956*, Ph.D. diss (New York University, 2003), 295. Kelley, *Hammer and Hoe*, 204–05.

49. Rosa Parks also served as E. D. Nixon's secretary. Nixon was president of the Montgomery branch of the Brotherhood of Sleeping Car Porters and the Voters League. He became president of the local branch of the NAACP in 1945 and served as a key organizer of the Montgomery bus boycott in 1955. For more on E. D. Nixon, see Thornton, *Dividing*, 28–32, 59–64 passim, and 99–102 passim; Taylor Branch, *Parting the Waters: America in the King Years, 1954–1963* (New York, 1988), 120–36 passim; Howell Raines, *My Soul Is Rested; Movement Days in the Deep South Remembered* (New York, 1977), 37–39, 43–51.

50. "Alabama Whites Attack Woman; Not Punished," *PC*, October 28, 1944, 2.

51. Gene Roberts and Hank Klibanoff, *The Race Beat: The Press, the Civil Rights Struggle, and the Awakening of a Nation* (New York, 2006), 22.

52. Ibid., 22. Timothy B. Tyson, "Wars for Democracy," in David S. Cecelski and Timothy B. Tyson, eds., *Democracy Betrayed: The Wilmington Race Riot of 1898 and Its Legacy* (Chapel Hill, N.C., 1998), 255; see also Harvard Sitkoff, "Racial Militancy and Interracial Violence in the Second World War," *Journal of American History* 58, no. 3 (December 1971): 661–82 passim.

53. FBI report on the Southern Negro Youth Conference, December 11, 1944, 2; see also Agent Abbaticchio's FBI report, dated November 30 to December 3, 1944, HK. See also "Delegation to Ask Alabama Governor for Justice for Rape Victim," *DW*, November 26, 1944, clipping found in Scrapbook Collection, ECC.

54. Eugene Gordon, "Alabama Authorities Ignore White Gang's Rape of Negro Mother," *Worker*, November 19, 1944, n.d.

55. Biondi states that New York City was the site of a postwar civil rights movement for jobs, equality, desegregation, and human dignity, which set the stage for the Southern movement a decade later. "With its large Black population, progressive race leadership, strong trade unions, and progressive print media," Biondi argues, New York City "became a major battleground in the postwar push for racial equality." It was also home to the United Nations, which "Black Popular Front" coalitions petitioned "seeking some form of assistance or intervention to aid the Black freedom struggle in the United States," especially the 1951 *We Charge Genocide* petition submitted by the Civil Rights Congress. Biondi, *Stand,* 37, 57.

56. "Press Release," November 20, 1944, folder 2, box 370, ECC.

57. Minutes from "Conference Held at Theresa Hotel, November 25, 1944 on Case of Mrs. Recy Taylor," series IV, reel 6, NNCP-M. See Charles A. Collins, executive secretary of the Negro Labor Victory Committee, to Governor Chauncey Sparks, November 30, 1944, folder 1, CS. The Negro Labor Victory Committee claimed to represent more than

300,000 black workers in more than one hundred affiliated CIO, AFL, and independent unions.

58. Moore was a Harlem activist, Garveyite, and member of the ILD and CPUSA, who fought on behalf of the Scottsboro boys in the 1930s. She headed up the New York branch of the Committee to Save Mrs. Rosa Lee Ingram, fought to desegregate major league baseball, and founded the first organization advocating black reparations in 1955. Biondi, *Stand,* 281; See also McDuffie, *Long Journeys.*

59. "Delegation to Ask Ala. Governor for Justice for Rape Victim," newspaper clipping, November 26, 1944, series IV, reel 6, NNCP-M.

60. Minutes from "Conference Held at Theresa Hotel," series IV, reel 6, NNCP-M. FBI reports show that at least fifty people participated in the panel discussion on "civil liberties" and Recy Taylor.

61. "Delegation to Ask Ala. Governor for Justice for Rape Victim," newspaper clipping, November 26, 1944, series IV, reel 6, NNCP-M.

62. Samuel L. Webb and Margaret E. Ambrester, eds., *Alabama Governors: A Political History of the State* (Tuscaloosa, Ala., 2001), 191.

63. Dan T. Carter, *The Politics of Rage: George Wallace, the Origins of the New Conservatism, and the Transformation of American Politics* (New York, 1995), 31.

64. While it is impossible to know exactly how many letters came in, the postcards, petitions, and personal letters in the Chauncey Sparks Papers number well over five hundred. If you count the number of signatures on the petitions sent in, they easily number in the thousands.

65. Mrs. Gretchen Coon to Governor Sparks, November 29, 1944, folder 1, CS.

66. A "Friend of the South" to Governor Sparks, December 3, 1944, folder 1, CS.

67. Charles A. Collins to Governor Sparks, November 30, 1944, folder 1, CS.

68. For an account of one of the worst racial pogroms in the United States during this period, see Cecelski and Tyson, *Democracy Betrayed.* See also David Fort Godshalk, *Veiled Visions: The 1906 Atlanta Race Riot and the Reshaping of American Race Relations* (Chapel Hill, N.C., 2009).

69. W. J. Cash, *The Mind of the South* (New York, 1991), 116.

70. Tyson, "Wars for Democracy," in Cecelski and Tyson, *Democracy Betrayed,* 262.

71. Kari Frederickson, *The Dixiecrat Revolt and the End of the Solid South, 1932–1968* (Chapel Hill, N.C., 2001), 33.

72. Cecelski and Tyson, *Democracy Betrayed,* 262. Howard W. Odum, *Race and Rumors of Race: The American South in the Early Forties* (Baltimore, Md., 1997), xi.

73. Odum, *Rumors,* 97–103.

74. Ibid.

75. Ibid., 55.

76. Ibid., 57.

77. Ibid., 57–58.

78. Ibid., 64.

79. Marilynn S. Johnson, "Gender, Race, and Rumours: Re-examining the 1943 Race Riots," *Gender and History* 10, no. 2 (August 1998): 259.

80. Ibid., 258.

81. Ibid., 258–59.

82. Ibid., 259.

83. Cecelski and Tyson, *Democracy Betrayed,* 267.

84. For more on the Detroit riot, see Dominic J. Capeci and Martha Wilkerson, *Layered Violence: The Detroit Rioters of 1943* (Jackson, Miss. 1991).

85. Odum, *Rumors,* 138. The rumors reflected reality. Banner headlines in African-American

and leftist newspapers detailed the injustices: "Negro WAC Beaten Up by Kentucky Cop, Faces Trial," *DW*, July 20, 1945; "Wife of Vet Beaten Twice," *BAA*, September 22, 1945; "Georgia White Men Beat 2nd Negro Woman," April 3, 1945, reel 91, frame 168, TCF; "White Soldiers Slug Two War Wives," *BAA,* September 22, 1945, 1; and "Three WACS Beaten by Cops Acquitted in Court Martial," *CD*, August 11, 1945, 8.

86. Letter signed by thirty-three soldiers from "Somewhere in Belgium" to Governor Sparks, January 27, 1945, folder 3, CS.

87. Eugene Henderson to Governor Sparks, January 16, 1945, folder 3, CS.

88. Ernest Scott to Governor Sparks, December 22, 1944, folder 3, CS.

89. Charles S. Seely to Governor Sparks, May 5, 1945, folder 4, CS.

90. Mr. and Mrs. Scott McCall to Governor Sparks, December 18, 1944, folder 3, CS.

91. Julius Crane to Governor Sparks, January 18, 1945, folder 3, CS.

92. Robert Norrell, *The Making of Modern Alabama* (Tuscaloosa, Ala., 1993), 141–42. According to Norrell, German POWs received the same food and shelter as U.S. troops, played sports, and took classes in English, music, and theater.

93. William Warren Rogers et al., *Alabama: The History of a Deep South State* (Tuscaloosa, Ala., 1994), 511.

94. "Alabama Officials Feel People's Pressure in Mrs. Taylor's Case," *DW*, December 12, 1944, 4.

95. Ibid.

96. Postcards and petitions for Recy Taylor, folder 2, 3, 4, CS.

97. "Taylor Case Is Now Nationwide," *Worker*, December 31, 1944, p. 12, clipping, folder 8, box 104, JBM.

98. Ibid.

99. Earl Conrad, "Dixie Sex Crimes Against Negro Women Widespread," *CD,* March 10, 1945, 5. Though the article keeps anonymous the African-American leader whom Conrad interviewed, I am confident it is E. D. Nixon—not only because he pledged support from his "organization" but also because he said he had a "dossier" of fifty similar cases. Given Rosa Parks's role in investigating racial violence, her meticulous record keeping, and her interest in rape cases, along with her close relationship to Nixon (she was his secretary), I believe there is enough evidence to conclude Conrad's source was Nixon. Since Conrad also interviewed E. G. Jackson, it is reasonable to assume that Jackson put Conrad in touch with his colleague and close ally Nixon. (When Nixon waged a fierce battle to oust Robert L. Matthews, the president of the Montgomery NAACP, throughout 1945, Jackson used his paper to aid his campaign. Nixon finally became president of the Montgomery branch in December 1945.) See Thornton, *Dividing,* 31.

100. John White, "Nixon Was the One: Edgar Daniel Nixon and the Montgomery Bus Boycott," in Brian Ward and Tony Badger, eds., *The Making of Martin Luther King and the Civil Rights Movement* (New York, 1996), 45.

101. Earl Conrad, "Dixie Sex Crimes Against Negro Women Widespread," *CD,* March 10, 1945, 5.

102. John H. McCray, "South's Courts Show New Day of Justice," *BAA*, July 11, 1959.

103. "Fayetteville White Man Sentenced to 15 Years for Raping a Negro Girl," *CT*, March 16, 1940. This case is interesting because of the relatively long sentence Davis received even after he was allowed to plead a lesser crime, attempted assault. Apparently sixteen-year-old black girls still could not be "raped." Still, the local NAACP raised enough money in order to wage a court battle and win. The clothes Davis casually threw out the window turned out to be the main evidence used against him.

104. "Young Woman Charges Crime at Rifle-Point," June 2, 1942, newspaper clipping, NAACP Papers, Alabama Chapter, 1940–1955, microfilm. See also Emory O. Jackson to Walter White, June 3, 1942, box C2, series II, NAACP Papers.

105. "Accused of Rape on Teen-Age Dunbar High School Girl," *ASP*, July 17, 1942, 1. Thanks to Story Matkin-Rawn for finding this article for me.

106. Reverend James M. Hinton to Thurgood Marshall, December 14, 1945; Thurgood Marshall to Reverend James M. Hinton, December 28, 1945; Milton Kemnitz to Thurgood Marshall, December 7, 1945; all letters in box 123, series III, NAACP Papers.

107. Lisa Lindquist Dorr, *White Women, Rape and the Power of Race in Virginia, 1900–1960* (Chapel Hill, N.C., 2004), 233–34. Strayhorn told her brother what happened and filed charges. Both men were arrested, tried, and ultimately convicted of rape. They were each sentenced to seven years in prison. The Virginia Supreme Court upheld the verdict. Ibid., 299n98.

108. Reverend V. E. Hilsman to Constance Baker Motley, January 12, 1950, box 123, series III, NAACP Papers.

109. "Two Denied Bail in Rape Case," *PC*, February 2, 1948, 5. The article about Berryhill and Gasque being held without bail was featured just above another article about a black man, titled "Stares Too Hard Gets Six Months." The juxtaposition of these two stories highlighted the unequal system of justice in the South. Richard Sutton, a nineteen-year-old African American from Plymouth, North Carolina, was sentenced to work six months on the county roads for "assault on a female" after he apparently frightened the woman by "staring at her in the County Courthouse Building." According to the report, Sutton had an appointment with the sheriff and stopped at the window of the recorder's office. He asked directions to the office but, according to the young white woman, "stared at her so hard she became frightened and ran."

110. Press release, February 25, 1948, box 123, Series III, NAACP Papers, Patterson managed to escape and told her story to the NAACP.

111. "I don't think it would be too much," Jones said, "if each branch in each state and each city . . . would ask each member to donate a small amount to see that this man is convicted." Franklin Williams, an assistant special counsel for the NAACP, assured Jones that "representatives of the Association are looking into the matter" and hoped to bring the "guilty person before the bar of justice." Mrs. Joy B. Jones to Arthur Springarn, July 31, 1947; Franklin H. Williams to Jones, July 31, 1947; Jones to Springarn, n.d.; "Rape of Girl, 11, Charged; No Action," n.d., newspaper clipping; "Alleged Rape on Girl Goes Unnoticed," n.d., newspaper clipping; all in box 123, series III, NAACP Papers.

112. Press release, "Negro Girl Beaten, Raped in Meridian," August 22, 1947; Edward Knott, Jr., to Walter White, August 19, 1947; Oliver W. Harrington to Robert Ratcliffe, August 21, 1947, box 123, series III, NAACP Papers. Press release states that "NAACP officials in this city were attempting to arouse sufficient public opinion to guarantee the prosecution" of Perry. See also, "Charge Woman's Rape to Mississippi Oil Man," *CD*, August 30, 1947, 8. Perry's strategy was similar to that employed by the Committee for Equal Justice for Mrs. Recy Taylor.

113. Charles Payne, *I've Got the Light of Freedom: The Organizing Tradition and the Mississippi Freedom Struggle* (Berkeley, Calif., 1995), 15.

114. Ibid., 15.

115. Marian Wynn Perry to Edward Knott, Jr., August 22, 1947, box 123, series III, NAACP Papers.

116. This strategy had proven relatively effective in the campaign to end lynching. Payne posits that negative nationwide publicity, coupled with the falling price of cotton, electoral changes wrought by mass migration out of the South, and pending federal anti-lynching legislation, made the South subject to more scrutiny than ever before. "By the 1930s, newspapers in larger southern cities typically criticized lynchings, at least in principle. By the 1940s, their criticisms were clearly linked to fear of such scrutiny." The fact that the United States was engaged in a global war against fascism and racism

abroad made lynching African Americans a foreign policy faux pas and helped to decrease the public "spectacle" lynchings popular in the early part of the twentieth century. See Payne, *Light of Freedom,* 19. Of course, these pressures did not end white violence against African Americans, as evidenced by the brutal murders and sexual attacks in Mississippi in the 1940s.

117. "Alabama Has No Race Problem, Claims Official," *CD,* March 31, 1945, 11. Conrad's articles appeared as a series of three separate essays in early spring 1945, but drafts found in his papers suggest that he conducted the interviews with residents in Montgomery, Abbeville, and Birmingham in late December 1944.

118. Mrs. (P. B.) Margaret H. Moss to Governor Sparks, n.d., folder 3, CS.

119. "Governor Sparks to Press Charges Against Rapists Following Protests," *PC,* December 23, 1944, 1.

120. "Report," 3–4.

121. "Report," 3–4; "Supplemental Report," 4.

122. Ibid., 5.

123. Ibid.

124. Ibid., 14.

125. Ibid., 9

126. "Supplemental Report," 4.

127. "Report," 4.

128. "Supplemental Report," 5–14.

129. Ibid., 10–12.

130. Agent Abbaticchio's FBI report, dated January 11 to January 27, 1945, box 45, HK.

131. "This Evening," *BN,* February 21, 1945, and "The Henry County Case," *BN,* February 25, 1945, 6, clippings, folder 2, CS.

132. "Second Henry County Grand Jury Finds No Bill in Negro's Charges," *DE,* February 15, 1945.

133. Esther Cooper Jackson to James Jackson, n.d., James E. Jackson and Esther Cooper Jackson Papers, Tamiment Library, New York City. Thanks to Sara Rzeszutek for mailing me a copy of the letter.

134. "Strange As It Is," n.d. clipping, NAACP-Alabama Files, 1940–55, microfilm. I-Corbitt 3; Corbitt verified the move. He said Rosa Parks came to Abbeville to move Taylor to Montgomery. Recy and her husband stayed in Montgomery for two to three months, living in a rooming house on South Jackson Street.

135. Clara Hard Rutledge was the wife of a state highway engineer. Her liberal views and actions were unusual at the time. Rutledge was joined by other white liberal women including Miss Juliette Gordon, a librarian; Mrs. Olive Andrews, the wife of a local insurance agent; Mrs. Bea Kaufman, the wife of a wholesale grocery executive; Mrs. Frances P. McLeod, the wife of a Methodist minister; and (after 1951) Virginia F. Durr, the wife of attorney and New Deal appointee Clifford Durr. See Thornton, *Dividing,* 36. Clara Hard Rutledge to Earl Conrad, n.d., folder 6, box 365, EC.

136. Henrietta Buckmaster to Dorothy Laing, March 1, 1945, folder 19, box 8, series II "Political Activities," AKL. Thanks to Jacki Castledine for finding this material for me.

137. Governor Sparks to Alexander Nunn, April 2, 1945, folder 1, CS.

138. Glenda Sullivan to executive board members, April 2, 1945, NNCP-M.

139. Press release, March 30, 1945, NNCP-M.

140. Glenda Sullivan to executive board members, April 2, 1945, NNCP-M.

141. Kelley, *Hammer and Hoe,* 224. For more on McCarthyism and anti-Communism, see Ellen Schrecker, *Many Are the Crimes: McCarthyism in America* (Boston, 1998); David Oshinsky, *A Conspiracy So Immense: The World of Joe McCarthy* (New York, 1983); David Caute,

The Great Fear: The Anti-Communist Purge Under Truman and Eisenhower (New York, 1978); and Richard Fried, *Nightmare in Red: The McCarthy Era in Perspective* (New York, 1990).

142. In Montgomery, for example, E. D. Nixon and Rufus A. Lewis organized competing voter-registration clubs. After *Smith v. Allwright* ended the white primary in 1944, Nixon's Alabama Voters League and Lewis's Citizens Club had helped 813 African Americans register to vote—3.7 percent of the city's black population. By 1955, the number had doubled. They also waged battles against police brutality and mobilized community action to defend other black women who were assaulted in the late 1940s and early 1950s. See Thornton, *Dividing,* 28–35.

CHAPTER 2. "NEGROES EVERY DAY ARE BEING MOLESTED"

1. Ella Ree Jones statement, July 12, 1942, Thurgood Marshall to T. T. Allen, president of the Montgomery, Alabama, NAACP, August 4, 1942, box 114, series II, NAACP Papers.

2. Lamont H. Yeakey, *The Montgomery, Alabama Bus Boycott, 1955–56,* Ph.D. diss. (Columbia University, 1979), 195.

3. See "Incidents and Complaints—Transportation Department, Race Question, Twelve Months Ending March 31st 1944"; "Report of Complaint Reports—Race Question, Twelve Months Ending June 30th 1943"; "Analysis of Complaints and Incidents Concerning Race Problems on Birmingham Electric Company's Transportation System, 12 Months Ending August 31, 1942," CP.

4. Ella Ree Jones statement, July 12, 1942, in Marshall to Allen, August 4, 1942, box 114, series II, NAACP Papers.

5. Juan Williams, *Thurgood Marshall: American Revolutionary* (New York, 1998), 130.

6. Thurgood Marshall to T. T. Allen, August 4, 1942, box 113, series II, NAACP Papers. It is unclear how Allen handled the case after Marshall alerted him to Jones's beating, but it is worth noting that Allen was considered by local activists a do-nothing leader, which caused blacks to oust him and elect E. D. Nixon in the next NAACP election. See Dorothy A. Autrey, *The National Association for the Advancement of Colored People in Alabama, 1913–1952,* Ph.D. diss. (University of Notre Dame, 1985), 244. See also Yeakey, *Boycott,* 62.

7. Thurgood Marshall to Hon. William H. Hastie, dean of Howard Law School, January 13, 1945, box 194, series II, NAACP Papers.

8. Ibid.

9. Barbara Ransby, *Ella Baker and the Black Freedom Movement: A Radical Democratic Vision* (Chapel Hill, N.C., 2003), 141–42.

10. Timothy B. Tyson, *Radio Free Dixie: Robert F. Williams and the Roots of Black Power* (Chapel Hill, N.C., 1999), 51. African Americans emerged from World War II determined to force the United States to reconcile the wartime rhetoric of democracy with the reality of Jim Crow. See Steven F. Lawson, ed., *To Secure These Rights: The Report of President Harry S. Truman's Committee on Civil Rights* (Boston, 2004), 5. World War II ushered in dramatic changes in the domestic political landscape. Two million African Americans left the South during the war as a result of many forces, including the mechanization of farming, which reduced Southern dependency on sharecroppers, and the lure of defense jobs, which pulled hundreds of thousands of African Americans north, dramatically altering electoral politics. By 1948 African Americans had enough voting power in the North to tip the balance in any presidential contest. Black ballots determined political victors in sixteen non-South states. In the South, *Smith v. Allwright* led to renewed registration efforts, and black registered voters rose from 250,000 in 1944 to more than a

million in 1952. See Steven F. Lawson, *Black Ballots: Voting Rights in the South, 1944–1969* (Lanham, Md., 1999), 139. For other ways the South changed during the war, see John Egerton, *Speak Now Against the Day* (New York, 1994), 347–61. The emerging Cold War rivalry between the United States and the Soviet Union, and the creation of the United Nations in 1945, presented African Americans with myriad opportunities to publicly address racial issues and call American practices into question on the world stage. See Mary Dudziak, *Cold War Civil Rights: Race and the Image of American Democracy* (Princeton, N.J., 2000), 11–13.

11. On "shock troops," see John Dittmer, *Local People: The Struggle for Civil Rights in Mississippi* (Urbana, Ill., 1994), 9.

12. Egerton, *Speak,* 366: "Georgia and Alabama were the principal killing fields." Each state had at least seven confirmed racial murders in 1946 alone.

13. Ibid., 362; Patricia Sullivan, *Days of Hope: Race and Democracy in the New Deal Era* (Chapel Hill, N.C., 1996), 197.

14. Egerton, *Speak,* 362–63.

15. Laura Wexler, *Fire in a Canebrake: The Last Mass Lynching in America* (New York, 2003), 51.

16. "In their place," Egerton, *Speak,* 367; Maceo Snipes story in Sullivan, *Days,* 213.

17. Wexler, *Fire,* 82.

18. Egerton, *Speak,* 369. Loy Harrison spoke freely about his role in the lynching in 1981 to Clinton Adams, who witnessed the murders when he was ten years old. Harrison and his accomplices were never prosecuted. In 1992 Adams broke his silence and told the FBI and reporters at the *Atlanta Constitution* what he had seen in 1946. He named four of the murderers (deceased at the time) and said that one of the five cars at the scene was a state police car.

19. Glenda E. Gilmore, "Murder, Memory and the Flight of the Incubus," in Cecelski and Tyson, *Democracy Betrayed,* 75.

20. Tyson, *Radio Free Dixie,* 58; see also Leon F. Litwack, "Hellhounds," in Hilton Als et al., eds., *Without Sanctuary: Lynching Photography in America* (Santa Fe, N.M., 2000).

21. Frederick Douglass quoted in Martha Hodes, *White Women, Black Men: Illicit Sex in the Nineteenth Century South* (New Haven, Conn., 1997), 206.

22. Egerton, *Speak,* 370.

23. Ibid., 371. See also Lawson, *To Secure,* 8. Harris survived and later identified five of the murderers. An all-white jury acquitted the men after deliberating five hours in February 1947.

24. Sullivan, *Days,* 214

25. Lawson, *To Secure,* 9.

26. Ibid., 9; See also Dudziak, *Cold War,* 23.

27. Dudziak, *Cold War,* 20.

28. Ibid., 31.

29. Steven F. Lawson, *Running for Freedom: Civil Rights and Black Politics in America Since 1941* (New York, 2008), 42.

30. Lawson, *To Secure,* 28–29.

31. Ibid., 179, 31.

32. Egerton, *Speak,* 476–77.

33. Thornton, *Dividing,* 59.

34. Parks with Haskins, *My Story,* 84.

35. Ibid., 85.

36. Tyson, *Radio Free Dixie,* 94.

37. Philip Dray, *At the Hands of Persons Unknown: The Lynching of Black America* (New York, 2002), 399.

38. Ibid.

39. Ibid., 397.

40. Ibid., 398.

41. The Civil Rights Congress was formed at a conference in Detroit on April 27–28, 1946. By the mid-1950s it consisted of sixty chapters across the nation, most on the East and West coasts; only ten chapters existed in the South. In the summer of 1948, black Communist William L. Patterson, former head of the ILD, became the national secretary of the organization. Patterson hoped to pattern the CRC protest strategies and tactics after those used in the defense of the Scottsboro boys. See Charles H. Martin, "The Civil Rights Congress and Southern Black Defendants," *Georgia Historical Quarterly* 71, no. 1 (Spring 1987): 25–52 passim; Gerald Horne, *Communist Front? The Civil Rights Congress* (London, 1988), 29–32.

42. Dray, *Persons Unknown,* 397: "no white man had ever been executed for rape in Mississippi."

43. Ibid., 402. Braden came as a representative of the Southern Conference Education Fund.

44. Willie McGee to Rosalie McGee, May 7, 1951, folder 14, box 48, ACB.

45. "Mississippi Whites Roar Approval as Willie McGee Dies in the Chair," *CD,* May 19, 1951, 5.

46. Eric Rise, *The Martinsville Seven: Race, Rape, and Capital Punishment* (Charlottesville, Va., 1995), 1.

47. Ibid., 2.

48. "Two Va. Cops Guilty of Raping Negro Woman Get 7 Years," *PC,* May 14, 1949, 1.

49. Tyson, *Radio Free Dixie,* 68.

50. "Assault . . . at 75 Feet," pamphlet distributed by the NAACP Legal Defense and Educational Fund, box 128, series IIB, NAACP Papers.

51. "Neighbors Say God Aiding Mack Ingram," *CD,* March 29, 1952, 3.

52. Dray, *Persons Unknown,* 405.

53. Parks with Haskins, *My Story,* 86.

54. Yeakey, *Boycott,* 182; See also Parks with Haskins, *My Story,* 85–86. The Montgomery NAACP challenged Reeves's sentence in the state supreme court, which upheld the death sentence. The U.S. Supreme Court struck down his conviction and returned the case to lower courts, which found him guilty again. The state supreme court reaffirmed the lower court's decision, and Reeves was executed in 1957. See also *Jeremiah Reeves, Jr. v. State of Alabama,* 246 Ala. 476; 88 So. 2d 561; 1956 Ala. Lexis 392.

55. Parks with Haskins, *My Story,* 86.

56. Martin Luther King, Jr., *Stride Toward Freedom: The Montgomery Story* (San Francisco, 1958), 32.

57. Tyson, *Radio Free Dixie,* 109.

58. Parks with Haskins, *My Story,* 94.

59. Marcel Reedus, George King, and Vertamae Grosvenor, *Cradle of the Confederacy,* episode 6 of WTCBUd.

60. Ibid.; S. S. Seay, *I Was There by the Grace of God* (Montgomery, Ala., 1990), 130–31. "All kinds of sexual relations," in Solomon Seay, Sr., interview by Worth Long with Randall Williams, http://unbrokencircle.org/focus_week03_seay.htm (accessed February 2, 2006); I-SS. See also *MA,* April 5, 1949, 8A; April 6, 1949, 1B; April 7, 1949, 2A; April 15, 1949, 8A; April 17, 1949, 3A; April 20, 1949, 3A; April 21, 1949, last page; May 3, 1949, 1A; May 21, 1949, 1A; May 27, 1949, 12A; *AT,* April 22, 1949, 1; April 29, 1949, 1; *PC,* June 4, 1949, 3. See also Thornton, *Dividing,* 34–35.

61. "Court Denies 2 Petitions in Rape Case; Mayor Needn't Identify, Nor Sheriff Arrest Accused Men," *MA,* April 29, 1949; "Drew Pearson Changes Mind; Criticizes City," *MA,* May 3, 1949, 1.

62. "Rape Cry Against Dixie Cops Falls on Deaf Ears," *BAA*, April 9, 1949, 1.

63. Yeakey, *Boycott,* 152. See also Stewart Burns, ed., *Daybreak of Freedom: The Montgomery Bus Boycott* (Chapel Hill, N.C., 1997), 7.

64. Seay, *Grace of God,* 131, 135, 136.

65. "Drew Pearson Changes Mind; Criticizes City," *MA*, May 3, 1949, 1.

66. "Mayor Denies Negro Raped," *MA*, April 15, 1949, 8; E. G. Jackson, "Attack Case Drags On; No Arrests Made," *AT*, April 22, 1949, 1.

67. Thornton, *Dividing,* 33, 591n28.

68. Ibid., 33–36 passim. Thornton documents a number of crimes white police officers committed against black men and women throughout the 1940s and claims that police brutality was the number-one issue affecting the black community in the decade preceding the bus boycott.

69. E. G. Jackson, "Attack Case Drags On; No Arrests Made," *AT*, April 22, 1949, 1. Chief King was finally relieved from his job by Mayor John L. Goodwyn in 1948. See Brenna Greer, *"Our Leaders Is Just We Ourself ": Black Women's Resistance in the Making of the Montgomery Bus Boycott,* master's thesis (University of Wisconsin, Madison, 2004), 19.

70. E. G. Jackson, "Attack Case Drags On: No Arrests Made," *AT*, 22 April 1949, 1.

71. "Racial Discord Is Promoted by NAACP, Says Mayor," *MA*, April 15, 1949. See also *MA*, April 5, 1940, 8A; April 6, 1949, 1B; April 7, 1949, 2A; April 15, 1949, 8A; April 17, 1949, 3A; April 20, 1949, 3A; April 21, 1949, last page; May 3, 1949, 1A; May 21, 1949, 1A; May 27, 1949, 12A.

72. Seay was arrested two weeks before the grand jury hearing for disorderly conduct during a public meeting about the Perkins affair. His arrest and short stint in jail roused the local ministers, who were relatively conservative and less outspoken than Reverend Seay. It served as a catalyst for more ministerial involvement in the Perkins protest.

73. Seay interview by Long and Williams, http://unbrokencircle.org/focus_week03_seay.htm (accessed April 2005).

74. Ibid.

75. Seay, *Grace of God,* 138–39.

76. "96 Indictments Returned Here," *MA*, May 21, 1949, 1.

77. Ibid.

78. An all-white jury sentenced John C. Howard and Jack Oliver to more than forty years in prison for raping Melinda Jackson, twenty-two, and Annie Grayson, twenty-four. Howard and Oliver robbed a group of African Americans at gunpoint on April 25, 1948, stealing money and a truck. They pushed Jackson and Grayson into the truck, drove them to a secluded area, and then raped them at gunpoint. They were arrested immediately and held without bail. County prosecutor U. G. Jones urged the jury to bring in a verdict that would "show the world that the Negro can get justice in the courts" and that the "people of Elmore County will not tolerate such conduct." The lengthy sentence was a first for Elmore County, if not Alabama as a whole. According to the *Chicago Defender*, the sentences "appeared to meet with full approval of both white and colored citizens, more than 300 of whom attended the trials." See "Alabama Lily-White Jury . . . JAILS 2 WHITE RAPISTS," *CD*, December 11, 1948, 1; "White Gets 45 Years for Raping a Negro," *NYT*, December 3, 1948, 28; "Man Gets 45 Year Term for Rape of Alabama Negro," *WP,* December 3, 1948, 1; "Found Guilty of Raping Negro; Gets 45 Years," *CDT*, December 3, 1948.

79. "Due Process of Law for Gertrude Perkins," *MA*, May 22 1949, 2B.

80. Seay interview by Long and Williams.

81. *Cradle of the Confederacy,* WTCBUd.

82. Yeakey, *Boycott,* 187.

83. Case 2, folder IV, box 30, 14, MLK; Townsend Davis, *Weary Feet, Rested Souls: A Guided History of the Civil Rights Movement* (New York, 1998), 34.

84. Thornton, *Dividing,* 30. See also *MA*, February 15, 22, March 1, May 24, June 7, 1951.

85. Yeakey, *Boycott,* 98.

86. Ibid., 95.

87. Case 2, folder IV, box 30, 14, MLK; Davis, *Weary Feet,* 34; Yeakey, *Boycott,* 85.

88. According to documents, Flossie Hardman died five years after her attack from shock "which her mother claims was caused by her never recovering from the ordeal she went through." See Case 2, folder IV, box 30, 14, MLK.

89. Thornton, *Dividing,* 35; Jo Ann Gibson Robinson, *The Montgomery Bus Boycott and the Women Who Started It* (Knoxville, Tenn., 1987), 21.

90. Robinson, *Montgomery,* 22.

91. Thomas Gilliam, "The Montgomery Bus Boycott of 1955–56," in Garrow, *Walking City,* 198. Yeakey, *Boycott,* argues that African Americans made up approximately 70 percent of riders, most of them being domestics, maids, cooks, service workers, and day laborers. African Americans made up 39.9 percent of Montgomery's 106,525 people in 1950. Montgomery was home to more black women than black men. The 23,847 black women accounted for 56 percent of the total black population. Of these, 54.5 percent worked in private households as domestics. Another 18.7 percent did "service work" (as attendants, beauticians, housekeepers, cleaners, janitors, cooks, waitresses, etc.). A total of 73 percent of these African-American women worked as domestics or service workers, and the majority relied on public transportation to get to work. Forty-eight percent of black men were common laborers or domestic or service workers. See Yeakey, *Boycott,* 9–13. Yeakey also notes that even a "cursory survey of those who had run-ins with bus drivers reveals a preponderance of women involved in such incidents" (226).

92. Yeakey, *Boycott,* 20. This information is taken from the 1950 census.

93. Ibid., 352; See also Greer, *Our Leaders,* 17.

94. Burns, *Daybreak,* 70.

95. Robinson, *Montgomery,* 26.

96. William H. Chafe, Raymond Gavins, and Robert Korstadt, eds., *Remembering Jim Crow: African Americans Tell About Life in the Segregated South* (New York, 2001), 9.

97. Robinson, *Montgomery,* 36.

98. Norman Walton, "The Walking City: A History of the Montgomery Bus Boycott" in Garrow, *Walking City,* 16–17.

99. See Yeakey, *Boycott,* 209–13. For information on similar bus conditions in Birmingham, Alabama, see Robin D. G. Kelley, *Race Rebels: Culture, Politics, and the Black Working Class* (New York, 1994), 55–70.

100. Yeakey, *Boycott,* 220. Certainly some women preferred not to sit anywhere near white men, given their historic mistreatment of black women.

101. Burns, *Daybreak,* 62.

102. Yeakey, *Boycott,* 209.

103. Ibid., 197, n. 2.

104. E. D. Nixon, interview, in Earl Selby and Miriam Selby, *Odyssey: Journey Through Black America* (New York, 1971), 53.

105. Yeakey, *Boycott,* 198.

106. Rosa Parks, interview, in Selby and Selby, *Odyssey,* 54.

107. Ibid.

108. Yeakey, *Boycott,* 47.

109. Ibid., 12–13, 48. Eight percent of Montgomery's female labor force could be classified as professionals in 1950. Most of the 671 professionals were elementary and secondary

school teachers, college professors, and librarians. Only two percent, just 161 black women, were stenographers, typists, secretaries, and file clerks.

110. Yeakey, *Boycott,* 54.

111. Ibid., 49.

112. Ibid., 100

113. Branch, *Parting the Waters*, 22, 24.

114. Yeakey, *Boycott,* 110.

115. For more on Vernon Johns, see Ralph E. Luker, "Murder and Biblical Memory: The Legend of Vernon Johns," in Joyce Appleby, ed., *The Best American History Essays, 2006* (New York: Macmillan, 2006), 201–30.

116. Mary Fair Burks, "Trailblazers: Women in the Montgomery Bus Boycott," in Vicki L. Crawford, Jacqueline Anne Rouse, and Barbara Woods, eds., *Black Women in the Civil Rights Movement, Trailblazers and Torchbearers: 1941–1965* (Bloomington, Ind., 1990), 79; "would take it over," in Belinda Robnett, *How Long? How Long? Black Women in the Struggle for Civil Rights* (New York, 1997), 56.

117. Burks, "Trailblazers," 78.

118. Ibid., 79. The date of the formation of the WPC is unclear. Burks says she formed the organization in 1946; Jo Ann Robinson concurs in her memoir. J. Mills Thornton claims the WPC was founded in 1949. Robinson became president in 1950, but Burks was president for at least a few years before Robinson took the reins. Therefore I am inclined to believe Burks and Robinson.

119. Burks, "Trailblazers," 79. Some of the women Burks recalled being present at the first meeting also became "pioneers" of the WPC. They are Cynthia Alexander, Elizabeth Arrington, Sadie Brooks, Albertine Campbell, Mary Cross, Faustine Dunn, Thelma Glass, Frizette Lee, Jewel Clayton Lewis, Thelma Morris, Geraldine Nesbitt, Ivy Pettus.

120. Ibid., 80.

121. Robinson, *Montgomery,* 29. It is important to point out that Lewis employed a number of canvassers, who went door to door signing people up to register to vote. Almost all of them were women: Mrs. Ethel Alexander, Mrs. Viola Bradford, Mrs. Hattie Carter, Mrs. Gloria Jean German, Mrs. Delores Glover, Mr. Leon Hall, Mrs. Bertha Howard and family, Mrs. Yvonne Jenkins, Mrs. Gwendolyn Patton, Mrs. Bertha Smith, and Mrs. Barbara Williams.

122. Burks, "Trailblazers," 80.

123. Thornton, *Dividing,* 32.

124. Burks, "Trailblazers," 74.

125. Greer, *Our Leaders,* 29, 30.

126. Robinson, *Montgomery,* 16.

127. "Shameful and deplorable," in *MA*, September 15, 1954, 1A. On the drive for better parks and recreational spaces, see Yeakey, *Boycott,* 158–67.

128. J. Mills Thornton, "Challenge and Response in the Montgomery Bus Boycott of 1955–1956," in Garrow, *Walking City*, 332.

129. Burks, "Trailblazers," 81.

130. "Digest of Proceedings: Sojourn for Truth and Justice—Washington, D.C., Sept. 29 thru Oct. 1, 1951," in box 12, LTP.

131. "A Call to Negro Women," pamphlet, box 13, LTP.

132. Here the STJ refers to Rosa Lee Ingram, a black sharecropper, widow, and mother of twelve, who was convicted and sentenced to death for the self-defense slaying of a white man in Ellaville, Georgia, on November 4, 1947. She had served four years of a commuted death sentence when "A Call" was issued. Ibid.

133. McDuffie, *Long Journeys,* 46.

134. "Digest of Proceedings, Sojourn for Truth and Justice, Washington, D.C., Sept. 29 thru Oct. 1, 1951," box 12, LTP.

135. For more on the Rosa Lee Ingram case, see Charles H. Martin, "Race, Gender and Southern Justice: The Rosa Lee Ingram Case," *American Journal of Legal History* 29, no. 3 (July 1985): 251–68; Virginia Shadron, *Popular Protest and Legal Authority in Post–World War II Georgia: Race, Class, and Gender Politics in the Rosa Lee Ingram Case,* Ph.D. diss. (Emory University, 1991).

136. Robert M. Ratcliffe, "He Tried to Go with Me," *PC*, March 20, 1948, 1.

137. Ibid.

138. Martin, "Race, Gender," 252. What exactly transpired the day Stratford died is hard to reconstruct. Whether Rosa Lee grabbed the gun from Stratford as they fought, and then beat him herself, or whether her sons used other farm tools to beat him to death is unclear. All the testimony used to sentence the Ingrams was provided by white men and women. The Ingrams each gave statements. Rosa Lee first claimed that she killed Stratford herself, but her sons told different stories after they were separated. None of them spoke to an attorney, and none were advised of their right to remain silent. While all the white officials involved in questioning the Ingrams swear they did not use coercion or intimidation to extract statements, the children were doubtless terrified. The trial record indicates that they were not defended in any meaningful way and that their interests were not represented. The trial began on Monday, January 26, 1948, and ended the same day, with a unanimous guilty verdict from an all-white, twelve-man jury. The guilty verdict, rendered without consideration of mercy, sentenced them to death. Throughout the trial, white prosecutors portrayed Mrs. Ingram as a kind of monster, brutish and overpowering, while Stratford was presented as a weak, wimpy old man who did not have the strength to fight. See transcript of supreme court case file 1624, 1623, *Rosa Lee Ingram v. The State of Georgia,* Georgia Archives, Atlanta. The question of whether Stratford attacked Ingram sexually never came up at the trial, but Ingram claimed later in an exclusive interview that Stratford had tried on numerous occasions to "go with her." "He was mad because I wouldn't go into the cotton house with him," she claimed. "He had tried three times to make me go into the cotton house and have something to do with him." He never tried to rape her, she said, "He just tried to compel me." Robert M. Ratcliffe, "He Tried to Go with Me," *PC*, March 20, 1948, 1. See also, Shadron, *Popular Protest,* 145–47, 151–53. The *Courier's* portrayal of Ingram as another victim of white men's lust rallied readers and supporters to the cause. The *Courier* made the Ingram story their main news item each day for the entire year of 1948, drawing new subscribers and $37,933 in donations for her defense. The NAACP fought the Ingrams' case in the courts, raised money for the family's well-being, and organized local campaigns to pressure state officials. In March 1948 the NAACP persuaded Judge W. M. Harper to commute their sentences, but could not convince him to grant the Ingrams a new trial altogether. As the NAACP appealed to the Georgia Supreme Court, the CRC used the Ingram case to mobilize left-wing pressure groups by presenting it to the Human Rights Commission of the United Nations. When the Georgia Supreme Court refused to reverse the life sentence and grant a new trial, the NAACP began to quietly pursue a strategy for parole or pardon. The NAACP also raised thousands of dollars to provide for Ingram's nine other children and built the family a new house. Rosa Lee Ingram was finally released from prison on August 26, 1959, long after the CRC and the STJ had dissolved. See Martin, "Race-Gender," 260–66, and Shadron, *Popular Protest,* 235–38.

139. "Proclamation of the Sojourners for Truth and Justice," box 12, LTP. The short-lived organization did not survive the Red Scare of the 1950s. For more on the Sojourners, see Erik S. McDuffie, "A 'New Freedom Movement of Negro Women': Sojourning for Truth,

Justice, and Human Rights during the Early Cold War," *Radical History Review* 101 (2008): 81–106.

140. Thornton, "Challenge and Response," in Garrow, *Walking City*, 332.

141. Robinson, *Montgomery*, 42.

CHAPTER 3. "WALKING IN PRIDE AND DIGNITY"

1. Burns, *Daybreak*, 74; Interview with Claudette Colvin, MBd, http://www .montgomeryboycott.com/profile_colvin.htm. (accessed December 18, 2007).

2. Claudette Colvin, testimony, May 11, 1956, in Burns, *Daybreak*, 75. See also Thornton, *Dividing*, 53.

3. Gary Younge, "She Would Not Be Moved," *Guardian*, December 16, 2000. Greer rightly notes in her master's thesis that this statement indicates that defying segregation laws on the buses was relatively common and that either Colvin had refused to give up her seat for whites in the past, or that she witnessed other black passengers refuse to abide by the segregation laws. See Greer, *Our Leaders*, 36.

4. Colvin testimony, in Burns, *Daybreak*, 75.

5. Claudette Colvin, interview, MBd.

6. Colvin testimony, in Burns, *Daybreak*, 75. See also Lynne Olson, *Freedom's Daughters: The Unsung Heroines of the Civil Rights Movement from 1830 to 1970* (New York, 2001), 93.

7. Younge, "She Would Not," *Guardian*, December 16, 2000; see also Colvin interview, MBd.

8. Most accounts of the Montgomery bus boycott portray Colvin as out of control. Brinkley claims Colvin was an "unruly tomboy with propensity for curse words" (*Rosa*, 89–90); Branch says she was "immature—prone to breakdowns and outbursts of profanity" (*Parting the Waters*, 122). Colvin denies swearing, screaming, or kicking. Testimony from the court trial, including testimony from the bus driver, Cleere, and the officers present, all corroborate Colvin's claim. The real question, then, is why is this characterization so persistent? Thornton, *Dividing*, 53; Younge, "She Would Not," *Guardian*, December 16, 2000.

9. Younge, "She Would Not," *Guardian*, December 16, 2000.

10. Yeakey, *Boycott*, 239.

11. Ibid., 245; King, *Stride Toward Freedom*, 41.

12. Robinson, *Montgomery*, 39.

13. Yeakey, *Boycott*, 246; Thornton, *Dividing*, 55.

14. King, *Stride Toward Freedom*, 26.

15. Parks with Haskins, *My Story*, 112.

16. Thornton, *Dividing*, 56.

17. Gray quoted in Olson, *Daughters*, 94.

18. Thornton, *Dividing*, 54, 55.

19. Yeakey, *Boycott*, 241, 242.

20. Ibid.

21. Thornton, *Dividing*, 54. See also *MA*, March 19, 1955, 7A.

22. Yeakey, *Boycott*, 244, 245.

23. Robinson, *Montgomery*, 42.

24. Ibid.

25. Mrs. A. W. West, interview by Willie M. Lee, January 23, 1956, box 4, folder 4, PBV.

26. John A. Salmond, *The Conscience of a Lawyer: Clifford J. Durr and American Civil Liberties, 1899–1975* (Tuscaloosa, Ala., 1990), 174.

27. Yeakey, *Boycott*, 269.

28. Robinson, *Montgomery*, 39.

29. Yeakey, *Boycott*, 270.

30. Ibid. Colvin states that she was not sexually active, but that her pregnancy was the result of statutory rape. Colvin interview, MBd.

31. Younge, "She Would Not," *Guardian*, December 16, 2000; Yeakey, *Boycott*, 270.

32. Younge, "She Would Not," *Guardian*, December 16, 2000.

33. Yeakey, *Boycott*, 271.

34. Ibid.

35. Raines, *Rested*, 38–39.

36. Greer, *Our Leaders*, 44.

37. Parks with Haskins, *My Story*, 112.

38. Branch, *Parting the Waters*, 123.

39. Olson, *Daughters*, 94.

40. Yeakey, *Boycott*, 271; Smith later denied this and argued that her father never drank, nor did they live in a dilapidated house.

41. See Branch, *Parting the Waters*, 123–28; Olson, *Daughters*, 94–95; Marissa Chappell, Jenny Hutchinson, and Brian Ward, " 'Dress modestly, neatly . . . as if you were going to church': Respectability, Class, and Gender in the Montgomery Bus Boycott and the Early Civil Rights Movement," in Peter J. Ling and Sharon Monteith, eds., *Gender in the Civil Rights Movement* (New York, 1999), 84. On respectability and the "culture of dissemblance," see Darlene Clark Hine, "Rape and the Inner Lives of Black Women in the Middle West: Preliminary Thoughts on a Culture of Dissemblance," *Signs* 14 (Summer 1989): 912–20. For more on the silencing of sexuality during this era, see Thaddeus Russel, "The Color of Discipline: Civil Rights and Black Sexuality," *American Quarterly* 60, no. 1 (2008): 101–28.

42. Joseph Crespino, *In Search of Another Country: Mississippi and the Conservative Counterrevolution* (Princeton, N.J., 2007), 20.

43. Charles Payne, *I've Got the Light of Freedom: The Organizing Tradition and the Mississippi Freedom Struggle* (Berkeley, Calif., 1995), 35.

44. The White Citizens' Councils counted approximately 250,000 members throughout the South. See Numan V. Bartley, *The Rise of Massive Resistance: Race and Politics in the South During the 1950s* (Baton Rouge, La., 1969), 83–84; Neil R. McMillen, *The Citizens' Council: Organized Resistance to the Second Reconstruction, 1954–1964* (Urbana, Ill., 1994), 184, 186; Tom P. Brady, *Black Monday: Segregation or Amalgamation, America Has Its Choice* (Winona, Miss., 1955).

45. For more on the ways respectability, dignity, manhood, and womanhood shaped the strategies and goals of the middle- and working-class black activists during Reconstruction and the Progressive Era, see Glenda Gilmore, *Gender and Jim Crow: Women and the Politics of White Supremacy in North Carolina, 1896–1920* (Chapel Hill, N.C., 1996); and Evelyn Brooks Higginbotham, *Righteous Discontent: The Women's Movement in the Black Baptist Church, 1880–1920* (Cambridge, Mass., 1993).

46. Hine, "Rape and Inner Lives," 915.

47. See Chapter 2 for more on Rosa Lee Ingram.

48. McMillen, *Citizens' Council*, 44.

49. Ibid., 159. State senators Walter Coats Givhan and Sam Englehardt were leaders of the Central Alabama Citizens' Council.

50. Thornton, *Dividing*, 60; Parks with Haskins, *My Story*, 115.

51. Brinkley, *Rosa*, 109.

52. Parks with Haskins, *My Story*, 115.

53. Ibid., 115–16.

54. Ibid., 101.
55. Ibid., 106.
56. Greer, *Our Leaders,* 49.
57. Olson, *Daughters,* 109.
58. See postcards and petitions signed by Leona McCauley in folder 3, CS.
59. Parks with Haskins, *My Story,* 121.
60. Olson, *Daughters,* 111.
61. Parks with Haskins, *My Story,* 125. See also the similar response Nixon gave to Steven M. Millner in an interview on July 27, 1977, in Garrow, *Walking City,* 546.
62. Olson, *Daughters,* 110.
63. Robinsin, *Montgomery,* 45.
64. Ibid., 45, 50.
65. Ibid., 45–46; italics mine.
66. Ibid., 46–47.
67. Sidney Rogers, interview, Pacifica Radio, April 1956, in Burns, *Daybreak,* 84.
68. Chappell, et al., " 'Dress modestly, neatly . . . ,' " 87.
69. Branch, *Parting the Waters,* 133.
70. Brinkley, *Rosa,* 128.
71. Olson, *Daughters,* 115.
72. Ibid., 114.
73. Robinson, *Montgomery,* 57.
74. Parks with Haskins, *My Story,* 132.
75. Brinkley, *Rosa,* 131.
76. Olson, *Daughters,* 115.
77. Brinkley, *Rosa,* 133.
78. E. D. Nixon, interview, in Selby and Selby, *Odyssey,* 60.
79. Ibid., 61.
80. Ibid.
81. On E. D. Nixon choosing King for the MIA leadership, see *Eyes on the Prize: America's Civil Rights Movement,* vol. 1, Blackside Productions, PBS Video, 1986, 2006, DVD.
82. Branch, *Parting the Waters,* 137.
83. Nixon interview in Selby and Selby, *Odyssey,* 60.
84. Branch, *Parting the Waters,* 136.
85. "The men took it over," in Jo Ann Robinson, interview by Steven Millner, August 10, 1977, in Garrow, *Walking City,* 570; "definitely decided to assume leadership," in Robinson, *Montgomery,* 64.
86. Branch, *Parting the Waters,* 139–41.
87. Ibid., 140.
88. Transcript of mass meeting at Holt Street Baptist Church, December 5, 1955. Martin Luther King Estate Collection, copy online at http://www.stanford.edu/group/King/publications/papers/vol3/551205.004-MIA_Mass_Meeting_at_Holt_Street_Baptist_Church.htm (accessed October 30, 2005).
89. Yeakey, *Boycott,* 274.
90. Ralph Abernathy, "The Natural History of a Social Movement: the Montgomery Improvement Association," in Garrow, *Walking City,* 124.
91. On Robinson's complaint about black men's failure to protect black women on the buses, see *Montgomery,* 37.
92. Burns, *Daybreak,* 15.
93. Robinson, *Montgomery,* 69.
94. Ibid., 66.
95. Rufus Lewis, interview by Donald T. Ferron, January 20, 1956, folder 7, box 3, PBV.

In a letter to Preston Valien on January 21, 1956, Ferron said, "Mrs. Jo Ann Robinson seems to have been the key organizer for the protest. She is the backbone of this collective effort." Folder 7, box 1, PBV.

96. Rosa Parks, interview by Sidney Rogers, Pacifica Radio, April 1956, transcript in Burns, *Daybreak,* 86.

97. Erna Dungee Allen, interview by Steven Millner, August 6, 1977, in Garrow, *Walking City*, 522–23.

98. Georgia Gilmore, interview, in Henry Hampton and Steve Fayer, *Voices of Freedom: An Oral History of the Civil Rights Movement from the 1950s through the 1980s* (New York, 1990), 29. Mrs. A. W. West argued that the "working people" were the "ones who keep this movement going . . . The leaders could do nothing by themselves. They are only the voice of thousands of colored workers." See Mrs. A. W. West, interview by Willie M. Lee, January 23, 1956, folder 4, box 4, PBV.

99. Willie M. Lee, "Statements heard in various places," January 27, 1956, folder 4, box 4, PBV.

100. Irene Stovall, interview by Willie M. Lee, February 1, 1956, folder 4, box 4, PBV. Lee notes that Mrs. Stovall is a "large woman of brown complexion" whose "eyes became narrow slits while talking about her previous employer."

101. Mrs. Beatrice Charles, interview by Willie M. Lee, January 20, 1956, folder 4, box 4, PBV.

102. Ibid.

103. Sam Englehardt, interview by Anna Holden February 8, 1956, folder 3/14, box 3, PBV.

104. Mrs. Beatrice Charles, interview by Willie M. Lee, January 20, 1956, folder 4, box 4, PBV.

105. Ibid.

106. Burns, *Daybreak,* 12. At a mass meeting on March 26, 1956, Jo Ann Robinson gave a pep talk and argued that whites deny African Americans a sense of dignity. "Look at our schools . . . we have no titles, we are not respected—every man is entitled to a certain dignity." She then went on to argue that the boycott was restoring that sense of dignity. "Transcript—Mass Meeting, MIA," March 26, 1956, folder 6, box 3, PBV.

107. Domestic, interview by Willie M. Lee, January 24, 1956, in Burns, *Daybreak,* 229.

108. Mrs. Allen Wright, interview by Willie M. Lee, January 24, 1956, folder 4, box 4, PBV.

109. Ibid.

110. Ibid.

111. Burns, *Daybreak,* 16.

112. Anna Holden, "Report from MIA mass meeting," March 22, 1956, folder 6, box 3, PVB.

113. Branch, *Parting the Waters*, 149.

114. Ibid.

115. Reedus, et al., *Cradle of the Confederacy,* WTCBU, episode 7.

116. Reedus, et al., *My Feet Is Tired, But My Soul Is Rested,* WTCBU, episode 9.

117. Yeakey, *Boycott,* 372.

118. Vernon Jarret, "Club from Nowhere Paid Way of Boycott," *ChT,* December 12, 1975, 1.

119. Greer, *Our Leaders,* 83.

120. Jarret, "Club from Nowhere," *ChT,* December 12, 1975, 1.

121. Ibid.

122. Ibid.

123. Burns, *Daybreak,* 16.

124. Jarret, "Club from Nowhere" *ChT,* December 12, 1975, 1.

125. Ibid.

126. Brinkley, *Rosa,* 147.

127. Erna Dungee Allen, interview by Steven Millner, August 8, 1977, in Garrow, *Walking*

City, 522–23. On "formal leadership," see Belinda Robnett, *How Long? How Long? African American Women in the Struggle for Civil Rights* (New York, 1997), 18.

128. Robnett, *How Long?,* 65.

129. Brinkley, *Rosa,* 147.

130. Ibid.

131. Yeakey, *Boycott,* 410.

132. Ibid., 389.

133. Robnett, *How Long?,* 65.

134. Robinson, *Montgomery,* 125.

135. Jo Ann Robinson, interview in Hampton and Fayer, *Voices of Freedom,* 31.

136. Willie M. Lee, "Statements heard in various places," January 27, 1956, folder 4, box 4, PBV.

137. Greer, *Our Leaders,* 98.

138. Martin Luther King, "The 'New Negro' of the South: Behind the Montgomery Story," *Socialist Call* 24, No. 6 (June 1956), in box 273, series III, A, NAACP Papers.

139. Clifford J. Durr to Mr. Nathan David, February 2, 1956, in Burns, *Daybreak,* 152.

140. Georgia Gilmore interview, in Hampton and Fayer, *Voices of Freedom,* 30–31.

141. Burns, *Daybreak,* 42.

142. Clifford J. Durr to Mr. Nathan David, February 2, 1956, ibid., 152.

143. Minutes of the Executive Board Meeting, February 2, 1956, in Burns, *Daybreak,* 148–50; "List of Persons and Churches Most Vulnerable to Violent Attack," folder IV, 14, MLK.

144. Branch, *Parting the Waters,* 168.

145. Brinkley, *Rosa,* 153–54; Burns, *Daybreak,* 153–54.

146. Burns, *Daybreak,* 153.

147. "Preview of the 'Declaration of Segregation,' " in Burns, *Daybreak,* 154.

148. Branch, *Parting the Waters,* 168; Brinkley, *Rosa,* 154.

149. Greer, *Our Leaders,* 104. Greer notes that Jo Ann Robinson, Irene West, and Euretta Adair, all key members of the WPC, were indicted. So were Ida Mae Caldwell, a local labor leader; Lottie Varner, owner of a beauty shop; Audrey Bell Lanford and Cora McHaney, both teachers; Lollie Boswell and Addie James Hamilton, a widow and house-wife respectively; Martha L. Johnson, a student at Alabama State College; and Alberta Judkins, Mrs. Jimmie Lowe, and Alberta James. See also, "Indicted in Bus Boycott," folder 1, box 3, PBV.

150. Branch, *Parting the Waters,* 169.

151. Bayard Rustin, "Montgomery Diary," *Liberation* 1, no. 2 (April 1956): 8. It was Bayard Rustin who instructed Nixon to turn the arrest into a badge of honor.

152. Robinsin, *Montgomery,* 150.

153. Branch, *Parting the Waters,* 177.

154. Robnett, *How Long?,* 151.

155. B. J. Simms, interview by Steven Millner July 16, 1977, in Garrow, *Walking City,* 579–80.

156. *Christian Century* 67, no. 10 (March 28, 1956): 387.

157. Transcript, *State of Alabama v. M. L. King Jr.,* March 19–22, 1956, folder 3, box 3, PBV.

158. Transcript, *State of Alabama v. M. L. King Jr.,* March 19–22, 1956, in Burns, *Daybreak,* 64–65 (Walker); 67 (Brooks); 69 (Brimson); 72 (Moore). See also folder 3, box 3, PBV.

159. Branch, *Parting the Waters,* 184.

160. "New Sounds in the Courthouse," *Time,* April 2, 1956, 24; see also Greer, *Our Leaders,* 105.

161. Transcript, *State of Alabama v. M. L. King Jr.,* March 19–22, 1956, folder 3, box 3, PBV.

162. Ibid.

163. Branch, *Parting the Waters,* 184.

164. Brinkley, *Rosa,* 160.

165. Branch, *Parting the Waters*, 184.

166. Brinkley, *Rosa,* 160.

167. Fellowship of Reconciliation, "Martin Luther King and the Montgomery Story: How 50,000 Negroes Found a New Way to End Racial Discrimination," n.d., box 207, series AIII, NAACP Papers.

168. *Gayle v. Browder,* 352 U.S. 903, Ralph Abernathy and Martin Luther King, Jr., to Alabama Clergy, November 30, 1956, in Burns, *Daybreak,* 305.

169. Branch, *Parting the Waters*, 194.

170. Martin Luther King, Jr., *Where Do We Go from Here: Chaos or Community?* (Boston, 1968), 123.

CHAPTER 4: "THERE'S OPEN SEASON ON NEGROES NOW"

1. Melba Patillo Beals, *Warriors Don't Cry: A Searing Memoir of the Battle to Integrate Little Rock's Central High* (New York, 1994), 22–25.

2. Ibid., 25–26.

3. Ibid., 26. At a distance of decades and in the absence of police reports and newspaper accounts of the incident, it is difficult to substantiate Melba Patillo Beals's story, but the attempted rape fits within a documented history. Beals declined to be interviewed.

4. Ibid., 26–27.

5. Ibid., 27.

6. Daisy Bates, *The Long Shadow of Little Rock* (Fayetteville, Ark., 1986), 15.

7. Ibid., 11–12, 15.

8. Robnett, *How Long?,* 77.

9. Ibid.

10. "Two City Policemen Indicted," *ASP,* July 17, 1942, 1; "Rape Case Ends in Mistrial," *AG*, July 29, 1942, 14.

11. Though not exhaustive, my research found at least eleven trials, reported in local newspapers, mainly the *State Press*, of white men accused of raping black women in and around Little Rock between 1942 and 1959. Of those eleven trials, three men were found guilty, but only one received a jail sentence (four years). The other two men received suspended sentences and were allowed to go free. Two trials resulted in a mistrial; two men were acquitted. Most cases, of course, never made it past a grand jury. Bates publicized many more reported rapes and attempted rapes: see the prominent trial of two white policemen accused of raping Rosa Lee Cherry, a black high school student, on June 15, 1942. The *Arkansas State Press* publicized the rape, placed photographs of the officers on the front page of the paper, and demanded they be held accountable. Vigilance by Bates and the black community forced a trial in July 1942. The case ended in a mistrial. See *State of Arkansas v. L. S. Mullinax, C. B. Eddie Jr., Dan Ellard*, No. 43862, Pulaski County Circuit Court, July 15, 1942; "Two City Police Men Indicted: Accused of Rape on Teenage Dunbar High School Girl," *ASP*, July 17, 1942, 1; "Keeping the Negro in His Place," *ASP*, July 17, 1942, 1; A. F. Cunningham, "A Disgrace in Disgrace," *ASP*, August 14, 1942, 4; "Grand Jurors Begin Probe of Two Cases," *AD*, July 15, 1942, 2; "Four Indicted on Capital Charges," *AG*, July 16, 1942, 11; "Assault Case Ends with 'Hung' Jury," *AD*, July 28, 1942, 16; "Rape Case Ends in Mistrial," *AG*, July 29, 1942, 14. Other headlines in *ASP* throughout the 1940s and 1950s indicate Bates's personal interest in securing justice for African-American women assaulted by white men. See, for example, "Expectant Mother Brutally Beaten by White Grocer," *ASP*, June 12, 1942, 1; "Still Pending!" *ASP*, November 20, 1942, 1; "Something Must Be Done," editorial, *ASP*, November 20, 1942, 6; "Girl Awarded Damages Against Kroger Grocery,"

ASP, May 21, 1943, 1; "Following Their Training," *ASP*, August 27, 1943, 1; "A 64$ '?,'"*ASP*, August 28, 1944; "Alleged White Rapists Freed by All-White Jury in Ashdown; Raping Negro Is No Offense if Rapist Is Drunken White Jury Finds," *ASP*, July 22, 1949, 1; "Bus Driver Beats Up Negro Woman in Heart of City; Knocks Her Down While Negro 'Men' Merely Look," *ASP*, September 16, 1949, 1; "Alleged Rape Laid to White Man; Seven Year Old Girl Is Victim," *ASP*, January 2, 1953, 1; "Attack on Girl Brings Sentence," *ASP*, April 3, 1953, 1; "White Attacker of Negro Girl Must Pay," *ASP*, October 23, 1953, 1; "Eight Year Old Girl Accuses White Man of Assault," *ASP*, November 20, 1953, 1; "Light of Approaching Car Prevents Rape of 11-Year-Old Girl," *ASP*, December 30, 1955, 1; "Rape Attempt on Negro Girl Charged to White Man," *ASP*, July 24, 1959, 1; "Jury Sees No Crime When Whites Rape Negro Girls," *ASP*, October 23, 1959, 1. Thanks to Story Matkin Rawn and John Adams for finding these articles for me.

12. *U.S. News & World Report* 40 (February 24, 1956): 134, 135, 138. Leander and Talmadge are quoted in Stephen J. Whitfield, *A Death in the Delta: The Story of Emmett Till* (Baltimore, Md., 1988), 9.

13. Michael J. Klarman, *From Jim Crow to Civil Rights: The Supreme Court and the Struggle for Racial Equality* (New York, 2004), 427.

14. McMillen, *Citizens's Council,* 185.

15. For more on the tension between "respectable" leaders and white vigilantes in Mississippi, see Crespino, *Another Country,* 24–28.

16. Klarman, *Jim Crow,* 427.

17. Crespino, *Another Country,* 20.

18. Ibid., 28

19. Annette Butler, testimony, in Charles B. Gordon, "Lurid Case Being Heard: Duncan Trial in 2nd Day—Signed Statement Admitted," *MCEJ*, March 28, 1957, 1.

20. Ibid.

21. Ibid.

22. "Brady to Hear Mississippi Rape Case," *CDD*, May 16, 1956, 6.

23. "Tom P. Brady," obituary, *Time*, February 12, 1973.

24. Charles B. Gordon, "Walthall Countian Cleared: Olen Duncan Acquitted by Pike Jury on Rape Count, Faces Kidnap Charge," *MCEJ*, March 29, 1957, 1.

25. Charles B. Gordon, "Court Bulletin," *MCEJ*, March 26, 1957, 1.

26. Charles B. Gordon, "Trial of Duncan Pending," *MCEJ*, April 4, 1957, 1.

27. Gordon, "Walthall Countian Cleared," *MCEJ*, March 29, 1957, 1.

28. Ibid. In the fall of 1957 he pleaded nolo contendre to the kidnapping charge and received a suspended two-year sentence. See "Duncans Freed from Jail on Suspended Sentences," *MJEC*, October 28, 1957; clipping, SCR ID # 10–67–0-3–1-1–1, MSSC-d (accessed February 12, 2008).

29. "Negro Women Ask That Statement Be Published," *MCEJ*, April 4, 1957, 4.

30. "Negro Committee Expresses Views of Alleged Rape of Colored Girl," *MCEJ*, May 17, 1956, 8.

31. Charles B. Gordon, "Ernest Dillon Is Sentenced to 20 Years at Hard Labor," *MCEJ*, April 5, 1957, 1.

32. "Testimony of Hollis Turner (Colored) McComb Mississippi, General Legislative Investigating Committee," May 14, 1958, SCR ID # 9–3-0–1-21–1-1, MSSC-d (accessed February 12, 2008).

33. Oliver Emmerich, "High-Lights in the Headlines," *MCEJ*, May 15, 1956, 1.

34. Brinkley, *Rosa,* 165.

35. Ibid., 174.

36. Payne, *Light of Freedom,* 36–40.

37. The best account of the Till murder remains Whitfield, *Death in the Delta.* William Bradford Huie. "The Shocking Story of Approved Killing in Mississippi," *Look,* January 24, 1956, 46–50.

38. Dittmer, *Local People,* 58.

39. Andrew M. Manis, *A Fire You Can't Put Out: The Civil Rights Life of Birmingham's Reverend Fred Shuttlesworth* (Tuscaloosa, Ala., 1999), 147. Aaron survived the attack but remained psychologically scarred for years.

40. Thornton, *Dividing,* 94. According to Thornton, Raymond Britt, Henry Alexander, Kyle Livingston, and James York were indicted for the murder in 1976, but after a series of lie detector tests cleared Livingston, the other indictments were "quashed as legally defective." The same men were charged with the bombings at the Graetz, King, and Abernathy homes. See Thornton, *Dividing,* 610–11n123.

41. "He Whistled at Me Says Witness to Slaying," *RAA,* September 1, 1956, 1.

42. "Mashers Molest Women, Police Look Other Way," *RAA,* September 1, 1956, 1.

43. Ibid.

44. "Freed in Wolf Whistle Death: Judge Suspends Sentence," *RAA,* November 11, 1956, 1.

45. Cash, *Mind,* 115–16.

46. Wendell Berry, *The Hidden Wound* (San Francisco, 1989), 59; see also Tyson, *Radio Free Dixie,* 94–95.

47. McMillen, *Citizens' Council,* 184.

48. Brian Ward, ed., *Media, Culture, and the Modern African American Freedom Struggle* (Gainesville, Fla., 2001), 5.

49. Glenn C. Altschuler, *All Shook Up: How Rock 'n' Roll Changed America* (New York, 2003), 37–38.

50. Bertrand, *Race, Rock,* 181.

51. Ibid., 188.

52. Altschuler, *All Shook,* 40.

53. Dan T. Carter, *From George Wallace to Newt Gingrich: Race in the Conservative Counterrevolution, 1963–1994* (Baton Rouge, La., 1996), 2. Carter reminds us that the *Southerner* was one of the "most racist magazines published in the 1950s." Asa Carter was also the organizer of a secret paramilitary force he called the "Original Ku Klux Klan of the Confederacy." When George Wallace launched a gubernatorial campaign in 1962, he chose Asa Carter to be his speechwriter.

54. Altschuler, *All Shook,* 38.

55. Ibid.

56. Bertrand, *Race, Rock,* 188.

57. John Oliver Killens, *Black Man's Burden* (New York, 1965), 127.

58. Gunnar Myrdal, *An American Dilemma: The Negro Problem and Modern Democracy* (New York, 1944), 587.

59. Tyson, *Radio Free Dixie,* 92–93., provides the best account of what came to be known as the "Kissing Case." See also George Weissman, "The Kissing Case," *Nation,* January 17, 1959, 46–49.

60. Tyson, *Radio Free Dixie,* 95.

61. Ibid., 95–96.

62. Ibid., 96.

63. Ibid., 92.

64. Ibid., 101.

65. Ibid., 117–19. The "Kissing Case" gained worldwide publicity due to Williams and the

Committee to Combat Racial Injustice's shrewd exploitation of America's Cold War politics. See Patrick D. Jones, *Communist Front Shouts "Kissing Case" to the World: The Committee to Combat Racial Injustice and the Politics of Race and Gender During the Cold War,* master's thesis (University of Wisconsin, Madison, 1996).

66. Tyson, *Radio Free Dixie,* 134–35.

67. For the impact of the Cold War on civil rights, see Mary L. Dudziak, *Cold War Civil Rights: Race and the Image of American Democracy* (Princeton, N.J., 2000); and Thomas Borstelmann, *The Cold War and the Color Line: American Race Relations in the Global Arena* (Cambridge, Mass., 2001). For more on the Little Rock crisis, see Elizabeth Jacoway, *Turn Away Thy Son: Little Rock, the Crisis that Shocked the Nation* (New York, 2007); John Kirk, *Epitaph for Little Rock* (Fayetteville, Ark., 2008); and Daisy Bates, *The Long Shadow of Little Rock* (Fayetteville, Ark., 1986).

68. Borstelmann, *Cold War,* 104.

69. Ibid., 103.

70. "Dwight Eisenhower's Radio and Television Address to the American People on the Situation in Little Rock," September 24, 1957, in Steven F. Lawson and Charles Payne, *Debating the Civil Rights Movement, 1945–1968* (Lanham, Md., 1998), 60–64.

71. Borstelmann, *Cold War,* 103.

72. Alabama, Arkansas, Florida, Georgia, Louisiana, Mississippi, South Carolina, Tennessee, and Virginia respectively. Nullification resolutions in all four states passed in 1957. See Bartley, *Resistance,* 131.

73. McMillen, *Citizens' Councils,* 267.

74. Harvard Sitkoff, *The Struggle for Black Equality, 1954–1992* (New York, 1993), 66; Editorial, *NYT,* June 16, 1959; Altschuler, *All Shook,* 37.

75. Adam Fairclough, *To Redeem the Soul of America: The Southern Christian Leadership Conference and Martin Luther King Jr.* (Athens, Ga., 2001), 37.

76. Branch, *Parting the Waters,* 207.

77. Bartley, *Resistance,* 215. Bartley claims that besides Alabama, in which the NAACP was legally barred from operating, Texas and Arkansas effectively stymied the NAACP during the 1950s and early 1960s.

78. Roy Wilkins to Mr. Barbee William Durham, February 14, 1957, box A273, series III, NAACP Papers.

79. Roy Wilkins to LeRoy Collins, May 6, 1959, box A91, series III, NAACP Papers.

CHAPTER 5. "IT WAS LIKE ALL OF US HAD BEEN RAPED"

1. "Report on Tallahassee Incident," May 9, 1959, box A91, series III, NAACP Papers. Thanks to Timothy B. Tyson for finding this small folder for me. For information on the Roy Hamilton concert, see *PC,* May 16, 1959.

2. *NYAN,* June 20, 1959, 37. Jimmy Carl Cooper, a white youth, testified that David Beagles told him he planned to go out and get "some nigger 'stuff' " and noted that "stuff was not the word used." See Trezzvant W. Anderson, "Rapists Missed Out on First Selection," *PC,* June 20, 1959, 3. A cleaned-up version reported that Beagles had plans to get a "Negro girl": "Four Convicted in Rape Case," *TD,* June 14, 1959, 7. "I Was Scared," *PC,* June 20, 1959, 1. "Four Begin Defense in Trial on Rape," *NYT,* June 13, 1959, A13. See also criminal case file 3445, *State of Florida v. Patrick Gene Scarborough, David Ervin Beagles, Ollie Odell Stoutamire, and William Ted Collinsworth, 1959,* Leon County Courthouse, Tallahassee, Fla.. Thanks to Leon County Courthouse for sending me the file. Because the original trial transcript is no longer available, I have had to rely on newspaper reports, particularly those in African-American news-

papers: the *Baltimore Afro-American*, the *Louisiana Weekly*, the *New York Amsterdam News*, the *Pittsburgh Courier*, and the South Carolina *Lighthouse and Informer*. The fact that the transcript is missing is verified in the case file notes of *Patrick G. Scarborough v. State of Florida*, 390 So. 2d 830 (Fla. Dist. Ct. App., 1980). See also Robert W. Saunders, "Report on Tallahassee Incident," May 9, 1959, box A91, series III, NAACP Papers.

3. "Deputy Tells of Confessions," *TD*, June 12, 1959.

4. Russell Anderson, interview by Jackson Lee Ice, July 1978, in Jackson Lee Ice Papers (JLI).

5. For more on the double lynching, see Walter T. Howard, "Vigilante Justice and National Reaction: The 1937 Tallahassee Double Lynching," *Florida Historical Quarterly* 67, no. 1 (July 1988).

6. Glenda Alice Rabby, *The Pain and the Promise: The Struggle for Civil Rights in Tallahassee, Florida* (Athens, Ga., 1999), 18, 30–31.

7. Saunders, "Report on Tallahassee Incident."

8. "Deputy Tells of Confessions," *TD*, June 12, 1959. Original reports stated that Owens was "bound and gagged," but she later testified that she was only blindfolded; after she pulled the blindfold down, she appeared to have been gagged.

9. "Four Whites Seized in Rape of Negro," *NYT*, May 3, 1959, A45.

10. On the Tallahassee bus boycott, see Rabby, *Pain*, 9–46.

11. Ibid., 13.

12. Ibid., 28.

13. Ibid., 17. For C. K. Steele on students in movement, see Robert M. White, *The Tallahassee Sit-ins and CORE: A Nonviolent Revolutionary Sub-movement*, Ph.D. diss. (Florida State University, 1964), 65.

14. White, *Sit-ins*, 65.

15. Ibid.

16. "Rapists Face Trial," *FAMUAN* 27 (May 1959), 1, 3; "Negroes Ask Justice for Co-ed Rapists," *AC*, May 4, 1959, 2; "Four Whites Seized in Rape of Negro," *NYT*, May 3, 1959, A45; ibid., May 5, 1959, A23; "Mass Rape of Co-ed Outrages Students," *LW*, May 9, 1959, 1; *L'Osservatore Romano*, June 12, 1959; *Herald Tribune—London*, June 13, 1959; "Jury to Take Up Rape of Negro Co-ed," *AC*, May 5, 1959, 5.

17. Patricia Stephens Due interview by author, March 4, 1999. See also Tananarive Due and Patricia Stephens Due, *Freedom in the Family: A Mother-Daughter Memoir of the Fight for Civil Rights* (New York, 2003), 40–41; White, *Sit-ins*, 65.

18. See Howard Smead, *Blood Justice* (New York: Oxford University Press, 1988); "Lynch Victim Mack Parker's Body Is Found," *NYT*, May 5, 1959; Tyson, *Radio Free Dixie*, 143.

19. "4 Indicted In Rape of Negro Co-Ed," *NYHT*, May 7, 1959, 5.

20. M. C. Williams quoted in "Packed Court Hears Not Guilty," *PC*, May 16, 1959, 1–2; "Judge Instructs Jury Here," *TD*, May 6, 1959, 1; "Indictment for Rape," criminal case file 3445, *Florida v. Scarborough, Beagles, Stoutamire, and Collinsworth*; "Four Plead Not Guilty to Rape," *TD*, n.d., clipping, folder 4, box 912, WMW.

21. Claude Sitton, "Negroes See Gain in Conviction of Four for Rape of Co-ed," *NYT*, June 15, 1959, A1; statistics are from David R. Colburn and Richard K. Scher, *Florida's Gubernatorial Politics in the Twentieth Century* (Gainesville, Fla., 1980), 13. Willis McCall is quoted in Steven F. Lawson, David R. Colburn, and Darryl Paulson, "Groveland: Florida's Little Scottsboro," in David R. Colburn and Jane L. Landers, eds., *The African American Heritage of Florida* (Gainesville, 1995), 298–325, esp. 312.

22. See Moses J. Newson, "The Wind Blew, the Sky Was Overcast," *BAA*, June 20, 1959; Moses J. Newson, "Abraham's Shadow Hangs Low Over Tallahassee," ibid.; and Moses J. Newson, "His Mother Can Never Forget Him," ibid.

23. "Another Dixiecrat Headache," *PC*, June 20, 1959; "The Other Story," n.d., clipping, folder 1, box 912, WMW.

24. William H. Chafe, "Epilogue from Greensboro, North Carolina," in Cecelski and Tyson, *Democracy Betrayed,* 281–82.

25. "Senate to Get Racial Measures," *TD*, June 14, 1959, 1; "Pent Up Critique on the Rape Case," ibid., May 14, 1959.

26. *PC*, May 30, 1959, 3; "Mr. Muhammad Speaks," *PC*, May 16, 1959.

27. Ella Baker quoted in *PC*, May 30, 1959, 3; see also Ransby, *Ella,* 210. "Enforce the Law," *NYAN*, May 9, 1959; "What Will Florida Do," *PC*, May 16, 1959.

28. "King Asks Ike to Go to Mississippi," *BAA*, May 23, 1959; see also Martin Luther King, Jr., to Clifford C. Taylor, May 5, 1959, in *The Papers of Martin Luther King,* vol. 6 (Berkeley, Calif., forthcoming). Thanks to Kieran Taylor for sending me this information. "Report from Europe," *BAA,* May 23, 1959.

29. "Report from Europe," *BAA*, May 23, 1959; "King Asks Ike to Go to Mississippi," ibid.; "Appeal to U.N. to Stop Race Violence," *LW*, May 9, 1959, 1.

30. Tyson, *Radio Free Dixie,* 148–50.

31. Ibid., 149

32. Ibid., 145–51, esp. 148, 149; 163–65.

33. Roy Wilkins to LeRoy Collins, May 6, 1959, box A91, series III, NAACP Papers.

34. *TD*, May 4, 1959. On the "fair maiden," see Hall, "Mind That Burns," 335.

35. "I Was Scared," *PC*, June 20, 1959; see also "Did Not Consent," *TD*, June 11, 1959; "Rape Co-ed's Own Story," *NYAN*, June 20, 1959, 1; *AC,* June 12, 1959; "Negro Girl Tells Jury of Rape by Four," *NYT*, June 12, 1959, A16. Coverage of Owens's testimony was nearly identical in newspapers cited.

36. "Did Not Consent," *TD*, June 11, 1959; "I Was Scared," *PC*, June 20, 1959, 1; *CO*, June 12, 1959, 1A.

37. "Did Not Consent," *TD,* June 11, 1959. "I Was Scared," *PC*, June 20, 1959, 1; "State's exhibits" (knife) in criminal case file 3445, *Florida v. Scarborough, Beagles, Stoutamire, and Collinsworth, 1959.*

38. "Rape Co-ed's Own Story," *NYAN*, June 20, 1959, 1; "I Was Scared," *PC*, June 20, 1959, 1; see also "Four Begin Defense in Trial on Rape," *NYT*, June 13, 1959, A13.

39. Doctors quoted in "Rape Co-ed's Own Story," *NYAN*, June 20, 1959, 1; also in "Four Begin Defense in Trial on Rape," *NYT*, June 13, 1959, A13; friends quoted in "Did Not Consent," *TD,* June 11, 1959; John Rudd and Richard Brown quoted in "Deputy Tells of Confessions," *TD*, June 12, 1959.

40. Trezzvant W. Anderson, "Rapists Missed Out on First Selection," *PC*, June 20, 1959, 3; "Four Begin Defense in Trial on Rape," *NYT*, June 13, 1959, A13; Howard Williams quoted in "Rape Defendants Claim Consent," *TD*, June 13, 1959.

41. "Negro Co-ed Gave Consent, Rape Defendants Tell Jury," *AC*, 13 June 1959.

42. "Four Convicted in Rape Case; Escape Chair; 2 hr 45 min Verdict Calmly Received in Court," *TD*, June 14, 1959, 1; Pearlie Collinsworth and friends quoted in "Rape Defendants Claim Consent," *TD*, June 13, 1959; Maudine Reeve's History of Ted Collinsworth, "States exhibit #15," criminal case file 3445, *Florida v. Scarborough, Beagles, Stoutamire, and Collinsworth, 1959;* Mrs. W. T. Collinsworth, letter, "State's exhibit #16," ibid.

43. W. M. C. Wilhoit, testimony, in "Motion for Leave to File Notice of Defense of Insanity," May 28, 1959, criminal case file 3445, *Florida v. Scarborough, Beagles, Stoutamire, and Collinsworth, 1959;* "Four Begin Defense in Trial on Rape," *NYT*, June 13, 1959, A13; John Rudd quoted in "Four Guilty of Raping Negro; Florida Jury Votes Mercy," *NYT*, June 14, 1959, A1; Arthur Everett, "Four Convicted in Florida Rape Case," *WP*, June

14, 1959; "Insanity Plea Prepared as Rape Case Defense," *TD*, May 28, 1959; "Mental Exam Set for Collinsworth," *TD*, May 29, 1959.

44. "Four Guilty of Raping Negro; Florida Jury Votes Mercy," *NYT*, June 14, 1959, A1; Charles U. Smith, interview by Jackson Lee Ice, 1978, in JLI; verified in I-CUS, March 9, 1999.

45. "Precedent Seen in Rape Trial," *TT*, June 15, 1959; *TD*, June 14, 1959, 1.

46. "Verdict," June 14, 1959, criminal case file 3445, *Florida v. Scarborough, Beagles, Stoutamire, and Collinsworth, 1959*; "Guilty as Charged," *BAA*, June 20, 1959; A. H. King quoted in "No Brutality Proof, Says Florida Jury," *AC*, June 15, 1959, 1.

47. "Mild Verdict Angers Negroes in Rape Case," *PC*, June 20, 1959; Claude Sitton, "Negroes See Gain in Conviction of Four for Rape of Co-ed," *NYT*, June 15, 1959, A1; "I'm Leaving Dixie," *NYAN*, June 20, 1959.

48. Apparently students at Florida A&M ostracized Thomas Butterfield and Richard Brown for failing to protect Betty Jean Owens and Edna Richardson; students thought they ought to have shown some "physical resistance" rather than run away from the "point of a knife and gun": "I'm Leaving Dixie," *NYAN*, June 20, 1959; "Hits Negro Men," *NYAN,* June 6, 1959, 8; "Williams Was Right," *BAA*, June 27, 1959; "Four Convicted in Rape Case," *TD*, June 14, 1959, 7.

49. Sitton, "Negroes See Gain in Conviction of Four for Rape of Co-ed," *NYT*, June 15, 1959, A1; "Negroes Say They Will Use Tallahassee Case as Precedent in Rape Trials," *TT*, June 15, 1959.

50. Trezzvant W. Anderson, "Four Florida Rapists Near Chair," *PC*, July 4, 1959; Trezzvant W. Anderson, "Fla. Rape Case Mercy Sought for Four Negroes," *PC*, June 27, 1959.

51. *BAA*, June 27, 1959.

52. "Hunt Convicted Rapist in Florida Woman's Murder," *CDD*, February 11, 1969, 4. This article is the only source that mentions Beagles's name and his relationship to the murder of Betty Jean Robinson Houston. His criminal record, available online, does not mention a second murder charge. I am reluctant to say with certainty that he committed this crime without other evidence. David Beagles currently lives in Alabama and is on supervised parole. Florida Department of Corrections inmate number DC 66792, http://offender.fdle.state.fl.us/offender/flyer.do?personD=31547 (accessed February 11, 2008). Patrick Scarborough was paroled in 1965, then sent back to prison for violating his parole in 1968. He was paroled again and then incarcerated again in 1993 for second-degree murder. He is currently serving out the remainder of his life sentence. DOC inmate number DC 022849, http://offender.fdle.state.fl.us/offender/flyer.do?personId =56126 (accessed February 11, 2008). Ollie Stoutamire was paroled in 1965 and currently lives in Grand Ridge, Florida. William T. Collinsworth was paroled in 1965; I do not know his whereabouts.

53. Roy Wilkins to Frederick Cunningham, June 23, 1959, box A91, series III, NAACP Papers; "This Is Not Equal Justice," *LW*, July 4, 1959; Editorial, *NYAN*, June 20, 1959, 8.

54. Fred G. Millette to Judge W. May Walker, June 15, 1959, folder 1, box 912, WMW; Mrs. Laura Cox to Judge Walker, June 15, 1959, ibid., Mrs. Bill Aren to Judge Walker, June 15, 1959, ibid.

55. On the "incubus," see Glenda Gilmore, "Murder, Memory, and the Flight of the Incubus," in Cecelski and Tyson, *Democracy Betrayed, 73–93*.

56. For information on Florida's moderate racial politics, see Thomas R. Wagy, *Governor LeRoy Collins of Florida: Spokesman of the New South* (Tuscaloosa, Ala., 1985); and "From Sit-in to Race Riot: Businessmen, Blacks, and the Pursuit of Moderation in Tampa,

1960–1967," in Elizabeth Jacoway and David Colburn, eds., *Southern Businessmen and Desegregation* (Baton Rouge, La., 1982), 257–81.

57. Cases cited in Kimberly R. Woodard, "The Summer of African-American Discontent," unpublished paper (Duke University, 1992). See also "Death to be Demanded in Rape Case," *BAA*, 4 July 1959; "S.C. Judge Makes History! Dooms Marine to Death in Chair," *CD*, July 11, 1959, 1; John H. McCray, "Marine Doomed to Electric Chair in S.C. Rape Case," *BAA*, July 11, 1959, 1; Clarence Mitchell, "Separate but Equal Justice," *BAA*, July 11, 1959; "Girlfriend Turns in Rape Suspect," *BAA*, August 1, 1959; "Two Win New Trials," *NYT*, November 15, 1961, 19; "Free Marine Doomed for Raping Negro," *CDT*, June 30, 1962, C10. Fred G. Davis appealed his death sentence to the South Carolina Supreme Court; they reversed the decision and returned it to the trial judge. See *State v. Fred G. Davis*, 239 SC 280; 122 SE 2d 633; 1961 Lexis 52. Ralph Lee Betts of North Carolina was incarcerated and made numerous escapes. See his record on the North Carolina Department of Corrections website: http://webapps6.doc.state.nc.us/apps/offender/offend1?DOCNUM=0030630&SENTENCEINFO=yes&SHOWPHOTO=yes (accessed February 11, 2008). At least one case did not follow the Tallahassee precedent. On July 15, Tommy Paul Daniels, a white man from Macon, Georgia, raped a black babysitter, then bragged about it to his friend's boss and told him he planned to take his brother back to the house for another round with the teenage girl. "I even threatened to kill her when she cried out," Daniels boasted. The police arrived as Daniels and his brother were about to assault the girl again. Two months later an all-white jury acquitted Daniels, despite a city-wide campaign by the NAACP. See Andrew M. Manis, *Macon, Black and White: An Unutterable Separation in the American Century* (Macon, Ga., 2004), 197–98; Trezzvant Anderson, "Negroes Weep as Georgia White Is Acquitted," *PC*, September 26, 1959; "Free White Georgian in Rape Case," *CD*, September 29, 1959, 9; "Freed in Racial Rape," *NYT*, September 16, 1959, 78. See also box 15, folder 83, and box 11, folder 36, TWA.

58. James Booker, "The Tallahassee Case—A Turning Point in the South," *NYAN*, July 18, 1959.

59. Editorial, "A Step Toward Equal Justice," *LW*, July 18, 1959.

60. "The Tallahassee Case: A Turning Point in the South," *NYAN*, July 18, 1959; John H. McCray, "South's Courts Show New Day of Justice," *BAA*, June 11, 1959.

61. Richard Haley, "Reports on Events in Tallahassee, October 1959-June 1960," folder 7, box 10, series 5, CORE Papers.

62. Ella J. Baker, "Bigger Than a Hamburger," in Clayborne Carson, ed., *The Eyes on the Prize Civil Rights Reader: Documents, Speeches and Firsthand Accounts from the Black Freedom Struggle, 1954–1990* (New York, 1991), 120.

63. For more on the sit-ins in Greensboro, see William H. Chafe, *Civilities and Civil Rights: Greensboro, North Carolina, and the Black Struggle for Freedom* (New York, 1981).

64. An electronic search of articles about white men who raped black women, in the *Chicago Defender* from 1950 to 1960, yielded thirty-one articles, while a similar search turned up only eleven articles in the same paper from 1960 to 1970.

65. Gerda Lerner, *Black Women in White America: A Documentary History* (New York, 1972), 172. See also Hall, "Mind That Burns," 328–49; and Leslie A. Schwalm, *A Hard Fight for We: Women's Transition from Slavery to Freedom in South Carolina* (Urbana, Ill., 1997), 37, 44–45, 119–21.

66. James W. Silver, *Mississippi: The Closed Society* (New York, 1964), 151.

CHAPTER 6. "A BLACK WOMAN'S BODY WAS NEVER HERS ALONE"

1. Chana Kai Lee, *For Freedom's Sake: The Life of Fannie Lou Hamer* (Urbana, Ill., 1999), 9, 11.

2. Ibid., 9–10.

3. Harriet A. Washington, *Medical Apartheid: The Dark History of Medical Experimentation on Black Americans from Colonial Times to the Present* (New York, 2006), 190. In 1973 the Southern Poverty Law Center (SPLC) filed a class-action lawsuit to end federal funding for involuntary sterilization. SPLC lawyers discovered that 100,000 to 150,000 women had been sterilized using federal funds; half of them were black women. Ibid., 202–4; According to Dorothy Roberts, "It was a common belief among Blacks in the south that Black women were routinely sterilized without their informed consent for no valid medical reasons," and "teaching hospitals performed unnecessary hysterectomies on poor black women as practice for their medical residents. This sort of abuse was so widespread," Roberts continues, that "these operations came to be known as Mississippi appendectomies." Dorothy Roberts, *Killing the Black Body: Race, Reproduction and the Meaning of Liberty* (New York, 1999), 90. U.S. Congress, "Hearing Before a Select Panel on Mississippi and Civil Rights, Testimony of Mrs. Fannie Lou Hamer," *Congressional Record*, 88th Cong., 2d sess., June 4 to June 16, 1964, vol. 110, pt. 10, 14001–2; Lee, *Freedom's Sake*, 20–21. Hamer was a lifelong opponent of birth control. The women's movement of the late 1960s and early 1970s fought to restrict the practice of coercive or forced sterilization. The Reproductive Rights National Network (R2N2) "investigated and documented thousands of cases of forced sterilization, especially of people of color; of welfare recipients threatened with cutoffs of stipends unless they submitted to sterilization; and of women asked to sign sterilization consent forms while in labor, either in pain or partly anesthetized." In 1974 the U.S. Department of Health, Education, and Welfare finally issued guidelines that required informed consent and prohibited sterilization of women under the age of twenty-one. See Rosalyn Baxandall and Linda Gordon, "Second Wave Feminism," in Nancy Hewitt, ed., *A Companion to American Women's History* (New York, 2002), 420.

4. Ibid., 21; Kay Mills, *This Little Light of Mine: The Life of Fannie Lou Hamer* (New York, 1993), 22.

5. Dittmer, *Local People*, 171.

6. Lee, *Freedom's Sake*, 49; See also "The Winona Incident: An Interview with Annelle Ponder and Fannie Lou Hamer, June 13, 1963," in Pat Watters and Reese Cleghorn, *Climbing Jacob's Ladder: The Arrival of Negroes in Southern Politics* (New York, 1967); SNCC Papers, microfilm, reel 40, frames 454–57.

7. Annell Ponder, interview by Jack Minnis, SNCC Papers, microfilm, reel 38, frame 502; Watters and Cleghorn, *Climbing*, 366.

8. Dittmer, *Local People*, 171.

9. Payne, *Light of Freedom*, 242.

10. Lee, *Freedom's Sake*, 9–10, 78–81, 51–52. Although Lee argues that Hamer was "inclined to dissemble when it came to sex, race and violence" (78–81), Lee's own evidence suggested that Hamer testified publicly to the sexualized aspects of her beating in Winona, Mississippi, and her forced sterilization as often as she kept them hidden (see 54, 59, 79, 80–81, 89, 198n42, 196n2).

11. Ibid., 52; Fannie Lou Hamer, interview, in Selby and Selby, *Odyssey*, 186. See also Jerry DeMuth, "Tired of Being Sick and Tired," *Nation*, June 1, 1964.

12. Lawrence Guyot, interview by John Rachal, 1996, transcript, vol. 673, COHCH. See also Lee, *Freedom's Sake*, 53.

13. Lee, *Freedom's Sake*, 59.

14. Ibid., 78–81.

15. WNEW Radio transcript, June 6, 1963, CORE Papers on microfilm, series III, reel 22, frames 219–29. See also "The Uses of Nonviolence," *Nation*, July 6, 1963, 2–3.

16. WNEW Radio transcript. Demonstrations in Jackson took place in the spring and early summer of 1963, just a few months after James Meredith integrated Ole Miss and just before Medgar Evers was assassinated. Between 1890 and 1920 middle-class black women active in the Baptist Church and Convention movement relied on the politics of respectability to counter negative stereotypes and to advance an agenda of racial equality. Strict adherence to "manners and morals" in public helped black women protect their sexual identities and assert themselves as dignified human beings in a white supremacist society that ridiculed them as lazy, dirty, and/or promiscuous. According to Darlene Clark Hine, middle-class black women also adopted a "culture of dissemblance" to shield themselves emotionally and physically from Jim Crow. As a result, clubwomen used respectability and dissemblance as political weapons to fight racism and win sympathetic white allies. See also Evelyn Brooks Higginbotham, *Righteous Discontent: The Women's Movement in the Black Baptist Church, 1880–1920* (Cambridge, Mass., 1993), 193–94.

17. WNEW Radio transcript, June 6, 1963, CORE Papers on microfilm, series III, reel 22, frames 219–29.

18. Olson, *Daughter,* 191.

19. Ibid., 192.

20. Robnett, *How Long?,* 134–35. SNCC released Turner's sworn affidavit on January 20, 1962.

21. Unita Blackwell, interview, in Tiffany Joseph and Gabriel Mendes, "Voter Registration and the Missisppi Freedom Democratic Party," on the *Freedom Now! Archival Project of Tougaloo College and Brown University* website, http://www.stg.brown.edu/projects/FreedomNow/themes/mfdp/index.html (accessed July 21, 2009).

22. "Police Brutality in Southwest Georgia, 1963," folder 2, box 47, CAB.

23. Ibid.

24. Medical Committee for Human Rights, Report, June 1965, folder 11, box 55, CAB. For more on the Medical Committee, see John Dittmer, *The Good Doctors: The Medical Committee for Human Rights and the Struggle for Social Justice in Health Care* (New York, 2009). For more on the abuse of black women in Southern prisons, see Douglas Blackmon, *Slavery by Another Name: The Re-enslavement of Black Americans from the Civil War to World War II* (New York, 2009); and Mary Ellen Curtin, *Black Prisoners and Their World: Alabama, 1865–1900* (Charlottesville, Va., 2000).

25. WNEW Radio transcript, June 6, 1963, CORE Papers on microfilm, series III, reel 22, frames 219–29. See also *Nation*, July 6, 1963, 3.

26. Dorothy Height, *Open Wide the Freedom Gates: A Memoir* (New York, 2003), 158; and Deborah Gray White, *Too Heavy a Load: Black Women in Defense of Themselves, 1894–1994* (New York, 1999), 194.

27. "Background: Atlanta, Jackson, London, Selma 1963–1966," folder 2, box 2, series 19, NCNWR. Thanks to Kenneth Chandler for his help locating this transcript.

28. Ibid.

29. Height, *Open Wide,* 158–59.

30. "Cowan, Polly—Writings," folder 22, box 4, series 19, NCNWR. Thanks to Kenneth Chandler for finding this document for me.

31. Height, *Open Wide,* 162.

32. Ibid., 169.

33. White, *Too Heavy,* 198.

34. For more on the Birmingham movement, see Glenn T. Eskew, *But for Birmingham: The Local and National Movements in the Civil Rights Struggle* (Chapel Hill, N.C., 1997); Andrew Manis, *A Fire You Can't Put Out* (Tuscaloosa, Ala., 1999); Diane McWhorter, *Carry Me Home: Birmingham, Alabama: The Climactic Battle of the Civil Rights Revolution* (New York, 2001); and Thornton, *Dividing.*

35. Dittmer, *Local People,* 157. Between 1962 and 1964, when the VEP organized throughout the South, black voter registration in Mississippi barely budged.

36. *Freedom on My Mind,* produced and directed by Connie Field and Marilyn Mulford, California Newsreel, 1994, videocassette.

37. Endesha Ida Mae Holland, *From the Mississippi Delta: A Memoir* (New York, 1997), 78.

38. Ibid., 83.

39. Ibid., 84.

40. Ibid., 86.

41. Ibid., 91, 90. It is unclear if Holland is suggesting that many Delta families were headed by single mothers, or if the oppressive racial environment made it difficult, if not dangerous, for black men to protect their wives and daughters.

42. Ibid., 85.

43. Ibid., 90.

44. Moses came to Mississippi as an SNCC volunteer in the federally sponsored Voter Education Project. President John F. Kennedy helped raise money from liberal philanthropic organizations to steer civil rights activists into voter registration, which he hoped would provoke less violence and fewer headlines than the nonviolent direct action strategies pursued by SNCC and CORE during the 1960 sit-ins and 1961 Freedom Ride. Major civil rights organizations—the NAACP, SCLC, CORE, and SNCC—agreed to participate, believing that the Kennedy administration would protect them from white violence. Between 1962 and 1964, they fanned out across the South to register black voters. Wiley Branton, director of the VEP, believed the "Justice Department would take all necessary steps to protect federal or constitutional rights," including the "elementary matter of protection." The Justice Department, however, had no intention of sending federal troops to the South "for fear of alienating powerful southern lawmakers whose cooperation the administration needed to pass its legislative program." When law enforcement was left up to hostile local officials, civil rights activists were often mistreated, beaten, sexually abused, and, in some cases, killed. See Lawson, *Running,* 86–90.

45. Holland, *Delta,* 210.

46. Ibid., 219. Holland went on to earn her Ph.D. from the University of Minnesota and became a professor at the University of Southern California and SUNY Buffalo. Her play, *From the Mississippi Delta*, was nominated for a Pulitzer Prize. Endesha Ida Mae Holland died January 25, 2006.

47. Even after Byron de la Beckwith assassinated Mississippi NAACP leader Medgar Evers on June 11, 1963, the Kennedy administration's solution to white violence was to get "black people off the streets" and negotiate with white leaders who continued to flout the constitution. According to Dittmer, the "Kennedys demonstrated once again that in the short run, at least, they preferred order to justice." Dittmer, *Local People,* 169. For more on the life and death of Medgar Evers, see Myrlie Evers, *For Us, the Living* (New York, 1967); Adam Nossiter, *Of Long Memory: Mississippi and the Murder of Medgar Evers* (Cambridge, Mass., 2002); Myrlie Evers-Williams, Manning Marable, and Medgar Wiley Evers, *The Autobiography of Medgar Evers: A Hero's Life and Legacy Revealed Through His Writings, Letters, and Speeches* (New York, 2005).

48. Olson, *Daughters,* 294.

49. Sally Belfrage, *Freedom Summer* (Charlottesville, Va., 1965), 10.

50. Dittmer, *Local People,* 263.

51. John Herbers, "Mississippi: A Profile of the Nation's Most Segregated State," *NYT,* June 28, 1964, E3.

52. Dittmer, *Local People,* 266; clipping, *Newsweek,* February 24, 1964, box 274, series IIIA, NAACP Papers.

53. Dittmer, *Local People,* 266.

54. "Went into State to Enroll Voters," *NYT,* December 5, 1964, 19.

55. Dittmer, *Local People,* 266.

56. Clipping, *Newsweek,* February 24, 1964, in box 274, series IIIA, NAACP Papers.

57. Ibid.

58. Robnett, *How Long?,* 127; Dittmer, *Local People,* 251.

59. Klansmen murdered Charles Moore, a twenty-year-old Alcorn College student, and Henry Dee, twenty-one, after beating them in the Homochitto National Forest on May 2, 1964. Bystanders also found the body of a black teenager wearing a CORE T-shirt floating in the Big Black River that summer. He was never identified. See Dittmer, *Local People,* 251–52.

60. Ibid., 251.

61. Often called the "Emmett Till generation," many SNCC workers remember the brutal lynching of Till and the image of his mutilated body printed in *Jet* magazine as a galvanizing force. Ibid., 58. Sally Belfrage saw pictures of Till in *Jet* for the first time during Freedom Summer. She remembered it being "the most awful picture I had ever seen." Belfrage, *Summer,* 159.

62. For more on the interracial tensions during Freedom Summer, see Sara Evans, *Personal Politics: The Roots of Women's Liberation in the Civil Rights Movement and the New Left* (New York, 1979); and Mary King, *Freedom Song: A Personal Story of the 1960s Civil Rights Movement* (New York, 1987), esp. chap. 12.

63. A number of scholars seem to be interested in whether interracial sex did actually occur during Freedom Summer and, if so, what it means. I am not interested in this issue, agreeing with Bernice Johnson Reagon that "a lot of it was nobody's business." Robnett, *How Long?,* 131; See also Renee C. Romano, *Race Mixing: Black-White Marriage in Postwar America* (Gainesville, Fla., 2006), 177–85; and Allen Matusow, "From Civil Rights to Black Power: The Case of SNCC, 1960–1966," in Barton J. Bernstein and Allen J. Matusow, eds., *Twentieth Century America: Recent Interpretations* (New York, 1969), 531–36.

64. Olson, *Daughters,* 267.

65. Ibid., 305; Robnett, *How Long?,* 124.

66. Olson, *Daughters,* 267.

67. Belfrage, *Summer,* 111.

68. Ibid.

69. "Innocent Plea in Rape Case," *JDN,* July 27, 1960, 5; "White Youth Guilty in Rape," *NYT,* July 28, 1960, 5.

70. Ibid. It is unclear whether the girl normally carried a penknife when in the company of white men, or if she was wary of Loden, but it is an interesting detail. Did black women carry small weapons when they went to work for whites? Did mothers and fathers warn their daughters and encourage them to protect themselves?

71. "Report on Rape Cases Beginning January 1, 1940, Through March 31, 1965, Compiled from the Records of the Mississippi State Penitentiary, Parchman, Mississippi," box 21, LSCRRCP. The report contains the name, charge, sentence, and status of each man charged with rape in every county of Mississippi, but it does not list the dates on which they were charged. Charles Coffee and Louis Coffee received life sentences for raping a "Negro age 5" and, as of March 31, 1965, were still in Parchman (see note 74 below). With the exception of Abraham Sloan and the Coffee brothers, none of the white men charged or sentenced were from the Delta. Eighty-nine African Americans in Delta counties were charged with rape or attempted rape and sentenced to prison between 1940 and 1965. Of those, the report indicates, seventeen were charged with rape or attempted rape of white women. The sentencing patterns indicate that when charged

with rape or attempted rape of white women, black men were sentenced to life in prison. They received paltry sentences for similar charges brought by black girls or women. The breakdown of the numbers of black men charged and sentenced in Delta counties: Bolivar, 11; Carroll, 2; Coahoma, 15; Humphreys, 3; Issaquena, 3; Leflore, 11; Sharkey, 7; Sunflower, 13; Tallahatchie, 2; Tunica, 3; Washington, 15; Yazoo, 4.

72. "Rapes Race Girl; Saved by Jury," *CD*, August 6, 1960, 1; "White Youth Guilty in Rape," *NYT*, July 28, 1960, 5.

73. "Rapes Race Girl; Saved by Jury," *CD*, August 6, 1960, 1. In 1965, when the NAACP Legal Defense Fund and the Law Students Civil Rights Research Council researched sentencing patterns for rape in the South, they compiled a record of rape cases in Mississippi from 1940 to 1965. The record indicates that as of March 31, 1965, L. J. Loden was still serving time in Parchman penitentiary. See "Report on Rape Cases Beginning January 1, 1940, Through March 31, 1965, Compiled from the Records of the Mississippi State Penitentiary, Parchman, Mississippi," box 21, LSCRRCP.

74. "White Youth Gets Life in Rape Case," *WP*, December 12, 1965, A3. On February 8, 1961, two white male pedophiles from Yazoo City, Mississippi, were convicted of raping a five-year-old African-American child on a plantation and sentenced to life in prison. The assailants, Louis Coffee, eighteen, and Charles Coffee, twenty, pleaded guilty. I do not include this in my calculation since pedophilia is a different and unique sex crime, but it is worth mentioning. See "Whites Get Life Sentences," *JA*, February 8, 1961, 1; and "Two Get Life for Rape," *NYT*, February 10, 1961, 15.

75. My research indicates that no white man was executed by the state of Mississippi—or any other Southern state, for that matter—for the crime of rape on a black woman between 1940 and 1975, the period this book covers.

76. The Civil Rights Act of 1964 outlawed discrimination in public accommodations, including hotels, restaurants, and theaters; banned discrimination based on race, color, religion, sex, or national origin in employment; created the Equal Employment Opportunity Commission (EEOC) to enforce this provision and investigate discrimination in the workplace; made federal funding contingent upon fair practices; barred unequal voter-registration requirements but failed to eliminate literacy tests; and enabled the Justice Department to file lawsuits to force states to desegregate their schools. The act contained no provision that could be used to protect civil rights activists from physical harm. See Lawson, *Running for Freedom*, 91, 95.

77. Fannie Lou Hamer and Victoria Gray were elected congresspersons in the November 1964 statewide mock elections. Payne, *Light of Freedom,* 321.

78. American Radio Works, "Fannie Lou Hamer Testimony in Front of the Credentials Committee, Democratic National Convention, Atlantic City, New Jersey, August 22, 1964," http://americanradioworks.publicradio.org/features/sayitplain/flhamer.html, accessed March 12, 2008; Lawson, *Running for Freedom*, 97; Dittmer, *Local People,* 272–302 passim; and Lee, *Freedom's Sake,* 99.

CHAPTER 7. SEX AND CIVIL RIGHTS

1. Thornton, *Dividing,* 488.

2. Dan T. Carter, *From George Wallace to Newt Gingrich* (Baton Rouge, La., 1999) 1; Branch, *At Canaan's Edge: America in the King Years, 1965–1968* (New York, 2006), 162.

3. Branch, *At Canaan's Edge,* 165; Lyndon Johnson signed the Voting Rights Act on August 6, 1965, after speedy action by Congress. The act banned literacy tests; authorized the use of federal registrars and observers to enforce voting rights; required states to have electoral changes approved to guarantee the rules; did not discriminate against black voters (known as preclearance); brought Alabama, Georgia, Louisiana, Mississippi, South

Carolina, Virginia, and parts of North Carolina under federal supervision; and enabled the Justice Department to bring suit against states that continued to use the poll tax. In order to avoid federal supervision, states have to appeal to federal district court in Washington, D.C., and prove that they did not use a "discriminatory test or device for the previous five years." Lawson, *Running,* 117–18.

4. Thornton, *Dividing,* 403–06.

5. Ibid., 399–401; on Jim Clark's posse, see 411.

6. For a good description of Clark, see "Jim Clark, Sheriff Who Enforced Segregation, Dies at 84," *NYT,* June 7, 2007. See also "Bridge to Freedom," *Eyes on the Prize* DVD. Approximately 14,000 blacks and 14,500 whites made up Selma's population in 1964; the county population was about 58 percent black in 1960. In 1970, 29,000 blacks and 26,500 whites lived in Dallas County. See Thornton, *Dividing,* 414, 498–89.

7. Branch, *At Canaan's Edge,* 8.

8. For more on the Jimmie Lee Jackson case and the current legal proceedings against James Bonard Fowler, see journalist John Fleming's investigative work at the *Anniston Star,* http://www.annistonstar.com (accessed April 23, 2008). See also Branch, *At Canaan's Edge,* 8, and Thornton, *Dividing,* 486.

9. "Bridge to Freedom," *Eyes on the Prize* DVD.

10. Al Turner, ibid.

11. Lawson, *Running,* 110–11. This was King's strategy in Birmingham, where he and the SCLC counted on "Bull" Connor to attack the respectable and nonviolent marchers, many of whom were children. For more on the way white violence attracted national media attention and thus compelled federal action, see Payne, *Light of Freedom,* 394–99.

12. David Garrow, *Bearing the Cross: Martin Luther King Jr. and the Southern Christian Leadership Conference* (New York, 1989), 381.

13. Branch, *At Canaan's Edge,* 46.

14. F. D. Reese, interview by Larry Vasser, box 121, series 4, TB.

15. Branch, *At Canaan's Edge,* 50.

16. Ibid., 52.

17. See film footage of the confrontation on "Bridge to Freedom," *Eyes on the Prize* DVD.

18. Branch, *At Canaan's Edge,* 56.

19. Thornton, *Dividing,* 488.

20. Mary Stanton, *From Selma to Sorrow: The Life and Death of Viola Liuzzo* (Athens, Ga., 1998), 143; Branch, *At Canaan's Edge,* 153.

21. "Alabamian in House Assails March," *NYT,* March 31, 1965, 17; "Says Sex Is Motive in Rights Movement," *CD,* March 31, 1965, 9.

22. Stanton, *From Selma,* 144.

23. "Photos Prove March Orgies, Says Solon," *BN,* April 4, 1965; "Godless riff-raff" quote from "Says Sex Is Motive in Rights Movement," *CD,* March 31, 1965, 9.

24. Stanton, *From Selma,* 144–45; Albert C. Persons, *Sex and Civil Rights: The True Selma Story* (Birmingham, Ala., 1965), 1.

25. Persons, *Sex,* 9.

26. Affidavits from Alabama Department of Public Safety, GW.

27. Ibid.

28. Ironically, an entire section of the book is devoted to "How 'Images' Are Created," detailing how media bias manipulates images to advance a pro–civil rights agenda.

29. Persons, *Sex,* 7.

30. Ibid., 4.

31. Ibid., 6.

32. On Bayard Rustin, see John D'Emilio, *Lost Prophet: The Life and Times of Bayard*

Rustin (New York, 2003); Jervis Andersen, *Bayard Rustin: Troubles I've Seen* (Berkeley, Calif., 1998).

33. Persons, *Sex,* 14.
34. Stanton, *From Selma,* 144.
35. Patricia Sullivan, ed., *Freedom Writer: Virginia Foster Durr: Letters from the Civil Rights Years* (New York, 2003), 328.
36. Virginia Durr to Carl and Anne Braden, May 3, 1965, folder 1, box 41, CAB. See also Virginia Foster Durr with Hollinger F. Barnard, ed., *Outside the Magic Circle: The Autobiography of Virginia Foster Durr* (New York, 1987), 327, 328.
37. Virginia Durr to Carl and Anne Braden, May 3, 1965, folder 1, box 41, CAB.
38. See the stack of telegrams sent to the NAACP, "Telegrams Relating to Selma-Montgomery March," box 274, series IIIA, NAACP Papers.
39. Al Kuettner, "Reporter Digs into Talk of Alabama Sex Orgies," *Mississippi Press Scimitar*, April 1, 1965.
40. "Clerics in March Rebut Dickinson," April 29, 1965, *NYT*, 16.
41. Branch, *At Canaan's Edge*, 153.
42. Durr with Barnard, *Outside,* 175.
43. Ibid., 326
44. Governor George Wallace to Congressman Malcolm Bethea, April 7, 1965, GW.
45. Stanton, *From Selma,* 147.
46. James G. Clark, *I Saw Selma Raped: The Jim Clark Story* (Birmingham, Ala., 1966). Clark's book recycles information found in Persons's magazine, *Sex and Civil Rights*, and offers up Lost Cause justifications for white oppression of African Americans.
47. Clark, *Selma Raped,* 42.
48. Branch, *At Canaan's Edge*, 173.
49. FBI report on murder of Liuzzo, March 26, 1965, folder 2, box 124, TB; Branch, *At Canaan's Edge*, 173–74.
50. "Action squad" in Branch, *At Canaan's Edge*, 178; "panicked" in Stanton, *From Selma,* 52.
51. Jack Anderson, "FBI Informer Was Traveling in Murder Car," *WP*, March 21, 1983, B13; Stanton, *From Selma,* 55.
52. Branch, *At Canaan's Edge*, 218; Seth Cagin and Philip Dray, *We Are Not Afraid: The Story of Goodman, Schwerner and Chaney and the Civil Rights Campaign for Mississippi* (New York, 1988), 442; "The Imperial Klonsel: Matt Murphy," *NYT*, May 7, 1965, 25.
53. Branch, *At Canaan's Edge*, 177. See also, "Memorandum for Mr. Tolson, Mr. Belmong, Mr. Deloach, Mr. Rosen," from J. Edgar Hoover, March 26, 1965, folder 2, box 124, TB.
54. Stanton, *From Selma,* 54.
55. Ibid., 55.
56. "Liuzzo Case Jury Retires for Night Without a Verdict," *NYT*, May 7, 1965, 1.
57. "Klansman Linked to Death Bullet," *NYT*, May 6, 1965, 1.
58. Eliza Heard, "Economics and a Murder Trial," *New South*, October, 1965, 5; Olson, *Daughters,* 346.
59. Virginia Foster Durr, *Freedom Winter,* ed. Patricia Sullivan (New York, 2003), 331; See also "Press Release," May 7, 1965, box 273, series IIIA, NAACP Papers.
60. Stanton, *From Selma,* 116.
61. Ibid., 55.
62. Ibid., 121; *Time*, May 14, 1965.
63. "Liuzzo Case Jury Retires for Night Without a Verdict," *NYT*, May 7, 1965, 1; Branch, *At Canaan's Edge*, 218.
64. "Liuzzo Case Jury Retires for Night," *NYT,* May 7, 1965, 1.

65. All of Liuzzo's murderers, Eugene Thomas, forty-three, of Bessemer; William Orville Eaton, forty-one, of Bessemer; Collie Leroy Wilkins, Jr., twenty-one, of Fairfield; and Gary Thomas Rowe (FBI informant), thirty-one, of Birmingham, were found not guilty of state murder charges. On December 3, 1965, Thomas, Eaton, and Wilkins were found guilty on federal charges of conspiracy to violate the civil rights of Liuzzo. See Thornton, *Dividing,* 489; Stanton, *From Selma,* 130.

66. Stanton, *From Selma,* 120–21.

67. Ibid., 121.

68. "FBI Has Drawn Cloak of Secrecy Around Arrests of Four Klansmen," *WP,* March 28, 1965, A2; Stanton, *From Selma,* 54.

69. Branch, *At Canaan's Edge,* 219; "Murder in Alabama: American Wives Think Viola Liuzzo Should Have Stayed Home," *Ladies' Home Journal,* July 1965, in folder 2, box 124, TB.

70. The "decaying structures of family life" are indicated by the statistics found in the report: "1/4 of all negro marriages dissolved; 1/4 of all negro births illegitimate; 1/4 of negro families headed by women; 90% higher infant mortality rate, heavy narcotics addiction and delinquency, and rampant poverty." See Office of Policy Planning and Research, U.S. Department of Labor, *The Negro Family: The Case for National Action* (U.S. Government Printing Office, No. 1965 0–794–628, March 1965). By August, the report had become headline news. "Inside Report," *WP,* August 18, 1965, A19. See also Branch, *At Canaan's Edge,* 370. For the definitive account of how Americans responded to the Moynihan report, see Lee Rainwater and William L. Yancey, *The Moynihan Report and the Politics of Controversy* (Cambridge, Mass., 1967).

71. "Race Problems Pointed Up in Moynihan Report," *LAT,* September 29, 1965, A4.

72. Peniel W. Joseph, *Waiting 'Til the Midnight Hour* (New York, 2006), 152.

73. Branch, *At Canaan's Edge,* 371.

74. Whites in the area were not nonviolent; only thirty miles away, in Poplarville, a mob kidnapped and lynched Mack Charles Parker in 1959. In Hattiesburg, only 25 of the 7,495 eligible black voters were registered in 1961. The Kennedy Justice Department filed a number of lawsuits in an attempt to force Lynd to at least permit blacks to attempt to register to vote. Lynd defied the Justice Department at every turn and even refused to obey a ruling by the Fifth Circuit Court of Appeals prohibiting him from discriminating against blacks. When the Supreme Court upheld the lower court's rulings, Lynd still did not comply. The lawsuits made Hattiesburg the "major testing ground in the battle for suffrage rights." Dittmer, *Local People,* 179–80, 184.

75. Ibid., 179.

76. Ibid., 182.

77. Ibid., 259.

78. Kennard's case was a frame-up organized and carried out by the State Sovereignty Commission with the full support of Governor J. P. Coleman and William D. McCain, president of USM. The commission spied on Kennard, used friendly blacks to dissuade him from applying to USM, and jailed him when he persisted. When Kennard was diagnosed with end-stage cancer in 1963, state leaders released him from prison to avoid any outside scrutiny should he die in custody. The trumped-up conviction and sentence were just "another example of racial justice in the closed society" and indicated whites were willing to do just about anything to thwart black advancement. Dittmer, *Local People,* 79–83 passim.

79. Ibid., 213.

80. *HA,* November 9, 1965, 2.

81. Dittmer, *Local People,* 217. Sam Bowers was convicted along with seven other Klansmen of federal civil rights violations in the murders of James Goodman, Michael Schwerner,

and James Chaney in October 1967. Bowers was finally convicted in 1998 of murdering Vernon Dahmer on January 10, 1966. After Dahmer announced he would help blacks register to vote by collecting poll taxes at his store, Bowers and two carloads of Klansmen firebombed Dahmer's home and business. Dahmer died shortly thereafter from burns and injuries sustained during the attack. See Dittmer, *Local People,* 391.

82. Laurie Pritchett was the chief of police in Albany, Georgia, from 1959 to 1966. When the SCLC launched a campaign to desegregate local institutions and register voters there in 1961, Pritchett declared he was in favor of nonviolence and ordered his officers to use restraint. Pritchett's decision kept negative nationwide publicity to a minimum, contributing to the "failure" of the SCLC's Albany campaign. For more on the Albany movement, see Branch, *Parting the Waters,* and Garrow, *Bearing the Cross.* Only one person was arrested during Freedom Day, a break from past practices. Dittmer, *Local People,* 221.

83. "Negro Girl Reports Rape by White Man," *HA,* July 14, 1965, 7; "Cannon Indicted, Pleads Innocent to Rape Charge," *HA,* July 17, 1965, 1.

84. Lois Miles interview by author, October 17, 2007, Hattiesburg, Mississppi.

85. "Negro Girl Reports Rape by White Man," *HA,* July 14, 1965, 7; "Cannon Indicted, Pleads Innocent to Rape Charge," *HA,* July 17, 1965, 1. Description of crime scene based upon author visit to Hattiesburg on October 17, 2007; I-JD.

86. "Cannon Indicted, Pleads Innocent to Rape Charge," *HA,* July 17, 1965, 1; "Southern White Found Guilty of Raping Negro," *LAT,* November 12, 1965, 12.

87. Yashuhiro Katagiri, *Mississippi State Sovereignty Commission: Civil Rights and States Rights* (Jackson, Miss., 2001), 173; see also "Press Release," n.d, in M191, folder 7, box 137, GPJ.

88. "White Convicted of Raping Negro," *NYT,* November 12, 1965, 1.

89. "Cannon Indicted, Pleads Innocent to Rape Charge," *HA,* July 17, 1965, 1; I-JD.

90. "Rape Trial Under Way; Grandmother Points to Cannon," *HA,* November 9, 1965, 1.

91. "Conflicting Stories Told," *HA,* November 10, 1965, 1.

92. "Southern White Found Guilty of Raping Negro," *LAT,* November 12, 1965, 12.

93. I-JD.

94. "Conflicting Stories Told," *HA,* November 10, 1965, 1; I-JD. Dukes described the language of the defense attorney as "rude" and "crass." He said that he asked inappropriate things and made everyone in court sick with his perverted language.

95. "Rape Trial Under Way; Grandmother Points to Cannon," *HA,* November 9, 1965, 1.

96. Ibid.

97. "Grandmother Points Out Man Accused of Assault," *CL,* November 10, 1965, 4.

98. I-JD.

99. "Conflicting Stories Told," *HA,* November 10, 1965, 1.

100. Ibid.

101. "Cannon Found Guilty of Rape, Jury Gives Him Life," *HA,* November 11, 1965, 1.

102. "Southern White Found Guilty of Raping Negro," *LAT,* November 12, 1965, 12.

103. "Cannon Found Guilty of Rape," 1; "White Convicted of Raping Negro," *NYT,* November 12, 1965, 1.

104. "State Man Gets Life for Rape of Negro Girl," *JA,* November 20, 1965, 1.

105. None of the movement activists I interviewed or contacted remembered the case, including Raylawni Branch, who desegregated USM in the fall of 1965, and Daisy Wade Harris, who housed movement activists and whose sons helped desegregate the public schools. I-RB, I-DWH. Joyce Ladner said hearing about Cannon's conviction "hit me like a bolt of lightning." Joyce Ladner to author, March 7, 2006. None of the oral histories collected at USM's Center for Oral History mention the case, except for Judge Stanton Hall, who claimed he sent Cannon to prison for life because "I have justice

in the back of my heart and justice is blind, we have no difference here between race, creed and color. And whoever you are, we try them on their merits." See "Interview with Judge Stanton Augustus Hall, Judge, 12th district, Mississippi Circuit," by Prof. Carl Willis, 1972, vol. III, 45, COHCH. Thanks to Curtis Austin for his assistance and hospitality.

106. Dittmer, *Local People,* 327.

107. The *Chicago Defender* ran a small paragraph issued by UPI that reported the guilty verdict but offered very little detail or commentary. "Dixie White Guilty in Rape of Negro Girl," *CD,* November 13, 1965.

108. I-JD.

109. "South Must Enforce Own Criminal Laws," *HA,* November 11, 1965, 1.

110. "Mississippi State Penitentiary, Parchman, Mississippi," November 23, 1965, M191, folder 4, box 138, GPJ.

111. Ibid.

112. "Rape Conviction Here Is Upheld," *HA,* October 3, 1966, 3; *Norman Cannon v. State of Mississippi,* 190 So 2d 848; 1966. Cannon appealed his conviction a number of times, most recently in 2001. Thanks to Jean Smith Vaughn, assistant attorney general, who shared the state's brief with me.

113. "Cite Southern Courts, Officers in CR Woes," *HA,* November 15, 1965, 1.

114. Branch, *At Canaan's Edge,* 382.

115. "White Convicted of Raping Negro," *NYT,* November 12, 1965, 1; "Southern White Found Guilty of Raping Negro," *LAT,* November 12, 1965, 12; "White Youth Gets Life in Rape Case," *WP,* November 12, 1965, A3.

116. "South Finds New 'Sense of Somebodiness,'" *LAT,* November 21, 1965, K3.

117. After the Tallahassee verdicts in 1959, the NAACP indicated it would focus on making sentencing in interracial rape cases more equal, especially in Florida, where a number of black men waited on death row for rape or attempted rape of white women. See Chapter 5. See also "Racial Double Standard Is Charged in Rape Cases," *WP,* September 22, 1966.

118. In January 1966, the Southern Regional Council (SRC) issued a special report reinforcing the NAACP's findings. The report used statistics from the U.S. Bureau of Prisons to show that "despite the fact that more than half of all convicted rapists are white, eighty-seven percent of all the persons executed for rape between 1930 and 1963 were Negroes convicted and sentenced by southern courts." According to the report, the skewed sentences were firmly rooted in the legal and customary exclusion of African Americans and women on Southern juries. The jury system in the South, the SRC argued, existed in a "crippled condition." Attorney General Nicholas Katzenbach told the *Chicago Defender* that he concurred with the SRC's findings. "The jury system as it now operates in most parts of the South," he said, "is grossly unfair." Harry Golden, "Southern Justice and the Negro," *CD,* January 15, 1966, 14. Because the death penalty for rape was a "peculiar product of Southern history and culture," the LDF announced a major study that would examine twenty-six hundred rape cases in eleven Southern states over the previous twenty years. With a grant of $100,000 from the LDF, Marvin Wolfgang, a University of Pennsylvania criminologist, and Anthony Amsterdam, a legal scholar at Stanford, supervised twenty-eight law students selected by the Law Students Civil Rights Research Council (LSCRRC) as they journeyed into 225 counties investigating every rape conviction after 1945 that they could find. Jack Greenberg, the director of the LDF's efforts, hoped the survey would yield information that could be used to "establish precedents on the sentencing issue" in eighteen capital punishment cases being handled by the LDF. "We are making the legal argument that the arbitrary discretion to choose between life and death, by southern juries, violates due process plus equal pro-

tection because, in the absence of any standards . . . southern juries are free to act arbitrarily and discriminatorily." A *Chicago Defender* headline neatly summarized the issue: "Rape Trap Helps Dixie Lynch Legally." See "Study Probes 'Bias' in Rape Cases," *CD*, April 25, 1966, 6; "Rape Penalties in South Studied," *NYT*, April 26, 1966. See also box 21, LSCRRCP; "Rape Trap Helps Dixie Lynch Legally," *CD*, February 11, 1967, 7. The LDF used results from the study to challenge a number of cases in which African-American men convicted of rape received the death penalty, many of which even reached the Supreme Court.

119. *Norman Cannon, Appellant, v. State of Mississippi, Appellee*, 816 So 2d 433; 2002 Miss. Cannon's appeal for post conviction relief and motion for habeas corpus were denied on April 30, 2002. Cannon may have died in prison, as he is no longer listed as an inmate at Parchman penitentiary and there is no record of his conviction being overturned.

120. Peter Wallenstein, *Tell the Court I Love My Wife* (New York, 2002), 15.

121. On the way gender and sexuality structured slavery, see Kathleen Brown, *Good Wives, Nasty Wenches, and Anxious Patriarchs* (Chapel Hill, N.C., 1996) 128–36; Kirsten Fischer, *Suspect Relations: Sex, Race and Resistance in Colonial North Carolina* (Ithaca, N.Y., 2002); and White, *Too Heavy*.

122. Romano, *Race Mixing*, 186; *Loving v. Virginia* 388 U.S. 1 (1967). Eleven former Confederate states plus five border states. See also, Wallenstein, *Tell the Court*, 232.

123. Romano, *Race Mixing*, 189. The Lovings violated the 1691 law established during slavery and its modern manifestations. However, the "only way in which the Lovings' case was clearly affected" by twentieth-century changes were in the penalties they faced. Before 1932, the penalty for violating the antimiscegenation laws was two to five years in prison. In 1932 the minimum penalty was reduced to just one year in prison. Wallenstein, *Tell the Court*, 216.

124. Wallenstein, *Tell the Court*, 216; Romano, *Race Mixing*, 189.

125. The Caroline County grand jury brought indictments in October 1958 and Circuit Court Judge Leon M. Bazile issued the one-year sentence. Wallenstein, *Tell the Court*, 217; Romano, *Race Mixing*, 189.

126. Wallenstein, *Tell the Court*, 217.

127. Ibid., 217, 219. The ACLU helped win *Perez v. Sharp*, a 1948 California Supreme Court decision that made miscegenation laws illegal under the state constitution. See Wallenstein, *Tell the Court*, 192–99, passim, 213, 240, 242. See also *Perez v. Sharp*, 32 Cal.2d 711, 198 P.2d 171 (1948). The ACLU also argued a case challenging the constitutionality of Oklahoma's ban on interracial marriage. The state supreme court ruled in 1965 that because the U.S. Supreme Court had not issued a ruling outlawing interracial marriage, the Oklahoma laws were constitutional. By the time the ACLU was ready to appeal to the Supreme Court, the plaintiff had married someone else. See Wallenstein, *Tell the Court*, 211–14.

128. Ibid., 224.

129. President Johnson signed the Civil Rights Act of 1968 on April 11 of that year, shortly after Martin Luther King was assassinated. Known as the Fair Housing Act, it banned discrimination in the rental, sale, and financing of housing and provided federal enforcement provisions. It also protected civil rights activists from intimidation, coercion, violence, and reprisals, something civil rights workers had been demanding for a long time. See Lawson, *Running for Freedom*, 133.

CHAPTER 8. "POWER TO THE ICE PICK!"

1. Joan's name is spelled several ways but is always pronounced *Jo-Ann*. See "Exhibit A," Medical Examiner's Report, folder 4, box 4, HH; James Reston, Jr., *The Innocence of Joan*

Little: A Southern Mystery (New York, 1977), 9–11. Little was serving a seven-to-ten-year sentence for breaking and entering and larceny and began serving time on June 6, 1974. See James Reston, Jr., "The Joan Little Case," *NYT Magazine*, April 6, 1975.

2. Reston, *Innocence,* 37.

3. Joan Little with Rebecca Ranson, "I Am Joan," *Southern Exposure* 6, no. 1 (1978), 46. See also Testimony of Joan Little, transcript, folder 2, box 1, JR.

4. Marjorie Wright, interview by James Reston audiocassette, JR.

5. Little with Ransom, "I Am Joan," 47.

6. For more on the Rosa Lee Ingram case, see Charles H. Martin, "Race, Gender and Southern Injustice: The Rosa Lee Ingram Case," *American Journal of Legal History* 29, no. 3 (July 1985), 251–68.

7. Karen Bethea-Shields quoted in Anne Blythe, "Role of Women in the Civil Rights Plight," *RNO*, July 23, 2005.

8. Lawson, *Running for Freedom,* 111. According to Lawson, four years after the passage of the Voting Rights Act, about three-fifths of Southern black adults had registered to vote. In Mississippi alone, black registration jumped from 6.7 percent in 1964 to 59.4 percent in 1968. In Alabama, black registration increased from 23 to 53 percent.

9. Joseph, *Waiting,* 157.

10. Steve M. Gillon and Cathy D. Matson, *The American Experiment: A History of the United States,* vol. 2 (Boston, 2002), 1155; Lawson, *Running for Freedom,* 127.

11. Lawson, *Running for Freedom,* 127. For more on urban riots during the 1960s, see Thomas J. Sugrue, *The Origins of Urban Crisis: Race and Inequality in Postwar Detroit* (Princeton, N.J., 1996).

12. Doug Rossinow, "The New Left: Democratic Reformers or Left-Wing Revolutionaries," in David Farber and Beth Bailey, eds., *The Columbia Guide to America in the 1960s* (New York, 2001), 92. For more on the origins and struggles of the New Left, see James Miller, *"Democracy Is in the Streets": From Port Huron to the Siege of Chicago* (New York, 1987); Todd Gitlin, *The Sixties: Years of Hope, Days of Rage* (New York, 1987); Terry H. Anderson, *The Movement and the Sixties: Protest in America from Greensboro to Wounded Knee* (New York, 1995).

13. Carter, *Wallace to Gingrich,* xii.

14. Ibid., 33. See also Dan T. Carter, *The Politics of Rage: George Wallace, the Origins of the New Conservatism, and the Transformation of American Politics* (New York, 1995).

15. Beth Tompkins Bates, "The Upheaval of Jim Crow: African Americans and the Struggle for Civil Rights in the 1960s," in Farber and Bailey, *Columbia Guide,* 85. For more on Memphis, see Michael K. Honey, *Going Down Jericho Road: The Memphis Strike, Martin Luther King's Last Campaign* (New York, 2008).

16. Joseph, *Waiting,* 227.

17. Ibid., 228; Lawson, *Running for Freedom,* 129.

18. Joseph, *Waiting,* 244. Joseph argues that the Panthers' gender politics became "more progressive rhetorically" but remained "conflicted internally." Women often did the cooking, cleaning, and secretarial work, while men served in public leadership roles. Still, things were beginning to change, and in the early 1970s Elaine Brown became party chair. For more on Brown and the role of women in the Black Panther Party, see Charles Jones, ed., *The Black Panther Party (reconsidered),* (Baltimore, Md., 1998); Elaine Brown, *A Taste of Power: A Black Woman's Story* (New York, 1992); Bobby Seale, *Seize the Time: The Story of the Black Panther Party and Huey P. Newton* (New York, 1970); and Hugh Pearson, *The Shadow of the Panther: Huey Newton and the Price of Black Power in America* (Reading, Mass., 1994).

19. Timothy B. Tyson, *Blood Done Sign My Name: A True Story* (New York, 2004), 118–29 passim.

20. Ibid., 257.

21. Ibid., 258.

22. Ibid., 258, 268–69. Tyson says the New Hanover County sheriff's department was "heavily infiltrated by the Ku Klux Klan" and notes that Sheriff Marion Millis admitted as much in the *RNO*, October 27, 1965, 342.

23. Chavis drew a thirty-five-year prison sentence. The Wilmington Ten garnered massive media attention, and in 1977 Amnesty International launched a campaign to have them declared "political prisoners." In 1980 a federal court reversed the verdicts after discovering that "the prosecution's tactics had worked hand in glove with the FBI's COINTELPRO (Counter Intelligence Program) operation to shut down the black freedom movement." See Tyson, *Blood Done Sign My Name*, 270. For more on the Wilmington Ten, see Bud Schultz and Ruth Schultz, *It Did Happen Here: Recollections of Political Repression in America* (Berkeley, Calif., 1989), 195–212; Larry Reni Thomas, *The True Story Behind the Wilmington Ten* (Chapel Hill, N.C., 1980); Ben Chavis, *Wilmington 10: Editorials and Cartoons* (New York, 1977).

24. Angela Davis, "The Struggle of Ben Chavis and the Wilmington 10," *Black Scholar*, April 1975, 29–31. It was because of her involvement with the Wilmington Ten that Davis first heard about Joan Little. For more on Davis's activism and involvement with the Black Power movement in the late 1960s and early 1970s, see Joseph, *Waiting*, 241–75 passim.

25. Reston, *Innocence*, 28. In Ayden, North Carolina, twenty-five miles to the west of Washington, white students bombed the high school bathroom, and months of turmoil followed the murder of a black laborer by a white policeman. In Williamston, twenty miles to the north, Golden Frinks, SCLC field secretary and the best-known and most experienced civil rights organizer in North Carolina, led the Williamston Freedom Movement from 1963 to 1965. National leaders in the SCLC eyed Williamston for a national campaign in 1965—it had a vibrant black community that was well organized, and a violent white leadership connected to an active Ku Klux Klan. According to David Cecelski, the SCLC chose Selma instead of the "small Tobacco Belt" town to make a national stand. "Bloody Sunday," Cecelski notes, "would become world famous; Williamston and Frinks, thus far, historical footnotes." See Cecelski, *Along Freedom Road: Hyde County, North Carolina and the Fate of Black Schools in the South* (Chapel Hill, N.C., 1994), 82–85.

26. Mark Pinsky, "The Innocence of James Reston, Jr.," *Southern Exposure* 6, no. 1 (1978): 40.

27. Cecelski, *Freedom Road*, 36, 185n70.

28. Reston, *Innocence*, 22.

29. Ibid., 6, 176.

30. Ibid., 14.

31. "Heavy lidded and shambling" from "Trial Gives New Twist to Old Racial Issues," *NYT*, August 12, 1975, 14.

32. Ibid.

33. Reston, *Innocence*, 73; "The Joan Little Case," *NYT Magazine*, April 6, 1975. See also Jerry Paul and Joan Little, interview by Reston, audiocassette, JR.

34. See Reston, *Innocence*, 284–89. See also Joan Little, interview by Reston audio cassette, JR.

35. Golden Frinks, interview by James Reston audiocassette, JR.

36. Baxandall and Gordon, "Second Wave Feminism," in Nancy Hewitt, ed., *A Companion to American Women's History* (Oxford, 2005), 417. For more on the women's movement see Rosalyn Baxandall and Linda Gordon, eds., *Dear Sisters: Dispatches from the Women's Liberation Movement* (New York, 2000); Sara M. Evans, *Tidal Wave: How Women Changed America at Century's End* (New York, 2003); and Ruth Rosen, *The World Split Open: How the Modern Women's Movement Changed America* (New York, 2000).

37. New York Women Against Rape (NYWAR) founded the first rape crisis center in October 1971; Maria Bevacqua, *Rape on the Public Agenda* (Boston, 2000), 33.

38. The Crenshaw Women's Center in Los Angeles organized an "anti-rape squad" and created a rape hotline; in Berkeley, California women organized the Bay Area Women Against Rape; In Washington D.C., women's rights activists created a rape crisis center; and in Chicago Women Against Rape organized a conference dedicated to rape. Bevacqua, *Rape,* 33, 36.

39. Reston, *Innocence,* 7.

40. Erskine Caldwell, *Tobacco Road* (New York, 1932).

41. For more on the "progressive mystique," see William H. Chafe, *Civilities and Civil Rights: Greensboro, North Carolina and the Black Struggle for Freedom* (New York, 1981).

42. "Justice in North Carolina: Once More Old South," *NYT,* March 9, 1975, B5E.

43. Reston, *Innocence,* 77.

44. Ibid., 13.

45. David Cecelski, "Karen Bethea-Shields: In Joan Little's Cell," *RNO,* January 12, 2003.

46. Reston, "The Innocence of Joan Little," *Southern Exposure* 6, no. 1 (1978): 37.

47. "Joanne Little: No Escape Yet," *Off Our Backs,* January 1975, folder 3, box 4, HH.

48. Angela Davis, "Forum: Joanne Little: The Dialectics of Rape," *Ms.* 3, no. 12 (June 1975): 74–77.

49. Julian Bond's letter soliciting funds, n.d., folder 3, box 4, HH.

50. Reston, "The Joan Little Case," *NYT Magazine,* April 6, 1975 folder 16, box 2, HH.

51. The file on Joan Little in the NAACP Legal Defense and Educational Fund Papers contains few documents, mainly letters to constituents indicating that it stood ready to support Little if she asked it to, but in the meantime, it deferred to the Southern Poverty Law Center. See "Memorandum to Mabel Smith from Mildred Bond," February 5, 1975; Nathanial R. Jones to Alfred Baker Lewis, March 11, 1975; and Charles E. Carter to Ms. L. Wailes, April 22, 1975. A draft of a memo to Joan Little offering the NAACP's assistance was crossed out and "not sent" was written on the top. All documents found in folder 2, part V, 1911, NAACP Papers.

52. Maulana Ron Karenga, "In Defense of Sister Joanne: For Ourselves and History," *Black Scholar,* July–August 1975, 40, 42.

53. "Minutes of the Joanne Little Defense Committee," folder 1, box 3, RLP. Thanks to William LeFevre for sending me these documents and to Jeanne Theoharis, who shared her find with me.

54. Genna Rae McNeil, "Joanne Is You, Joanne Is Me," in Bettye Collier Thomas and V. P. Franklin, eds., *Sisters in the Struggle: African American Women in the Civil Rights Black Power Movement* (New York, 2001), 271.

55. Christina Greene, *Our Separate Ways: Women and the Black Freedom Movement in Durham, North Carolina* (Chapel Hill, N.C., 2005), 225.

56. Ibid., 225–26.

57. McNeil, "Joanne," in Thomas and Franklin, *Sisters,* 270.

58. Ibid., 270.

59. Newsletter, n.d., box 1, "Southern Poverty Law Center," JLP, and n.d., JLP; "Funds Sought for Miss Little's Defense," *Durham Morning Herald,* n.d., box 1, "Ann and Raymond Cobb," in JLP, and n.d., JLP.

60. Reston, *Innocence,* 180.

61. See "Motion for Change of Venue," *State of North Carolina v. Joan Little,* folder 4, box 4, HH. Mullin later published her findings. See John B. McConahay, Courtney J. Mullin, and Jeffrey Frederick, "The Uses of Social Science in Trials with Political and Racial Overtones: The Trial of Joan Little," *Law and Contemporary Problems* 41, no. 1, (1977): 205–29; See also "A Case of Rape or Seduction?" *Time,* July 28, 1975, 19.

62. Ginny Carroll, "500 Stage Courthouse Rally," *RNO*, July 15, 1975, 1. "Trial of decade," quoted in Michael Coakley, "The Joan Little Trial Is Over, but the Issues Remain," *ChT*, August 24, 1975, B1. The rally included members of NOW, the National Black Feminist Organization, the Black Panther Party, and local members of the Free Joanne Little Defense Fund, as well as other individuals and groups.

63. Rick Nichols, "Stage Set to Weigh a Killing," *RNO*, July 27, 1965, 1.

64. Wayne King, "Jury Selection Challenged by Joan Little's Lawyers," *NYT*, July 15, 1975, 20.

65. "Joan Little Trial Begins: First Juror Is Selected," *RNO*, July 27, 1965, 1, 5B. Chalmers claimed he was associated with the Klan only because they asked him to represent them. "It was not an ideological thing, it was a professional thing. They paid a fee and are entitled to a lawyer," another attorney said in his defense. But Chalmers also represented Klan members in local legal matters. Before the HUAC hearings, Chalmers established a considerable reputation as a criminal prosecutor. As Wake County solicitor, he "successfully prosecuted North Carolina's notorious basketball point-fixing case involving prominent college teams." Chalmers also admitted becoming a "severe alcoholic" in the late 1960s and attempted suicide in 1968 "by shooting a small caliber rifle into his mouth." "Prosecutor Bristles at Klan Stereotype; Points to Record," *RNO*, July 16, 1975, 1–2.

66. "Jury Seated in Murder Trial of Joan Little," *RNO*, July 24, 1975, 1. The newspaper featured pictures of the jurors after the trial. "Jurors Say Evidence Too Thin to Convict," *RNO*, August 16, 1975, 1, 5B.

67. The defense exploited the lax practices of the small-town Southern policemen, their lack of education and experience, and their careless collection of evidence, creating the perception that they had bungled the investigation from the start. State's witnesses added to the impression that the investigation had been incompetent. For example, according to Reston, "the local detective could produce no identifiable fingerprint from the bars or the bed or the sink or the clothes or the ice pick. The SBI chemist's test of Joan Little's scarf, found underneath Alligood's body, was inconclusive." Photographs were splattered with developing chemicals, making it impossible to tell the difference between blood spatters and chemical dots. Worse, "from the technical legal standpoint," the prosecution could not even establish Joan Little's presence in the jail cell where Alligood was murdered. See Reston, *Innocence*, 259, 260–76 passim.

68. Testimony of Joan Little, transcript, folder 2, box 1, JR.

69. Frances B. Kent, "Joan Little's Lawyers to Show Jailer Made Frequent Sexual Advances," *LAT*, August 8, 1975, B20.

70. "Ex-Inmates Testify in Little Case," *RNO*, August 8, 1975, 1, folder 3, box 3, HH. See also Hobgood's trial notes, folder 4, box 3, HH.

71. Ibid.

72. Reston, *Innocence*, 113.

73. Ibid., 114.

74. Reston, "Innocence of Joan Little," *Southern Exposure*, 36.

75. Rick Nichols, "Charge Is Reduced in Joan Little Trial," *RNO*, August 7, 1975, 1.

76. "Little Says She Stabbed Jailer," *NYT*, August 12, 1975.

77. Testimony of Joan Little, transcript, folder 2, box 1, JR.

78. Rick Nichols, "Testifies at Trial," *RNO*, August 12, 1975, 1.

79. Testimony of Joan Little, transcript, folder 2, box 1, JR.

80. Ibid. Little used the word "sex" at first and admitted that Alligood said "pussy" only after Griffin harassed her. "Is that what you said yesterday? What did you say he said yesterday? Did he say sex or use some other term?" Little replied calmly, "I am using the word sex because I don't want to use any other word because it's still embarrassing to

me." Griffin's point was to raise questions about why, if Alligood wanted to "get some pussy," did he accept oral sex instead? At best, the line of questioning made Griffin look like he was subjecting Little to unnecessary harassment. Worse, it forced Griffin into admitting that Alligood asked for sex—it didn't matter what kind.

81. Ibid. See also Michael Coakley, "Admits She Stabbed Him," *ChT*, August 12, 1975, 1.

82. Testimony of Joan Little, folder 2, box 1, JR; Coakley, "Admits She Stabbed Him," *ChT*, August 12, 1975, 1; "Testifies at Trial," *RNO*, August 12, 1975, 1.

83. Wayne King, "Defense Closes for Joan Little," *NYT*, August 13, 1975, 68.

84. Testimony of Joan Little, transcript, folder 2, box 1, JR.

85. Hobgood ruled that the question about whether she had a sexually transmitted disease was "irrelevant." Testimony of Joan Little, folder 2, box 1, JR; "Defense Closes," *NYT*, August 13, 1975, 68. John A. Wilkinson, who was retained by the Alligood family to act in their interests, gave a closing statement as well, arguing that oral sex, or "unnatural sex," was not rape. "It is a detestable, horrible thing, but it's not the statutory crime of rape, and it's not punishable by death." Wilkinson argued that what Alligood allegedly did to Joan Little was only "mistreatment," for which he did not deserve to be murdered. See "Jury Argument of John A. Wilkinson," transcript, folder 10, box 2, JR.

86. "Joan Little Case Goes to Trial Today," *LAT*, August 15, 1975, B5; "Mr. Griffin's Argument to the Jury," transcript, folder 8, box 2, HH.

87. "Final Arguments Heard in Trial of Joanne Little," n.d., clipping, folder 12, box 3, HH.

88. "Prosecutor and Defense Present Final Arguments in Joan Little Case," *NYT*, August 15, 1975; "Final Arguments Heard in Trial of Joanne Little," n.d., clipping, folder 12, box 3, HH.

89. Reston, *Innocence*, 320–21. A transcript of Galloway's closing argument was not in the Judge Hamilton Hobgood Papers or the James Reston Collection. It is interesting that of all the people Reston interviewed for his book, he did not speak to Karen Galloway, who could have shed the most light on the racial and sexual dynamics of the Little trial. When Reston refers to Galloway in his book, it is only in passing.

90. "Mr. Paul's Argument to the Jury," transcript, folder 9, box 2, JR. See also Lerner, *Black Women*, 166–69.

91. "Final Arguments heard in trial of Joanne Little," n.d., clipping, folder 12, box 3, HH. Paul's portrayal of Little as a civil rights heroine was a stretch, but it helped counter the negative images the prosecution presented to the jury. It also set up expectations that Little could not meet. After the trial, supporters hoped she would become a political activist, and she often pledged to fight racism, sexual violence, and prison abuse. Instead, in the months and years after her acquittal, she moved in and out of prison. In December 1975 she missed a court date, and a warrant was issued for her arrest. She then served twenty-one months in prison for the original breaking and entering charge. In October 1977 she escaped from prison and was finally captured in Brooklyn two months later. Little refused to return to North Carolina until the Supreme Court ordered her to do so. Beginning in February 1979, she served four months in the women's prison in Raleigh, North Carolina. She was arrested again ten years later in New York for driving a car with a stolen license plate and possession of an illegal weapon. See Melynn Glusman, "Forgetting Joan Little: The Rise and Fall of a Mythical Black Woman," unpublished paper in author's possession.

92. "Mr. Paul's Argument to the Jury," transcript, folder 9, box 2, JR.

93. Wayne King, "Joan Little Acquitted in Jailer's Slaying," *NYT*, August 16, 1975, 49.

94. Ibid.

95. Rick Nichols, "Wake Jury Acquits Joan Little, Says State Didn't Prove Its Case," *RNO*, August 16, 1975, 1.

96. "Joan Little Says Jurors Just," *RNO*, August 16, 1975, 5B.

97. Michael Coakley, "The Joan Little Trial Is Over, but the Issues Remain," *ChT*, August 24, 1975, B1.

98. Ibid.

99. "Mr. Paul's Argument to the Jury," folder 9, box 2, JR.

100. Bevacqua, *Rape,* 56. Bevacqua argues that the first "speak-out" held by the New York Radical Feminists on January 24, 1971, served as a catalyst for the antirape movement. See also Flora Davis, *Moving the Mountain: The Women's Movement in America Since 1960* (New York, 1991), 310–11; Ruth Rosen, *The World Split Open: How the Modern Women's Movement Changed America* (New York, 2000), 181–83; Estelle B. Freedman, *No Turning Back: The History of Feminism and the Future of Women* (New York, 2002), 282–87. I would argue that silence, even among white women, was not nearly as ubiquitous as historians suggest, since hundreds of men had been arrested, thrown in jail, and even executed for rape and attempted rape before the women's movement took root.

101. "Joan Little Says Jurors Just," *RNO*, August 16, 1975, 5B.

102. "Dixie Racism," cartoon in *BAA*, August 19–23, 1975, 4, clipping, folder 13, box 3, HH.

EPILOGUE. "WE ALL LIVED IN FEAR FOR YEARS"

1. William Faulkner, *Requiem for a Nun* (New York, 1987).

2. I-Corbitt.

3. Ibid.

4. R. J. Corbitt, interview by author, January 19, 2009, Abbeville, Ala.

5. Arthur Corbitt, interview by author, January 19, 2009, Abbeville, Ala.

6. Mary Murry, interview by author, January 19, 2009, Abbeville, Ala.

7. I-Corbitt.

8. Alma Daniels, interview by author, January 19, 2009, Abbeville, Ala.

9. I-RTC 30.

10. I-Corbitt 3.

11. I-RTC 30.

12. I-Corbitt.

13. I-RTC.

14. Ibid.

15. Shailagh Murray, "A Family Tree Rooted in American Soil," *WP*, October 2, 2008, C1.

Bibliography

MANUSCRIPT COLLECTIONS

Atlanta, Georgia

Archives and Special Collections, Robert W. Woodruff Library, Atlanta University Center

TWA	Trezzvant W. Anderson Papers
SCHW	Southern Conference for Human Welfare Papers
RM	Ralph McGill
GWR	Glenn W. Rainey Papers, Congress of Interracial Cooperation
CSP	Claude Sitton Papers
PS	Interviews by Patricia Sullivan

Manuscripts, Archives, and Rare Books Library, Emory University

MECP	Matt N. and Evelyn Graves Crawford Papers
HK	Harvey Klehr Papers
LTP	Louise Thompson Patterson Papers
CSP-E	Claude Sitton Papers
LS	Lillian Smith Papers

The Georgia Archives

Rosa Lee Ingram v. State of Georgia

Auburn, New York

Cayuga Community College Library

ECC	Earl Conrad Collection

Birmingham, Alabama

Department of Archives, Birmingham Public Library

BPSF	Birmingham Police Surveillance Files, 1947–80
BWOF	*Birmingham World* Office Files
EBCP	Eugene "Bull" Connor Papers
CP	Cooper Green Papers
NAACP-m	NAACP Papers, Alabama Chapter, 1940–55, microfilm

Boston, Massachusetts

Howard Gotleib Archival Research Center, Boston University

MLK   Martin Luther King, Jr., Papers

Chapel Hill, North Carolina

Southern Historical Collection, Manuscript Department, Wilson Library, University of North Carolina, Chapel Hill

HH   Judge Hamilton H. Hobgood Papers
JR   James Reston Collection
TB   Taylor Branch Papers

Detroit, Michigan

Archives of Labor and Urban Affairs, Walter P. Reuther Library, Wayne State University

RLP   Rosa L. Parks Collection

Durham, North Carolina

Rare Book, Manuscript, and Special Collections Library, Duke University

JHC   John Hope Franklin Collection
WHC   William H. Chafe Oral History Collection
BTV   Behind the Veil: Documenting African American Life in the Jim Crow South
               Collection
JBM   J. B. Matthews Papers
JLP   Joan Little Papers, 1973–75 and n.d.

Hanover, New Hampshire

Rauner Special Collections Library, Dartmouth University

AKL   Alexander Kinnan Laing Papers

Hattiesburg, Mississippi

COHCH   Center for Oral History and Cultural Heritage, University of Southern
               Mississippi

McCain Library and Archives, University of Southern Mississippi

GPJ   Governor Paul Johnson Papers

Madison, Wisconsin

State Historical Society of Wisconsin

CAB   Carl and Braden Papers
CORE   Congress of Racial Equality Papers
CIC   Commission on Interracial Cooperation Papers
DB   Daisy Bates Papers
HRC   Highlander Research and Education Center Records

Montgomery, Alabama

Alabama Department of Archives and History

CS   Governor Chauncey Sparks Papers, Recy Taylor Case, Administrative Files

GW   Governor George Wallace Papers, Administrative Files
TCF   Tuskegee Clipping File, microfilm

New Orleans, Louisiana

Amistad Research Center, Tulane University
PBV   Preston and Bonita Valien Papers

New York, New York

Schomburg Center for Research in Black Culture
NNCP-M   National Negro Congress Records, microfilm
ILD   International Labor Defense Papers
EG   Eugene Gordon Papers
BJD   Benjamin J. Davis, Jr., Papers
ECHT   Earl Conrad/Harriet Tubman Collection

Princeton, New Jersey

Seeley G. Mudd Manuscript Library, Princeton University
LSCRRCP   Law Students Civil Rights Research Council Papers

Tallahassee, Florida

Leon County Courthouse

State of Florida v. Patrick Gene Scarborough, David Erwin Beagles, Ollie Odell Stoutamire, William Ted Collinsworth, 1959

Special Collections, Robert Manning Strozier Library, Florida State University
GLC   Governor LeRoy Collins Papers, in Florida Governors Manuscript Collection
JLI   Jackson Lee Ice Papers
WMW   W. May Walker Papers

Samuel H. Coleman Library, Special Collections, Florida A and M University
FAMUANA   FAMUana Collection

Washington, D.C.

Library of Congress
NAACP   National Association for the Advancement of Colored People Papers
APR   A. Philip Randolph Papers
UL   Papers of the Urban League
BR   Bayard Rustin Papers

Mary McLeod Bethune Council House NHS and National Archives for Black Women's History
NCNWR   National Council of Negro Women Records, Wednesdays in Mississippi Series

Moorland-Springarn Research Center, Howard University
SNYC   Southern Negro Youth Congress Papers

Selected Manuscripts on Microfilm

CORE-M   Congress of Racial Equality Papers, 1941–67 (Sanford, N.C.: Microfilm Corporation of America, 1980)

FBI-VL   FBI File on Klu Klux Klan murder of Viola Liuzzo (Wilmington, Del.: Scholarly Resources, 1990)

SRC   Southern Regional Council Papers, 1944–68 (Ann Arbor, Mich.: University Microfilms International, 1984)

SNCC   Student Non-Violent Coordinating Committee Papers, 1959–72 (Sanford, N.C.: Microfilm Corporation of America, 1982)

DIGITAL SOURCES

EOPI   *Eyes on the Prize Interviews,* Washington University Special Collections, http://library.wustl.edu/units/spec/filmandmedia/hampton/eyesIinterviews.html

MSSC-d   Mississippi State Sovereignty Commission Records, 1994–2006, Mississippi Department of Archives and History, http://www.mdah.state.ms.us

CRMd   Civil Rights in Mississippi Digital Archive, University of Southern Mississippi, http://www.lib.usm.edu/~spcol/crda

MBd   "They Changed the World: The Story of the Montgomery Bus Boycott," http://www.montgomeryboycott.com

NCDCd   North Carolina Department of Corrections, Offender Information, http://www.doc.state.nc.us/offenders/

FDCd   Florida Department of Corrections, Offender Search, http://www.dc.state.fl.us/InmateInfo/InmateInfoMenu.asp

Progenealogists   http://www.progenealogists.com/parks/aqwg01.htm

FLHTd   Fannie Lou Hamer Testimony in front of Credentials Committee, Democratic National Convention, Atlantic City, N.J., August 22, 1964, http://americanradioworks.publicradio.org/features/sayitplain/flhamer.html (accessed March 12, 2008)

WCBUd   *Will the Circle Be Unbroken?* Radio Series, www.unbrokencircle.org (accessed April 2005); transcripts have since been acquired by Emory University in Atlanta, http://marbl.library.emory.edu/findingaids/content.php?id=src-circle 934_106912#descriptiveSummary

HSBd   Transcript, mass meeting at Holt Street Baptist Church, Montgomery, Ala., December 5, 1955, http://www.stanford.edu.libproxy.lib.unc.edu/group/King/publications/papers/vol3/551205.004-MIA_Mass_Meeting_at_Holt_Street_Baptist_Church.htm (accessed October 30, 2005)

SELECTED NEWSPAPERS AND PERIODICALS

BAA   *Baltimore Afro-American*
              The Black Scholar
AT   *Alabama Tribune*
AC   *Atlanta Constitution*

ADW	*Atlanta Daily World*
AD	*Arkansas Democrat*
AG	*Arkansas Gazette*
ASP	*Arkansas State Press*
BN	*Birmingham News*
BW	*Birmingham World*
CT	*Carolina Times*
CO	*Charlotte Observer*
CDT	*Chicago Daily Tribune*
CD	*Chicago Defender*
ChT	*Chicago Tribune*
CL	*Clarion Ledger* [Mississippi]
	Crisis
DW	*Daily Worker*
DE	*Dothan Eagle*
	Ebony
FAMUAN	Florida A&M University
	The Guardian
HA	*Hattiesburg American* [Mississippi]
JA	*Jackson Advocate* [Mississippi]
JDN	*Jackson Daily News {Mississippi}*
	Jet
LLC	*Laurel-Leader Call* [Mississippi]
LI	*Lighthouse and Informer* [South Carolina]
LAT	*Los Angeles Times*
LW	*Louisiana Weekly*
MEJ	*McComb Enterprise Journal* [Mississippi]
	Messenger
MA	*Montgomery Advertiser*
	The Nation
	Newsweek
NYAN	*New York Amsterdam News*
NYHT	*New York Herald-Tribune*
NYT	*New York Times*
OOB	*Off Our Backs*
PC	*Pittsburgh Courier*
RNO	*Raleigh News and Observer* [North Carolina]
	Signs: Journal of Women in Culture and Society
SE	*Southern Exposure*
SD	*Tallahassee Democrat*
TT	*Tampa Tribune*
	Time
US	*U.S. News & World Report*
WP	*Washington Post*

INTERVIEWS BY AUTHOR

Correspondence, audiotapes, video recordings, and/or transcripts in author's possession

I-TB	Theralene Beachem, Birmingham, Ala., March 19, 2003
I-JB	Joanne Bland, Selma, Ala., March 15, 2004
I-MB	Martha Boyer, Birmingham, Ala., March 18, 2003
I-RB	Raylawni Branch, Hattiesburg, Miss., with Patricia Buzzard, June 3, 2006
I-JC	Johnnie Carr, Montgomery, Ala., March 17, 2004
I-JL	J. L. Chestnutt, Selma, Ala., March 15, 2004
I-AC	Arthur Corbitt, Abbeville, Ala., January 19, 2009
I-Corbitt	Robert Corbitt, Abbeville, Ala., January 19, 20, 2009
I-Corbitt 3	Robert Corbitt, telephone interview, December 3, 2008
I-Corbitt 8	Robert Corbitt, telephone interview, December 8, 2008
I-RJC	R. J. Corbitt, Abbeville, Ala., January 19, 2009
I-RTC	Recy Taylor Courtney, Abbeville, Ala., January 19, 20, 2008
I-RTC 30	Recy Taylor Courtney, telephone interview, December 30, 2008
I-AD	Alma Daniels, Abbeville, Ala., January 19, 2009
I-GD	Gloria Dennard, Birmingham, Ala., March 19, 2003
I-PSD	Patricia Stephens Due, telephone interview, March 4, 1999
I-JD	James Dukes, Hattiesburg, Miss., October 17, 2007
I-FG	Fred Gray, Montgomery, Ala., March 15, 2004
I-DWH	Daisy Wade Harris, Hattiesburg, Miss., with Patricia Buzzard, June 5, 2006
I-LSH	Linda S. Hunt, Birmingham, Ala., March 19, 2003
I-LMJ	Lucille M. Johnson, Birmingham, Ala., March 16, 2003
I-LK	Lillie Kinsey, Abbeville, Ala., January 19, 2009
I-JL	Joyce Ladner, correspondence, March 7, 2006
I-LM	Lois Miles, Hattiesburg, Miss., October 17, 2007
I-ALM	Annie Lois Murry, Abbeville, Ala., January 19, 2009
I-MM	Mary Murry, Abbeville, Ala., January 19, 2009
I-SS	Solomon Seay, Jr., telephone interview, March 9, 1999
I-SPS	Sam Pat Skipper, telephone interview, January 5, 2009
I-CUS	Charles U. Smith, telephone interview, March 9, 1999

BOOKS

Als, Hinton, John Lewis, Leon F. Litwack, and James Allen, eds. *Without Sanctuary: Lynching Photography in America.* Santa Fe, N.M.: Twin Palms, 2000.

Altschuler, Glenn C. *All Shook Up: How Rock 'n' Roll Changed America.* New York: Oxford University Press, 2003.

Anderson, Jervis. *A. Philip Randolph.* New York: Harcourt Brace, 1973.

———. *Bayard Rustin: Troubles I've Seen: A Biography.* New York: HarperCollins, 1997.

Anderson, Karen. *Wartime Women: Sex Roles, Family Relations, and the Status of Women During World War II.* Contributions in Women's Studies, vol. 20. Westport, Conn.: Greenwood Press, 1981.

Anderson, Terry H. *The Movement and the Sixties: Protest in America from Greensboro to Wounded Knee.* New York: Oxford University Press, 1995.

Appleby, Joyce Oldham, ed. *The Best American History Essays 2006.* New York: Macmillan, 2006.

Ayers, Edward L. *The Promise of the New South: Life After Reconstruction.* New York: Oxford University Press, 1992.

Baldwin, James. *The Fire Next Time.* 1963; reprint. New York: Vintage Books, 1993.

————. *The Price of the Ticket: Collected Nonfiction, 1948–1985.* New York: St. Martin's Press, 1985.

Bardaglio, Peter Winthrop, and Nancy Bercaw. *Gender and the Southern Body Politic: Essays and Comments.* Jackson: University Press of Mississippi, 2000.

Bartley, Numan V. *The Rise of Massive Resistance: Race and Politics in the South During the 1950s.* Baton Rouge: Louisiana State University Press, 1969.

Bates, Daisy. *The Long Shadow of Little Rock: A Memoir.* Fayetteville: University of Arkansas Press, 1986.

Baxandall, Rosalyn, and Linda Gordon, eds. *Dear Sisters: Dispatches from the Women's Liberation Movement.* New York: Basic Books, 2000.

Beals, Melba Patillo. *Warriors Don't Cry: A Searing Memoir of the Battle to Integrate Little Rock's Central High.* New York: Washington Square Books, 1994.

Belfrage, Sally. *Freedom Summer.* Charlottesville: University Press of Virginia, 1965.

Berlin, Ira. *Many Thousands Gone: The First Two Centuries of Slavery in North America.* Cambridge, Mass.: Belknap Press of Harvard University Press, 1998.

Berry, Wendell. *The Hidden Wound.* San Francisco: North Point Press, 1989.

Bertrand, Michael T. *Race, Rock and Elvis.* Urbana: University of Illinois Press, 2000.

Bevacqua, Maria. *Rape on the Public Agenda: Feminism and the Politics of Sexual Assault.* Boston: Northeastern University Press, 2000.

Biondi, Martha. *To Stand and Fight: The Struggle for Civil Rights in Postwar New York City.* Cambridge, Mass.: Harvard University Press, 2003.

Block, Sharon. *Rape and Sexual Power in Early America.* Chapel Hill: University of North Carolina Press, 2006.

Boles, John B. *The South Through Time: A History of an American Region.* Englewood Cliffs, N.J.: Prentice Hall, 1995.

Borstelmann, Thomas. *The Cold War and the Color Line.* Cambridge, Mass.: Harvard University Press, 2001.

Bourke, Joanna. *Rape: Sex Violence History.* London: Virago Press, 2007.

Boyle, Kevin. *Arc of Justice: A Saga of Race, Civil Rights and Murder in the Jazz Age.* New York: Henry Holt and Co., 2004.

Brady, Tom P. *Black Monday: Segregation or Amalgamation, America Has Its Choice.* Winona, Miss.: Association of Citizens' Councils, 1955.

Branch, Taylor. *Parting the Waters: America in the King Years, 1954–1963.* New York: Simon and Schuster, 1988.

———. *Pillar of Fire: America in the King Years, 1963–1965.* New York: Simon & Schuster, 1998.

———. *At Canaan's Edge: America in the King Years, 1965–1968.* New York: Simon and Schuster, 2006.

Breines, Winifred. *The Trouble Between Us: An Uneasy History of White and Black Women in the Feminist Movement.* New York: Oxford University Press, 2006.

Brinkley, Douglass. *Rosa Parks.* New York: Penguin Press, 2000.

Brown, Elaine. *A Taste of Power: A Black Woman's Story.* New York: Pantheon, 1992.

Brown, Kathleen. *Good Wives, Nasty Wenches, and Anxious Patriarchs.* Chapel Hill: University of North Carolina Press, 1996.

Brownmiller, Susan. *Against Our Will: Men, Women and Rape.* New York: Ballantine, 1975.

Brundage, W. Fitzhugh. *Lynching in the New South: Georgia and Virginia.* Urbana: University of Illinois Press, 1993.

Burns, Stewart. *Daybreak of Freedom: The Montgomery Bus Boycott.* Chapel Hill: University of North Carolina Press, 1997.

Cagin, Seth, and Philip Dray. *We Are Not Afraid: The Story of Goodman, Schwerner and Chaney and the Civil Rights Campaign for Mississippi.* New York: Macmillan, 1988.

Cahn, Susan. *Sexual Reckonings: Southern Girls in a Troubling Age.* Cambridge, Mass.: Harvard University Press, 2007.

Caldwell, Erskine. *Tobacco Road.* New York: First Edition Library, 1932.

Capeci, Dominic J., and Martha Wilkerson. *Layered Violence: The Detroit Rioters of 1943.* Jackson: University Press of Mississippi, 1991.

Caraway, Nancie. *Segregated Sisterhood: Racism and the Politics of American Feminism.* Knoxville: University of Tennessee Press, 1991.

Carson, Clayborne. *In Struggle: SNCC and the Black Awakening of the 1960s.* Cambridge, Mass.: Harvard University Press, 1981.

———, ed. *The Eyes on the Prize Civil Rights Reader: Documents, Speeches, and Firsthand Accounts from the Black Freedom Struggle.* New York: Penguin Books, 1991.

Carter, Dan T. *Scottsboro: An American Tragedy.* Baton Rouge: Louisiana State University Press, 1979.

———. *The Politics of Rage: George Wallace, the Origins of the New Conservatism and the Transformation of American Politics.* New York: Simon and Schuster, 1995.

———. *From George Wallace to Newt Gingrich: Race in the Conservative Counterrevolution, 1963–1994.* Baton Rouge: Louisiana State University Press, 1999.

Cash, Wilbur J. *The Mind of the South.* New York: Vintage Books, 1941.

Caute, David. *The Great Fear: The Anti-Communist Purge Under Truman and Eisenhower.* New York: Simon and Schuster, 1978.

Cecelski, David. *Along Freedom Road: Hyde County, North Carolina and the Fate of Black Schools in the South.* Chapel Hill: University of North Carolina Press, 1994.

Cecelski, David, and Tim Tyson, eds. *Democracy Betrayed: The Wilmington Race Riot of 1898 and Its Legacy.* Chapel Hill: University of North Carolina Press, 1994.

Chafe, William Henry. *Civilities and Civil Rights: Greensboro, North Carolina, and the Black Struggle for Freedom.* New York: Oxford University Press, 1986.

———. *The Paradox of Change: American Women in the Twentieth Century.* New York: Oxford University Press, 1991.

———. *The Unfinished Journey: America Since World War II.* 5th ed. New York: Oxford University Press, 2000.

———. *The Achievement of American Liberalism: The New Deal and Its Legacies.* New York: Columbia University Press, 2003.

Chafe, William Henry, Raymond Gavins, and Robert Korstadt, eds. *Remembering Jim Crow: African Americans Tell About Life in the Segregated South.* New York: New Press, 2001.

Chalmers, David M. *Hooded Americanism: The History of the Ku Klux Klan.* Durham, N.C.: Duke University Press, 1981.

Chappell, David L. *A Stone of Hope: Prophetic Religion and the Death of Jim Crow.* Chapel Hill: University of North Carolina Press, 2004.

Chateauvert, Melinda M. *Marching Together: Women of the Brotherhood of Sleeping Car Porters, 1925–1957.* Urbana: University of Illinois Press, 1998.

Chavis, Ben. *Wilmington 10: Editorials and Cartoons.* New York: United Church of Christ, Commission for Racial Justice, 1977.

Chestnut, J. L., Jr., and Julia Cass. *Black in Selma: The Uncommon Life of J. L. Chestnut, Jr.: Politics and Power in a Small American Town.* New York: Farrar, Straus and Giroux, 1990.

Civil Rights Congress. *We Charge Genocide: The Historic Petition to the United Nations for Relief from a Crime of the United States Government Against the Negro People.* New York: International Publishers, 1970.

Clark, James G. *I Saw Selma Raped: The Jim Clark Story.* Birmingham: Selma Enterprises, 1966.

Cobble, Dorothy Sue. *The Other Women's Movement: Workplace Justice and Social Rights in Modern America.* Princeton, N.J.: Princeton University Press, 2003.

Colburn, David R. *Racial Change and Community Crisis: St. Augustine, Florida, 1877–1980.* New York: Columbia University Press, 1985.

Colburn, David R., and Jane L. Landers. *The African American Heritage of Florida.* Gainsville: University Press of Florida, 1995.

Colburn, David R., and Richard K. Scher. *Florida's Gubernatorial Politics in the Twentieth Century.* Tallahassee: University Press of Florida, 1980.

Collier-Thomas, Bettye, and V. P. Franklin, eds. *Sisters in the Struggle: African American Women in the Civil Rights Movement.* New York: New York University Press, 2001.

Collins, Patricia Hill. *Black Feminist Thought: Knowledge, Consciousness and the Politics of Empowerment.* New York: Routledge, 1991.

————. *Black Sexual Politics: African Americans, Gender and the New Racism.* New York: Routledge, 2005.

Conrad, Earl. *Jim Crow America.* New York: Duell, Sloan and Pearce, 1947.

Crawford, Vicki L., Jacqueline Rouse, and Barbara Woods, eds. *Women in the Civil Rights Movement: Trailblazers and Torchbearers.* Bloomington: University of Indiana Press, 1990.

Crespino, Joseph. *In Search of Another Country: Mississippi and the Conservative Counterrevolution.* Princeton, N.J.: Princeton University Press, 2007.

Curry, Constance. *Silver Rights.* New York: Algonquin Books, 1995.

Curry, Constance, Joan Browning, et al., eds. *Deep in Our Hearts: Nine White Women in the Freedom Movement.* Athens: University of Georgia Press, 2000.

Dailey, Jane. *Before Jim Crow: The Politics of Post-emancipation Virginia.* Chapel Hill: University of North Carolina Press, 2000.

Dailey, Jane, Glenda Gilmore, and Bryant Simon, eds. *Jumpin' Jim Crow: Southern Politics from Civil War to Civil Rights.* Princeton, N.J.: Princeton University Press, 2000.

Daniel, Pete. *Standing at the Crossroads: Southern Life in the Twentieth Century.* New York: Hill and Wang, 1986.

————. *Lost Revolutions: The South in the 1950s.* Chapel Hill: University of North Carolina Press, 2000.

Davidson, Osha Gray. *The Best of Enemies: Race and Redemption in the New South.* New York: Scribner, 1996.

Davies, David, ed. *The Press and Race: Mississippi Journalists Confront the Movement.* Jackson: University of Mississippi Press, 2001.

Davis, Angela. *If They Come in the Morning: Voices of Resistance.* San Francisco: National United Committee to Free Angela Davis, 1971.

————. *An Autobiography.* New York: Random House, 1974.

————. *Women, Race, and Class.* New York: Random House, 1983.

Davis, Townsend. *Weary Feet, Rested Souls: A Guided History of the Civil Rights Movement.* San Francisco: Norton, 1998.

De Jong, Greta. *A Different Day: African American Struggles for Justice in Rural Louisiana, 1900–1970.* Chapel Hill: University of North Carolina Press, 2002.

D'Emilio, John. *Sexual Politics, Sexual Communities: The Making of a Homosexual Minority in the United States, 1940–1970.* Chicago: University of Chicago Press, 1983.

————. *Lost Prophet: The Life and Times of Bayard Rustin.* New York: Free Press, 2003.

————, ed. *Making Trouble: Essays on Gay History, Politics, and the University.* New York: Routledge, 1992.

Dent, Tom. *Southern Journey: A Return to the Civil Rights Movement.* New York: Morrow, 1997.

Deslippe, Dennis A. *"Rights Not Roses": Unions and the Rise of Working-Class Feminism, 1945–1980.* Urbana: University of Illinois Press, 2000.

Dittmer, John. *Local People: The Struggle for Civil Rights in Mississippi.* Urbana: University of Illinois Press, 1994.

Dollard, John. *Caste and Class in a Southern Town.* Madison: University of Wisconsin Press, 1988.

Dorr, Lisa Linquist. *White Women, Rape and the Power of Race in Virginia, 1900–1960.* Chapel Hill: University of North Carolina Press, 2004.

Douglas, Davidson M. *Reading, Writing, and Race: The Desegregation of the Charlotte Schools.* Chapel Hill: University of North Carolina Press, 1995.

Doyle, William. *An American Insurrection: The Battle of Oxford Mississippi, 1962.* New York: Doubleday, 2001.

Draper, Alan. *Conflict of Interests: Organized Labor and the Civil Rights Movement in the South, 1954–1968.* Ithaca, N.Y.: ILR Press, 1994.

Dray, Philip. *At the Hands of Persons Unknown: The Lynching of Black America.* New York: Random House, 2002.

Du Bois, W. E. B. *The Souls of Black Folk.* New York: Vintage Books, 1990.

Dudziak, Mary L. *Cold War Civil Rights : Race and the Image of American Democracy.* Princeton, N.J.: Princeton University Press, 2000.

Due, Patricia, and Tananarive Due. *Freedom in the Family: A Mother-Daughter Memoir of the Fight for Civil Rights.* New York: Ballantine, 2003.

Durr, Virginia Foster. *Outside the Magic Circle: The Autobiography of Virginia Foster Durr,* ed. Hollinger F. Barnard. New York: Simon and Schuster, 1987.

———. *Freedom Writer: Virginia Foster Durr, Letters from the Civil Rights Years,* ed. Patricia Sullivan. New York: Routledge, 2003.

Dyson, Michael Eric. *I May Not Get There with You: The True Martin Luther King, Jr.* New York: Free Press, 2000.

Eagles, Charles W. *The Civil Rights Movement in America.* Jackson: University of Mississippi Press, 1986.

———. *Outside Agitator: Jon Daniels and the Civil Rights Movement in Alabama.* Chapel Hill: University of North Carolina Press, 1993.

Egerton, John. *Speak Now Against the Day: The Generation Before the Civil Rights Movement in the South.* Chapel Hill: University of North Carolina Press, 1994.

Eskew, Glenn T. *But for Birmingham: The Local and National Movements in the Civil Rights Struggle.* Chapel Hill: University of North Carolina Press, 1997.

Estes, Steve. *I Am a Man! Race, Manhood, and the Civil Rights Movement.* Chapel Hill: University of North Carolina Press, 2005.

Evans, Sara M. *Personal Politics: The Roots of Women's Liberation in the Civil Rights Movement and the New Left.* New York: Vintage, 1979.

———. *Tidal Wave: How Women Changed America at Century's End.* New York: Free Press, 2003.

Evers, Myrlie. *For Us, the Living.* Garden City, N.Y.: Doubleday, 1967.

Fager, Charles E. *Selma, 1965.* New York: Scribner, 1974.

Fairclough, Adam. *To Redeem the Soul of America: The Southern Christian Leadership Conference and Martin Luther King, Jr.* Athens: University of Georgia Press, 1987.

———. *Martin Luther King, Jr.* Athens: University of Georgia Press, 1995.

———. *Race and Democracy: The Civil Rights Struggle in Louisiana, 1915–1972.* Athens: University of Georgia Press, 1995.

———. *Better Day Coming: Blacks and Equality, 1890–2000.* New York: Viking, 2001.

Fairstein, Linda A. *Sexual Violence: Our War Against Rape.* New York: Morrow, 1993.

Farber, David, and Beth Bailey. *The Columbia Guide to America in the 1960s.* New York: Columbia University Press, 2001.

Feldman, Glenn, ed. *Before Brown: Civil Rights and White Backlash in the Modern South.* Tuscaloosa: University of Alabama Press, 2004.

Feldstein, Ruth. *Motherhood in Black and White: Race and Sex in American Liberalism, 1930–1965.* Ithaca, N.Y.: Cornell University Press, 2000.

Fischer, Kristen. *Suspect Relations: Sex, Race and Resistance in Colonial North Carolina.* Ithaca, N.Y.: Cornell University Press, 2002.

Fleming, Cynthia Griggs. *Soon We Will Not Cry: The Liberation of Ruby Doris Smith Robinson.* Lanham, Md.: Rowan and Littlefield, 1998.

Forman, James. *The Making of Black Revolutionaries.* Seattle: University of Washington Press, 1997.

Fosl, Catherine. *Subversive Southerner: Anne Braden and the Struggle for Racial Justice in the Cold War South.* New York: Palgrave, 2002.

Frady, Marshall. *Martin Luther King Jr.* New York: Penguin, 2002.

Frederickson, Kari. *The Dixiecrat Revolt and the End of the Solid South, 1932–1968.* Chapel Hill: University of North Carolina Press, 2001.

Fried, Richard M. *Nightmare in Red: The McCarthy Era in Perspective.* New York: Oxford University Press, 1990.

Gaillard, Frye. *Cradle of Freedom: Alabama and the Movement That Changed America.* Tuscaloosa: University of Alabama Press, 2004.

Gardner, Michael. *Harry Truman and Civil Rights.* Carbondale, Ill.: Southern Illinois University Press, 2002.

Garrow, David. *Bearing the Cross: Martin Luther King Jr. and the Southern Christian Leadership Conference.* New York: Morrow, 1986.

———. *The Walking City: The Montgomery Bus Boycott: 1955–1956.* New York: Carlson, 1989.

Gates, Henry Louis, and Nellie Y. McKay, eds. *The Norton Anthology of African American Literature.* New York: Norton, 1997.

Giddings, Paula. *When and Where I Enter: The Impact of Black Women on Race and Sex in America.* New York: Morrow, 1984.

————. *Ida: A Sword Among Lions: Ida B. Wells and the Campaign Against Lynching.* New York: Amistad, 2008.

Gilmore, Glenda. *Gender and Jim Crow: Women and the Politics of White Supremacy in North Carolina, 1896–1920.* Chapel Hill: University of North Carolina Press, 1996.

————. *Defying Dixie: The Radical Roots of Civil Rights, 1919–1950.* New York: Norton, 2008.

Gitlin, Todd. *The Sixties: Years of Hope, Days of Rage.* New York: Bantam Books, 1987.

Graetz, Robert S. Montgomery: *A White Preacher's Memoir.* New York: Fortress Press, 1991.

Grant, Colin. *Negro with a Hat: The Rise and Fall of Marcus Garvey.* New York: Oxford University Press, 2008.

Grant, Joanne. *Ella Baker: Freedom Bound.* New York: John Wiley and Sons, 1998.

Green, Ben. *Before His Time: The Untold Story of Harry T. Moore, America's First Civil Rights Martyr.* New York: Free Press, 1999.

Green, Laurie B. *Battling the Plantation Mentality: Memphis and the Black Freedom Struggle.* Chapel Hill: University of North Carolina Press, 2007.

Greenberg, Cheryl. *A Circle of Trust: Remembering SNCC.* New Brunswick, N.J.: Rutgers University Press, 1998.

Greene, Christina. *Our Separate Ways: Women and the Black Freedom Movement in Durham, North Carolina.* Chapel Hill: University of North Carolina Press, 2005.

Goings, Kenneth. *The NAACP Comes of Age: The Defeat of Judge John Parker.* Bloomington: Indiana University Press, 1990.

Goodman, James. *Stories of Scottsboro.* New York: Pantheon Books, 1994.

Guralnick, Peter. *Sweet Soul Music: Rhythm and Blues and the Southern Dream of Freedom.* New York: Harper and Row, 1986.

Halberstam, David. *The Children.* New York: Random House, 1998.

Hale, Grace Elizabeth. *Making Whiteness: The Culture of Segregation in the South, 1890–1940.* New York: Pantheon, 1998.

Hall, Jacquelyn Dowd. *Revolt Against Chivalry: Jessie Daniel Ames and the Women's Campaign Against Lynching.* New York: Columbia University Press, 1993.

Hampton, Henry, and Steve Fayer. *Voices of Freedom: An Oral History of the Civil Rights Movement from the 1950s to the 1980s.* New York: Bantam, 1990.

Harmon, David A. *Beneath the Image of the Civil Rights Movement and Race Relations: Atlanta, Georgia, 1946–1981.* New York: Garland, 1996.

Height, Dorothy I. *Open Wide the Freedom Gates: A Memoir.* New York: Public Affairs, 2003.

Hernton, Calvin C. *Sex and Racism in America.* New York: Grove Press, 1965.

Hewitt, Nancy A., ed. *A Companion to American Women's History.* Oxford: Blackwell Publishing, 2005.

Higginbotham, Evelyn Brooks. *Righteous Discontent: The Women's Movement in the Black Baptist Church, 1880–1920.* Cambridge, Mass.: Harvard University Press, 1993.

Hill, Lance. *The Deacons for Defense: Armed Resistance and the Civil Rights Movement.* Chapel Hill: University of North Carolina Press, 2004.

Hill, Ruth Edmonds, ed. *The Black Women Oral History Project.* Westport, Conn.: Meckler, 1991.

Hine, Darlene Clark. *Black Women in United States History.* New York: Carlson, 1990.

————. *Black Women in White: Racial Conflict and Cooperation in the Nursing Profession, 1890–1950.* Bloomington: Indiana University Press, 1990.

Hine, Darlene Clark, Wilma King, and Linda Reed, eds. *We Specialize in the Wholly Impossible: A Reader in Black Women's History.* New York: Carlson, 1995.

Hine, Darlene Clark, and Kathleen Thompson, eds. *A Shining Thread of Hope: History of Black Women in America.* New York: Broadway Books, 1998.

Hodes, Martha. *White Women, Black Men: Illicit Sex in the 19th Century South.* New Haven, Conn.: Yale University Press, 1997.

————, ed. *Sex, Love, Race.* New York: New York University Press, 2000.

Holland, Endesha Ida Mae. *From the Mississippi Delta: A Memoir.* New York: Simon and Schuster, 1997.

Holt, Len. *The Summer That Didn't End: The Story of the Mississippi Civil Rights Project of 1964.* New York: Da Capo Press, 1992.

Honey, Maureen. *Creating Rosie the Riveter: Class, Gender and Propaganda During World War II.* Amherst: University of Massachusetts Press, 1984.

————. *Bitter Fruit: African American Women in World War II.* Columbia: University of Missouri Press, 1999.

Honey, Michael. *Southern Labor and Black Civil Rights.* Chicago: University of Chicago Press, 1993.

Horne, Gerald. *Communist Front? The Civil Rights Congress.* Rutherford, N.J.: Fairleigh Dickinson University Press, 1988.

Hunter, Tera. *To 'Joy My Freedom: Southern Black Women's Lives and Labors After the Civil War.* Cambridge, Mass.: Harvard University Press, 1997.

Jackson, George. *Soledad Brother: The Prison Letters of George Jackson.* Chicago: Bantam, 1970.

Jacoway, Elizabeth, and David R. Colburn. *Southern Businessman and Desegregation.* Baton Rouge: Louisiana State University Press, 1982.

Jenkins, McKay. *The South in Black and White: Race, Sex, and Literature in the 1940s.* Chapel Hill: University of North Carolina Press, 1999.

Jones, Charles, ed. *The Black Panther Party Reconsidered.* Baltimore: Black Classic Press, 1998.

Jones, Jacqueline. *Labor of Love, Labor of Sorrow: Black Women, Work, and the Family from Slavery to the Present.* New York: Basic Books, 1985.

Jordan, Winthrop. *White over Black: American Attitudes Toward the Negro, 1550–1812.* Chapel Hill: University of North Carolina Press, 1968.

Joseph, Peniel E. *Waiting 'Til the Midnight Hour: A Narrative History of Black Power in America.* New York: Henry Holt, 2006.

Katagiri, Yashuhiro. *Mississippi State Sovereignty Commission: Civil Rights and States Rights.* Jackson: University of Mississippi Press, 2001.

Kelley, Robin D. G. *Hammer and Hoe: Alabama Communists During the Great Depression.* Chapel Hill: University of North Carolina Press, 1990.

———. *Race Rebels: Culture, Politics, and the Black Working Class.* New York: Free Press, 1994.

Kelley, Robin G., and Earl Lewis, eds. *To Make Our World Anew: A History of African Americans.* New York: Oxford University Press, 2000.

Kennedy, Randall. *Interracial Intimacies: Sex, Marriage, Identity and Adoption.* New York: Pantheon, 2003.

Key, V. O. *Southern Politics in State and Nation.* New York: Knopf, 1949.

King, Martin Luther, Jr. *Stride Toward Freedom: The Montgomery Story.* New York: Harper and Row, 1958.

———. *Where Do We Go from Here? Chaos or Community.* Boston: Beacon Press, 1967.

King, Martin Luther, Jr., and Clayborne Carson. *Autobiography of Martin Luther King Jr., 1929–1968.* New York: Warner Books, 1998.

King, Mary. *Freedom Song: A Personal Story of the 1960s Civil Rights Movement.* New York: Morrow, 1987.

Kirk, John A. *Redefining the Color Line: Black Activism in Little Rock, Arkansas, 1940–1970.* Gainesville: University Press of Florida, 2002.

Klarman, Michael J. *From Jim Crow to Civil Rights: The Supreme Court and the Struggle for Racial Equality.* New York: Oxford University Press, 2004.

Kluger, Richard. *Simple Justice: The History of* Brown v. Board of Education *and Black America's Struggle for Equality.* New York: Knopf, 1976.

Korstadt, Robert Rogers. *Civil Rights Unionism: Tobacco Workers and the Struggle for Democracy in the Mid-Twentieth-Century South.* Chapel Hill: University of North Carolina Press, 2003.

Kreuger, Thomas A. *And Promises to Keep: The Southern Conference for Human Welfare, 1938–1948.* Nashville, Tenn.: Vanderbilt University Press, 1967.

Lau, Peter F. *Democracy Rising: South Carolina and the Fight for Black Equality Since 1985.* Lexington: University Press of Kentucky, 2006.

Lawson, Steven F. *Black Ballots: Voting Rights in the South, 1944–1969.* New York: Columbia University Press, 1976.

———. *Running for Freedom: Civil Rights and Black Politics in America Since 1941.* New York: McGraw-Hill, 1991.

———, ed. *To Secure These Rights: The Report of President Harry S. Truman's Committee on Civil Rights.* Boston: Bedford/St. Martin, 2004.

Lawson, Steven F., and Charles Payne. *Debating the Civil Rights Movement, 1954–1968.* New York: Rowan and Littlefield, 1998.

Lee, Chana Kai. *For Freedom's Sake: The Life of Fannie Lou Hamer.* Urbana: University of Illinois Press, 1999.

Lerner, Gerda. *Black Women in White America: A Documentary History.* New York: Pantheon Books, 1972.

Levine, Daniel. *Bayard Rustin and the Civil Rights Movement.* New Brunswick, N.J.: Rutgers University Press, 2000.

Lewis, David L. and Charles W. Eagles. *The Civil Rights Movement in America: Essays.* Jackson: University Press of Mississippi, 1986.

Lewis, John. *Walking with the Wind: A Memoir of the Movement.* New York: Simon and Schuster, 1998.

Ling, Peter, and Sharon Monteith, eds. *Gender in the Civil Rights Movement.* New York: Garland, 1999.

Litwack, Leon. *Trouble in Mind: Black Southerners in the Age of Jim Crow.* New York: Knopf, 1998.

Logan, Rayford W. *The Betrayal of the Negro: From Rutherford B. Hayes to Woodrow Wilson.* New York: Da Capo Press, 1997.

MacLean, Nancy. *Behind the Mask of Chivalry.* New York: Oxford University Press, 1994.

Manis, Andrew M. *A Fire You Can't Put Out.* Tuscaloosa: University of Alabama Press, 1999.

———. *Macon Black and White: An Unutterable Separation in the American Century.* Macon, Ga.: Mercer University Press, 2004.

Manis, Andrew M., and Marjorie L. White, eds. *Birmingham Revolutionaries: Fred Shuttlesworth and the Alabama Christian Movement for Human Rights.* Macon, Ga.: Mercer University Press, 2000.

Marsh, Charles. *God's Long Summer: Stories of Faith and Civil Rights.* Princeton, N.J.: Princeton University Press, 1997.

Martin, Linda, and Kerry Segrave. *Anti-Rock: The Opposition to Rock 'n' Roll.* New York: De Capo Press, 1993.

Mason, Gilbert R. *Beaches, Blood, and Ballots: A Black Doctor's Civil Rights Struggle.* Jackson: University Press of Mississippi, 2000.

Matusow, Allen J. *The Unraveling of America: A History of Liberalism in the 1960s.* New York: Harper, 1984.

McAdam, Doug. *Freedom Summer.* New York: Oxford University Press, 1988.

McMillen, Neil. *The Citizens' Council: Organized Resistance to the Second Reconstruction, 1954–1964.* Urbana: University of Illinois Press, 1994.

———, ed. *Remaking Dixie: The Impact of World War II on the American South.* Jackson: University Press of Mississippi, 1997.

McMurray, Linda O. *To Keep the Waters Troubled: The Life of Ida B. Wells.* New York: Oxford University Press, 1999.

McWhorter, Diane. *Carry Me Home: Birmingham, Alabama: The Climactic Battle of the Civil Rights Revolution.* New York: Simon and Schuster, 2001.

Meier, August, and Elliot Rudwick. *CORE: A Study in the Civil Rights Movement, 1942–1968.* Urbana: University of Illinois Press, 1975.

Meyer, Leisa D. *Creating G.I. Jane: Sexuality and Power in the Women's Army Corps.* New York: Columbia University Press, 1996.

Meyerowitz, Joanne, ed. *Not June Cleaver: Women and Gender in Postwar America, 1945–1960.* Philadelphia: Temple University Press, 1994.

Milkman, Ruth. *Gender at Work: The Dynamics of Job Segregation by Sex During World War II.* Urbana: University of Illinois Press, 1987.

Miller, James. *"Democracy Is in the Streets": From Port Huron to the Siege of Chicago.* Cambridge: Harvard University Press, 1994.

Mills, Kay. *This Little Light of Mine: The Life of Fannie Lou Hamer.* New York: Dutton, 1993.

Mills, Nicholaus. *Like a Holy Crusade: Mississippi 1964: The Turning of the Civil Rights Movement in America.* Chicago: University of Chicago Press, 1992.

Minchin, Timothy. *Hiring the Black Worker: The Racial Integration of the Southern Textile Industry, 1960–1980.* Chapel Hill: University of North Carolina Press, 1999.

———. *The Color of Work: The Struggle for Civil Rights in the Southern Paper Industry: 1945–1980.* Chapel Hill: University of North Carolina Press, 2001.

Moody, Anne. *Coming of Age in Mississippi.* New York: Dell, 1968.

Moore, Brenda L. *To Serve My Country, To Serve My Race: The Story of the Only African American WACS Stationed Overseas During World War II.* New York: New York University Press, 1996.

Moran, Rachel. *Interracial Intimacies: The Regulation of Race and Romance.* Chicago: University of Chicago Press, 2001.

Morgan, Edmund S. *American Slavery, American Freedom: The Ordeal of Colonial Virginia.* New York: Norton, 1975.

Morris, Aldon D. *The Origins of the Civil Rights Movement: Black Communities Organizing for Change.* New York: Free Press, 1984.

Morrison, Toni. *Race-ing Justice, En-gendering Power: Essays on Anita Hill, Clarence Thomas and the Construction of Reality.* New York: Pantheon, 1992.

Murray, Pauli. *Proud Shoes: The Story of an American Family.* New York: Harper and Row, 1978.

———. *Song in a Weary Throat: The Autobiography of a Black Activist, Feminist, Lawyer, Priest and Poet.* Knoxville: University of Tennessee Press, 1989.

Myrdal, Gunnar. *An American Dilemma: The Negro Problem and Modern Democracy.* New York: Harper and Brothers, 1941.

Nelson, Bruce. *Divided We Stand: American Workers and the Struggle for Black Equality.* Princeton, N.J.: Princeton University Press, 2001.

Newbeck, Phyl. *Virginia Hasn't Always Been for Lovers: Interracial Marriage Bans and the Case of Richard and Mildred Loving.* Carbondale, Ill.: Southern Illinois University Press, 2004.

Newman, Louise Michele. *White Women's Rights: The Racial Origins of Feminism in the United States.* New York: Oxford University Press, 1999.

Norrell, Robert J. *Reaping the Whirlwind: The Civil Rights Movement in Tuskegee.* New York: Knopf, 1985.

———. *The Making of Modern Alabama: State History and Geography.* Tuscaloosa, Ala.: Yellowhammer Press, 1993.

Nossiter, Adam. *Of Long Memory: Mississippi and the Murder of Medgar Evers.* New York: De Capo, 2002.

O'Brien, Gail. *The Color of the Law: Race, Violence, and Justice in the Post–World War II South.* Chapel Hill: University of North Carolina Press, 1999.

Odum, Howard W. *Race and Rumors of Race: The American South in the Early Forties.* Baltimore, Md.: The Johns Hopkins University Press, 1997.

Olson, Lynne. *Freedom's Daughters: The Unsung Heroines of the Civil Rights Movement from 1830 to 1970.* New York: Scribner, 2001.

O'Reilly, Kenneth. *Racial Matters: The FBI's Secret File on Black America.* New York: Free Press, 1989.

———. *Nixon's Piano: Presidents and Racial Politics from Washington to Clinton.* New York: Free Press, 1995.

Oshinsky, David. *A Conspiracy So Immense: The World of Joe McCarthy.* New York: Free Press, 1983.

Painter, Nell Irvin. *Creating Black Americans: African American History and Its Meaning, 1619 to the Present.* New York: Oxford University Press, 2006.

Parker, Frank R. *Black Votes Count: Political Empowerment in Mississippi after 1965.* Chapel Hill: University of North Carolina Press, 1990.

Parks, Rosa, and Jim Haskins. *Rosa Parks: My Story.* New York: Dial Press, 1992.

Patterson, James T. *Brown v. Board of Education: A Civil Rights Milestone and Its Troubled Legacy.* New York: University of Oxford Press, 2001.

Patterson, Toby Graham. *A Right to Read: Segregation and Civil Rights in Alabama's Public Libraries.* Tuscaloosa: University of Alabama Press, 2002.

Payne, Charles. *I've Got the Light of Freedom: The Organizing Tradition and the Mississippi Freedom Struggle.* Berkeley: University of California Press, 1995.

Pearson, Hugh. *Shadow of the Panther: Huey Newton and the Price of Black Power in America.* Reading, Mass.: Addison-Wesley, 1994.

Persons, Albert. *Sex and Civil Rights: The True Selma Story.* Birmingham, Ala.: Esco Publishers, 1965

Powledge, Fred. *Free at Last? The Civil Rights Movement and the People Who Made It.* Boston: Little, Brown, 1991.

Pratt, Robert. *We Shall Not Be Moved: Desegregation of the University of Georgia.* Athens: University of Georgia Press, 2002.

Rabby, Glenda Alice. *The Pain and the Promise: The Struggle for Civil Rights in Tallahassee, Florida.* Athens: University of Georgia Press, 1999.

Raines, Howard. *My Soul Is Rested: Movement Days in the South Remembered.* New York: Putnam, 1977.

Rainwater, Lee, and William L. Yancey. *The Moynihan Report and the Politics of Controversy: A Trans-Action Social Science and Public Policy Report.* Cambridge, Mass.: MIT Press, 1967.

Ransby, Barbara. *Ella Baker and the Black Freedom Movement: A Radical Democratic Vision.* Chapel Hill: University of North Carolina Press, 2003.

Raper, Arthur F. *Preface to Peasantry: A Tale of Two Black Belt Counties.* Columbia: University of South Carolina Press, 2005.

Reed, Linda. *Simple Decency and Common Sense: The Southern Conference Movement, 1938–1963.* Bloomington: Indiana University Press, 1997.

Reed, Merl E. *Seedtime for the Modern Civil Rights Movement: The President's Committee on Fair Employment Practice, 1941–1968.* Baton Rouge: Louisiana State University Press, 1991.

Reston, James, Jr. *The Innocence of Joan Little: A Southern Mystery.* New York: Times Books, 1977.

Rise, Eric. *The Martinsville Seven: Race, Rape and Capital Punishment.* Charlottesville: University of Virginia Press, 1995.

Roberts, Dorothy. *Killing the Black Body: Race, Reproduction and the Meaning of Liberty.* New York: Vintage, 1999.

Robinson, Armstead L., and Patricia Sullivan, eds. *New Directions in Civil Rights Studies.* Charlottesville: University of Virginia Press, 1991.

Robinson, Jo Ann. *The Montgomery Bus Boycott and the Women Who Started It.* Knoxville: University of Tennessee Press, 1987.

Robnett, Belinda. *How Long? How Long? African American Women in the Struggle for Civil Rights.* New York: Oxford University Press, 1997.

Roche, Jeff. *Restructured Resistance: The Silbey Commission and the Politics of Desegregation in Georgia.* Athens: University of Georgia Press, 1998.

Rogers, Kim Lacy. *Righteous Lives: Narratives of the New Orleans Civil Rights Movement.* New York: New York University Press, 1993.

Rogers, William Warren, Robert David Ward, Leah Rawls Atkins, and Wayne Flynt. *Alabama: The History of a Deep South State.* Tuscaloosa: University of Alabama, 1994.

Romano, Renee C. *Race Mixing: Black-White Marriage in Postwar America.* Cambridge, Mass.: Harvard University Press, 2003.

Rose, Tricia. *Longing to Tell: Black Women Talk About Sexuality and Intimacy.* New York: Farrar, Straus and Giroux, 2003.

Rosen, Hannah. *Terror in the Heart of Freedom: Citizenship, Sexual Violence and the Meaning of Race in the Postemancipation South.* Chapel Hill: University of North Carolina Press, 2008.

Rosen, Ruth. *The World Split Open: How the Modern Women's Movement Changed America.* New York: Viking, 2000.

Ross, Rosetta. *Witnessing and Testifying: Black Women, Religion, and Civil Rights.* Minneapolis: Fortress Press, 2003.

Ruiz, Vicki L., and Ellen Carol Dubois. *Unequal Sisters: A Multicultural Reader in U.S. Women's History,* 3rd ed. New York: Routledge, 2000.

Salmond, John A. *The Conscience of a Lawyer: Clifford J. Durr and American Civil Liberties, 1899–1975.* Tuscaloosa: University of Alabama Press, 1990.

Savage, Barbara. *Broadcasting Freedom: Radio, War, and the Politics of Race, 1938–1948.* Chapel Hill: University of North Carolina Press, 1999.

Schechter, Patricia A. *Ida B. Wells-Barnett and American Reform, 1880–1930.* Chapel Hill: University of North Carolina Press, 2001.

Schrecker, Ellen. *Many Are the Crimes: McCarthyism in America.* Boston: Little, Brown, 1998.

Schulz, Bud, and Ruth Schultz. *It Did Happen Here: Recollections of Political Repression in America.* Berkeley: University of California Press, 1989.

Schwalm, Leslie. *A Hard Fight for We: Women's Transition from Slavery to Freedom in South Carolina.* Urbana: University of Illinois Press, 1997.

Scott, Anne Fior. *The Southern Lady: From Pedestal to Politics, 1830–1930.* Chicago: University of Chicago Press, 1970.

Scott, Joan W. *Gender and the Politics of History.* New York: Columbia University Press, 1988.

Seale, Bobby. *Seize the Time: The Story of the Black Panther Party and Huey P. Newton.* New York: Vintage, 1970.

Seay, S. S., Sr. *I Was There by the Grace of God.* Montgomery, Ala.: S. S. Seay Educational Foundation, 1990.

Selby, Earl, and Miriam Selby. *Odyssey: Journey Through Black America.* New York: Putnam and Sons, 1971.

Sellers, Cleveland. *The River of No Return: The Autobiography of a Black Militant and the Life and Death of SNCC.* New York: Morrow, 1973.

Shapiro, Herbert. *White Violence and Black Response: From Reconstruction to Montgomery.* Amherst: University of Massachusetts Press, 1988.

Silver, James W. *Mississippi: The Closed Society.* New York: Harcourt, 1964.

Smead, Howard. *Blood Justice: The Lynching of Mack Charles Parker.* New York: Oxford University Press, 1988.

Smith, Lillian. *Killers of the Dream.* New York: Norton, 1994.

Smith, Merril, ed. *Sex Without Consent: Rape and Sexual Coercion in America.* New York: New York University Press, 2003.

Snitow, Ann, Christine Stansell, and Sharon Thompson, eds. *Powers of Desire: The Politics of Sexuality.* New York: Monthly Review Press, 1983.

Sommerville, Diane Miller. *Rape and Race in the Nineteenth Century South.* Chapel Hill: University of North Carolina Press, 2004.

Stanton, Mary. *From Selma to Sorrow: The Life and Death of Viola Liuzzo.* Athens: University of Georgia Press, 2001.

Stember, Charles Herbert. *Sexual Racism: The Emotional Barrier to an Integrated Society.* New York: Elsevier, 1976.

Sugrue, Thomas J. *The Origins of the Urban Crisis: Race and Inequality in Postwar Detroit.* Princeton, N.J.: Princeton University Press, 1996.

Sullivan, Patricia. *Days of Hope: Race and Democracy in the New Deal Era.* Chapel Hill: University of North Carolina Press, 1996.

———, ed. *Freedom Writer: Virginia Foster Durr, Letters from the Civil Rights Years.* New York: Routledge, 2003.

Takaki, Ronald. *Double Victory: A Multicultural History of America in World War II.* Boston: Little, Brown, 2000.

Terborg-Penn, Rosalyn. *African American Women in the Struggle for the Vote, 1850–1920.* Bloomington: Indiana University Press, 1998.

Thornton, J. Mills. *Dividing Lines: Municipal Politics and the Struggle for Civil Rights in Mont-gomery, Birmingham, and Selma.* Tuscaloosa: University of Alabama Press, 2002.

Townsend, Davis. *Weary Feet, Rested Souls: A Guided History of the Civil Rights Movement.* New York: Norton, 1998.

Tuck, Stephen G. N. *Beyond Atlanta: The Struggle for Racial Equality in Georgia, 1940–1980.* Athens: University of Georgia Press, 2001.

Tyson, Timothy B. *Radio Free Dixie: Robert F. Williams and the Roots of Black Power.* Chapel Hill: University of North Carolina Press, 2000.

———. *Blood Done Sign My Name: Murder, Grace and Growing Up Southern.* New York: Random House, 2004.

Van Deburg, William L. *New Day in Babylon: The Black Power Movement and American Culture.* Chicago: University of Chicago Press, 1992.

———. *Modern Black Nationalism: From Marcus Garvey to Louis Farrakhan.* New York: New York University Press, 1997.

Wagy, Tom R. *Governor LeRoy Collins of Florida: Spokesman of the New South.* Tuscaloosa: University of Alabama Press, 1985.

Wallace, Michelle. *Black Macho and the Myth of the Superwoman.* New York: Verso, 1990.

Wallenstein, Peter. *Tell the Court I Love My Wife: Race, Marriage, and Law—An American History.* New York: Palgrave, 2002.

Ward, Brian. *Just My Soul Responding: Rhythm and Blues, Black Consciousness and Race Relations.* Berkeley: University of California Press, 1998.

———, ed. *Media, Culture, and the Modern African American Freedom Struggle.* Gainesville: University Press of Florida, 2001.

Ward, Brian, and Anthony Badger, eds. *The Making of Martin Luther King the Civil Rights Movement.* New York: New York University Press, 1996.

Warren, Robert Penn. *Segregation: The Inner Conflict in the South.* New York: Random House, 1956.

Washington, Harriet A. *Medical Apartheid: The Dark History of Medical Experimentation on Black Americans from Colonial Times to the Present.* New York: Doubleday, 2006.

Watters, Pat, and Reese Cleghorn. *Climbing Jacob's Ladder: The Arrival of Negroes in Southern Politics.* New York: Harcourt, 1967.

Webb, Clive, ed. *Massive Resistance: Southern Opposition to the Second Reconstruction.* New York: Oxford University Press, 2005.

Webb, Sheyann, and Rachel West Nelson. *Selma, Lord, Selma: Girlhood Memories of the Civil Rights Days.* Tuscaloosa: University of Alabama Press, 1980.

Weisbrot, Robert. *Freedom Bound: A History of America's Civil Rights Movement.* New York: Norton, 1990.

Wells-Barnett, Ida B. *On Lynchings: Southern Horrors, a Red Record, Mob Rule in New Orleans.* Salem: Ayer Company, 1991.

Werner, Craig. *A Change Is Gonna Come: Race, Music, and the Soul of America.* New York: Plume, 1998.

Wexler, Laura. *Fire in a Canebrake: The Last Mass Lynching in America.* New York: Scribner, 2003.

White, Deborah Gray. *Arn't I a Woman? Female Slaves in the Plantation South.* New York: Norton, 1985.

————. *Too Heavy a Load: Black Women in Defense of Themselves, 1894–1994.* New York: Norton, 1999.

White, Walter. *Rope and Faggot: A Biography of Judge Lynch.* New York: Knopf, 1929.

Whitfield, Stephen J. *A Death in the Delta: The Story of Emmett Till.* Baltimore: Johns Hopkins University Press, 1991.

Williams, Myrlie Evers, Manning Marable, and Medgar Wiley Evers. *The Autobiography of Medgar Evers: A Hero's Life and Legacy Revealed Through His Writings, Letters and Speeches.* New York: Basic Books, 2005.

Wilson, Bobby M. *Race and Place in Birmingham: The Civil Rights and Neighborhood Movements.* New York: Rowan and Littlefield, 2000.

Wirt, Frederick M. *We Ain't What We Was: Civil Rights in the New South.* Durham, N.C.: Duke University Press, 1997.

Wolcott, Victoria. *Remaking Respectability: African American Women in Interwar Detroit.* Chapel Hill: University of North Carolina Press, 2001.

Woodward, C. Vann. *The Strange Career of Jim Crow.* New York: Oxford University Press, 1966.

The WPA Guide to 1930s Alabama. Tuscaloosa: University of Alabama Press, 2000.

Zinn, Howard. *SNCC: The New Abolitionists.* New York: Beacon Press, 1965.

ARTICLES

Anderson, Karen. "Last Hired and First Fired: Black Women Workers During World War II." *Journal of American History* 69 (June 1982).

Boris, Eileen. "You Wouldn't Want One of 'Em Dancing with Your Wife': Racialized Bodies on the Job in World War II." *American Quarterly* 50 (1998).

Braukman, Stacy. " 'Nothing Else Matters but Sex': Cold War Narratives of Deviance and the Search for Lesbian Teachers in Florida, 1959–1963." *Feminist Studies* 27, no. 3 (Fall 2001).

Brown, Elsa Barkley. "Womanist Consciousness: Maggie Lena Walker and the Independent Order of Saint Luke." *Signs* 14 (1989).

————. " 'What Has Happened Here': The Politics of Difference in Women's History and Feminist Politics." *Feminist Studies* 18 (Summer 1992).

————. "Negotiating and Transforming the Public Sphere: African American Political Life in the Transition from Slavery to Freedom." *Public Culture* 7 (1994).

Campbell, Kirsten. "Legal Memories: Sexual Assault, Memory, and International Humanitarian Law." *Signs* 28, no. 1 (2002).

Cardyn, Lisa. "Sexualized Racism/Gendered Violence: Outraging the Body Politic in the Reconstruction South." *Michigan Law Review* (February 2002).

Davis, Angela. "The Struggle of Ben Chavis and the Wilmington Ten." *Black Scholar* (April 1975).

————. "Joanne Little: The Dialectics of Rape." *Ms.* 3, no. 12 (June 1975).

Dorr, Lisa Lindquist. "Black-on-White Rape and Retribution in 20th Century Virginia: 'Men, Even Negroes, Must Have Some Protection,' *Journal of Southern History* 66, no. 4 (November 2000).

Edwards, Alison. "Rape, Racism and the White Women's Movement: An Answer to Susan Brownmiller." Sojourner Truth Organization, pamphlet, n.d.

Edwards, Laura F. "Sexual Violence, Gender, Reconstruction, and the Extension of Patriarchy in Granville County, North Carolina." *North Carolina Historical Review* 68, no. 3 (July 1991).

Fine, Michelle, and Lois Weis. "Disappearing Acts: The State and Violence Against Women in the Twentieth Century." *Signs* 25, no. 4 (2000).

Flood, Dawn Rae. " 'They Didn't Treat Me Good': African American Rape Victims and Chicago Courtroom Strategies During the 1950s." *Journal of Women's History* 17, no. 1 (2005).

Freedman, Estelle B. " 'Uncontrolled Desires': The Response to the Sexual Psychopath, 1920–1960." In Kathy Peiss and Christina Simmons, eds., *Passion and Power: Sexuality in History.* Philadelphia: Temple University Press, 1989.

Goldblatt, Beth. "Special Hearing Women: May 1996." Truth and Reconciliation Commission of South Africa, Report, 4.

Hall, Jacquelyn Dowd. "The Mind That Burns in Each Body: Women, Rape and Racial Violence." In Ann Snitow, Christine Stansell, and Sharon Thompson, eds., *Powers of Desire: the Politics of Sexuality.* New York: Monthly Review Press, 1983.

Helliwell, Christine. " 'It's Only a Penis': Rape, Feminism and Difference." *Signs* 25, no. 3 (2000).

Hengehold, Laura. "Remapping the Event: Institutional Discourses and the Trauma of Rape." *Signs* 26, no. 1 (2000).

Higginbotham, Evelyn Brooks. "African-American Women's History and the Metalanguage of Race." *Signs* 17, no. 2 (1992).

Hine, Darlene Clark. "Rape and the Inner Lives of Black Women in the Middle West: Preliminary Thoughts on a Culture of Dissemblance." *Signs* 14, no. 4 (Summer 1989).

Johnson, Marilynn S. "Gender, Race and Rumours: Re-Examining the 1943 Race Riots." *Gender and History* 10, no. 2 (August 1998).

Kaplan, Temma. "Reversing the Shame and Gendering the Memory." *Signs* 28, no. 1 (Summer 2002).

Karenga, Maulana Ron. "In Defense of Sister Joanne: For Ourselves and History." *Black Scholar* (July–August 1975).

Lawson, Steven F. "Freedom Then, Freedom Now: The Historiography of the Civil Rights Movement." *American Historical Review* 96 (1991).

————. "Civil Rights and Black Liberation." In Nancy Hewitt, ed., *Blackwell's Companion to Women's History.* Malden, Mass.: Blackwell, 2002.

Lawson, Steven F., David R. Colburn, and Darryl Paulson, "Groveland: Florida's Little Scottsboro." In David R. Colburn and Jane L. Landers, eds., *The African American Heritage of Florida.* Gainesville: University of Florida Press, 1994.

Martin, Charles H. "Race, Gender and Southern Justice: The Rosa Lee Ingram Case." *American Journal of Legal History* 29, no. 3 (July 1985).

―――. "The Civil Rights Congress and Southern Black Defendants." *Georgia Historical Quarterly* 71, no. 1 (Spring 1987).

Matthews, Nancy A. "Surmounting a Legacy: The Expansion of Racial Diversity in a Local Anti-Rape Movement." *Gender and Society* 3, no. 4 (December 1989).

McNeil, Genna Rae. "Joanne Is You, Joanne Is Me." In Bettye Collier Thomas and V. P. Franklin, eds., *Sisters in the Struggle: African American Women in the Civil Rights Black Power Movement.* New York: New York University Press, 2001.

Morgan, Jennifer. "Some Could Suckle over Their Shoulder: Male Travelers, Female Bodies and Gendering Racial Ideology, 1500–1700," *William and Mary Quarterly* 54 (1997).

Nasstrom, Kathryn L. "Down to Now: Memory, Narrative, and Women's Leadership in the Civil Rights Movement in Atlanta, Georgia." *Gender and History* 11, no. 1 (April 1999).

Novkov, Julie. "Racial Constructions: The Legal Regulation of Miscegenation in Alabama, 1890–1934." *Law and History Review* 20, no. 2 (Summer 2002).

Pascoe, Peggy. "Miscegenation Law, Court Cases, and Ideologies of 'Race' in Twentieth-Century America." *Journal of American History* 44 (June 1996).

Rosen, Hannah. " 'Not That Sort of Woman:' Race, Gender and Sexual Violence During the Memphis Riot of 1866." In Martha Hodes, ed., *Sex, Love, Race: Crossing Boundaries in North American History.* New York: New York University Press, 1999.

Sitkoff, Harvard. "Racial Militancy and Interracial Violence in the Second World War." *Journal of American History* 58 (December 1971).

Sommerville, Diane Miller. "The Rape Myth in the Old South Reconsidered." *Journal of Southern History* 61, no. 3 (August 1995).

Stiglmayer, Alexandra. "The Rapes in Bosnia-Herzegovinia." In Alexandra Stiglmayer, ed., *Mass Rape: The War Against Women in Bosnia-Herzegovinia.* Lincoln: University of Nebraska Press, 1994.

Swiss, Shana, and Joan E. Giller. "Rape as a Crime of War: A Medical Perspective." *Journal of the American Medical Association* 270, no. 5 (August 4, 1993).

Walker, Alice. "Advancing Luna and Ida B. Wells." In Henry Louis Gates and Nelly Y. McKay, eds., *The Norton Anthology of African American Literature.* New York: Norton, 1997.

DISSERTATIONS AND THESES

Block, Sharon. *Coerced Sex in British North America: 1700–1820.* Ph.D. diss., Princeton, 1995.

Greer, Brenna. *"Our Leaders Is Just We Ourselves": Black Women's Resistance in the Making of the Montgomery Bus Boycott.* Master's thesis, University of Wisconsin, Madison, 2004.

Jones, Patrick D. *Communist Front Shouts "Kissing Case" to the World: The Committee to Combat Racial Injustice and the Politics of Race and Gender During the Cold War.* Master's thesis, University of Wisconsin, Madison, 1996.

Matthews, Tracye. *"No One Ever Asks What a Man's Place in the Revolution Is": Gender and Sexual Politics in the Black Panther Party, 1966–1971.* Ph.D diss., University of Michigan, 1998.

McDuffie, Erik S. *Long Journeys: Four Black Women and the Communist Party USA, 1930–1956.* Ph.D. diss., New York University, 2003.

McGuire, Danielle. *Race, Rape, and Resistance: The Tallahassee Story.* Master's thesis, University of Wisconsin, Madison, 1999.

Shadron, Virginia. *Popular Protest and Legal Authority in Post–World War II Georgia: Race, Class and Gender Politics in the Rosa Lee Ingram Case.* Ph.D. diss., Emory University, 1991.

White, Robert M. *The Tallahassee Sit-ins and CORE: A Nonviolent Revolutionary Sub-movement.* Ph.D. diss., Florida State University, 1964.

Woodard, Kimberly R. "The Summer of African-American Discontent." Unpublished paper, Duke University, 1992.

Yeakey, Lamont H. *The Montgomery, Alabama, Bus Boycott, 1955–1956.* Ph.D. diss., Columbia University, 1979.

Index

Page numbers in *italic* refer to illustrations.

A NOTE ON THE TYPE

The text of this book was set in Garamond No. 3. It is not a true copy of any of the designs of Claude Garamond (ca. 1480–1561), but an adaptation of his types. It probably owes as much to the designs of Jean Jannon. Jannon's matrices came into the possession of the Imprimerie nationale, where they were thought to be by Garamond himself. This particular version is based on an adaptation by Morris Fuller Benton.

Composed by
North Market Street Graphics, Lancaster, Pennsylvania

Printed and bound by
Berryville Graphics, Berryville, Virginia

Designed by
Maggie Hinders